ONLINE SEARCHING

ONLINE SEARCHING:
A Scientist's Perspective

A Guide for the Chemical and Life Sciences

Damon D. Ridley

University of Sydney
Australia

JOHN WILEY & SONS

Chichester • New York • Brisbane • Toronto • Singapore

             National   01243 779777
             International (+44) 1243 779777
             e-mail (for orders and customer service enquiries): cs-books@wiley.co.uk
             Visit our Home Page on http://www.wiley.co.uk
                     or http://www.wiley.com

Other Wiley Editorial Offices

John Wiley & Sons, Inc., 605 Third Avenue,
New York, NY 10158-0012, USA

Weinheim · Brisbane · Singapore · Toronto

Library of Congress Cataloging-in-Publication Data

Ridley, D. D. (Damon D.)
    Online searching : a scientist's perspective / D. D. Ridley
        p.   cm.
    Includes bibliographical references and index
    ISBN 0-471-96520-0 (cloth : alk. paper). — ISBN 0-471-96521-9
    (paper : alk. paper)
      1. Information storage and retrieval systems — Science.
    2. Information storage and retrieval systems — Technology. 3. Online
    bibliographic searching. 4. Science — Databases. 5. Technology –
    – Databases. I. Title
    Z699.5.S3R53   1966   95–54160
    025.06′5 — dc20   CIP

British Library Cataloguing in Publication Data

A catalogue record for this book is available from the British Library

ISBN 0 471 96520 0 (cloth)
ISBN 0 471 96521 9 (paperback)

Typeset by the author
Printed and bound in Great Britain by Bookcraft (Bath) Ltd
This book is printed on acid-free paper responsibly manufactured from sustainable forestation,
for which at least two trees are planted for each one used for paper production

Contents

Preface   **xiii**

Introduction   **xv**

PART 1   FOCUS ON KEYWORDS

Chapter 1   Online Searching   3

1.1   Changes in scientific publishing   3
1.2   Electronic database producers   4
1.3   Online vendors   4
1.4   How these changes affect scientists and information specialists   5
    1.4.1   Instant and worldwide access   5
    1.4.2   Access versus ownership   5
    1.4.3   The different approach   6
    1.4.4   Costs   7
1.5   Types of databases   7
1.6   The principal roles of information specialists and scientists   7
1.7   Realistic expectations of databases   8
1.8   The future of electronic databases   9
    1.8.1   Online networks   9
    1.8.2   Localised computer databases and CD-ROMs   9
    1.8.3   Public domain networks - for example, the INTERNET   10
    1.8.4   "Front end packages"   10
Summary   11

Chapter 2   Basic Commands and Tools   12

2.1   Making the connection to the host   12
2.2   Commands and subcommands; command defaults   14
2.3   Basic search tools   17
    2.3.1   Boolean operators   17
    2.3.2   Proximity operators: greater precision in the use
          of AND and NOT   18
    2.3.3   Truncation symbols: simplifying the use of OR   19
2.4   Two examples   20
    Case 1. Find information reporting studies relating to the origin of life   20
    Case 2. Find information on asymmetric tandem additions   22
Summary   23

Chapter 3   Bibliographic Databases: Structure and Content   25

3.1   Hierarchy of bibliographic databases   26
3.2   Clusters   26
3.3   Structure of bibliographic databases   26

3.4   CAPlus File   28
3.5   BIOSIS File   31
3.6   Other files in which this article was indexed   32
3.7   Example from the physical sciences   35
3.8   Entries within fields   37
3.9   Bibliographic files: similarities and differences   38
Summary   39

Chapter 4   Bibliographic Databases: Non-index Fields   40

4.1   General entry of data: individual words and stop words   40
4.2   General entry of data: checking postings   41
4.3   Notes on the entry of data: specific fields   44
        4.3.1   Title Field   44
        4.3.2   Author Field   44
        4.3.3   Corporate Source Field   45
        4.3.4   Source Field   46
        4.3.5   Other bibliographic fields   48
        4.3.6   Abstract Field   48
Summary   49

Chapter 5   Bibliographic Databases: Index Fields   51

5.1   General structure of indexing   51
5.2   The location of index entries   52
5.3   The online thesaurus   53
        5.3.1   The structure of a thesaurus   53
5.4   Section codes and index headings   56
5.5   Indexing hierarchy: Chemical Abstracts Database   56
        5.5.1   Section codes   56
        5.5.2   Index headings   57
5.6   Indexing in other major bibliographic databases   61
5.7   Database Summary Sheets   61
Summary   63

Chapter 6   Bibliographic Databases: Search Outline   64

6.1   The principles   64
6.2   Scope and intent of the search   65
6.3   Natural language concepts   66
6.4   File selection   67
6.5   Search terms and fields   68
6.6   Preliminary search; review of results   68
6.7   Revision of search profile   69
6.8   Full search   69
6.9   Display of answers   70
        6.9.1   Delivery methods   70
        6.9.2   Display formats   71
Summary   72

Chapter 7   Bibliographic Databases: Search Terms   73

7.1   Choosing initial search terms   74
    7.1.1   Look up the print index guides: CAplus and EMBASE Files   75
    7.1.2   Search for the record for a known article of particular relevance:
           BIOSIS and CAPlus Files   80
    7.1.3   Perform a quick general (or casual) search: EMBASE File   83
    7.1.4   Expand in the index heading field, and, if possible,
           use the online thesaurus: MEDLINE File   87
7.2   Preliminary search and review of results   90
7.3   Revise search profile   92
    7.3.1   Proximity operators   92
    7.3.2   Concepts and fields   93
    7.3.3   Terms: synonyms, thesaurus   94
7.4   Full search   95
7.5   Display of answers   96
Summary   99
Summary of commands commonly used in bibliographic file searches on STN   100

Chapter 8   Full Text Files   101

8.1   The primary and the secondary literature   101
8.2   Full text: electronic versus hardcopy   102
8.3   Full text databases   102
8.4   Online records of full text scientific databases   103
8.5   When to search full text databases   105
8.6   Comparing full text records with indexed records   106
8.7   Searching full text databases   109
8.8   Displays in full text databases   110
8.9   Linking with other databases   114
8.10   Business and news databases   115
Summary   119

Chapter 9   Patent Information   120

9.1   The importance of patent databases   120
9.2   Patent databases   122
9.3   Indexing of Patents   124
    9.3.1   Indexing of the legal aspects   125
    9.3.2   Indexing of the technical aspects   128
    9.3.3   Abstracts and claims   132
9.4   Searching of the patent databases   133
    9.4.1   Subject searching (general)   134
    9.4.2   Searches based on classification codes   135
    9.4.3   Patent superfields   135
    9.4.4   Crossfile searching: patent families   136
    9.4.5   Determining patent competition   139
    9.4.6   Legal status information   141
Summary   143

Chapter 10   Special Topics   144

10.1   The commands on STN   144
    10.1.1   The HELP command   145
    10.1.2   The FILE and INDEX commands   148
    10.1.3   The SELECT command and SmartSELECT   151
10.2   Select CHEM   154
10.3   Current awareness searching   156
10.4   Citations   157
    10.4.1   Finding citations to a particular article   158
    10.4.2   Finding citations to a particular author   159
10.5   Searching for numeric properties   161
10.6   Costs and saving money   163
    10.6.1   Connect hour fees   164
    10.6.2   Search term fees   165
    10.6.3   Display costs   166
    10.6.4   Learning files   166
Summary   166

PART 2   FOCUS ON SUBSTANCES

Chapter 11   Chemical Substances: Structure and Indexing   171

11.1   The variety of substances   171
11.2   Finding information on substances   172
11.3   A brief description of some basic chemical concepts   175
    11.3.1   Atoms, elements and the Periodic Table   176
    11.3.2   Chemical substances   176
    11.3.3   How atoms are connected in molecules: the two main types of
            bonds   177
    11.3.4   Valence Bond structures   177
    11.3.5   Areas of chemistry   178
    11.3.6   Functional groups   179
11.4   Indexing of substances in the REGISTRY File   179
    11.4.1   Single substances   179
    11.4.2   Alloys   181
    11.4.3   Coordination compounds   182
    11.4.4   Incompletely defined substances   184
    11.4.5   Minerals   185
    11.4.6   Mixtures   186
    11.4.7   Polymers   188
    11.4.8   Proteins   190
    11.4.9   Nucleic acids   191

11.4.10 Salts   192
    a Salts which do not contain carbon   193
    b Salts from organic acids and Periodic Table Group I/II bases   194
    c Salts with nitrogen-containing bases   195
    d Salts from organic acids and organic bases   195
11.4.11 Isotopes   196
11.4.12 Isomers   198
    a Constitutional isomers   199
    b Stereoisomers   199
11.5   Class Identifiers and File Segments   202
11.6   Multicomponent substances   203
11.7   Searching for substances   203
Summary   204

Chapter 12   Finding Substances: Name Based Terms   205

12.1   Nomenclature   205
12.2   Systematic names   205
    12.2.1   IUPAC   205
    12.2.2   Chemical Abstracts Index Nomenclature   206
    12.2.3   Beilstein Nomenclature   206
    12.2.4   How systematic nomenclature works   206
12.3   Trade names and common names   207
12.4   Indexing in name based fields   207
    12.4.1   Single substance   207
    12.4.2   Multicomponent substances   208
12.5   Special symbols in CN fields   210
12.6   Name based search fields   210
12.7   Search tools in name based fields   212
    12.7.1   Proximity operators and truncation   212
    12.7.2   Restricting searches to special name fields   212
    12.7.3   Left-hand truncation in CNS Field   212
12.8   Search strategies in name based fields   213
    12.8.1   Single substance   213
    12.8.2   Multicomponent substances   215
12.9   When name based searches must be done   217
Summary   219

Chapter 13   Finding Substances: Formula Based Terms   220

13.1   The representation of molecular formulas   220
13.2   Indexing in the Molecular Formula Field   221
13.3   Molecular formula search fields   222
    13.3.1   Molecular Formula Field   222
    13.3.2   Basic Index   223
    13.3.3   Fields based on molecular formulas   223

13.4   Search strategies in molecular formula fields   224
     13.4.1   Proximity operators   224
     13.4.2   Numeric search fields   225
     13.4.3   Single substance   225
     13.4.4   Single multicomponent substance   227
     13.4.5   Multicomponent substances containing specific components   227
     13.4.6   Isotopic substances   227
     13.4.7   Other applications of searches based on molecular formulas   228
Summary   229

Chapter 14 How Structure Searching Works   230

14.1   Connection tables   231
14.2   What is the nature of the screening process?   232
14.3   Augmented Atom screens   233
14.4   Bond values   234
14.5   Normalized bonds   234
     14.5.1   Alternating single and double bonds in a ring with an even
           number of atoms   234
     14.5.2   Tautomers   235
14.6   Other cases in which the valence bond theory does not directly apply   237
     14.6.1   π-bonds   237
     14.6.2   Donor bonds   237
14.7   Other structure based screens   238
     14.7.1   Atom Sequence   238
     14.7.2   Type of Ring   238
     14.7.3   Bond Sequence   239
14.8   Screens which are number-based and Graph Modifier screens   240
14.9   The search process: types and scopes of searches   240
14.10   Files in which structures may be searched and displayed   241
Summary   242

Chapter 15 Searching by Structure   243

15.1   Define the query   244
15.2   Build the structure   246
     15.2.1   Traps for the unwary - particularly experienced chemists!   246
     15.2.2   Structure building defaults: system level   246
          a Chain default   246
          b Ring default   247
     15.2.3   Special cases: system definitions and STN Express defaults   249
15.3   System options   251
     15.3.1   Options within the DRAW menu of STN Express   251
          a Shortcut symbols   252
          b Variable   252
          c G-groups   253
          d Variable point of attachment   253
          e Repeating groups   254
     15.3.2   Options with the QueryDef Menu of STN Express   254

15.4   Perform a SAMPLE search and evaluate answers   254
15.5   Revise query and perform new SAMPLE search; evaluate answers   256
    15.5.1   Ways to narrow answer sets   257
    15.5.2   Being more specific in the structure query   257
        a Block substitution by adding hydrogens   257
        b Isolate rings   257
        c Define bonds and atoms more exactly   258
        d Search a larger structure   258
    15.5.3   Restricting the search to a subset of the file   258
        a Adding screens manually   258
        b Subset searches   259
    15.5.4   Exceeding system limits   259
15.6   Perform a FULL file search   260
15.7   Display answers; find information on the substances   261
15.8   Examples of searches   262
    15.8.1   The EXACT search   262
    15.8.2   The FAMILY search   264
    15.8.3   The SUBSTRUCTURE search   265
15.9   Stereosearch   269
15.10   Other structure-searchable files   272
    15.10.1 The MARPAT Files   273
    15.10.2 Structure search in the BEILSTEIN File   275
Summary   276

Chapter 16 Substance Files with Property Information   277

16.1   Substance-based files   277
16.2   Types of property information   278
16.3   Database Summary Sheets   279
16.4   Field Availability   279
16.5   Specific files: contents and notes   283
    16.5.1   BEILSTEIN File   283
        a Finding substances in the BEILSTEIN File   286
        b Chemical information   287
        c Physical property information   288
    16.5.2   CHEMLIST File   291
    16.5.3   CSCHEM File   293
    16.5.4   GMELIN File   294
    16.5.5   HODOC File   296
    16.5.6   HSDB File   297
    16.5.7   MRCK File   299
    16.5.8   MSDS Files   301
    16.5.9   RTECS File   302
    16.5.10 SPECINFO File   305
    16.5.11 Other substance-based files   306
Summary   307

Chapter 17   Searching for Chemical Reactions   308

17.1   What does a chemical reaction involve?   308
17.2   Electronic chemical reaction databases   310
17.3   Indexing in the CASREACT File   312
17.4   Searching in the CASREACT File   315
    17.4.1   Conversion of a specific substance A to a specific substance B   316
    17.4.2   Reaction of a specific substance A with a specific reagent C   318
    17.4.3   Conversion of a group of substances A to a group of
             substances B, or reactions of a group of substances A with a
             specific (or group of) reagent(s) C   319
    17.4.4   Conversion of one functional group to another   323
    17.4.5   Reaction involving a specific reagent or a group of related reagents   324
17.5   Other online chemical reaction files   325
Summary   326

Appendix 1 Command Comparison:
           STN, Dialog, Orbit/Questel   329

Appendix 2 The Periodic Table of Elements   331

Appendix 3 Functional Groups in the CASREACT File   332

Index   335

Preface

Welcome to the world of computerized literature searching! If you have a telephone or a network link, then all you need is a computer, a "black box" called a modem which helps the computer to send your messages down the line to a computer somewhere else in the world, and an account which allows you to talk to this computer .....

..... and you can access the world's scientific literature!

You can find out the latest research on any area you wish. In *agriculture* you can find the latest information on plant and animal breeding; in the *biosciences* you can find research on the mountain lions of America; and in *chemistry* you can find out about each of the 10,000 new substances discovered each week!

You can find information on *computers* and *electrical engineering*, on *building materials* and *energy sources*, on *pharmacology* and *health*, and on *safety issues*.

Want to know about the latest research in *medicine*? In *physics*? In *geology* and *geophysics* and *geography*? Actually, do you also want to know about research done over 100 years ago?

How about information on the latest materials, for example, for building, for medical applications, or for aeroplanes? Or what company is researching *environmental issues*, and what are the latest *Government regulations* applying to the use, transport and disposal of chemicals? What are the *business* prospects for your proposed product range, and what are the *legal* implications?

The scientific literature is at your fingertips, but of course you have to know how to search it. That's what this text is about.

The information is stored on computers, but how it is stored? What does it look like? Who determines what is there and how it is presented? We consider these questions first, that is, we learn about electronic databases, and how the information is presented in fields.

We learn what parts are written by the original authors and what parts are written by the people who make the databases. All of this takes us up to Chapter 7 where finally we learn how to search for the information using simple keywords, carefully connected in such a way, and using special "tools", that we obtain precise answers. Indeed in Chapter 7 we explore different ways in which we may find about research into chemical substances which lower blood cholesterol levels!

We then proceed to the issues relating to searching full text databases, to searching patents, and finally to a number of special topics which are important in the general searching of keyword files. Indeed Part 1 focuses on words, that is, the words in the records, the words used in search terms, and the commands and tools needed to tell the computer to find the words we want.

In Part 2 the focus is on chemical substances. We learn how to find information on chemical substances, but of course this means that we have to learn how to find the substances first. Actually there are many ways to find substances and we need to know them all so that we can choose the best one for the specific substances we need to find. This takes five chapters, but if you do not have a chemical background then don't worry since, as we are learning about how to find chemical substances, we explore what they are and how they are represented. As the world, and life on it, evolved over its 4 billion year history, great varieties of substances have been produced and somehow we have to establish rules and principles for representing these substances in a way which we, and our computers, understand. Indeed, many of the sections in these chapters are particularly important for those who do have a chemical background, since the ways in which computers understand structures sometimes are quite different from the ways in which chemists represent them, and the knowledge of these differences is absolutely vital in order to retrieve the substances required.

The penultimate chapter deals with searching for information on substances (in files which are arranged by substances), while the last chapter addresses some of the aspects of searching for chemical reactions.

One of the issues with online searching is that there is such a vast amount of information available. Potentially we are searching well over 100 million scientific records. Online searching presents a real intellectual challenge because of its size alone, but as we shall see in this text the size is just *one* of the *many* challenges!

However, it is a challenge which professional scientists, and the information specialists and librarians who work with them, must take up. A poorly conceived literature search can produce misleading results which could be very costly in the long run. Besides, if you are undertaking research in a particular area, the more you know about the related research of others then the better you can apply known information and known techniques to solve your problem.

Searching the computerised scientific literature is vastly superior to searching for information in the print version. There is so much more that may be done, and it may be done much more efficiently. This text introduces you to the techniques which are used today to "search the literature properly".

It is just as important
to search the literature properly
as it is to conduct proper research!

Introduction

I became involved with online searching in the early 1980s for two main reasons. First, I could see that online searching would greatly help in retrospective searching of the literature, which was a necessary part of any research program but which I found very tiresome and inefficient in the print materials. Further, it was obvious that the problems encountered then would increase as the size of the scientific literature increased!

Second, I found online searching an intellectual challenge! Even in those earlier days, it was by no means a trivial exercise, and indeed it offered challenges and opportunities well beyond those of searching the hardcopy literature. The ability to be able to search by structure, or part-structure, fascinated me not only because of the unique results which could be achieved, but also because of the very nature of the process and the manner in which structural information was input in an electronic database.

From the outset it was clear that considerable effort would be needed to gain expertise in online searching and I did not want to learn one system, and then have to relearn other online systems. So I took the decision to become involved with CASONLINE since I considered that the Chemical Abstracts Service (CAS) would always be at the forefront of information technology in my general area of research.

In 1985 CASONLINE grew into STN International which is an online network specialising in science and technology. It started with two files, the CAS REGISTRY File and the PHYSICS File. Now it has over 200 files and I had the advantage of "growing up" with the network. The intellectual challenges I faced then were only a fraction of the challenges which now are before those who wish to gain expertise in online searching.

While I had those two original motives for becoming involved with online searching, while I have reaped the benefits with respect to my research work, and while I certainly have enjoyed the intellectual challenge, the unforeseen bonus has been that my experiences in online searching have taken me around the world on a number of occasions. In lecturing on online searching, in presenting user meetings, and in teaching many hundreds of workshops, I have met many people from whom I have learnt and whom I also have started off on the path to becoming online searchers.

The people who have attended the workshops have ranged from professional scientists with no knowledge of online searching, through librarians who have had little online experience and virtually no formal training in the sciences, to information specialists who were familiar with other systems but now required detailed knowledge of STN.

Online searching in the *sciences* currently is done *mainly* through the networks known as Knight Ridder Information Services (formerly Dialog), Orbit/Questel (a merger of the former Orbit and Questel systems both of which were major vendors with particular strengths in patent searching), or STN. I am well aware of the competitiveness between the networks, and the strong feelings some end-users have about the policies they pursue.

I do not want to go into any of these issues here. Suffice it to say that this keen competitiveness ensures the highest quality products at the most competitive prices. It so happens that CASONLINE, and then STN, served my purposes best at the start, and it continues to do so. However, it is my opinion that STN has many unique features which apply virtually right across the sciences and that these make it the *network* which should at least be consulted first when information in the sciences is required.

Actually, online searching in the sciences is arguably the most challenging of all since not only does it have the complexities of searching bibliographic files that also apply to online searching in the humanities, but also the sciences have such complicated concepts which generally are unfamiliar to the non-specialist. The terminology, and the indexing, present special problems which need to be overcome.

Further, many new areas of science are continually developing so indexing policies are frequently changing. What started out as a small endeavor later may become a huge branch so complete revision of indexing is required, and this needs to be addressed by the searcher.

However online searching in the sciences uniquely involves searching by structure, numeric searching and even searching for chemical reactions. Each involves quite different procedures - all of which are relatively simple once the principles are understood.

Database producers and online vendors publish excellent search guides and conduct excellent workshop programs, and it is valid to question the need for a text in the area. I have a number of answers.

First, the materials produced generally target specific areas while the problems the beginner searcher confronts may be very diverse. For example, as an organic chemist I am well aware of the need to gain a perspective on my subject. There are too many individual chemicals, and too many different reactions to ever hope to remember many individual events. So we teach the details of organic chemistry as parts of broad concepts. The experienced chemist has developed this overall perspective which makes the understanding of the subject so much easier. In the same way this text is intended to give an *overall perspective* of online searching and from this base the searcher may solve specific problems by applications of specific techniques.

Looked at another way, and using the STN network as an example, the detailed STN search guides and workshop materials in my office occupy over three meters of shelf space. That's fine for me since I am familiar with the basics and I know where to look on the shelf for the specific materials I may want at any one time. However, the beginner searcher may find the detailed manuals overwhelming and most scientists simply do not have the time to study them. So this text provides information on the basics and refers users to the detailed guides when needed.

Second, most basic workshops focus on search mechanics using databases for illustrative examples. There *are* indeed two components to online searching: the search mechanics and the database content, and workshops tend to concentrate on the former.

However, the better the knowledge of the database, and of its construction and of its policies, then the better the search results. Indeed I consider the *preferred starting point* is from the knowledge of the database and then to work towards how to search it. Accordingly, whenever appropriate, each chapter in this text starts with information on the database and then points to search opportunities.

Third, the scope of searching is limited to the searcher's breadth of knowledge of the possibilities (and, of course, to the searcher's inventiveness). If only name-based searching of chemical substances is learnt then the searcher may attempt searches in this area when in fact a molecular formula or structure search might be far preferable. So this book brings together in the one place many of the features of online databases. Online searching requires a meeting of three minds: of the author who writes the original article, of the indexer who prepares the online record, and of the searcher. This text tries to facilitate this process of getting the minds together, by giving the searcher an overall perspective particularly of the issues at the indexing stage.

For example, scientists often approach me for advice on searches. However, the final search query we use often is very different from that suggested in their initial proposal. It is just that there are so many different ways to approach the problem and it is only through having breadth of knowledge of the science and of the database that an initial reasonable attempt may be made. It is a matter of getting into the right ball game first; once there the problem may be tackled in depth.

Fourth, when I give workshops to information specialists they often approach me afterwards and ask what scientific texts (or even courses) they might study in order to better understand the scientific concepts. This applies particularly to areas of chemistry which has so many fascinating, albeit at times somewhat difficult to understand, concepts which affect the everyday life of the researcher, if not the everyday lives of us all. This book also attempts to explain some of the science which the concepts represent.

Lastly, I sometimes feel that the teachers of online services focus a little too much on the system, and on the ways in which computers can manipulate the data. To my mind computers are tools and while they certainly affect our lives they should not dominate us. There never will be a substitute for human intelligence and computers should be used to do the tasks they are good at - namely mechanical manipulations particularly those of a repetitive kind. On the other hand, creativity comes from the human mind. Online searching is a creative art, and a science, and to be done well it certainly needs the ingenuity of the human mind.

Much of the information in this text relates to indexing issues and to general online strategies, and is relatively independent of specific online networks. For example, many of the major databases are common to the different networks, and indeed the database producers mostly supply the same tapes to the different vendors. So in this sense most of this text is of relevance to searchers *independent of the specific system they use*.

However, the vendors organise the material a little differently, and they use slightly different commands. As the searcher becomes more experienced in online searching, it soon is realised that these subtle differences may significantly affect the actual mechanics of the search. So a decision had to be taken from the outset as to whether this text would attempt to illustrate search mechanics, and examples, for the three major networks covering the sciences, or whether it would focus mainly on one network.

In the end, to choose the latter option was a relatively easy decision to make purely on practical grounds, and for a number of reasons. First, to cover all networks effectively would mean a substantially larger text. Second, although the general implementations now are quite stable, the search mechanics for each network are constantly under review and changes are made, often several times a year, to some specific implementations. So eventually, in any case the searcher would need to consult the vendors for detailed information. Third, as I have already mentioned, it is my opinion that one network, the STN network, covers the databases in the sciences very effectively and the specific features, and the databases which uniquely it has, make it the network of choice *at least in the first instance*.

I realise that some searchers may be disappointed initially that this text focuses on the STN network, and I know that many people ask for details of comparisons between vendors, both with respect to the content and the search mechanics. I also realise that many searchers, who became familiar with the older networks many years ago, are somewhat reluctant to change vendors. Indeed, initially in this text I did include a number of "system comparisons" and I did discuss them with many others who are expert searchers. Further, I did include notes to the effect that this feature was available only on specific networks, and in specific instances, but by doing this it became very apparent that I was often writing: "this feature, or this database, is available only on the STN network." So in writing this text it became even more apparent to me that STN is the network of choice for scientists.

Still, I must emphasise that this text mainly covers general issues and principles which are applicable across all the networks. For example, all of Chapter 1 (general issues relating to online searching), most of Chapter 2 (basic commands and tools), and Chapters 3-7 (content of databases and general keyword search principles and applications) contain information which is highly relevant to all systems. Chapter 8 (full text files) is generally applicable, although currently most of the full text scientific databases mentioned are available only on STN. The sections relating to the content of patent databases in Chapter 9, and some of the specific search options, have general application since many of the major patent databases are available on the three systems. However, many of the special topics in Chapter 10 are specific to STN, although the other networks sometimes have comparable implementations.

Chapter 11 discusses general aspects of chemical substances and chemistry (which certainly are independent of online networks!), and discusses details of the indexing of the Chemical Abstracts Registry Database which is used by all systems. Next, Chapters 12 and 13 discuss aspects of retrieval of substances by name- and formula-based searches and while generally applicable it must be pointed out that there are some specific implementations of the different systems which need to be addressed in certain instances.

While structure searches are possible on the Orbit/Questel network the implementation is quite different from that on STN. This presents no problem for those who access both STN and Orbit/Questel using the STN Express communications software, but it must be said that nearly all of Chapters 14 and 15 (how structure searching works, and searching by structure) address options available only on STN. While I am well aware that substances may be found exclusively by name and formula-based searches, and that some feel that they never will need to understand or perform structure searches, I believe the majority of searches for substances should at very least consider structure search options. While this statement may alarm some searchers, I can assure them that structure searches are not difficult and indeed are much easier than searching for text based terms!

The key to most of Chapter 16 (substance files with property information) is to be able to find the substances in the first place and thus the searcher needs to understand all about the options in the preceding four chapters. Finally, the majority of Chapter 17 (searching for chemical reactions) relates to the CASREACT database which is exclusive to STN, although the general principles are applicable to alternative chemical reaction databases, for example those available through in-house networks or through CD-ROM products.

Next, while substantial parts of the text relate to issues in chemistry and allied sciences, this book is for all who need to search generally in the sciences. Thus issues relating to chemical substances need very special consideration, and information on chemical substances is required across a very wide range of disciplines. On the other hand, issues relating to keyword searches in the sciences are less complex and the principles involved in any case are the same regardless of the discipline in which the keyword searches are done.

Online networks have changed dramatically in the last decade, and will continue to change but perhaps not at such a fast rate. While the basic rules, on which the text focuses, have now been established, nevertheless some of the technology will have advanced by the time this text appears in print. Vendors produce monthly news bulletins and these should be as essential a part of the scientist's current reading as is the primary literature.

At times, the text has been written in point form since I consider that a few "bullet points" can say more than extensive prose. Bullet points also can highlight, and can encourage critical thought on, the matters being addressed. I hope readers take up this challenge to critically review the suggestions and examples presented!

In this text, those parts which display information from online records are listed as screens, and this clearly differentiates them from tables or figures. These screens were taken from the STN network during the latter part of 1995, and so are current in that general time period. All the screens were not recorded on the same day, so there may be some listings which are not absolutely consistent throughout. It should also be mentioned here that the screens displayed in this text may be a little different from the actual appearance of the entries in the databases, and that many screens have been edited. Such editing has been necessary for publication purposes in this print format, but all attempts have been made to preserve the important points in the screens where such editing has occurred. However, as mentioned many times, this text focuses on general principles and so the precise number of records retrieved, and indeed the details of individual searches, are of much lesser importance.

Acknowledgments

Over the years I have been fortunate to learn about online searching and its techniques from many people, particularly those at the Chemical Abstracts Service in Columbus, Ohio. However, I also have learnt much from the many thousands of people who have attended the workshops and user meetings I have presented, and from those who regularly call me as part of my function as STN Help Desk operator in Australia. I thank you all.

I particularly thank Brian Cannan, Ed Hueckel, Beth Langstaff, Bernie Losekamp, Ken Ostrum, Kirk Schwall, Joe Uffner, and Fred Winer from the Chemical Abstracts Service, and Tony Graddon from the CSIRO Information Services Unit in Australia. All of these people, in various ways, have been both helpers and inspirers!

I thank also those in STN, and the various database producers, who have given me access to the databases and have given permission to display the various online records shown in this book. While I have given specific acknowledgments to the owners of the materials in the screens I have displayed, there are many other tables and figures which derive from information provided by the database producers. As I mention in Chapter 8, the producers of the secondary literature enhance the original literature significantly and searching the scientific literature effectively is possible because of their contributions.

I acknowledge also others who have assisted with the writing of this text including Paul Peters (Science Information International Ltd, The Netherlands), and Tony Smith (President, Magdalen College Oxford). However, special thanks go to Fred Winer (Chemical Abstracts Service) who worked through the manuscript with me at its various stages of preparation and who offered so much valuable technical advice.

Part 1

Focus on Keywords

1

Online Searching

In this chapter we learn:

- *How the scientific literature has changed.*
- *Electronic databases (what types of databases there are, who makes them, and how we access them).*
- *How the changes affect those who search the literature.*
- *The different versions of the electronic databases (online, in-house, and CD-ROM).*
- *And we consider some likely future developments in searching electronic databases.*

1.1   Changes in scientific publishing

The modern era of the scientific literature began in the early parts of the 19th century when a handful of scientific societies in Europe produced the first journals. These journals were collections of works by different authors rather than complete works in book form, and they reported the most recent discoveries. At this time most research groups were able to collect the full relevant literature in their personal libraries. In a way they had immediate access to the world's literature!

By the beginning of the 20th century many hundreds of journals were being produced and organizations saw the need for indexes, particularly in the major fields of chemistry, medicine and physics.

One of these organizations was the American Chemical Society which set up a special division, the Chemical Abstracts Service, in 1907. The mission of CAS was "to be the world leader in providing chemical information" and this it has done very effectively in the traditional print version. By the early 1960s there were almost three million abstracts and Chemical Abstracts were increasing at a rate of nearly 200,000 entries per year. (Currently the Chemical Abstracts Service indexes around 9000 serials and other document types, and the database is increasing by over 500,000 entries per year.) It was becoming very evident that a new version was needed - if only to save space on the burgeoning library shelves!

First the literature was produced additionally in cassettes, and then in microfiche, but the process of searching remained the same. It involved a very tedious manual search of the indexes which now covered many thousands of journals and other publications.

1.2   Electronic database producers

In 1963 CAS decided to invest heavily in the new computer technology. In making the decision that they would produce their abstracts in machine readable form, CAS became one of the world's first electronic database producers.

The new technology required a different approach to database construction and in those early years CAS made a number of key policy decisions which were to change the concept of searching the literature.

Many other organizations, who also traditionally had produced hardcopy abstracts, soon became electronic database producers as well (Table 1.1). So by the late 1960s a number of electronic databases were available, but access to them was restricted to those few who were able to lease copies of the databases, and load them on their own computers.

Table 1.1   Some major electronic database producers[a]

ORGANIZATION	MAJOR BIBLIOGRAPHIC FILE	YEARS RECORDS (for the electronic version)	
BIOSIS	BIOSIS	1969-	9.5M
Chemical Abstracts Service	CA/CAplus	1967-	12M
Engineering Information Inc	COMPENDEX	1970-	4M
Elsevier	EMBASE	1974-	6M
US Department of Energy	ENERGY	1974-	3M
American Geological Institute	GeoRef	1785-	2M
IFI/Plenum	IFICDB IFIPAT IFIUDB	1950-	3M
Int. Atomic Energy Agency	INIS	1970-	2M
European Patent Office	INPADOC	1968-	23M
Institution Electrical Engineers	INSPEC	1969-	5M
Japan Info Centre Science/Tech	JICST-E	1985-	2M
Cambridge Scientific Abs	LIFESCI	1978-	1.5M
FIZ Karlsruhe	MATH	1972-	1M
US National Library of Medicine	MEDLINE TOXLINE TOXLIT	1966-	8M
Materials Information	METADEX	1966-	1M
Nat Tech Info Service	NTIS	1964-	2M
Deutsches Patent amt	PATDPA	1968-	2.5M
Institute for Scientific Information	SCISEARCH	1974-	13M
US Patent and Trademark Office	USPATFULL	1971-	2M
Derwent Information Ltd	WPI Files	1963-	7M

[a]This list contains some of the major electronic database producers of the late 1960s. Since then a number of traditional hardcopy producers, for example the Beilstein Institute, have converted their databases into electronic versions.

1.3   Online vendors

In the early 1970s another important development occurred. Satellite links enabled cheaper telecommunications and a new business grew. This was the business of the online vendors who loaded several databases on host computers which could be accessed remotely. At last, online searching was a reality for anyone who was prepared to make a small investment in a desk-top computer, and in a means of linking this computer through a telecommunications network to the host.

The online vendors started with relatively few databases, but quickly more were added so that currently the major vendors have well in excess of 100 databases. They now cover all areas of the literature, and indeed there are a number of different databases which cover various aspects of a single area.

By far the major online vendors of information in the *sciences* are the networks known as Dialog which is owned by Knight Ridder Information Services, the Orbit/Questel network which is a combination of the former Orbit and Questel networks, and STN, which originally commenced as the CASONLINE network. Many of the same science databases are available through each of these networks, although at times in somewhat different versions. Each vendor also has a number of unique files, and searchers should study the advantages and disadvantages of each network, and study the latest options being offered.

1.4 How these changes affect scientists and information specialists

The changes affect scientists, and the information specialists who support them, in many ways.

1.4.1 Instant and worldwide access

Once again the full literature is available to the researcher at a location near to the laboratory. All that is needed is a computer and a connection to an international telecommunications network which serves the online vendor. However, one major difference between this situation and that in the late 19th century is the size of the literature. Today the online searcher is often overloaded with information, and special strategies now have to be used to retrieve only the most relevant records.

1.4.2 Access versus ownership

Another major difference is that the library of the late 19th century was owned by the end-user. While library resources actually have expanded in the latter part of the 20th century, they have not expanded at anywhere near the same rate as the expansion of the literature. Critical scrutiny of library budgets has meant the number of hardcopy materials owned has increasingly diminished in proportion to the size of the literature.

Ownership of materials protects the interests of future scientists in the organization, but if this is done at the expense of adequate provision of services to the present scientists, then the policy needs changing. Indeed the long debate of access to, versus ownership of, the literature in the sciences essentially now is over. The best science libraries are those which provide the best *access* to the literature.

Somewhat related to this is the whole question of pricing. During the 20th century, the hardcopy literature served the supplier and the user in a way which was beneficial to both, and for which both groups could establish, and work within, budgets. However, with the availability first of photocopiers and now of relatively cheap computers with very cheap memory storage, the financial aspects of the well-established relationship between supplier and user are volatile to say the least!

Like it or not, the scientist is being forced to change in the way the literature is searched. Further, as scientists increasingly are going to learn about each other's work through electronic databases, then scientists have to *rethink the way they write those parts of their papers,* which are their major source of input into the electronic record. This issue, which particularly relates to the importance of the titles and abstracts, is discussed in Section 3.9.

1.4.3   The different approach

The approach to searching the literature online is vastly different from the approach to searching the hardcopy, and it differs with the different types of files. There are a number of issues and they are discussed in detail in the chapters which follow. It is sufficient at this stage merely to note that online searching is vastly different from searching print materials in ways which may be summarized:

- in text files, many different concepts, including those entered by authors and by indexers, can be searched and linked simultaneously;
- in many text files, the most comprehensive and efficient searching for substances is performed with Registry Numbers rather than name based terms and this applies particularly to those files, like those produced by CAS, in which CAS Registry Numbers are the primary index terms. (CAS Registry Numbers also facilitate searching for substances in many other files, although at times there may be some limitations which will be mentioned later in this text);
- in chemical substance files, structures may be searched and either exact, or substructure, matches of the structure search query may be sought (there is no counterpart to structure searching in the print materials);
- information about many substances may be searched simultaneously;
- in numeric files, it is possible to find numeric values for substances or to find substances which have specific numeric properties;
- in full text files, individual words, or words connected in specified ways, may be searched in a way not possible in the hardcopy; and
- it is very easy through online networks to search across a number of databases and to obtain unique answer sets (for example, to eliminate duplicate answers).

Online searching provides opportunities not possible through hardcopy searching, but there is a price to pay. The first relates to the problems inherent with reliance on access to materials where at least in part outside organizations have control; the second relates to the fact that to become an effective online searcher requires a considerable investment in learning the skills of online searching, in learning the command language of the online vendor, and in understanding the editorial policies of the database producers.

Online searching is very different from searching print materials. You have to think in a very different way, so change your way of thinking!

1.4.4 Costs
It is unfortunate that in many organizations the costs of online searching have been directed towards the end-user, whereas the costs of the hardcopy library have been built into the institutional infrastructure. This has given an entirely false impression of the relative cost of online services to the end-users. It is difficult to estimate the real costs of online searching versus searching the hardcopy (and all the infrastructure required to support it in the first instance), and in any case these costs will vary for older and for newer institutions, and across the research disciplines being studied. However, a conservative estimate is that online costs are only 25% of the real costs of searching and maintaining the hardcopy library. Naturally, online networks also allow coverage of a much wider range of literature than that which can be purchased and maintained in a library of print materials.

From the outset it must be said that anything of any value costs money to produce, so whoever makes the investment in indexing and providing access to the scientific literature will need to recover costs. Accordingly end-users should consider the value of the information they obtain through online networks as well as the costs, and must understand that nothing comes free!

1.5 Types of databases

There are a variety of types of databases, and the broad types are listed in Table 1.2. The general contents of the databases are given, but there are differences with the different databases, for example some chemical substance databases may have very extensive bibliographic and numeric information.

Table 1.2 Broad database classes

TYPE OF DATABASE	CONTENT
Bibliographic	title of article, names of authors and their organizations, source of article (journal name, volume, publication year, page number), abstract, index entries
Chemical substance	substance names, molecular formulas, chemical structure
Chemical reaction	primarily based on chemical reactions, particularly on the conversion of one substance to another
Directory	products and suppliers
Numeric	chemical, physical and toxicology property information
Full text	full text of the original article

Quite different techniques are needed to search and display information in the different types of databases. However, as online searching is considerably more complicated than hardcopy searching, the scientist must rely to a great extent on the expertise of the information specialist.

1.6 The principal roles of information specialists and scientists

Indeed online searching is best conducted through a close association between the information specialist and the scientist, and each has special roles.

In general the principal roles of the information specialist are:

*   to maintain the local hardware and software;
*   to maintain the access to the online networks and to conduct all administrative tasks;
*   to have full knowledge of the network commands and techniques for online searching;
*   to obtain copies of original publications;
*   to be familiar with database policies across a wide range of scientific disciplines and to alert scientists to the limitations of the databases; and
*   to alert scientists to system options and to conduct general training programs on online searching within the organization.

The principal roles of the scientist are:

*   to be familiar with general issues relating to database policies, particularly for those databases central to the research area;
*   to be familiar with basic network commands and techniques for online searching; and
*   to advise the information specialist on the intent and scope of the search requirements, and on the scientific aspects of the search query.

Currently there often is too big a gap in knowledge between the information specialist and the scientist. It is just as unreasonable to expect the information specialist to become expert in the scientific disciplines of the end-user scientists, as it is to expect the scientist to become fully conversant with all the technical details of online searching. However, scientists really should become more familiar with database policies, and, in particular, to be fully aware of those relatively few instances when these policies mean the actual contents of the databases differ from the usual representations scientists use.

1.7   Realistic expectations of databases

There often is no single "correct" way to effect online searching, but there are basic rules to be followed. Different approaches, particularly to keyword searches, will achieve slightly different results but searchers cannot expect online networks to provide all the answers. Commonly references cited in key publications retrieved from online searches are still needed to help fill in some of the gaps.

It must also be realized that electronic databases are far from perfect and that inconsistencies and errors occur. Database producers are under considerable time pressure to keep the information up to date, and errors necessarily occur. While the database producers could, in time, work towards an error-free product, this would be at considerable extra cost, which in turn would be passed onto the end-user.

However, the deficiencies are few and in any case the skilled searcher can overcome most of them. Nevertheless it must be said that online searching is an extremely efficient process, particularly when compared with the efficiency with which searching the print materials is achieved.

1.8   The future of electronic databases

Computers and information technology will play an increasing role in communications between scientists and in library operations, but the question remains as to the version through which they will best serve the end-user scientist and information specialist in the access to the scientific literature. Online networks are only one electronic medium, but others include localized in-house systems, CD-ROM products, and public domain networks.

While the future is difficult to predict, a number of points may be made about the strengths and weaknesses of the various electronic options. A summary of the points follows and the advantages or disadvantages specified are relative to the type of the electronic version (online networks, localized computer networks, CD-ROMs) and are not relative to hardcopy versions. There can be no debate that electronic versions are vastly superior!

1.8.1   Online networks
The advantages of online networks are that they:

- have ease of access;
- have minimal infrastructure requirements;
- have ease of updating;
- have standardized formats;
- enable easy crossover of information between databases (to be able to correlate information in a number of databases is a key feature of online networks);
- have sophisticated search software which enables very extensive databases to be searched and in quite unique ways (for example, by chemical structure);
- provide breadth and depth of information; and
- don't depend on lease or contract arrangements.

The disadvantages of online networks are that they:

- incur telecommunication expenses;
- have direct costs associated with each use;
- require extensive training workshops; and
- require closely supervised access.

1.8.2   Localized computer databases and CD-ROMs
The advantages of in-house computer databases and CD-ROM products are that they:

- have ease of access;
- do not incur telecommunication expenses;
- do not have costs associated with each use; and
- require minimal supervised access.

The disadvantages are that they:

- have substantial infrastructure requirements both in equipment and personnel;
- may experience delays in updating;
- may not have standardization of formats;
- may not have ease of crossover between databases;

- may have less sophisticated (and hence limited) search software;
- may provide less breadth and depth of information, but then user-selection of databases will probably mean only the most relevant databases are held;[*]
- depend on lease and contract arrangements and have substantial subscription costs; and
- require some training workshops.

1.8.3   Public domain networks - for example, the INTERNET
Scientific publishing is a very complex process and the infrastructure developed over time, through which authors present their works to editors of serials who in turn call upon expert refereeing prior to publication, both safeguards the quality of the research and the quality of the way it is reported. Publishers also provide the necessary distribution networks.

Access to both the primary and secondary (indexed) literature through public domain networks like the INTERNET will become increasingly popular, but valuable information will never be free. It is difficult to see how different databases might be *networked* over the INTERNET in a way which will make this arrangement competitive with the commercial online vendors. The other current difficulty with the INTERNET is that, when used in the interactive mode, it is very slow in many parts of the world, and this can cause seemingly long and sometimes expensive delays.

1.8.4   "Front-end packages"
Without doubt a major limitation of online networks is the extensive training required to become proficient in the use of the network. Accordingly, online vendors are directing significant resources into the development of "front-end packages" which incorporate some of the intelligences of how databases are put together and some of the index issues, and which eliminate the need to learn the command language and the various online techniques and tools.

The STN Express software and the front end package Scifinder produced by STN, and ProBase and SciBase produced by Knight Ridder Information Services achieve the aim of making online searching more user-friendly and obviating the need for extensive training - at least for some applications. Indeed currently Scifinder is an excellent package which links the CAplus and REGISTRY Files (that is, the major bibliographic and substance files produced by CAS), and which involves a "point and click" mode of operation that requires essentially no prior training. Further, it has an attractive pricing package. However, currently it is limited to a few files (although more are being considered) and there are issues relating to the speed of the INTERNET, on which it relies, in some countries.

---

[*]However, not all relevant databases might be provided in formats suitable for in-house use. It must be realized that the electronic information provided by database producers is very different and that online vendors make very substantial investments in standardizing the tapes to produce a relatively consistent format between files (particularly to facilitate cross-file searching and to simplify the level of knowledge of search and display commands required).

Yet, with all these front-end packages there still are issues relating to indexing, and indeed to the content of the databases, and an elementary knowledge of these is helpful to say the least.* It will be some years before the packages fully take over, and in any event this will occur only when all the databases are available in forms which lend themselves more readily to manipulation by such techniques. Indeed, as is mentioned in Section 1.8.1, online networks require extensive training workshops and require closely supervised access, and this is partly due to the different constructions of, and consistencies within, the databases!

Summary

- *Electronic database producers* create databases in electronic versions.
- *Online vendors* standardize the formats and make many databases available worldwide through telecommunications networks.
- *Online searching requires a very different approach* to hardcopy searching, and offers opportunities not possible through the hardcopy versions.
- There are six *major types of databases* (bibliographic, chemical substance, chemical reaction, directory, numeric and full text) each of which requires special search and display techniques.
- *Online networks have many advantages* over alternative electronic versions and are likely to remain as the major source for information retrieval.

---

*Learning databases and searching the literature should be a part of all university and college courses but usually less than 1% of the course curriculum is given to these aspects even though most courses involve many hundreds of hours of teaching the scientific aspects!

2

Basic Commands and Tools

In this chapter we learn:

- *How to obtain your connection to the online network.*
- *How to tell the host computer what you want it to do (that is, the way you enter your instructions).*
- *The difference between a command and a subcommand prompt, and the implications of default options.*
- *The basic search tools which are the Boolean and proximity operators, and truncation.*

We conclude by looking at two actual records, one in a very general, and one in a very specific, area of research.

Before the content of the various types of databases[*] can be explored it is necessary to gain some familiarity with how the process works, and with the basic online techniques. Accordingly this chapter outlines some of the most commonly used commands and tools, which will be used as the databases are being discussed. Other commands will be introduced as needed throughout the text.

2.1   Making the connection to the host

The basic components of the process to make the online connection are given in Figure 2.1. As essentially any computer may be used, the first critical choice involves the communications software. Most vendors produce their own software, while independent software manufacturers also market communications packages.

12

---

[*]The word *file* is sometimes restricted to refer to the electronic version of a *database* which in turn is a collection of materials regardless of the format. However, the two terms are used interchangeably throughout this text.

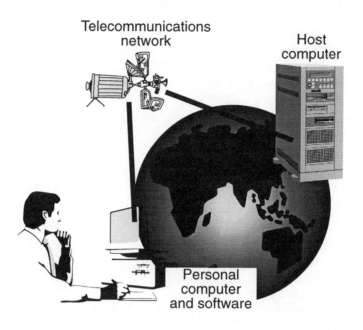

Figure 2.1 Components of the online connection

The searcher needs a computer and communications software with which to connect, via a communications network, to the host computer. To enter the system, a loginid and password are required.

Software may be divided into two types, namely those which support text only, and those which support text and graphics. If the searcher requires searching by structure, structure displays, or downloading of graphic images, then software which supports text and graphics is essential. While currently there are a few communications software packages which support graphics, the communications software STN Express, available from STN, has an excellent interface with the search engines used for searching chemical structures. STN Express also has facilities for connecting to other vendors, for interfacing with the QUESTEL structure connection tables, and for capturing graphic images.

Access to online vendors may be made through telecommunications networks like INTERNET, CompuServe, SprintNet and BT Tymnet, or through local networks or direct dial. (Searchers should check with the vendor on the connection procedure, and seek assistance from them in the event of any difficulties arising, since sometimes it can be a tricky process to make connections through local area networks.) An account is needed with the host vendor and when this has been set up a loginid and password are given to the account holder. All communications software programs have facilities for autologin, but, if used, it is necessary to maintain adequate security within the local network in order to allow access to authorized users only.

2.2   Commands and subcommands; command defaults

Upon completion of the login, the system gives the command prompt which on STN is the arrow, => (Screen 2.1).

Screen 2.1[a]   STN   login

* * * * * * * * * Welcome to STN International * * * * * * * * * *

NEWS 1 Dec 18 STN Seminar Schedule - N. America
NEWS 2 Sep 21 MAC & DOS STN Express Users
NEWS 3 Aug 4 Macintosh STN Express Users of C(O)CH3 Shortcut
NEWS 4 Dec 8 Discount Change for STN Karlsruhe Academic Program
NEWS 5 Dec 21 PATOSEP now more convenient for English speaking searchers.
NEWS 6 Dec 21 NEWCRYST and NEI No Longer Available
NEWS 7 Dec 22 Recent Internet Congestion Relieved
NEWS 8 Jan 2 DRUGPAT added to STN with one FREE connect hour in January

NEWS HOURS STN Operating Hours Plus Help Desk Availability
NEWS INTER General Internet Information
NEWS LOGIN Welcome Banner and News Items
NEWS PHONE Direct Dial and Telecommunication Network Access to STN
NEWS WWW   CAS World Wide Web site (general information)

Enter NEWS followed by the item number or name to see news on that
specific topic.

* * * * * * * * * * * * * * STN Columbus * * * * * * * * * * * * * * *
FILE 'HOME' ENTERED AT 19:42:43 ON 02 JAN 96
=>

---

[a]Copyright STN and Reprinted with Permission

It is necessary now to enter a command, then the searcher's instructions followed by a carriage return. The format is:

=>   **COMMAND   < USER INSTRUCTIONS>   RETURN**[*]

While there are over 30 commands used on the different networks, the 5 most common are the commands to enter the file, to display an alphabetical listing of terms, to conduct a search, to view answers online, and to end the online session. All networks have commands for these purposes and the actual commands used by STN are given in Table 2.1. (The corresponding commands on Dialog and Orbit/Questel are given in Appendix 1.)

---

[*]In this text all user entries are typed in bold - for convenience in interpreting the online screens.

Table 2.1 The five most commonly used commands

FULL NAME OF COMMAND	ABBREV- IATION	FUNCTION	EXAMPLE (STN)
FILE	**FIL**	to enter a file (database)	**FIL BIOSIS**
EXPAND	**E**	to display an alphabetical list of terms	**E NUTRITION**
SEARCH	**S**	to conduct a search	**S NUTRITION**
DISPLAY	**D**	to view answers online	**D L1 1-5 BIB**
LOGOFF	**LOG**	to end the online session	**LOG Y**

All commands must be followed by the user's instructions. If insufficient or incorrect instructions are given, the system either assumes defaults (see below) or gives the subcommand prompt, which on STN is the colon, **:** . Subcommands always appear if the full name of the command is entered. With many subcommands there are default options, which are shown in parentheses before the subcommand prompt, and on STN the default options may be selected either by typing in the option or by typing in a period. To illustrate this, if a search has been conducted and if an answer set L1[*] of 15 answers has been obtained in a bibliographic database, then the subcommands under the DISPLAY command appear:

> => **DISPLAY**
> ENTER (L1), L# OR ?: .
> ENTER ANSWER NUMBER OR RANGE (1): **1-3, 8, 15**
> ENTER DISPLAY FORMAT (BIB): **BIB IND**

There are many points to note here:

- the three defaults are in parentheses, that is, (L1), (1), and (BIB);
- in the DISPLAY command the last answer set obtained is listed as the default L-number;
- any L# (L-number) may be entered as required;
- online help may always be obtained by typing in the query mark, ? (see also Section 10.1.1);
- the default in the first subcommand above (L1) may be chosen either by typing in L1 or a period (default options on STN always are given in parentheses and may be chosen by entering a period at the subcommand);
- the default answer number (of the 15 in the above example) is answer number 1 (which always is the most recent answer in answer sets from bibliographic databases);
- any single answer, or range of answers (with numbers separated by a hyphen) may be displayed and commas (or spaces) may be typed between the individual answers or ranges (as shown);
- all answers may be displayed if required (here either by entering 1-, or 1-15); and
- the format of the answer is the part of the record the searcher requires (the various options will be discussed in later sections).

---

[*]Each information unit is given an L-number on STN. It is a reference number which may be used as a search term, or as an identifier for further instructions, for example to indicate which answer set is to be displayed.

However, if the abbreviation of the command is entered the command defaults are chosen automatically by the system, although any individual subcommand may be overridden if required. Some examples are given in Table 2.2.

Table 2.2 Some examples of the display command in a typical bibliographic file (in which the default display format is the BIB format)

ENTRY	OUTCOME
D	answer 1 from last answer set displayed in BIB format
D 5-7	answers 5,6,7 from last answer set displayed in BIB format
D 1- TI ABS	titles and abstracts of all answers from last answer set displayed
D 2 7 IALL	answers 2 and 7 from the last answer set in the indented all format
D L4 2,7 AU	Author field entries in answers 2 and 7 from answer set L4

Most commands have subcommand defaults and naturally they vary with the different commands. It is handy to know the defaults, although since they always represent the most common choices then few problems result if they are used automatically. The defaults for the five main commands on STN are given in Table 2.3.

Table 2.3 Command default options on STN

COMMAND	DEFAULT
FILE	HOME File
EXPAND	Twelve alphabetical listings in the Basic Index[a]
SEARCH	Search conducted in the Basic Index[a]
DISPLAY	Answer 1, of last answer set, in default format for the file
LOGOFF	No default, confirmation of command always required

[a]All files have a number of fields, and those which are most commonly searched are collectively grouped in the Basic Index (which differs from file to file).

Important notes:
- **Commands may be entered as the full word or as an abbreviation.**
- **Commands have a number of subcommand options.**
- **There are system determined defaults for many subcommands.**
- **If you enter the full word for the command you will be prompted for the subcommands (and the defaults will be in parentheses).**
- **If you enter the abbreviation, the system will execute the defaults unless you override them.**

2.3   Basic search tools

Bibliographic databases may contain records with several hundreds of words, and may include many different concepts. One of the great advantages of online searching is that a number of different concepts may be searched simultaneously, and this is possible partly because *words in records are treated as individual entries.* The searcher merely picks out the keywords in the record and connects them in any way desired with either Boolean or proximity operators.

2.3.1   Boolean operators

The AND operator (example: => S ACID AND RAIN) requires that the terms both be present in the record, while the NOT operator (example: => S ACID NOT RAIN) requests that only records which have the first term and not the second term be retrieved. The NOT operator should be used with caution since it is all-exclusive and may eliminate answers of interest in certain circumstances. That is, if the term is to be excluded (NOT operator used) the record will be eliminated even though other parts of the record may contain terms required. However, as will be seen later, care must be exercised in the use of *all* operators!

The OR operator requires that at least one of the terms be present in a record in order for it to be retrieved. It is used to link synonyms, and terms connected with the OR operator should always be enclosed in parentheses, since terms in parentheses are considered first in the execution of the search statement by the system. (Systems define the order of execution of the operators and the OR operator always has the *lowest* priority.) Synonymous terms always have this requirement of priority execution!

For example, the search: => S ACID AND RAIN OR SNOW would execute the AND operator first then the OR operator (since the normal priority of execution is AND before OR). Accordingly any record with ACID and RAIN, and then, independently, any record with SNOW would be retrieved.

However, the search: => S ACID AND (RAIN OR SNOW) would achieve the desired aim since any record which had the term ACID, and either of the synonymous terms RAIN and SNOW, would be retrieved.[*]

> **Important notes:**
> - **There are often a number of synonyms for the various scientific terms, and great care should be taken to ensure that all relevant synonyms are incorporated in the search statement in order to obtain comprehensive answers.**
> - **Synonyms are connected with the OR operator and terms must be in parentheses.**

---

*The use of parentheses here to achieve priority in execution of operators is analogous to their use in mathematics. For example, $4 + 4 \div 2$ gives 6 (division has priority over addition) whereas $(4+4)\div 2$ gives 4 since operators in parentheses have priority.

Use of the Boolean operators AND and NOT requires that the terms be anywhere in the record (actually, the operators require the terms to be anywhere in the fields being searched), but frequently greater precision in the connection between the terms is required. This greater precision is achieved by use of *proximity operators*. Meanwhile connecting all possible synonyms with the OR operator could involve lengthy search entries but luckily many synonyms have the same word stem (for example, ACID, ACIDS, ACIDIC) and so *truncation symbols* are used. Proximity operators and truncation symbols are often used in search statements instead of the three Boolean operators.

2.3.2 Proximity operators: greater precision in use of AND and NOT

Bibliographic databases contain a number of fields. For example, the title of the article is placed in the Title Field (TI), the authors in the Author Field (AU), where they work in the Corporate Source Field (CS), the abstract is in the Abstract Field (AB), and the index entries are in the Index Fields (IT, CC, ST, CT). Details of bibliographic search fields are discussed in Chapters 5 and 6, but at this stage all that is necessary to know is that there are a number of different and independent fields in which searches may be conducted.

The Boolean operators AND or NOT apply to the fields searched. In bibliographic databases searches are mainly performed in the default field, called the Basic Index, which usually includes individual words from the title, abstract, keywords and index fields.

So the search: => **S ACID AND RAIN** retrieves answers where the two terms are *anywhere* in the Basic Index. ACID may appear only in the title, while RAIN may appear only in the abstract.

In many searches it is necessary to have a more restricted connection between the terms in order to avoid false hits. For example, the above search would retrieve answers in which IODIC ACID SALTS were used in seeding RAIN, and these would be irrelevant if the search intended to retrieve only records in which ACID RAIN (that is, rain which is acidic - usually because of sulfuric acid present) is reported.

More restricted connections are achieved through the use of proximity operators, which are listed in Table 2.4 together with their broad definitions. (In some files the operators have special meanings and these will be discussed in subsequent chapters, while issues relating to the use of proximity operators are discussed in Section 7.3.1.)

Table 2.4 Proximity operators on STN

OPERATOR	ALLOWS ANSWERS WHEN
AND	terms are anywhere in the fields searched
(L)	terms are in the same information unit[a]
(P)	terms are in the same paragraph
(S)	terms are in the same sentence
(A)	terms are immediately adjacent (any order)
(W)	terms are adjacent in the order specified

[a]This generally applies to a single field, or a single field repetition in cases, like index fields, where many headings are used.

Notes on proximity operators:

• The list of operators in Table 2.4 requires that terms linked be present, that is a search: => **S ACID (L) RAIN** requires both terms be in the same information unit. However, just like the NOT operator requires that the terms following the operator be excluded, then (NOTL), (NOTP), (NOTS), (NOTA), and (NOTW) require that the terms following the operator be excluded within the restriction imposed by the proximity specified.

- The operators (P), (S), (A), and (W) may be further qualified by numbers, so that (nA) requires that the terms have not more than n intervening words. So an article with a string of words, "....this concentration of sulfuric acid in rain can affect growth of plants ....", would be retrieved with the search: => **S ACID (1A) RAIN**, but not with the search: => **S ACID (A) RAIN**.

- Most systems use implied proximity in cases where search terms are separated by blanks, that is, the (W) operator is assumed. Accordingly it is perfectly acceptable to conduct a search: => **S AUTOMOBILE ENGINE**, but only since the system automatically interprets the instruction as: => **S AUTOMOBILE (W) ENGINE**. (Remember words are entered individually, and there would be no *single* word AUTOMOBILE ENGINE!)

- While it is essential to insert a "space" before and after Boolean operators (**S ACID AND RAIN**), it is optional to insert a "space" before and after proximity operators (**S ACID(L)RAIN, S ACID (L) RAIN** both are acceptable).

- While upper-case letters have been used for instructions following command and subcommand prompts throughout this text, either upper- or lower-case letters always are acceptable.

2.3.3 Truncation symbols: simplifying the use of OR

The three truncation symbols used on STN are given in Table 2.5. The ? is used to represent any number of characters (including zero). In most files only "right-hand" truncation may be used, that is, the symbol may be used only after the word stem. However, some files permit the use of "left-hand" truncation as well. (The Database Summary Sheets, which are discussed in Section 5.7 and which are provided free of charge for each File, indicate when left-hand truncation may be used.) For example, the search: => **S ?SYNTHE?** would retrieve, *inter alia*, **SYNTHE*SIS*, SYNTHE*TIC***, and *PHOTO***SYNTHE*SIS***.

Table 2.5 Truncation symbols on STN

SYMBOL	USED FOR	EXAMPLE	RETRIEVES
?	zero or any number of characters	**S ACID?**	ACID, ACIDS ACIDIC, ACIDIFY ACIDIFICATION
#	zero or one character	**S ACID##**	ACID, ACIDS, ACIDIC
!	one character (within word only)	**S POLYMERI!E**	POLYMERISE, POLYMERIZE

Truncation should not be chosen too early in the word stem (otherwise non-synonymous terms might be searched: for example, SYN? would search SYNONYM as well as SYNTHESIS), nor too late (otherwise synonyms might be excluded, for example, SYNTHES? would retrieve SYNTHESIS but not SYNTHETIC). It is to be noted that the use of truncation may be cost-effective in files which have search term pricing, since only one search fee is incurred even though a number of terms are effectively searched. That is, even though: => **S ANTICHOLESTER?** searches for many terms (which if entered individually would each constitute a search term and incur a fee when search term charges apply) there is only one search term charge.

Truncation also is used to retrieve singular and plural forms of words and while users sometimes request systems to allow for "automatic plurals", this is not a good use of computer technology. Many false hits would be obtained and many unnecessary terms would be used if computer algorithms were used for this purpose!

> **Important notes:**
> - **Operators connect individual terms; the proximity operators give greater precision than the Boolean operators AND and NOT.**
> - **Truncation symbols simplify the use of the OR operator.**

2.4 Two examples

Searches may be conducted on any topic! While in subsequent chapters the details of how to search and then how to display answers are discussed, it is worth exploring now two simple searches in order to become familiar with the overall procedure and with the type of information that is available.

Case 1: Find information reporting studies relating to the origin of life
While studies on the origin of life may come from a variety of scientific areas, one important area of research involves the study of fossils and the GeoRef File, which has information from across the earth sciences, is a particularly good starting point.

Relevant articles might contain words like: origin of life; origins of life; original life forms; and original forms of life (plus, of course, many other terms, but at this stage the exercise is simply to obtain a sample record in order to gain some familiarity with what is involved in a search), so one search term might be ORIGIN## and the second one might be LIFE. In order to retrieve records in which the two terms are near each other in the text, the (L) proximity operator is tried in the first instance, and the results are shown in Screen 2.2.

Screen 2.2[a]   Sample search on the origins of life in the GeoRef File

```
=> FIL GEOREF
.... b
=> S     ORIGIN##(L)LIFE
         59436        ORIGIN##
          4796        LIFE
L1        1652        ORIGIN##(L)LIFE
```

[b]Throughout this text many online displays are abbreviated and four periods (....) are often used to indicate when this occurs. The text omitted here is the system response to acknowledge the GeoRef File has been entered, to indicate the progressive cost of the current session, and to advise on the copyright restriction.

---

[a]Copyright American Geological Institute and Elsevier Scientific Publishers, and reprinted with permission

After the search: => **S ORIGIN## (L) LIFE** is entered, the system lists the postings for the terms searched, that is the number of records which have the individual terms. In this case there are 59,436 records in the file which have the word stem ORIGIN with up to two additional letters (remember each # allows for one or zero characters at the end of a word), and 4796 records which have the word LIFE. Then the system looks through these records, identifies all those which have both the terms present in the same information unit (this restriction is imposed by the searcher through the use of the (L) operator), and puts them into an answer set which it labels L1. As seen in Screen 2.2, 1652 records satisfy this criterion.

Any of these answers may be displayed in a variety of formats, and a sample answer is shown in Screen 2.3. This answer was retrieved since the required terms appear in the last line of the record, and, for convenience, the system "highlights" these terms (generally in bold as shown here, although highlighting may appear between asterisks ***, or squares ▯).

Screen 2.3[a]   Sample answer from the GeoRef File (ALL display format)

AN	95:31971 GeoRef ND 95-29188
TI	Role of major terrestrial cratering events in dispersing life in the solar system
AU	Wallis, Max K.; Wickramasinghe, N. C.
CS	University of Wales College of Cardiff, School of Mathematics, Cardiff, United Kingdom; University of the West Indies, Kingston, Jamaica
SO	Earth and Planetary Science Letters, 130(1-4). Pub. date: Feb 1995. p. 69-73. 20 refs. Publisher: Elsevier, Amsterdam, Netherlands CODEN: EPSLA2
DT	Serial
BL	Analytic
FS	NEW; Bibliography and Index of Geology
LA	English
AB	The larger and most energetic cratering events from comet and asteroid collisions with the Earth are probably associated with ejection of solid material faster than escape speeds every 100 Myr or so. Metre-sized boulders, we estimate, may have been ejected directly into Venus-crossing and perhaps Mars-crossing orbits from comet impacts at ....
CC	4 (Extraterrestrial Geology)
CT	asteroids; comets; cratering; Earth; ejecta; exobiology; impacts; Jupiter; **life origin**; Mars; solar system; theoretical studies

---

Of course, there are too many answers (1652) in this initial answer set and the search would need to be refined, but at least this example illustrates how information is obtained. The various options for refining initial answer sets are discussed later (in Chapters 6 and 7).

Case 2: Find information on asymmetric tandem additions
However, information on very specific research may be obtained just as easily and a
particularly interesting, but specific, chemical process involves asymmetric tandem
addition.[*] The CAplus File is a good source of such chemical information, and the display
of a record from a search: => **S ASYMMETRIC TANDEM ADDITION#** is shown
in Screen 2.4.

All that needs to be noted here is that while the record in Screen 2.4 is quite different
from the record in Screen 2.3, in both records the information is presented in a number of
fields. For example, some of the fields are the Title Field (TI), Author Field (AU), and
Abstract Field (AB).

Screen 2.4[a] Sample record from search in the CAplus File

ACCESSION NUMBER:	1990:98170 CAPLUS
DOCUMENT NUMBER:	112:98170
TITLE:	Intramolecular **asymmetric tandem additions** to chiral naphthyloxazolines
AUTHOR(S):	Meyers, A. I.; Licini, Giulia
CORPORATE SOURCE:	Dep. Chem., Colorado State Univ., Fort Collins, CO, 80523, USA
SOURCE:	Tetrahedron Lett. (1989), 30(31), 4049-52 CODEN: TELEAY; ISSN: 0040-4039
DOCUMENT TYPE:	Journal
LANGUAGE:	English
CLASSIFICATION:	25-27 (Benzene, Its Derivatives, and Condensed Benzenoid Compounds)
OTHER SOURCE(S):	CASREACT 112:98170
GRAPHIC IMAGE:	

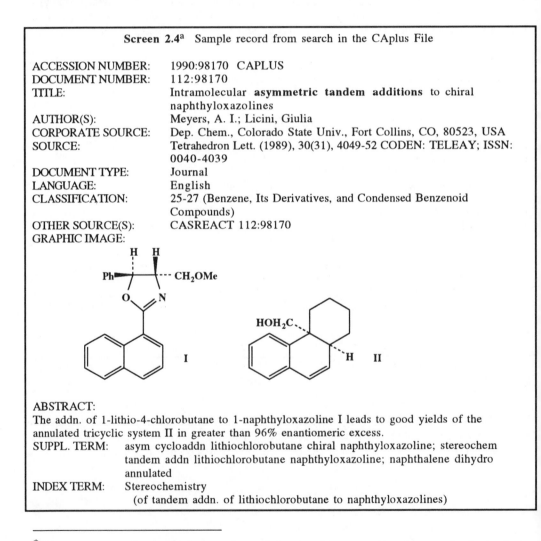

ABSTRACT:
The addn. of 1-lithio-4-chlorobutane to 1-naphthyloxazoline I leads to good yields of the
annulated tricyclic system II in greater than 96% enantiomeric excess.

SUPPL. TERM:	asym cycloaddn lithiochlorobutane chiral naphthyloxazoline; stereochem tandem addn lithiochlorobutane naphthyloxazoline; naphthalene dihydro annulated
INDEX TERM:	Stereochemistry (of tandem addn. of lithiochlorobutane to naphthyloxazolines)

---

[*]It is not necessary for the reader to understand the chemistry now, since this exercise is simply to
obtain a quite different type of record in order to show the variety of information which is
available in bibliographic files.

Screen 2.4 (continued)	
INDEX TERM:	Cycloaddition reaction
	(stereoselective, of lithiochlorobutane to chiral naphthyloxazoline)
INDEX TERM:	87306-64-7 89043-90-3
	ROLE: PROC (Process)
	(cycloaddn. of, with lithiochlorobutane, stereochem. of)
INDEX TERM:	125425-83-4
	ROLE: PROC (Process)
	(cycloaddn. of, with naphthyloxazolines, stereochem. of)
INDEX TERM:	125425-86-7P
	ROLE: RCT (Reactant); SPN (Synthetic preparation); PREP (Preparation)
	(prepn. and decarbonylation of)
INDEX TERM:	125425-89-0P
	ROLE: RCT (Reactant); SPN (Synthetic preparation); PREP (Preparation)
	(prepn. and hydride redn. of)
INDEX TERM:	125425-85-6P
	ROLE: RCT (Reactant); SPN (Synthetic preparation); PREP (Preparation)
	(prepn. and hydrolysis or redn. of)
INDEX TERM:	125425-88-9P
	ROLE: RCT (Reactant); SPN (Synthetic preparation); PREP (Preparation)
	(prepn. and hydrolysis-acetylation of)
INDEX TERM:	1013-08-7P, 1,2,3,4-Tetrahydrophenanthrene 125425-84-5P 125425-87-8P
	125474-05-7P
	ROLE: SPN (Synthetic preparation); PREP (Preparation)
	(prepn. of)
INDEX TERM:	10297-05-9, 1-Chloro-4-iodobutane
	ROLE: RCT (Reactant)
	(sequential lithium-iodide exchange and cycloaddn. of, with
	naphthyloxazolines)

The next five chapters discuss the different types of information, and then the different techniques required in searching bibliographic databases!

Summary

*   *Connections* to online networks require several steps, and details are available through the Customer Service Centers for the vendors.
*   The system has *two levels of prompts*: command level and subcommand level.
*   All interactions with the host computer require the format:

    => COMMAND   \<INSTRUCTIONS>   RETURN

*   When *full commands* are entered, subcommand prompts appear automatically; subcommand defaults then appear in parentheses.
*   When *abbreviated forms* of the commands are entered, subcommand defaults will be executed unless they are overridden by the user.
*   Files contain entries in *fields*.

- In most fields *individual words* are entered, although in a few fields (particularly the Author Field and index heading fields) terms are entered as bound phrases.
- *Boolean operators* AND and NOT are used to connect terms in records, although more specific *proximity operators* often are required.
- Boolean operator OR is used to search for synonyms and *terms must be enclosed in parentheses*.
- *Truncation symbols* are used to search for terms with common stems. Right-hand truncation is always allowed, while left-hand truncation is allowed in some fields in some files, and the Database Summary Sheets always should be consulted to check on file-specific features.

3

Bibliographic Databases: Structure and Content

In this chapter we learn that:

- *Bibliographic databases are grouped into subject areas, then within each database there are individual records which are further divided into fields and, eventually, into individual words or into bound phrases.*
- *A single record has bibliographic fields, abstracts and index fields.*
- *In bibliographic databases, entries are based on author text (in title and abstract fields) and on index text (in index fields).*
- *The records in different electronic databases for a single original journal article will have similar entries in bibliographic and abstract fields, but very different entries in index fields.*

Bibliographic databases vary from the comprehensive databases which abstract many thousands of articles annually across broad scientific areas, to those selective databases which cover very specific areas. The choice of database depends ultimately on the search requirements; if comprehensive search results are needed then one or more of the large databases should be searched, while if there is a specific database whose indexing policies correspond closely with the requirements of the searcher then that database may often suffice.

In many ways, searchers are tertiary database producers: the original articles constitute the primary literature, which then is abstracted and indexed, and appears in what is known as the secondary literature. From this the searcher builds a third, and very specialized, database. To do this effectively not only requires considerable knowledge of the science, the scientific databases, and the methods to search them, but also requires many policy decisions to be made along the way. These next four chapters are intended to help the searcher build the "tertiary" database and in so doing to help the searcher understand precisely the limitations that have been imposed on this database.

3.1   Hierarchy of bibliographic databases

As mentioned in Chapter 1, bibliographic databases are just one of the types of electronic databases available. There are well over 100 major bibliographic databases in the sciences, and they are conveniently grouped into clusters which cover broad discipline areas. Each cluster will contain a number of different files which report studies in the discipline area, and each file will have many individual records.

As already seen in Screens 2.3 and 2.4, each record is divided into a number of fields and sometimes there are many field repetitions. (For example, there are 10 repetitions of the Index Term Field in the record in Screen 2.4.) Sometimes a single field is divided instead into separate paragraphs and sentences (for example, the abstract field in Screen 2.3 has 1 paragraph and 5 sentences) and finally, each word in all of these fields is considered as an individual term (although some words are left grouped together in bound phrases, see Section 4.3.2). The hierarchy of bibliographic databases is thus represented in Figure 3.1, and it is very important for the searcher to understand that there are a number of different levels in which searches may be performed, and to use the appropriate strategies for searching the different levels.

1.   CLUSTERS
2.   FILES
3.   RECORDS
4.   FIELDS
5.   FIELD REPETITIONS or PARAGRAPHS
6.   SENTENCES
7.   INDIVIDUAL WORDS or BOUND PHRASES

Figure 3.1   The hierarchy of bibliographic databases

3.2   Clusters

For example, on STN, some of the cluster names, and the number of databases included in the clusters, are given in Table 3.1. This list is not comprehensive but covers all areas most commonly searched.

Naturally, many of the databases, which contain literature from broad areas, appear in a number of clusters, and, for example, the INSPEC File currently appears in 15 clusters on STN (ALLBIB, AUTHORS, CHEMDATA, CHEMENG, CHEMISTRY, COMPUTER, CORPSOURCE, ELECTRICAL, ENGINEERING, FUELS, MATDATA, MATERIALS, METALS, METDATA, and PHYSICS).

The special techniques which must be used to search a number of databases simultaneously are discussed in Chapters 7 and 10, and some of these techniques help identify relevant databases in areas unfamiliar to the searcher. However, before such searches, or indeed before any search in any file is conducted, it is necessary to understand the structure and content of bibliographic databases.

3.3   Structure of bibliographic databases

All bibliographic databases have fields which are broadly grouped into bibliographic fields, abstracts, and index fields. These are best illustrated by a specific example, but first it is valuable to look at an original article and follow the procedure whereby the primary article enters the secondary literature.

Table 3.1 Clusters of databases[a]

CLUSTER	NUMBER OF DATABASES	AREA COVERED
AGRICULTURE	22	Agriculture and related sciences
BIOSCIENCE	37	Biosciences
BUSINESS	21	Sci-Tech and business news
CHEMENG	16	Chemical engineering and applied chemistry
CHEMISTRY	37	Chemistry and related areas (excludes structure files)
COMPUTER	14	Computer sciences
CONSTRUCTION	9	Building and construction
ELECTRICAL	24	Electrical engineering sciences
ENGINEERING	46	Engineering and technology
ENVIRONMENT	37	Environment and environmental issues
FUELS	26	Energy sources
GEOSCIENCE	15	Earth and geosciences
GOVREGS	20	Governmental regulations
HEALTH	33	Health sciences
MATDATA	13	Numeric data for materials
MATERIALS	35	Materials sciences
MEDICINE	24	Medicine and medical sciences
METALS	14	Metals
METDATA	8	Numeric data for metals
NUMERIC	24	All files with numeric data
PATENTS	16	Patent files and bibliographic files with patent data
PETROLEUM	17	Petroleum and petrochemicals
PHARMACOLOGY	31	Pharmacology and pharmaceutical sciences
PHYSICS	16	Physics and physical sciences
POLYMERS	15	Polymer sciences
SAFETY	16	Occupational health and safety
TOXICOLOGY	26	Toxicological information

[a]As more databases are being added to the networks, the numbers of databases in the various clusters increase. Searchers should check with the vendors on up-to-date numbers. This information is also available online (on STN: **HELP CLUSTER**), and in the annual catalogues produced by the vendor.

The example chosen for this discussion is the article by Professor Gordon Lowe, and co-workers from the Dyson Perrins Laboratory at the University of Oxford, published in *Nucleic Acids Research* in 1992. Part of the first page of this article is reproduced in Figure 3.2.

When the article is received by the abstracting service it is analysed by a specialist in the area, and eventually the electronic record is produced. To illustrate how different databases index the article, the records for this article appearing in the CAplus, BIOSIS, EMBASE, MEDLINE and SCISEARCH Files are now discussed. (The CAplus and BIOSIS Files are two major files in the chemical and biological sciences respectively; EMBASE and MEDLINE are files which feature medicine and medical sciences; the SCISEARCH File covers all areas in the sciences.)

3.4   CAplus File

For example, the major database producer in chemistry and related sciences, the Chemical Abstracts Service, publishes the Chemical Abstracts database in 80 different sections.* Each of these 80 sections deals with a particular aspect of the database, and each in turn has a specialist team responsible for the indexing. In this way consistency in indexing is achieved.

Evidence for cross-linking DNA by bis-intercalators with rigid and extended linkers is provided by knotting and catenation

Nikoi K.Annan, Peter R.Cook[1], Stephen T.Mullins[2] and Gordon Lowe*

Dyson Perrins Laboratory, Oxford University, South Parks Road, Oxford OX1 3QY, [1]Sir William Dunn School of Pathology, Oxford University, South Parks Road, Oxford OX1 3RE and [2]Department of Chemistry, Brunel University, Uxbridge, Middlesex UB8 3PH, UK

Received January 9, 1992; Revised and Accepted February 5, 1992

ABSTRACT

A new series of DNA bis-intercalators is reported in which acridine moieties are connected by rigid and extended pyridine-based linkers of varied length. Cross-linking of DNA by bis-intercalation is inferred from the unwinding and folding of linear DNA induced by the compounds; after ligation and removal of the bis-intercalator, superhelical circles, catenanes and knots that bear a residual imprint of the bis-intercalator are observed. These novel bis-intercalators are of interest because they can be used to probe the spatial organization of DNA, especially near sites of replication, recombination or topoisomerase action where two duplexes must be in close proximity. Preliminary results on the effects of the various compounds on the cloning efficiency of bacteria and replication by permeabilized human cells are also presented.

INTRODUCTION

Although a large number of DNA bis-intercalators are known,[1,2,3,4] the two intercalating moieties usually bind to the same DNA duplex because they can rotate freely about the connecting linker. Binding of one intercalating moiety inevitably leaves the other in close proximity to other binding sites in the same duplex, leading to intramolecular cross-linking (Scheme 1, upper). However, if the linker is rigid with an extended configuration, binding of both intercalators into the same duplex will be impossible, unless the duplex is long enough to fold back on itself. Therefore, bis-intercalators with rigid and extended linkers should cross-link DNA duplexes, forming intermolecular links (Scheme 1, lower). Previously, we made two series of such bis-intercalators with rigid, extended and cleavable linkers connecting the two intercalating groups, based on the phenanthridinium and acridinium ions respectively.[5] Although these compounds were all intercalating agents, they were only weak cross-linking agents: they were also not very water soluble.

We now report a new series of compounds based on acridine as the intercalator which have improved cross-linking power and solubility. The rigid linkers terminate in pyridine at each end and are cleavable. Such molecules are of interest because they can be used to probe the spatial organization of DNA, especially near sites of replication, recombination or topoisomerase action where two duplexes must be in close proximity. We also present preliminary results on the effects of these compounds on the cloning efficiency of bacteria and on replication by permeabilized human cells.

The detection of intermolecular bis-intercalation poses a special problem. Hydrodynamic methods (including electrophoretic methods) generally provide strong circumstantial evidence for intercalation,[6,7,8] before formal proof is obtained using X-ray crystallography or n.m.r. spectroscopy.[9,10,11] However, bis-intercalators that cross-link different DNA molecules affect the hydrodynamic properties of DNA in ways that complicate analysis. After mono-intercalation, the second intercalating group protrudes from DNA so that mobility depends on the number

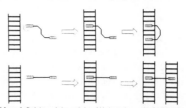

Scheme 1. Both intercalating moieties of bis-intercalators with flexible linkers generally bind to the same DNA molecule, because binding of one leaves the other close to other binding sites in the same duplex (upper). But if the linker connecting the two moieties is rigid and points the intercalating groups in opposite directions, binding to different duplexes is favoured (lower); binding to the same duplex is impossible, unless the duplex is long enough to fold back on itself.

---

* To whom correspondence should be addressed

---

*The main *summary* guides published by the Chemical Abstracts Service are: *CHEMICAL ABSTRACTS Index Guide*, and, *Subject Coverage and Arrangement of Abstracts by Sections in Chemical Abstracts*. CAS also publishes: CA HEADINGS LISTS in two volumes: *General*, and *Plants and Animals*, and these particularly assist with finding headings for online searches in the CAplus File (see Section 7.1.1).

Often a single article will cross section barriers, but eventually a primary section will be identified. In this case the article by Lowe and co-workers ended up in Chemical Abstracts Section 1 (Pharmacology). The entry becomes part of the database which then is available both in print and an electronic version.

The electronic version is available through a variety of networks, although different systems have different sections of the database, and the individual implementations vary. On STN, the complete electronic version is available, and variously appears in the files: CAplus (enhanced version of the CA File containing additionally *inter alia*, for 1300 key journals in chemistry, bibliographic information for all Table of Contents entries and author abstracts for all journal articles - even those not selected for inclusion in the CA File), CA (1967 to present), CApreviews (most recent entries) and CAOLD (records relating to the period 1957-1966).

The full online record (CAplus File) for this article is shown in Screen 3.1 and it is important to see how this record relates to the original document and to understand what indexing has been applied.

Screen 3.1[a] Record from the CAplus File

The display format used here is the format IALL, that is, all of the online record in indented format (which also spells out the full name of the fields).

ACCESSION NUMBER:	1992:400379 CAPLUS
DOCUMENT NUMBER:	117:379
TITLE:	Evidence for cross-linking DNA by bis-intercalators with rigid and extended linkers is provided by knotting and catenation.
AUTHOR(S):	Annan, Nikoi K.; Cook, Peter R.; Mullins, Stephen T.; Lowe, Gordon
CORPORATE SOURCE:	Dyson Perrins Lab., Oxford Univ., Oxford, OX1 3QY, UK
SOURCE:	Nucleic Acids Res. (1992), 20(5), 983-90 CODEN: NARHAD; ISSN: 0305-1048
DOCUMENT TYPE:	Journal
LANGUAGE:	English
CLASSIFICATION:	1-6 (Pharmacology) Section cross-reference(s): 28

ABSTRACT: A new series of DNA bis-intercalators is reported in which acridine moieties are connected by rigid and extended pyridine-based linkers of varied length. Crosslinking of DNA by bis-intercalation is inferred from the unwinding and folding of linear DNA induced by the compds.; after ligation and removal of the bis-intercalator, superhelical circles, catenanes and knots that bear a residual imprint of the bis-intercalator are obsd. These novel bis-intercalators are of interest because they can be used to probe the spatial organisation of DNA, esp. near sites of replication, recombination or topoisomerase action where two duplexes must be in close proximity. Preliminary results on the effects of the various compds. on the cloning efficiency of bacteria and replication by permeabilized human cells are also presented.

SUPPL. TERM:	DNA intercalator prepn antitumor antibacterial
INDEX TERM:	Deoxyribonucleic acids (intercalators, rigid, prepn. and cytoxic activity of)
INDEX TERM:	Bactericides, Disinfectants, and Antiseptics Neoplasm inhibitors (rigid DNA intercalators as, prepn. of)

```
┌──────────────────────────────────────────────────────────────────────────┐
│ Screen 3.1 (continued)                                                     │
│ INDEX TERM:    20141-87-1P   141889-88-5P, APPA   141889-90-9P   141889-91-0P│
│                ROLE: SPN (Synthetic preparation); PREP (Preparation)       │
│                (prepn. and DNA intercalation by)                           │
│ INDEX TERM:    3095-81-6P                                                   │
│                ROLE: RCT (Reactant); SPN (Synthetic preparation); PREP (Preparation)│
│                (prepn. and reaction of, with chloroacridine)               │
│ INDEX TERM:    110-86-1, Pyridine, reactions                               │
│                ROLE: RCT (Reactant)                                         │
│                (reaction of, with 9-chloroacridine)                        │
│ INDEX TERM:    553-26-4, 4,4'-Dipyridyl    13362-78-2                       │
│                ROLE: RCT (Reactant)                                         │
│                (reaction of, with chloroacridine)                          │
│ INDEX TERM:    623-27-8, 1,4-Benzenedicarboxaldehyde                       │
│                ROLE: RCT (Reactant)                                         │
│                (reaction of, with methylpyridine)                          │
│ INDEX TERM:    108-89-4, 4-Methylpyridine                                  │
│                ROLE: RCT (Reactant)                                         │
│                (reaction of, with terephthaldicarboxaldehyde)              │
│ INDEX TERM:    1207-69-8, 9-Chloroacridine                                 │
│                ROLE: RCT (Reactant)                                         │
│                (reactions of, DNA intercalator prepn. in relation to)      │
└──────────────────────────────────────────────────────────────────────────┘
```

Accordingly, information from the original document is placed in the following fields within the online record in the CAplus File.

ACCESSION NUMBER
The format is VOLUME:RECORD NUMBER and this field merely gives the database identifier for the record.

TITLE
The title here is exactly as in the original article although editorial modifications may be made in other cases. For example, titles are changed to American-English spelling, Greek letters are spelt out with periods before and after (example: α-helix becomes .alpha.-helix), and superscripts and subscripts are entered in normal type (example: $GABA_A$ becomes GABAA). These modifications to author-based entries, and to the symbols used in the scientific literature, are essentially standard across all databases.

AUTHOR
The format in the CAplus File is: SURNAME, GIVEN NAME INITIAL(S). Initials only are entered if the given name is not indicated in full in the original article.

CORPORATE SOURCE
In the CAplus File the corporate source is entered for the principal author as in the article, and a number of words are abbreviated (examples: Lab. and Univ.).

SOURCE
This field contains the document reference, and usually the name of the journal title is abbreviated.

DOCUMENT TYPE
Here the document type is journal. This is the most common type of entry in the CAplus File, and the next most common is patent, although the CAplus File lists 14 different document types (see Section 4.3.5).

LANGUAGE
This field gives the language of the original document. Original documents in non-English languages are translated and entered in the File with American-English spellings.
CLASSIFICATION
This field refers to the primary Section Code in which the article is entered, while cross-references refer to other Section Codes to which the content of the article relates.
ABSTRACT
The abstract gives the abstract from the original article, although CAS Standard Abbreviations are applied. Only a few abbreviations appear in this record (compds, obsd, esp), but the full list of standard abbreviations is in the booklet: *CAS Standard Abbreviations*. While the abstract here is very similar to the abstract in the original article, this is not always the case and CAS editorial staff will rewrite abstracts which do not meet CAS requirements.
SUPPLEMENTARY TERMS
The field lists either author provided keywords, or keywords added by the indexer, but based on author terminology in the original article.
INDEX TERMS
Each index heading is entered in a separate field repetition. CAS has approximately 90,000 Index Headings of which about 80% refer to specific plant or animal names. The format of entries in the INDEX TERM fields is:
   INDEX HEADING(S)
      (aspect of the article which related to the index heading).

It is necessary to realize that this record has two basic parts: those which were part of the original document (and which are based on author terminology), and those which have been added by the indexer. The searcher needs to be very aware of this particularly since the style of these entries may vary considerably (see Section 7.1).
   Information added by the database producer appears in the fields: ACCESSION NUMBER, CLASSIFICATION, SUPPLEMENTARY TERMS and INDEX TERMS, while information from the original document appears in the TITLE and ABSTRACT Fields. The remainder of the original article is condensed into the relatively few terms which have been indexed!

   Important notes:
   - **Bibliographic databases have three basic sections: bibliographic; abstract; index entries.**
   - **You need to be aware which parts within these sections are direct from the primary literature (author terminology) and which parts have been added by the database producers.**

3.5   BIOSIS File

The full online record in the BIOSIS File for the same article is given in Screen 3.2. The structure of the record is similar to that in the CAplus File, although from comparison of Screens 3.1 and 3.2 a number of differences are evident. In particular it is noted that this BIOSIS File record does not contain indexing to any of the substances which were indexed (as CAS Registry Numbers) in the CAplus record. (However, this is an unusual case and CAS Registry Numbers *are* in many BIOSIS File records, although Registry Numbers for different substances from the same original article often appear.)

Screen 3.2[a]   Record from the BIOSIS File (ALL format)

AN 92:254130 BIOSIS
TI EVIDENCE FOR CROSS-LINKING DNA BY BIS-INTERCALATORS WITH RIGID AND
    EXTENDED LINKERS IS PROVIDED BY KNOTTING AND CATENATION.
AU ANNAN N K; COOK P R; MULLINS S T; LOWE G
CS DYSON PERRINS LAB., OXFORD UNIVERSITY, SOUTH PARKS ROAD, OXFORD OX1 3QY.
SO NUCLEIC ACIDS RES 20 (5). 1992. 983-990. CODEN: NARHAD ISSN: 0305-1048
LA English
AB A new series of DNA bis-intercalators is reported in which acridine moieties are connected by
    rigid and extended pyridine-based linkers of varied length. Cross-linking DNA by bis-
    intercalation is inferred from the unwinding and folding of linear DNA induced by the
    compounds; after ligation and removal of the bis-intercalator, superhelical circles, catenanes
    and knots that bear a residual imprint of the bis-intercalator are observed. These novel bis-
    intercalators are of interest because they can be used to probe the spatial organisation of
    DNA, especially near sites of replication, recombination or topoisomerase action where two
    duplexes must be in close proximity. Preliminary results on the effects of the various
    compounds on the cloning efficiency of bacteria and replication by permeabilized human
    cells are also presented.
ST HUMAN BACTERIA
CC Biochemical Studies-General   10060
    Biochemical Studies-Nucleic Acids, Purines and Pyrimidines *10062
    Biophysics-Molecular Properties and Macromolecules *10506
    Physiology and Biochemistry of Bacteria *31000
    Genetics of Bacteria and Viruses 31500
BC Bacteria-General Unspecified 05000
    Hominidae 86215

[a]Copyright by BIOSIS and Reprinted with Permission

3.6   Other files in which this article was indexed

This article was also indexed in the EMBASE File (medical sciences database produced by Elsevier Science Publishers), the MEDLINE File (medical sciences database produced by the US National Library of Medicine), the SCISEARCH File (general database produced by the Institute for Scientific Information, ISI), and the TOXLIT File (general database which specializes in toxicology and which is produced by the US National Library of Medicine).

The bibliographic and indexing fields for the online records in the EMBASE, MEDLINE, and SCISEARCH Files are shown in Screens 3.3, 3.4, and 3.5 respectively. (The TOXLIT File contains the bibliographic entries and abstract identical to that in the CAplus File, but in the index fields, only the CA Classification Code and those CAS Registry Numbers included in the CAplus record are given.)

Screen 3.3[a] Record from the EMBASE File

AN	92105895 EMBASE
TI	Evidence for cross-linking DNA by bis-intercalators with rigid and extended linkers is provided by knotting and catenation.
AU	Annan N.K.; Cook P.R.; Mullins S.T.; Lowe G.
CS	Dyson Perrins Laboratory, Oxford University, South Parks Road, Oxford OX1 3QY, United Kingdom
SO	NUCLEIC ACIDS RES., (1992) 20/5 (983-990). ISSN: 0305-1048 CODEN: NARHAD
CY	United Kingdom
DT	Journal
FS	022 Human Genetics
LA	English
AB	..... *(identical to the abstract in Screen 3.2)*
CT	EMTAGS: genetic engineering and gene technology (0108); heredity (0137); mammal (0738); human (0888); nonhuman (0777); human tissue, cells or cell components (0111); priority journal (0007); article (0060); enzyme (0990)

Medical Descriptors:

*dna cross linking	*dna structure
dna denaturation	dna replication
dna recombination	molecular cloning
cell membrane permeability	dna supercoiling
human	nonhuman
human cell	
priority journal	article

Drug Descriptors:

*intercalating agent	acridine
dna topoisomerase: EC, endogenous compound	pyridine

RN	260-94-6; 80449-01-0; 110-86-1

Screen 3.4[a] Record from the MEDLINE File

AN	92195869 MEDLINE		
TI	Evidence for cross-linking DNA by bis-intercalators with rigid and extended linkers is provided by knotting and catenation.		
AU	Annan N K; Cook P R; Mullins S T; Lowe G		
CS	Dyson Perrins Laboratory, Oxford University, UK. SO Nucleic Acids Res, (1992 Mar 11) 20 (5) 983-90. Journal code: O8L. ISSN: 0305-1048.		
CY	ENGLAND: United Kingdom		
DT	Journal; Article; (JOURNAL ARTICLE)	LA	English
FS	Priority Journals; Cancer Journals	EM	9206
AB	....*(identical to the abstract in Screen 3.2)*		

CT	Check Tags: Human; Support, Non-U.S. Gov't	Acridine Orange: CH, chemistry
	Acridine Orange: PD, pharmacology	Cell Division: DE, drug effects
	Cloning, Molecular	*DNA, Superhelical: CH, chemistry
	Electrophoresis	Ethidium: CH, chemistry
	Ethidium: PD, pharmacology	Hela Cells
	*Intercalating Agents: CH, chemistry	Intercalating Agents: PD, pharmacology
	Nuclear Magnetic Resonance	Nucleic Acid Conformation

RN	3546-21-2 (Ethidium); 65-61-2 (Acridine Orange)
CN	0 (DNA, Superhelical); 0 (Intercalating Agents)

Screen 3.5[a]   Record from the SCISEARCH File

AN	92:196585 SCISEARCH
GA	The Genuine Article (R) Number: HK001
TI	EVIDENCE FOR CROSS-LINKING DNA BY BIS-INTERCALATORS WITH RIGID AND EXTENDED LINKERS IS PROVIDED BY KNOTTING AND CATENATION
AU	ANNAN N K; COOK P R; MULLINS S T; LOWE G (Reprint)
CS	UNIV OXFORD, DYSON PERRINS LAB, S PARKS RD, OXFORD OX1 3QY, ENGLAND; UNIV OXFORD, SIR WILLIAM DUNN SCH PATHOL, OXFORD OX1 3RE, ENGLAND; BRUNEL UNIV, DEPT CHEM, UXBRIDGE UB8 3PH, MIDDX, ENGLAND
CYA	ENGLAND
SO	NUCLEIC ACIDS RESEARCH, (11 MAR 1992) Vol. 20, No. 5, pp. 983-990. ISSN: 0305-1048.
DT	Article; Journal
FS	LIFE
LA	ENGLISH
REC	Reference Count: 26
AB	....(identical to the abstract in Screen 3.2)
CC	BIOCHEMISTRY & MOLECULAR BIOLOGY
STP	KeyWords Plus (R): BINDING; LUZOPEPTIN; NUMBER; DRUGS
RF	91-4817 001; LIPASE GENE; CDNA FOR STIMULATORY GDP/GTP EXCHANGE PROTEIN; EXPRESSION OF MESSENGER-RNA 91-7315 001; DNA ETHIDIUMBROMIDE FLUORESCENCE; EXTERNAL BINDING MODES; INTERACTION OF ANTITUMORAL DRUG MITOXANTRONE
RE	

Referenced Author (RAU)	|Year |(RPY)	| VOL (RVL)	| PG |(RPG)	| Referenced Work | (RWK)
CANNELAKIS E S	|1976	|418	|277	|BIOCHIM BIOPHYS ACTA
COOK P R	|1976	|22	|303	|J CELL SCI
DEAN F B	|1985	|260	|4975	|J BIOL CHEM
DEPEW R E	|1975	|72	|4275	|P NATL ACAD SCI USA
ESTEVE M E	|1981	|18	|1061	|J HETEROCYCLIC CHEM...

It is noted that the bibliographic and abstract entries in these files are similar to those in the CAplus and BIOSIS Files, although there are subtle differences - which nevertheless can substantially affect the search statements required. However, the indexing in each of these files is very different, and this reflects the different emphases of the different database producers.

Some of the more notable similarities and differences in the records shown in Screens 3.1 to 3.5 are:

- Title Fields: some entries are capitalized but this is of no consequence to searching since upper- and lower-case characters are treated equally.
- Author Fields: given names are in full in the CAplus record only.
- Corporate Source Fields: addresses are presented quite differently, and only in the SCISEARCH File are the addresses of the non-principal authors (that is, authors other than the author from whom reprints are available) given.

- Cited references are given in the SCISEARCH File only. As noted in the Reference Count Field (REC) there are 26 cited references but only 5 of these are shown in Screen 3.5.
- There are 11 CAS Registry Numbers in the CAplus record, 3 in the EMBASE record, and 2 in the MEDLINE record, and the only one in common is 110-86-1 (pyridine) which appears in the CAplus and EMBASE records. (Not always are the differences so pronounced, and in some cases there are good correlations between the CAS Registry Numbers listed.)
- There are many subtle differences, for example, the index entry in the EMBASE File is "molecular cloning" while in the MEDLINE File the corresponding entry is "cloning, molecular." (This has important implications, for example see Sections 2.3.2 and 4.1.)

It should also be noted that indexing in the SCISEARCH File mentions the antitumoral drug mitoxantrone which is not listed in the other records. Indeed in the original article over 20 substances are mentioned, and more than anything else this highlights the point that records in bibliographic databases are not only very condensed versions of the original documents but also are the outcome of very extensive indexing policies. However, provided these points are understood, and that search strategies are designed accordingly, the databases offer access to the world's scientific literature in a way just not possible through the print versions.

3.7   Example from the physical sciences

While the example above comes from the life sciences, the same picture emerges in all other areas of science. For example, records for the article titled "Gamma-ray-induced loss of Er3+-doped silica-core optical fiber" by Koyama *et al.* in the *Japanese Journal of Applied Physics* appear in the INSPEC, ENERGY, SCISEARCH and COMPENDEX Files. The bibliographic information and the abstract are very similar, and are shown in Screen 3.6 only for the INSPEC File. The only major difference for entries in the bibliographic and abstract fields is in the SCISEARCH File which additionally identified the author from whom reprints could be obtained, and the addresses of all the authors rather than just that of the first named author. There are a number of minor differences, for example the title of the entry in the COMPENDEX File has "Er3 plus -doped" rather than "Er3+-doped, and the "plus" is spelt out each time in the abstract.

Screen 3.6[a] Bibliographic information and abstract in record from the physical sciences (INSPEC File)

AN	94:4766459 INSPEC
DN	A9421-4281-002; B9411-4125-003
TI	Gamma-ray-induced loss of Er3+-doped silica-core optical fiber.
AU	Koyama, T.; Dohguchi, N.; Ohki, Y. (Dept. of Electr. Eng., Waseda Univ., Tokyo, Japan); Nishikawa, H.; Kusama, Y.; Seguchi, T.
SO	Japanese Journal of Applied Physics, Part 1 (Regular Papers & Short Notes) (July 1994) vol.33, no.7A, p.3937-41. 24 refs. CODEN: JAPNDE ISSN: 0021-4922
DT	Journal
TC	Experimental
CY	Japan

Screen 3.6 (continued)
LA   English
AB   Erbium-doped silica optical fibers were irradiated by gamma -rays, and their loss-
          increasing characteristics were analyzed. The loss is mainly induced by Er2+ created by
          the reduction of Er3+. It does not show a simple dependence on the Er3+ concentration.
          The loss increase is described by the sum of several saturating exponential terms and one
          linear term, which can be derived from the yield equation of E' gamma centers or other
          species induced from precursors by hole trapping. It is considered that hole trapping
          supplies electrons to induce the reduction, and plays an important role in the loss
          increase.

[a]Copyright by the Institution of Electrical Engineers and Reprinted with Permission

Meanwhile, Screen 3.7 shows the indexing for the records in the four files.

Screen 3.7[a] Index entries in records from the physical sciences
(INSPEC, ENERGY, SCISEARCH and COMPENDEX Files)

INSPEC File
CC   A4281D Optical propagation, dispersion and attenuation in fibres;
          A6180E Gamma rays; B4125 Fibre optics; FtL6 Qical waveguides
CT   ERBIUM; GAMMA -RAY EFFECTS; OPTICAL FIBRES;
          OPTICAL LOSSES; SILICON COMPOUNDS
ST   Er3+-doped silica-core optical fiber; gamma-ray-induced loss; loss increase;
          saturating exponential terms; yield equation; hole trapping; SiO2:Er3+; SiO2:Er
CHI   SiO2:Er ss, SiO2 ss, Er ss, O2 ss, Si ss, O ss, SiO2 bin, O2 bin, Si bin, O bin,
          Er el, Er dop
ET   Er; Er3+; Er ip 3; ip 3; Er2+; Er ip 2; ip 2; Er*O*Si; Er sy 3; sy 3; O sy 3; Si sy 3;
          SiO2:Er; SiO2:Er3+; Er3+ doping; doped materials; Si cp; cp; O cp; Er doping; O*Si;
          SiO; O; Si

ENERGY File
CC   *360605; B2460
CT   ABSORPTION SPECTROSCOPY; CONCENTRATION RATIO; DOSE-RESPONSE
          OPTICAL FIBERS; PHYSICAL RADIATION EFFECTS; TIME DEPENDENCE
          *OPTICAL FIBERS: *PHYSICAL RADIATION EFFECTS; *OPTICAL FIBERS:
          *GAMMA RADIATION
BT   COLOR CENTERS; CRYSTAL DEFECTS; CRYSTAL STRUCTURE;
          ELECTROMAGNETIC RADIATION; FIBERS; IONIZING RADIATIONS; POINT
          DEFECTS; RADIATION EFFECTS; RADIATIONS; SPECTROSCOPY; VACANCIES
ET   Er; Er3+; Er ip 3; ip 3; Er2+; Er ip 2; ip 2

SCISEARCH File
REC   Reference Count: 24
CC   PHYSICS, APPLIED
ST   Author Keywords: ER3+ DOPED OPTICAL FIBER; ERBIUM; RARE-EARTH
          ELEMENT; RADIATION-INDUCED OPTICAL ABSORPTION; E'GAMMA CENTER;
          HOLE TRAP
STP   KeyWords Plus (R): DEFECT CENTERS; AMORPHOUS SIO2; LASERS
RF   92-1192 002; ERBIUM-DOPED FIBER AMPLIFIERS; OPTICAL PROGRAMMABLE
          TRANSVERSAL FILTERS; LASER ENERGY-BANDS

Screen 3.7 (continued)
RE

Referenced Author (RAU)	Year (RPY)	VOL (RVL)	PG (RPG)	Referenced Work (RWK)
EEKS R A	1970	53	1176	J AM CERAM SOC
FRIEBELE E J	1974	45	3424	J APPL PHYS
GALEENER F L	1985	71	1373	J NON-CRYST SOLIDS

. . . .

(all 24 citations appeared, but only the first three are shown here)

COMPENDEX File
CC   741.3 Optical Devices and Systems; 547.2 Rare Earth Metals; 932.1 High Energy
          Physics; 921.6 Numerical Methods; 717.1 Optical Communication Systems; 941.3
          Optical Instruments
CT   *Optical fibers; Absorption spectroscopy; Silica; Electrons; Mathematical models;
          Rare earth elements; Optical communication; Spectrometers; Erbium; Gamma rays
ST   Erbium doped silica; Gamma ray induced loss; Yield equation; Hole trapping; Radiation
          induced optical absorption; Hole trap

---

[a]Copyright by the Institution of Electrical Engineers, US Department of Energy OSTI and its IEA
ETDE Contracting Parties, Institute for Scientific Information, and Engineering Information Inc,
and Reprinted with Permission

The Database Summary Sheets (see Section 5.7) for the individual files contain the full
descriptions for the indexing field codes. (The different files clearly have different indexing
hierarchies and terminologies, and some of those shown in Screen 3.7 include: CC =
Classification Code, CT = Controlled Term; ST = Supplementary Term, CHI = Chemical
Indexing, ET = Element Terms, BT = Broader Term, REC = Reference Count, STP =
Supplementary Term Plus.) The summary sheets also explain the various symbols
associated with the CHI and ET Fields in the INSPEC and ENERGY Files, and some of the
key terms are: bin = binary system; ss = system with 3 or more components; dop = dopant;
ip = ions positive, and cp = compounds. However, even without knowing these details it is
again apparent that the indexing in the files is very different.

3.8   Entries within fields

Sections 3.3 through 3.7 outline the fields of information, but as shown in Figure 3.1, fields
can be divided further into field repetitions or paragraphs, sentences and ultimately into either
individual words or bound phrases. In nearly all bibliographic fields the entries are as
individual words, except in the Author Field and, where they occur, in the Index Headings.
In these cases the entries are as bound phrases, that is, the entire phrase is recorded as a single
term.

It is important to recognize when each of these situations occurs since the proximity
operators have special meanings in the various instances. While the application of
proximity operators may be different in the different files, general rules may be stated:

1.   the (L) operator applies to the whole field, except when there are field repetitions in
      which case each field repetition is treated as a separate information unit;
2.   when they are implemented, the (P) and (S) operators apply to paragraphs and sentences
      in a single field (commonly in the Abstract Field); and

3. the operators cannot be used to connect terms in bound phrases which instead must be searched as an exact, and single, term in the Index Heading, or Author Field (however, individual words in Index Headings may be searched in the Basic Index in some files and again the Database Summary Sheets provide such information).

3.9   Bibliographic files: similarities and differences

While the structures of bibliographic files are similar, there very important differences. What does this mean to the original author and to the searcher?

First, since in the future publications will be retrieved increasingly through online networks, authors need to pay particular attention to the parts of the online records to which they directly contribute, that is, to the title and abstract. (Author contributed text is often referred to as "free text". Thus, searching "free text" refers to searching the parts of the records effectively written by the author.) In particular, the abstracts should include as many key words and phrases as required to fully convey to a searcher the type of research achieved, and these words and phrases should range from general terms to the specific terms which characterize the particular article. Authors should not attempt to be indexers, but they should be aware that the titles and the abstracts provide them with the opportunity to make important inputs into what will be a critical part of the electronic record.

Second, searchers should be aware that database policies apply to all parts of the online record. Even titles and abstracts may be modified differently, while Corporate Source and Source Fields frequently contain quite different abbreviations.

Third, searchers must have a good knowledge of database indexing policies in order to utilize fully index entries. Most database producers supply index guides upon request, and guides for the most used files should be studied carefully before attempting a search online.

Fourth, searchers should be particularly cautious in attempting multifile searches, and either a few very general terms or an adequate number of synonyms to cover different database terminologies should be used.

> **Important notes:**
> - **Titles and abstracts in records for journal articles are similar across files, but indexing is very different.**
> - **The implication for *authors* is that you must be very careful in the way you write your abstracts and you should mention all key points using relatively generic terminology for the discipline.**
> - **The implication for *searchers* is that you must have a good knowledge of the indexing policies of the database producers in order to achieve effective searches.**
> - **And you must remember that online records are much abridged versions of the original literature, so searches should initially be approached using relatively few concepts and relatively general terminology.**

Summary

- *Bibliographic files contain three general sections:*
  - bibliographic information;
  - abstracts;
  - indexing.
- Bibliographic information is subjected to database *editorial policies* and this relates mainly to the use of abbreviated terms, particularly for Corporate Source and Source (journal title) Fields.
- Entries in the online record which are mainly author written (titles, abstracts) are called *"free text" fields.*
- *Database indexing* is entered in SC, CC, IT, and ST Fields.
- There are major differences in the indexing policies of the different databases, so while titles and abstracts in bibliographic records for scientific articles usually are very similar, the index entries usually are very different.

4

Bibliographic Databases: Non-index Fields

In this chapter we learn:

- *System features which are used to identify possible search terms.*
- *How entries are actually posted in non-index fields.*
- *Some of the issues relating to searches in the non-index fields.*

In Chapter 3 the content of different bibliographic databases was outlined, and it is apparent that there are many similarities in the entries in the bibliographic and abstract fields. Accordingly the most frequently used searches in these fields are discussed in this chapter for the different databases. On the other hand, information in indexing fields is very different, and these fields are discussed in Chapter 5 for some representative databases.

4.1   General entry of data: individual words and stop words

Most bibliographic databases count text entries as *individual terms*. That is, each word, each sentence and each paragraph in the field is numbered sequentially and this enables proximity operators to apply. As mentioned already in Section 3.7 different databases may treat certain characters differently, but the most common situation relates to hyphenated words and fortunately all databases treat hyphenations uniformly, that is, the words are considered as two individual words and, for example, X-ray becomes two "words" X and ray.

Accordingly, if the (A) operator is used, the system looks for the first word number, and then if the second word number is +- 1 removed, a hit is recorded. The operator (4A) retrieves records in which the second word is +- 5 word counts removed. Similarly, the (nW) operator looks for the first word number, and then if the second word number is n+1 removed, a hit is recorded. However, neither of these operators cross field or sentence boundaries, that is, they operate only within a single information unit or a single sentence.

(It was noted in Section 3.6 that "molecular cloning" and "cloning, molecular" were index entries in the EMBASE and MEDLINE Files respectively and such inverted index entries are used very frequently. So unless the searcher is very aware of the entries in the database, it is better as a general rule to use the (A) operator to connect two words of this type. This simple trick usually is sufficient to cover both free text and index entries for the same concept.)

Some words, called "stop words", cannot be searched. Stop words are system- and file-specific but similar stop words occur across files within a single system. Some typical stop words in STN bibliographic files are listed in Figure 4.1.

AN	AND	AS	AT	BY
FOR	FROM	IN	NOT	OF
ON	OR	THE	TO	WITH

Figure 4.1 Typical stop words (which occur across a number of files)
Stop words vary across the files. However, file-specific stop words may be found on STN by entering **HELP CONTENT** at a command prompt in the file

Although stop words cannot be searched, they are present in the record and are counted for the purposes of the application of proximity operators.

4.2   General entry of data: checking postings

Even in a single database, entries in the Author, Corporate Source, and Source Fields may differ for the same author, work place or reference. Part of the problem here is that database producers can enter only the information they have available, and since editors of the various primary literature sources in turn have different policies then the bibliographic entries in journals differ. Thus, at times, authors' full given names are spelt out at the heading of the original article, while at other times only the surname and initials are given. (Because of the latter, most databases only enter initials even when full names are in the article. While this is done so that all entries are in the same format, it does mean that some potentially useful information is not present.)

Additionally databases do contain typographical errors which might have arisen either in the primary literature or in the indexing. It must be pointed out, however, that errors are very minor and in any case if a word is misspelt it may appear, correctly spelt, elsewhere in the record. It is inappropriate to focus on errors, instead it is sufficient merely to recognize they do occur and, when detected, to take steps to overcome them.

For all of these reasons a check of the postings of terms in the file is recommended before any search is performed, and this check is achieved through the EXPAND command on STN. The format for the command is:

=>   E   <TERM> / FIELD   <NUMBER OF LISTINGS REQUIRED>

and any number of listings between (and including) 5 and 25 may be used at one time.

Examples of the use of the EXPAND command in the Basic Index and in the Author Field in the CAplus File are shown in Screen 4.1.

There are many features of the EXPAND command on STN:

- The command asks for an alphabetical listing of the terms in the database, each term is given an E-number and the number of postings is indicated.

Screen 4.1[a] Examples of the EXPAND command in the CAplus File

```
=>   E  ANTICHOLESTER    10
E1       1    ANTICHOLESTATICS/BI      E2       1    ANTICHOLESTEMIC/BI
E3       1->  ANTICHOLESTER/BI         E4       1    ANTICHOLESTERAMIC/BI
E5       1    ANTICHOLESTERAMICS/BI    E6       7    ANTICHOLESTERASE/BI
E7       1    ANTICHOLESTERASIC/BI     E8       3    ANTICHOLESTEREMIA/BI
E9    2055    ANTICHOLESTEREMIC/BI     E10   4787    ANTICHOLESTEREMICS/BI

=>   E   LOWE G/AU
E1       1      LOWE FRANKLIN C/AU     E2       1    LOWE FREDERIC C/AU
E3      41->    LOWE G/AU              E4       2    LOWE G B/AU
E5      45      LOWE G D O/AU          E6       2    LOWE G E/AU
E7      14      LOWE G H/AU            E8       1    LOWE G M/AU
E9       1      LOWE G R JR/AU         E10      1    LOWE G Y/AU
E11      1      LOWE GEOFF/AU          E12      1    LOWE GEOFFREY/AU

=> E
E13     1     LOWE GEORGE B/AU         E14      2    LOWE GEORGE BERNARD/AU
E15     1     LOWE GEORGE E/AU         E16      1    LOWE GEORGE FREDERICK/AU
E17     1     LOWE GEORGE H/AU         E18      1    LOWE GEORGE H III/AU
E19     1     LOWE GILDA H/AU          E20      1    LOWE GISA/AU
E21   130     LOWE GORDON/AU           E22      1    LOWE GORDON D/AU
E23     8     LOWE GORDON D O/AU       E24      2    LOWE GORDON M/AU
```

[a]Copyright by the American Chemical Society and Reprinted with Permission

- Expansion of terms may be done in the Basic Index (no field specified as in the first instance in Screen 4.1) or in any one of the fields in the database (for example, the second expansion in Screen 4.1 is done in the Author Field).
- The default number of terms listed is 12, although any number of terms between 5 and 25 may be listed by entering the required number after the term (example: => **E ANTICHOLESTEMIC** 15 will list 15 terms).
- Further expanded terms in continued alphabetical order may be listed by typing **E** at the next arrow prompt (or, for example, => **E 25**, will ask for the next 25 listings).
- The term entered is always listed as E3 (so in the default number of expanded terms the two terms before and the nine terms after the term specified will be listed).
- The command asks for actual entries (so there is no point using truncation symbols in the term requested, or using proximity operators in attempts to connect terms).
- Only single terms may be expanded in fields where terms are entered individually (so there is no point expanding on "cholesterol lowering agents", that is, on three terms).
- Fields with bound phrases give expanded terms as the bound phrases only, although some fields contain both the bound phrases and the single terms. Generally, it is not

necessary to know this in advance, since it becomes very apparent once the information is displayed.

- E-numbers may be used as search terms (they effectively are system-generated synonyms for the terms).
- If the initial expanded term happens to be too late in the alphabet and required entries are not seen, then a term earlier in the alphabet may be chosen or else the command, **E BACK <TERM>** will produce a list in which E3 will be the term as entered and E4, E5, etc., will be terms immediately preceding the term in the alphabet (Screen 4.2).

Screen 4.2[a] Different forms for the EXPAND command (CAplus File)

=> **E BACK ANTICHOLESTEREMIA 6**

E1	4787	ANTICHOLESTEREMICS/BI	E2	2055	ANTICHOLESTEREMIC/BI
E3	3->	ANTICHOLESTEREMIA/BI	E4	1	ANTICHOLESTERASIC/BI
E5	7	ANTICHOLESTERASE/BI	E6	1	ANTICHOLESTERAMICS/BI

=> **E LEFT CHOLESTEREM**

E1	1	NORMOCHOLESTERE/BI	E2	1	CHOLESTEREL/BI
E3	0->	CHOLESTEREM/BI	E4	1	HYPERCHOLESTEREMI/BI
E5	98	CHOLESTEREMIA/BI	E6	3	ANTICHOLESTEREMIA/BI
E7	2	ANTIHYPERCHOLESTEREMIA/BI	E8	332	HYPERCHOLESTEREMIA/BI
E9	51	HYPOCHOLESTEREMIA/BI	E10	1	HYPRCHOLESTEREMIA/BI
E11	1	NORMOCHOLESTEREMIA/BI	E12	23	CHOLESTEREMIC/BI

=> **E 8**

E13	1	AINTICHOLESTEREMIC/BI	E14	2	AMTICHOLESTEREMIC/BI
E15	1	ANCHOLESTEREMIC/BI	E16	1	ANTCHOLESTEREMIC/BI
E17	1	ANTHCHOLESTEREMIC/BI	E18	1	ANTHIHYPERCHOLESTEREMIC/BI
E19	2055	ANTICHOLESTEREMIC/BI	E20	85	ANTIHYPERCHOLESTEREMIC/BI

[a]Copyright by the American Chemical Society and Reprinted with Permission

---

- In fields which allow left-truncation then **E LEFT <TERM>** will produce an alphabetical list on terms which have the stem embedded later in the term (Screen 4.2).
- There is no charge for the EXPAND command (only normal connect hour charges operate).
- However, in databases (in some systems) with search term pricing, each E-number constitutes a search term whereas use of a single term stem with truncation, which often effects the same result as searching a range of E-numbers, constitutes a single search term (Section 10.6.2).
- On STN the QUERY command may be used to store E-numbers for future searches and this is particularly useful when the searcher wishes to expand on a number of different terms before executing the search (the default implementation is that each time the EXPAND command is executed on a different term then E-numbers commence from E1). For example, if E1 through E5 need to be saved then: => **QUERY E1-E5** will create an L-number for these terms, and subsequently a search on this L-number may be performed. (Alternatively the searcher may enter=> **SET EXPAND CONTINUOUS** in which case E-numbers from earlier expands will not be deleted.)

In the event, it is apparent from Screen 4.1 that probably the most appropriate search term for the concept surveyed in Screen 4.1 is **ANTICHOLESTER?**[*] while publications by Gordon Lowe will be retrieved with the search: => **S (LOWE GORDON/AU OR LOWE G/AU)**.

> **Important notes:**
> - **There are many features available for listing the relevant search terms, and many rules apply.**
> - **You should always check postings for possible terms first, particularly in those databases where search-term pricing applies.**

4.3   Notes on the entry of data: specific fields

4.3.1   Title Field (individual terms posted)
The Title Field contains individual words from the title as it appears in the original article with the usual editorial modifications. For example, American-English spelling appears (non-English language articles are translated), Greek letters are spelt out with periods before and after (example: α-helix becomes .alpha.-helix), and superscripts and subscripts are entered in normal type in most databases although they are hyphenated in other databases (example: $GABA_A$ becomes GABAA or GABA-A; in the latter case it is posted as two words and this can have search implications).

Sometimes the easiest way to find the online record for a known document is to include a few words in a Title Field search (see Section 7.1.2).

4.3.2.   Author Field (each author posted as bound phrase)
Each individual author's name (usually up to 9 in total) is entered as a bound phrase, in the inverted format. Depending on the database, and depending on the entry in the original article, the author's name will appear either as:

SURNAME   GIVEN NAME   INITIAL(S)   or
SURNAME   INITIAL(S).

In order to identify all entries for the given author it is essential to expand on the author name in the Author Field (AU) prior to performing a search (see Screen 4.1). Some examples of how author names are entered in the CAplus File are shown in Figure 4.2.

While a comma may appear after the surname in the record, most searches in most databases may be performed without the comma and this is an exception to the general rule, that searches on bound phrases will only retrieve records which have identical bound phrase entries (including the punctuation).

---

[*]Note, however, that in Screen 4.2 there are 85 postings for ANTIHYPERCHOLESTEREMIC. This is a significant number and this term might need to be added in the search.

1 .   Normal representation, SURNAME GIVEN NAME INITIAL(S)
            Linus Pauling appears as:
            PAULING   LINUS/AU   **PAULING   L/AU**

2 .   Names with punctuation - replace punctuation with a blank
            John H O'Donnell appears as:
            O DONNELL   JOHN H/AU

3 .   Names with prefixes - try with and without blanks
            J Van der Maas appears as:
            VAN DER MAAS   J/AU   **VANDER MAAS   J/AU**
            VANDERMAAS   J/AU   **MAAS   JVD/AU**

4 .   Names with hyphens - replace hyphen with blank
            Patricia D C Brown-Woodman appears as:
            BROWN WOODMAN   PATRICIA   D   C/AU

5 .   Names with German umlaut - try AE, OE, UE for Ä, Ö, Ü
            A C Müller appears as:
            MUELLER   A   C/AU   **MULLER   A   C/AU**

Figure 4.2   Examples of entries for Author Names
These examples are taken from the CAplus File. Most other files have initials for given names
only, although in other respects the rules given in this figure apply

4.3.3   Corporate Source Field (individual terms posted)

Individual terms are entered, so the procedure is to expand on individual terms in the
Corporate Source Field to identify potential search terms which then are connected in the
search query with proximity operators. Here usually the AND, (L) or (S) operators suffice,
although more restrictive operators may be used. However, it should be noted that the
Boolean and the proximity operators relate to the individual words, so a search: => S
HARVARD AND BOSTON/CS would search for HARVARD in the Basic Index and
BOSTON in the Corporate Source! The correct entry is: => S **(HARVARD AND
BOSTON)/CS.**

Entries in the Corporate Source Field correspond with those in the original article
although some words may be abbreviated (Figure 4.3). However, abbreviations vary within
and between databases.

ENTRY and COMMON ABBREVIATION

Advanced	Adv	Chemistry	Chem
Division	Div	Engineering	Eng
Faculty	Fac	Institute	Inst
Laboratory	Lab	Department	Dep
Manufacturing	Mfg	Medical/Medicine	Med
Petroleum	Pet	Physical	Phys
Research	Res	University	Univ

Figure 4.3   Examples of abbreviations in the Corporate Source Field
However, entries vary and expansions should always be performed before searches are conducted

Sometimes original articles also have quite different representations for the same organization, and naturally these differences continue into the database entry. For example, an expansion on the organization 3M in the CAplus File shows that 3M is a heavily posted term in the CS Field. The searcher would also need to check on "MINNESOTA MINING" but it must be remembered that an expand: **E (MINNESOTA MINING)/CS** would be of no value (because entries are as individual words). Nevertheless expansions on MINNESOTA/CS and on MINING/CS would show they were heavily posted, so the search shown in Screen 4.3 would be performed. In this case, the system applies "implied proximity" when the terms are separated by spaces and, as seen in Screen 4.3, the (S) operator is assumed. This is acceptable since the CS Field usually has only one "sentence", but it may be that the (S) operator is too broad in which case it may be better to connect the terms with the (W) operator.

Note that in Screen 4.3 another display format, D HIT, is introduced. This display gives the fields, in the record, in which the search terms appear (see also Section 6.9.2).

Screen 4.3[a]   Search in the Corporate Source Field (CAplus File)

```
=> S (3M OR MINNESOTA MINING)/CS
          1588      3M/CS
         32678      MINNESOTA/CS
         16111      MINING/CS
          3967      MINNESOTA MINING/CS
                    ((MINNESOTA(S)MINING)/CS)
L1        5617      (3M OR MINNESOTA MINING)/CS
=> D 1-2 HIT
L1 ANSWER 1 OF 5617 CAPLUS COPYRIGHT 1995 ACS
CS       Rochester Tech Cent., 3M Co.
L1 ANSWER 2 OF 5617 CAPLUS COPYRIGHT 1995 ACS
PA[b]    Minnesota Mining  and Mfg. Co., USA
```

[a]Copyright by the American Chemical Society and Reprinted with Permission
[b]In patent records, the CS heading field name is replaced by PA (Patent Assignee). See Chapter 9.

> **Important note:**
> * **As with so many searches in bibliographic databases, the individual words in the records may vary considerably and if comprehensive searches are required it usually is necessary to search on a number of "synonyms".**

4.3.4   Source Field (individual terms posted; some fields are numeric)
The Source Field, which contains the document reference, actually consists of a number of fields each of which may be searched separately. Accordingly, the Source Field entry for a journal article: *Organometallics* (1995), 14 (1), 207-13 CODEN: ORGND7; ISSN: 0276-7333, also has information posted in the fields shown in Table 4.1. (Patents are referenced in an entirely different way and the issues are discussed in Chapter 9.)

Table 4.1 Posted fields within the Source Field

FIELD	ABBREV-IATION	POSTED TERMS	
JOURNAL TITLE	JT	Organometallics/JT	Organometallics/SO
PUBLICATION YEAR	PY	1995/PY	1995/SO
VOLUME NUMBER	VL	14/VL	14/SO
ISSUE NUMBER	IS	1/IS	1/SO
PAGE NUMBER	SO		207/SO
CODEN	SO	ORGND7/ISN	ORGND7/SO
ISSN	ISN	0276-7333/ISN	

Terms in each of these fields may be searched, although abbreviations for Journal Titles may vary and it is advisable to expand in the Journal Title Field first. However, since entries in this field are posted individually a number of expanded terms may be required, and it is often easier to search for journals as their CODENs or ISSN numbers in the Source Field. CODENs and ISSN numbers may be found on the cover pages of serials or in a variety of catalogues available in most libraries. However, some files do not list CODENs, but list only ISSN numbers - and, again, the procedure is either to check the Database Summary Sheet, or to try an expansion in the field when online.

Searches in the Source Field may also be used to retrieve the online record for a known article. Generally only a few terms are required, for example the article mentioned above may be retrieved with the search: => **S (ORGANOMETALLICS AND 14 AND 207)/SO**.

It should be noted that some of the fields within the Source Field are text fields, and that some are numeric fields. The search format for entries in text fields on STN is always: => **S <TEXT TERM> / FIELD CODE** and while the search format for entries in numeric fields may be in the same format, that is:

> => **S <NUMERIC VALUE> / FIELD CODE**
> (example: => **S 1995/PY**)

there is another general format in which the numeric term and the field code are linked with any one of the numeric operators shown in Table 4.2. These operators may be more convenient to use in many numeric searches, and apply in all numeric search fields (see also Section 10.4.2).

Table 4.2 Numeric operators and meanings

OPERATOR	SYMBOL	EXAMPLE	MEANING
EQUAL	=	PY=1990	Published in 1990
LESS THAN	<	PY<1990	Published in 1989 or earlier
GREATER THAN	>	PY>1990	Published in 1991 or later
LESS THAN/EQUALS	=<	PY=<1990	Published in 1990 or earlier
GREATER THAN/EQUALS	>=	PY>=1990	Published in 1990 or later
RANGE	-	1990-1994/PY	Published in 1990-1994 inclusive
(ANY COMBINATIONS ALLOWED)		1989<PY<1995	Published in 1990-1994 inclusive

4.3.5   Other bibliographic fields (individual terms posted)
Searches in the Document Type and Language Fields may be particularly useful if only some document types or languages are of interest, or need to be excluded. For example, a search query which includes the search term, **AND ENGLISH/LA**, will retrieve English-language articles only, while addition of the term, **NOT J/DT**, will exclude journal articles. (Some systems provide limit features so that entire answer sets are quickly limited to the specific document type or language without using search terms. This may also be file-specific within systems.)

The most common document types are journals (entry: J/DT) and patents (P/DT) but some databases also frequently describe review articles as a special document type (generally REVIEW/DT may be used as well as the keyword term REVIEW). Again, these are general comments to alert searchers to the possibilities, although individual files may have specific entries. To check in a file it is necessary merely to expand: **E REVIEW/DT** or **E REVIEW**, and from the numbers of postings listed the appropriate terms become obvious. (Review articles only might be required, for example if a very large answer set is obtained it might be better in the first instance to read a few general review articles on the topic.)

Other document types include books (B/DT), conference proceedings (C/DT), dissertations (D/DT) and technical reports (T/DT), but the full list of document types in a file is very easily obtained through an expand: **E A/DT**.

The language of the original document is posted in the Language Field and may be searched in most databases either as the full name or as an abbreviation (usually two or three letters). Again it is always advisable to expand first to determine the appropriate term, and an example is given in Screen 4.4. (Note the appearance of full names and abbreviations: EN, ENGLISH; EO, ESPERANTO; ET, ESTONIAN; FR, FRENCH; either form may be used as the search term.)

Screen 4.4[a] Entries in the Language Field in the BIOSIS File				
=> **E ENGLISH/LA** 14				
E1	882	EL/LA	E2	6309909	EN/LA
E3	6309909-->	ENGLISH/LA	E4	8	EO/LA
E5	56442	ES/LA	E6	8	ESPERANTO/LA
E7	39	ESTONIAN/LA	E8	39	ET/LA
E9	89	FA/LA	E10	236	FI/LA
E11	901	FINNISH/LA	E12	129107	FR/LA
E13	129107	FRENCH/LA	E14	313	GEORGIAN/LA

[a]Copyright by BIOSIS and Reprinted with Permission

4.3.6   Abstract Field (individual terms posted)
If there is an abstract in the original article, then the text in the Abstract Field usually corresponds closely, although database producers may make some changes which may include database standard abbreviations, and text only entries for certain characters (Greek letters are spelt with periods before and after and mathematical symbols are spelt in abbreviated form, for example >= becomes gtoreq (**greater than or equal** to)). If there is no abstract in the original article then the indexer will write the abstract and this particularly applies to patent documents (see Chapter 9).

Since abstract text usually is "free text" (author written) it may differ very substantially from index entries which are written by indexers to comply with database policies.

Accordingly the abstract text is a very important complement to the index text, and searches in both abstracts and indexes always should be considered.

Terms in the Abstract Field are posted individually so proximity operators must be used. If the (L) operator is used to connect terms they can be anywhere in the text for the Abstract Field, while the (S) operator permits connections only when terms are in the same sentence.[*] The (nA) and (nW) operators also apply in the abstract text, but do not cross sentence boundaries, that is, searches on words at the end of the first sentence and beginning of the second sentence will not retrieve records if the (A) or (W) operators are used.

It should be noted that many files do not have a separate abstract field. Indeed in most files on STN, the abstract text is placed in the Basic Index and cannot be searched separately in the AB Field. As usual, the Database Summary Sheets indicate the content of the Basic Index and indicate whether searches in the AB Field may be conducted separately.

Summary

- There are a *number of fields* which contain bibliographic information and, in general, for bibliographic records of journal articles, the entries are similar in the major bibliographic databases.
- However, there are *subtle differences* both between, and within, databases and the searcher should take great care to ensure that all relevant search terms are used.
- It is important to *check on postings* before searches are performed; these checks are used to identify potential search terms.
- On STN the *EXPAND command* is used to check postings, and there are many important applications of this command.

A general summary of search possibilities is given in Table 4.3.

---

[*]Not all databases allow use of the (S) operator in the Abstract Field in which cases the AND operator is assumed. A warning of this limitation always appears immediately prior to the display of the L-numbered answer set. Note also that the (S) operator is system-specific.

Table 4.3 Summary of search possibilities in the bibliographic fields

FIELD	COMMENTS
ACCESSION NUMBER	Search: **NUMBER/AN** (e.g., **S 122:106087/AN**)
TITLE[a]	Search: **TERM/TI**.[a] Individual terms entered. Sometimes the easiest way to find the online record for a known document is to include a few words in a search in the Title Field. => **S (EVIDENCE AND CROSS AND LINKING AND KNOTTING)/TI**
AUTHOR	Use EXPAND command to identify correct search terms. Each author name entered as bound phrase. Hence search: **S LOWE/AU** retrieves no answers; **S LOWE ?/AU** retrieves all records by those with surname LOWE; **S LOWE G?/AU** retrieves all records by those with given name starting with G (or with initial G); **S LOWE GORDON/AU** retrieves all records with entry LOWE., GORDON
CORPORATE SOURCE	Search: **TERM/CS**. Individual terms entered. Use EXPAND command to identify correct terms. Many synonyms may be present for the same organization.
SOURCE	Search: **TERM/SO**. Individual terms entered. SO Field contains many component fields: JT, VL, PY, ISN.
DOCUMENT TYPE	Search: **TERM/DT**. Mainly used with journals, patents, reviews (J/DT, P/DT, REVIEW/DT)
LANGUAGE	Search: **TERM/LA**. Full name or abbreviation acceptable. Use EXPAND command to identify terms.
ABSTRACT[a]	Search: **TERM/AB**.[a] (L) operator connects any two terms in the Abstract Field, while many databases additionally allow the more restrictive sentence operator, (S).

[a]Indicates the field is also included in Basic Index (in *most* files). However, there are exceptions and Database Summary Sheets should be consulted to find the list of all fields included in the Basic Index of the database. When included in the Basic Index, field codes are not required in the search statement.

5

Bibliographic Databases: Index Fields

In this chapter we learn:

• *About indexing!*
• *How to use a thesaurus (we show a simple geographical example involving broader and narrower terms based on the country, Australia).*
• *About Section Codes and Index Headings.*

We look briefly at the hierarchy of indexing in the Chemical Abstracts Database. We cannot tell you all about the indexing for all the files on every system, but at least we can give an overview of the issues involved!

5.1   General structure of indexing

It is apparent from the records shown in Chapter 3 that indexing policies vary greatly between the different databases. This not only has very considerable implications in cross-file searching (that is, when searches are being conducted either simultaneously or sequentially across files), but also it highlights the fact that a reasonable knowledge is required of indexing before any single database is searched. All databases will supply information on their indexing policies upon request, and it certainly is advisable to have index guides readily available for those databases most commonly searched.

The overall structure of indexing applied by most databases is similar, and is represented in Figure 5.1. Database producers first determine policies on the general areas to be covered and choose those parts of the primary scientific literature to be indexed. For bibliographic databases this generally means a portfolio of journals and patent classifications, but any associated literature considered relevant will be included.

GENERAL AREA
PORTFOLIO OF PRIMARY LITERATURE
(Journals, Patents, Books, Dissertations etc)
BROAD CLASSIFICATIONS
SECTION CODES
SUBSECTIONS
INDEX HEADINGS
ARTICLE-SPECIFIC TEXT

Figure 5.1   General structure of index entries

Lists of the journals indexed are published, but this does not mean that every article in the journal eventually appears in the database. Rather only those articles which relate to the database policies are indexed. For example, the *Scandinavian Journal of Metallurgy* is indexed by, *inter alia,* the CAplus, COMPENDEX, INSPEC, METADEX and SCISEARCH Files (all of these files have information in the general area of metallurgy, and, indeed, appear in the METALS CLUSTER on STN) but for the publication year 1993 when the journal published 46 articles, the number of articles appearing in the databases mentioned above is 43, 39, 7, 29, and 45 respectively. This picture is repeated with *all* journals, so it should not be assumed that all the articles in the original journal will be covered through searching just one database! However, some databases now include information from all articles in a journal regardless of whether they meet database content policies, and, for example, the CAplus File contains bibliography and abstracts (if available) for all articles in 1300 key journals.

> **Important note:**
> • **In searching one database you are searching the records for only those articles indexed by the database. You are not necessarily performing a comprehensive search of the literature!**

5.2   The location of index entries

Database producers set up a hierarchical structure of entries starting with very broad discipline areas and progressively becoming more specific until the relevant aspects of the actual article are indexed.

Indexing entries may be put in a number of different fields but the main ones are listed in Table 5.1. Generally the fields which include the word "code" will have both a numeric code and a text equivalent. For example, Screen 3.2 shows that the BIOSIS Classification Code 10060 refers to "Biochemical Studies-General".

On the other hand, fields which include the word "term" will generally have text-only entries, and these may often be based on author terminology (in the Supplementary Term Field), or on database headings (in the Controlled Term Field). However, mostly the distinction between "codes" and "terms" is of little consequence to the searcher, except that it is worth noting that numeric codes may be a little simpler to enter as search terms.

Table 5.1 Fields with indexing entries in some representative databases

FIELD CODE	FIELD NAME
BC	Biosystematic Code
CC	Classification Code
CN	Chemical Name
CT	Controlled Term
IT	Index Term
RF	Research Front
RN	Registry Number
SC	Section Code
ST	Supplementary Term
STP	Supplementary Term Plus

The structure of the indexing used by bibliographic databases falls into one of two categories. Either the database producer sets up a thesaurus, or sets up a series of section codes and subcodes (often accompanied by index headings).

5.3 The online thesaurus

Currently about one quarter of the databases on STN have an online thesaurus (which generally will be contained within a single index field) and these are readily identified either from the STN Database Catalogue, or from the Database Summary Sheets. The full thesaurus list contains indexing terms or classification codes in a hierarchical arrangement from broadest terms to narrowest terms, so general or specific searches may be executed by suitable choice of indexing terms.

5.3.1 The structure of a thesaurus
To illustrate the structure and use of a thesaurus, consider the CIN (Chemical Industry Notes) File which has a thesaurus based on geographic terms (GT). (It should be noted that a thesaurus can be set up on any hierarchical order of concepts, and the geographic thesaurus is chosen here simply because its structure may very easily be seen by all who have some familiarity with geography, and because it avoids difficult scientific concepts.)

On STN the procedure is first to expand on a relevant term in the thesaurus field using the EXPAND command in the normal manner. If the actual term used is not present then the list of E-numbers obtained will probably include some terms which may be used in the next stage. Screen 5.1 shows the expanded terms and indicates that AUSTRALIA *is* an entry in the thesaurus field, that there are 19,095 records in the file in which AUSTRALIA appears as a Geographic Term, and that there are 32 Associated Terms (AT).

Screen 5.1[a] Locating the thesaurus entries (Chemical Industry Notes Database)

=> **E AUSTRALIA/GT   7**

E#	FREQUENCY	AT		TERM
-----	-------------	------		-------------
E1	0	1		ATOLL/GT
E2	256	27		AUSTRALASIA/GT
E3	19095	32	-->	AUSTRALIA/GT
E4	0	1		AUSTRALIAN/GT
E5	0	4		AUSTRALIAN ANTARCTIC TERRITORY/GT
E6	1	1 2		AUSTRALIAN CAPITAL TERRITORY/GT
E7	3416	1 8		AUSTRIA/GT

---

[a]Copyright by the American Chemical Society and Reprinted with Permission

A second expansion (expansions on thesaurus listings are often referred to as explosions) on the term may now be undertaken to display the associated terms. The format for this second expansion on STN is: => **E <TERM>+RCODE / FIELD** where the options for the RCODE (relationship code) to be entered are given in Table 5.2 (here the Field GT is used as explained above although different databases have the thesaurus in different fields, usually the CT Fields, and the appropriate field code should be entered).

Table 5.2 Examples of explosions within the thesaurus

RCODE	EXAMPLE	OUTCOME
ALL	E AUSTRALIA+ALL/GT	all associated terms are listed
BT	E AUSTRALIA+BT/GT	all broader terms are listed only
NT	E AUSTRALIA+NT/GT	all narrower terms are listed only
NT2	E AUSTRALIA+NT2/GT	narrower terms down to the second level are listed

An actual explosion is shown in Screen 5.2 in which all associated terms are displayed. Note that there are indeed 32 E-numbers, that is, a total of 32 associated terms (as listed in Screen 5.1), and that, in common with all thesaurus terms, a NOTE appears which comments on the definition used with the term.

Screen 5.2[a] Display of all associated terms

=> **E E3+ALL/GT**

E1	17782	BT3	World/GT
E2	1359	BT2	Pacific Rim/GT
E3	17782	BT2	World/GT
E4	256	BT1	Australasia/GT
E5	10	BT2	Organizations/GT
E6	0	BT1	Commonwealth of Nations/GT
E7	10	BT2	Organizations/GT
E8	929	BT1	OECD/GT
E9	10	BT2	Organizations/GT
E10	1325	BT1	UN/GT
E11	19095	-->	Australia/GT

Screen 5.2 (continued)			
		NOTE Officially Commonwealth of Australia.	
		Australia is the only country that is also a continent. It is	
		geographically divided into 2 territories and 6 states.	
E12	5	NT1	Ashmore and Cartier Islands/GT
E13	1	NT1	Australian Capital Territory/GT
E14	59	NT1	Christmas Island/GT
E15	0	NT1	Cocos (Keeling) Islands/GT
E16	0	NT1	Coral Sea Islands/GT
E17	1	NT1	Heard and McDonald Islands/GT
E18	915	NT1	New South Wales/GT
E19	0	NT1	Norfolk Island/GT
E20	359	NT1	Northern Territory/GT
E21	1608	NT1	Queensland/GT
E22	451	NT1	South Australia/GT
E23	395	NT1	Tasmania/GT
E24	586	NT1	Victoria/GT
E25	1897	NT1	Western Australia/GT
E26	5	DP	Ashmore and Cartier Islands/GT
E27	0	DP	Australian Antarctic Territory/GT
E28	59	DP	Christmas Island/GT
E29	0	DP	Cocos (Keeling) Islands/GT
E30	0	DP	Coral Sea Islands/GT
E31	1	DP	Heard and McDonald Islands/GT
E32	0	DP	Norfolk Island/GT

Commonly there are several sets of broader, and of narrower, terms (since any single term can be part of a number of different hierarchies) and each set is grouped together. The different sets here relate to geographical area, and to political and to trading partners, so the broader terms in Screen 5.2 might also be visualized as below:

BT3	BT2	BT1	TERM
World	=> Pacific Rim	=> Australasia	=> Australia
	Organizations	=> Commonwealth of Nations	=> Australia
	Organizations	=> OECD	=> Australia
	Organizations	=> UN	=> Australia

On the other hand, while there are a number of narrower terms, in this case they all are at the same hierarchical level (NT1). (Further narrower terms might have been first cities (NT2) and then suburbs within cities (NT3) within any of the States of Australia but it happened that the hierarchy in the CIN File did not extend to such detail.)

The search strategy may now be completed. If the searcher is particularly interested in news on Australia related to the United Nations, the search: => S UN/GT AND AUSTRALIA/GT may be conducted. Sample answers would then be evaluated and the search would be revised if some important free text terms were uncovered. Meanwhile, for more specific information on New South Wales, the search statement may include the term: NEW SOUTH WALES/GT.

The online thesaurus is a very useful indicator of index terms and the database records may be narrowed quickly to key areas. As more such aids become available online, then searching on indexing terms will become easier.

Important notes:
- Find out whether the file has an online thesaurus (from the Database Catalogue or Database Summary Sheet).
- If there is an online thesaurus, expand on a possible term in the field with the thesaurus capability.
- A suitable term will soon be found in which case it can be expanded further (with the preferred relationship code).
- Next choose the most appropriate index code or term, using broader terms or narrower terms for more general or more specific searches respectively.

5.4   Section codes and index headings

Databases which do not have a specific thesaurus usually follow a classification system which involves Section Codes and Index Headings. In many ways Section Codes work like a thesaurus; it is just that the hierarchical links between the codes are not made in a way which allows easy expansions to show the different hierarchical levels. On the other hand, Index Headings constitute a parallel system of classification. They relate to specific topics in the subject which commonly cross Section Code boundaries.

5.5   Indexing hierarchy: Chemical Abstracts Database

5.5.1   Section codes
The Chemical Abstracts database is segmented as indicated in Figure 5.2. (Details of the sections are found in the manual: *Subject Coverage and Arrangement of Abstracts by Sections* in *Chemical Abstracts*, which is available from the CAS.) The database has 5 broad classifications: BIOCHEMISTRY; ORGANIC CHEMISTRY; MACROMOLECULAR CHEMISTRY; APPLIED CHEMISTRY and CHEMICAL ENGINEERING; and PHYSICAL, INORGANIC and ANALYTICAL CHEMISTRY, and each of these contains a number of section codes which in turn have subsections.

CHEMICAL ABSTRACTS DATABASE
(covers chemistry and related sciences in 80 section codes)
BROAD CLASSIFICATIONS

BIOCHEMICAL	ORGANIC	MACROMOLECULAR	APPLIED	PIA[a]

SECTION CODES

1. Pharmacology	21. General Organic Chemistry	etc
2. Mammalian Hormones	22. Physical Organic Chemistry	
3. Biochemical Genetics	23. Aliphatic Compounds	
4. Toxicology	24. Alicyclic Compounds	
5. etc	25. etc	

SUB-SECTIONS

1.1	Methods
1.2	Drug matabolism
1.3	Structure-activity
1.4	Adverse drug interactions and general pharmacology
1.5	etc

Figure 5.2 Indexing in the Chemical Abstracts Database
Note that only some of the entries are shown [a]PHYSICAL/INORGANIC/ANALYTICAL

Searches may be performed at any of these levels and Figure 5.3 gives some representative examples. Searches in Section Codes add another concept to the search statement and generally are used to narrow large answer sets to specific areas defined by the database producers. For example, if the searcher is interested in the synthesis of cholesterol in biochemical pathways the addition of the search term, **BIO/SC,**[*] will limit the search to the biochemical sections of the database. On the other hand, if the searcher is interested in the organic synthesis of cholesterol, the search term, **ORG/SC**, or even **32/SC** (Section Code 32: Steroids) might be used. Note that the CAS Roles may be used also to solve this problem (see below.)

However, it must be remembered that while such searches may lead to more precise answers, they rely greatly on specific indexing used by the database, and while the topic of interest may be characterized within a single section code, more commonly it will cross a number of areas in which case cross-section codes are listed in the SX Field.

SEARCH TERM	AREAS SEARCHED
S **MAC/SC**	all Section Codes in the MACROMOLECULAR CHEMISTRY class (Section Codes 35-46)
S **60/SC**	Section Code 60 (Waste Treatment and Disposal)
S **31-33/SC**	Section Codes 31 through 33 (Alkaloids to Steroids)
S **50.2/SC**	Section Code 50.2: Propellants and Explosives (Explosives, ignitors and detonators)

Figure 5.3   Examples of Section Code search terms in the CAplus File

5.5.2   Index headings

The Chemical Abstracts Database has over 10,000 Index Headings which define specific topics, while there are approximately 80,000 additional index headings which refer to animal or plant names. It should be noted that index headings change over time to reflect changes in the subject, so care should be taken to ensure that the correct index headings, for the time period being search, are used. While some databases (like MEDLINE) update all records with new indexing schemes, others (like CAplus) do not.

A common procedure is for the searcher to first consult the Index Guide before attempting a search, or to retrieve Index Headings online, since in this way important keywords, in the form of the Index Headings, may be identified and used in the preliminary search (see Section 7.1.1).

In the Chemical Abstracts Database each Index Heading is followed by a summary of the aspect of the original article which relates to the Heading. This is particularly valuable since specific research may be directly related to the index entry. (It is relevant to note here that terms in a single index entry in the CAplus File are treated as if in a single sentence. For example, the record shown in Screen 5.3 would be retrieved through all of the searches in which **REARRANGEMENT/CT** was linked with **STABLE** using either the (L), (A), or (W) operators.) However, most databases do not have specific text entries immediately following the index heading (for example, see Screen 3.2), and in these cases free text search terms may be linked with the index headings only through the AND operator (with possible loss of precision).

---

[*]The 5 broad classifications in Figure 5.2 are abbreviated BIO, ORG, MAC, APP, and PIA, and these abbreviations may be used as search terms in the SC Field.

Screen 5.3[a]   CAS Registry Numbers as Index Headings in the CAplus File

ACCESSION NUMBER: 1995:328426 CAPLUS
SUPPL. TERM: crystal structure phosphinoferrocene oxabutenyl palladium complex; mol
        structure phosphinoferrocene oxabutenyl palladium complex; phosphinoferrocene
        palladium platinum aryl complex; Heck cyclization aryl iodide palladium complex
INDEX TERM: Crystal structure
        Molecular structure
         (of phosphinoferrocene oxabutenyl palladium complex)
INDEX TERM: Rearrangement
        (stable arylpalladium iodides and reactive arylpalladium trifluoromethanesulfonates in
        intramol. Heck reaction)
INDEX TERM: Ring closure and formation
        (Heck, stable arylpalladium iodides and reactive arylpalladium
        trifluoromethanesulfonates in intramol. Heck reaction)
INDEX TERM: 159626-87-6P
        ROLE: PRP (Properties); RCT (Reactant); SPN (Synthetic preparation); PREP
        (Preparation) (crystal structure; stable arylpalladium iodides and reactive arylpalladium
        trifluoromethanesulfonates in intramol. Heck reaction)
INDEX TERM: 106-95-6, Allyl bromide, reactions 1730-25-2, Allylmagnesium bromide
        5159-41-1, 2-Iodobenzyl alcohol   14221-01-3, Tetrakis(triphenylphosphine)palladium
        16188-57-1, 2-Iodo-4-methylphenol 37609-69-1, Dilithium cyclooctatetraenide
        40400-13-3, 2-Iodobenzyl bromide   72287-26-4 123860-23-1
        ROLE: RCT (Reactant)
        (stable arylpalladium iodides and reactive arylpalladium trifluoromethanesulfonates in
        intramol. Heck reaction)
INDEX TERM: 24892-64-6P 57056-91-4P 159625-86-2P 159626-88-7P
        ROLE: RCT (Reactant); SPN (Synthetic preparation); PREP (Preparation)
        (stable arylpalladium iodides and reactive arylpalladium trifluoromethanesulfonates in
        intramol. Heck reaction)
INDEX TERM: 159626-89-8P 159626-90-1P 159626-91-2P 159626-92-3P 159626-93-4P
        159626-94-5P 159626-95-6P
        ROLE: SPN (Synthetic preparation); PREP (Preparation)
        (stable arylpalladium iodides and reactive arylpalladium trifluoromethanesulfonates in
        intramol. Heck reaction)

[a]Copyright by the American Chemical Society and Reprinted with Permission

    A further and most important aspect of Index Headings in the CAplus File is that each
chemical substance indexed is listed as an index entry, but only through its CAS Registry
Number. An example of the way in which substances are indexed is given in Screen 5.3
which shows the index fields for a record in the CAplus File.

There are a few important aspects to note. First, in index entries, CAS Registry Numbers appear only as controlled index terms. For example, they do not appear within the first three entries (which have their own Index Headings) and this has important consequences relating to the use of appropriate proximity operators. For example, a search: => S **MOLECULAR STRUCTURE AND 159626-87-6**[*] would retrieve this record, but the record would not be retrieved if the (L) operator was used.

Second, when CAS Registry Numbers appear in index entries, some descriptive information relating to the substances appears in the same index field (in parentheses), and naturally the (L) or (S) operator can be used to retrieve answers in these cases.

Third, some CAS Registry Numbers are followed by nomenclature terms, but they apply only to author specified terms (not systematic nomenclature), to trade and common names, and apply only from 1987 onwards (earlier records have CAS Registry Numbers only). Finally, when the original article reports a significant preparation of the substance the suffix P is added after the CAS Registry Number in the index term.

CAS Registry Numbers are listed only for those substances in the original article for which some new or significant discovery is reported. They are not listed for every substance mentioned in the original article (for example for solvents of reactions) unless the solvent has some special role. It is important to recognize this point since in many instances only some of the substances in the original article will be indexed in the online record.

A recent enhancement of the CAplus File has involved the assignment of roles after the CAS Registry Numbers in the record. There are 7 broad roles (super roles) and 38 specific roles, some of which are posted within more than one super role. The list of roles is given in Table 5.3.

CAS Registry Numbers are usually found in the REGISTRY File (the searching for CAS Registry Numbers, and their use as search terms in other files is discussed extensively in Part 2) and the REGISTRY File answer set is crossed over to the file(s) of interest. In this simple process the CAS Registry Numbers are automatically used as search terms in the new file. For example, if the answer set (which of course relates to substances) in the REGISTRY File is L1, then the search in the CAplus File: => **S L1**, will retrieve all records in which the CAS Registry Numbers appear.

While these records may always be narrowed with the addition of any text term, and may be narrowed with the search: => **S L1/P** to limit answers to those in which preparations for the substances of interest are reported, they now may be further narrowed using any of the super or specific roles given in Table 5.3. So the search: => **S L1/THU**, will retrieve only those records in which the therapeutic use of the substance is reported. Note that searching with roles is a *precision tool*, and may be very useful to focus on specific studies particularly when large numbers of entries occur for individual substances. On the other hand, it must be recognized that roles provide an additional level of indexing, and unless a precise role fully covers the area of interest, the searcher should consider using a number of roles, or the super roles, or otherwise scan through a number of the records retrieved from general searches on the substances.

---

[*]The Registry Number for the "phosphinoferrocene oxabutenyl palladium complex" mentioned in the first index entry is 159626-87-6.

Table 5.3   Role assignments in the CAplus File

SUPER ROLE CODE	FULL NAME	SPECIFIC ROLE CODE	NAME
ANST	Analytical Study	ANT	Analyte
		AMX	Analytical Matrix
		ARG	Analytical Reagent Use
		ARU	Analytical Role, Unclassified
BIOL	Biological Study	ADV	Adverse Effect, Including Toxicity
		AGR	Agricultural Use
		BMF	Bioindustrial Manufacture
		BAC	Biol. Activ. or Effector, Except Adverse
		BOC	Biological Occurrence
		BPR	Biological Process
		BUU	Biological Use, Unclassified
		BSU	Biological Study, Unclassified
		BPN	Biosynthetic Preparation
		FFD	Food or Feed Use
		MFM	Metabolic Formation
		THU	Therapeutic Use
FORM	Formation, Nonpreparative	FMU	Formation, Unclassified
		GFM	Geological or Astronomical Occurrence
		MFM	Metabolic Formation
OCCU	Occurrence	BOC	Biological Occurrence
		GOC	Geolog. or Astronom. Occurrence
		OCU	Occurrence, Unclassified
		POL	Pollutant
PREP	Preparation	BMF	Bioindustrial Manufacture
		BPN	Biosynthetic Preparation
		BYP	Pyproduct
		IMF	Industrial Manufacture
		PUR	Purification or Recovery
		PNU	Preparation, Unclassified
		SPN	Synthetic Preparation
PROC	Process	BPR	Biological Process
		GPR	Geological or Astronomical Process
		PEP	Physical, Eng., or Chem. Process
		REM	Removal or Disposal
USES	Uses	AGR	Agricultural Use
		ARG	Analytical Reagent, Use
		BUU	Biological Use, Unclassified
		CAT	Catalytic Use
		DEV	Device Component Use
		FFD	Food or Feed Use
		MOA	Modifier or Additive Use
		NUU	Nonbiological Use, Unclassified
		POF	Polymer in Formulation
		TEM	Technical or Engineering Material Use
		THU	Therapeutic Use
(Specific Roles not upposted to super roles)		MSC	Miscellaneous
		PRP	Properties
		RCT	Reactant

Roles have been assigned by the indexers from October 1994, while roles in the records in the CAplus File prior to that time have been assigned "algorithmically". That is, the roles have been assigned by computer-based searches which involved combinations of searches in Section Codes, Controlled Terms, and keywords. Backdating files in this way may not necessarily be as precise as indexing of the original articles, but nevertheless at least an additional entry point to the literature is available. At issue here is human intelligence versus (a form of) artificial intelligence, and while computerized scanning techniques are valuable, they need to be evaluated. However, a most important point is that the searcher needs to understand how entries are input, and then to adjust search strategies accordingly.

5.6   Indexing in other major bibliographic databases

Section 5.5 discusses just some of the issues relating to indexing in the Chemical Abstracts database. However, all the issues are a study in themselves and clearly the better the searcher understands the indexing, the better the search results which will be obtained.

Other databases have quite different indexing policies, and it is essential that they are understood. The first step is to obtain the index guides from the database producer and the question is: How do I find out the name and address of the database producer? The easiest answer is: through the Database Summary Sheets!

5.7   Database Summary Sheets

With so many different databases and so many fields, the resource materials provided by the database producer and the vendor become invaluable. An initial reference material is the Database Summary Sheet. Database Summary Sheets for each file are provided free of charge and it is essential that the complete set is kept up to date. They contain information on:

- Subject Coverage;
- Sources (that is, the primary literature indexed);
- File Data (time period covered, number of records);
- User Aids (print materials and online help available);
- Database Producer (contact information for the producer);
- Search and Display Field Codes (names and codes of search fields, search examples and display codes);
- DISPLAY and PRINT Formats (system-defined display formats, their contents and examples);
- SELECT and SORT Fields (list of fields for which the SELECT and SORT commands operate);[*]
- other information relevant to the File (for example, Thesaurus Fields); and
- Sample Records.

For example, the first page of the Database Summary Sheet for the TOXLINE File is shown in Figure 5.4 and the addresses of the database producer and supplier, and list of the "User Aids", are immediately identified. Subsequent pages of the Summary Sheet contain listings of the other items described above.

Many of the immediate questions the searcher may have concerning the mechanics of searching the File may be answered by a quick reference to the Database Summary Sheet. However, more detailed information, and indeed information on indexing, is found in the Database Descriptions and Index Guides.

In these last three chapters the database content and the tools and techniques required for searching online databases have been discussed. This is the *information* that is available to work with, and it is essential that its nature is fully understood. The next two chapters consider the strategies that are needed to *obtain the information* required from the searches.

---

[*]Details of the SELECT and SORT commands are given in the manual: *Guide to Commands*. Some summary information is given in Chapter 10.

TOXLINE

STN Database Summary Sheet

STN is operated in North America
by Chemical Abstracts Service

The **TOXLINE**® File (Toxicology Literature Online 1965 - present) is a bibliographic database produced by the U.S. National Library of Medicine (NLM). The database covers the pharmacological, biochemical, physiological, and toxicological effects of drugs and other chemicals. TOXLINE is composed of the following subfiles, shown with acronyms searchable in the /FS (File Segment) field and dates of coverage by publication year:

ANEUPL	Aneuploidy File, Environmental Mutagen Information Center, Oak Ridge National Laboratory (1970-1986)
BIOSIS	Toxicological Aspects of Environmental Health, BIOSIS from 1970
CIS	CIS Abstracts, International Labour Office, International Occupational Safety and Health Information Center, 1981 to present.
CRISP	Toxicology Research Projects, National Institutes of Health FY89-91
DART	Developmental and Reproductive Toxicology File, 1989 to the present
EMIC	Environmental Mutagen Information Center File, Oak Ridge National Laboratory, from 1950
EPIDEM	Epidemiology Information System, FDA Center for Food Safety, 1940 to present
ETIC	Environmental Teratology Information Center File, Oak Ridge National Laboratory, from 1950
FEDRIP	Federal Research in Progress, 1984 to the present
HMTC	Hazardous Materials Technical Center File, Defense Logistics Agency, 1982 to present
IPA	International Pharmaceutical Abstracts, American Society of Hospital Pharmacists, from 1969
NTIS	Toxicology Document and Data Depository File, National Technical Information Service, from 1979
PESTAB	Pesticides Abstracts (formerly Health Aspects of Pesticides Abstract Bulletin), Environmental Protection Agency, 1968-1981
PPBIB	Poisonous Plants Bibliography, a special collection of mostly pre-1976 material on this subject prepared especially to complement more recent coverage by other subfiles
TOXBIB	Toxicity Bibliography, National Library of Medicine, from 1966
TSCATS	Toxic Substances Control Act Test Submissions, pre-1988 to the present

The TOXBIB and BIOSIS (since August 1985) subfiles may be searched using the U.S. National Library of Medicine's Medical Subject Headings (MESH®). The records in these two subfiles are updated annually with the current version of MeSH headings. Online thesauri are available for the MeSH Tree Numbers (/MN), Controlled Terms (/CT), and Chemical Names (/CN).

Subject Coverage

TOXLINE contains references to published material and research in progress in the following areas:

- Adverse Drug Reactions
- Air Pollution
- Animal Venom
- Antidotes
- Carcinogenesis via Chemicals
- Chemically Induced Deseases
- Drug Evaluations
- Environmental Pollution
- Food Contamination
- Mutagenesis
- Occupational Hazards
- Pesticides and Herbicides
- Radiation
- Teratogenesis
- Toxicological Analysis
- Waste Disposal

Sources

TOXLINE includes primarily English-language items with international coverage of journal articles, letters, meeting abstracts, monographs, papers, research and project summaries, technical reports, theses, and unpublished material.

File Data

- Over 1,850,000 records (5/94)
- Updated monthly (approximately 10,000 records)
- Reloaded annually
- Automatic current-awareness searches (SDI's) are run monthly

User Aids

- Medical Subject Headings-ANNOTATED ALPHABETIC LIST (available in print and online)
- Medical Subject Headings-TREE STRUCTURES (available both in print and online)
- STNGUIDE
- Online Helps (HELP DIRECTORY lists all help messages available)
- PERMUTED Medical Subject Headings (available both in print and online)

Database Producer

National Library of Medicine (NLM)
8600 Rockville Pike
Bethesda, MD 20894 USA
Phone: 301-496-6193
        800-638-8480
Telefax: 301-496-0822
Email: mms@nlm.nih.gov

Database Supplier

Chemical Abstracts Service
2540 Olentangy River Road
P.O. Box 3012
Columbus, Ohio 43210-0012 USA
Phone: 614-447-3600
Telefax: 614-447-3713
Telex: 6 842 086 CHMAB

In Europe
STN International
c/o FIZ Karlsruhe
Postfach 2465
76012 Karlsruhe
Federal Republic of Germany
Phone: (+49) 7247/808-555
Telex: 17724710+
Telefax: (+49) 7247/808-131
STNmail: HLPDESKK

In Japan
STN International
c/o The Japan Information Center of
    Science and Technology (JICST)
5-2, Nagatacho 2-chome
Chiyoda-ku, Tokyo 100 Japan
Phone: (+81) 03-3581-6448
Telex: 02223604 JICST J
Telefax: (+81) 03-3581-6446
STNmail: HLPDESKT

In North America
STN International
c/o CAS
P.O. Box 3012
Columbus, Ohio 43210 U.S.A.
Phone: (614) 447-3731
Telex: 6842086 chmab
Telefax: (614) 447-3751
STNmail: HLPDESKC

July 1994

Figure 5.4   First page of Database Summary Sheet for the TOXLINE File

Summary

- Database producers set up a *hierarchical index structure* and sometimes this is built into a *thesaurus*. A thesaurus can be particularly useful since it directly indicates how the index codes are related, and broader or narrower terms can be identified easily.
- *Index headings and index terms* constitute a parallel form of classification. Terms based on author terminology are placed in ST Fields, while terms based on database policies are placed in CT (or IT) Fields.
- Searches based on index headings can immediately target key areas, although it must be understood that the headings are very much the result of index policies.
- *CAS Registry Numbers are used as the primary index entries* for substances in the CAS Files, and they commonly appear in index listings in other files on STN. In the Chemical Abstracts database, it is possible to assign *roles* to substances and such searches are very valuable when precise answers are required.
- *Database Summary Sheets* are an extremely valuable basic resource and they contain most of the immediate information usually needed relating to search and display of the databases.

6

Bibliographic Databases: Search Outline

*In this chapter we learn the **principles** of online searching! That is:*

- *To state concepts in "natural language".*
- *What needs to be considered to "convert" concepts into search terms.*
- *Issues relating to the evaluation of a preliminary search through to the display of the final answer set.*

6.1   The principles

There are a number of *principles* involved in setting up the search query through to the retrieval of the final answer set. This chapter outlines these principles, while Chapter 7 applies the steps in this chapter and shows alternative approaches to solve a particular problem.

The principles are listed in Figure 6.1. While the principles are numbered, and will be discussed separately in this chapter, these numbers do not necessarily follow the sequence in which the actual search is conducted because sometimes the principles are tightly interrelated. For example, the choice of search terms is closely connected with the file selection, while the principles of review of results (from the preliminary search) and revision of search profile may have to be applied a number of times before the final search is undertaken.

1.	SCOPE AND INTENT OF SEARCH
2.	"NATURAL LANGUAGE" CONCEPTS
3.	FILE SELECTION
4.	SEARCH TERMS
5.	PRELIMINARY SEARCH and REVIEW OF RESULTS
6.	REVISION OF SEARCH PROFILE
7.	FULL SEARCH
8.	DISPLAY OF ANSWERS

Figure 6.1   The principles of online searching in bibliographic files

However, it is really important to realize that a number of key steps need to be considered every time a search is conducted. Failure to do so is the single most common reason why disappointing search results are attained.

6.2   Scope and intent of the search

Many types of searches may be performed. They range from very narrow searches on specific topics through to very general searches in broad areas. Sometimes merely a few key references are required, and at other times it is essential to perform searches in which all information on the topic is retrieved. While the approaches to these different types of searches are similar, nevertheless it is valuable to be clear about the search expectations from the outset. (However, particularly in the very large databases, only the most experienced searchers may be able to reasonably predict the search outcome. So, usually, the initial intention may need modifying, for example when it is unexpectedly found that very extensive information is reported in the area of interest.)

Whether the search is broad or narrow, it should retrieve everything within the limitations set. In a sense every search should be comprehensive! There is a big difference between a comprehensive search in a narrowly defined area, and an incomplete search, for example, one in which insufficient thought was given to the construction of the search query - even though only a few answers might be retrieved in each case.

One of the features of online searching is the breadth and depth of the literature available, and sometimes very large numbers of hits are obtained. However, if required, these should be narrowed down in a *planned manner in which it clearly is understood what is being included and what is being excluded.* So, even if "merely a few key references are required" the search still should be comprehensive, and this means that the approaches to the types of searches mentioned above should be similar!

Limitations may be set in a number of ways. First, *a comprehensive search may be conducted in a single database* in which case it is being recognized that this might not constitute a comprehensive search of the *literature.* However, it is far better to do a thorough search of a single database than an ill-conceived search across a number of databases. In the former case the parameters merely have been set to coincide with the subjects and policies defined by the database producer. Provided these are understood then a so-defined comprehensive search can be conducted.

Second, *within a single database a number a limitations may be set.* The procedure here normally is to perform a comprehensive search of terms in the Basic Index of the file (additionally with terms in a specialized index like the Author Field or the Corporate Source

Field if terms in these fields are essential to the requirements of the search). If the answer set obtained is too large then planned restrictions may be added.

There are a number of ways in which answer sets may be restricted and some options are given in Figure 6.3 while a more detailed discussion appears in Section 7.3. In making these restrictions it should be recognized that comprehensive searches still are being performed but it is just that they are being done in specifically defined subsets of the database!

6.3   Natural language concepts

First, the searcher should prepare a spreadsheet as shown in Figure 6.2. The different concepts are written at the head of columns and eventually (but not first) possible search terms are added in rows under the headings.

CONCEPT A	CONCEPT B	CONCEPT C	CONCEPT D
search term A1	search term B1	search term C1	search term D1
search term A2	search term B2	search term C2	search term D2
search term A3		search term C3	

Figure 6.2   Setting out the concepts

In general the concepts are linked in the search statement by the Boolean operators AND and NOT, or the proximity operators such as (L), (P), and (S). The synonyms are linked by the OR operator and of course always are nested in parentheses.

While the full list of concepts should be stated, it is not necessary to search for all concepts in the first instance. For example, it may be quite unlikely that four different concepts may be mentioned in the one record, even if the searcher has allowed for a number of possible synonyms for each concept. While the *original article* might contain the information required, all the original details might not have been indexed in the database record which after all is a much abridged version of the original publication.

The concepts specified at the column headings should be those defined by the searcher, in the searcher's natural language. At this stage it is best not to get confused by indexing issues, or search terms. For example, if the searcher wishes to find information on the use of simvastatin for lowering cholesterol levels in the blood, then the concepts should be written in this natural language. For example:

CONCEPT A	CONCEPT B	CONCEPT C	CONCEPT D
simvastatin	lowering	cholesterol	blood

Important note:
- **Concepts should be stated in natural language form. The synonyms and hence search terms to be used depend very much on the database to be searched, so avoid confusion with indexing issues at this stage!**

6.4 File selection

Next it is necessary to select an appropriate file. If the searcher is completely unfamiliar with the search area (and this can happen even with experienced searchers who are confronted at times with problems on quite unfamiliar topics), then there are ways to determine relevant files online (for example, the INDEX command may be used, see Section 10.1.2). However, the searcher usually is aware of one or two of the major files in the area but if in doubt the hardcopy database descriptions, database summary sheets, or index guides should be checked.

Four of the major databases which will have records reporting research in the area of cholesterol lowering agents are the BIOSIS, CAplus, EMBASE and MEDLINE Files The EMBASE and MEDLINE Files are more likely to focus on aspects of clinical treatment of hypercholesterolemia (high cholesterol), while the BIOSIS and CAplus Files are more likely to deal with the pre-clinical aspects, particularly research into drug development. As seen in Chapter 3, while the free text components of these four databases are similar, there are big differences in their indexing so quite different spreadsheets need to be set up for each file.

While the development of the actual searches is discussed in Chapter 7, even at this stage some preliminary thoughts on the concepts shown at the end of Section 6.3 may be made. Even though four concepts have been identified there clearly is no need to include all four in the query. For example, the search term "blood" can be omitted (particularly in the early stages of the development of the search query), since cholesterol-lowering agents virtually always apply to blood cholesterol levels. The more concepts included, the narrower the search and indeed, in this case, inclusion of "blood" may exclude many valuable answers simply because it may not be an indexed term or may not appear in the title or abstract written by the author.

On the other hand, it is necessary to include terms relating to the substance simvastatin, since the intent of the search clearly is to find reports on the use of this substance to reduce blood cholesterol levels. However, while the concept is "simvastatin", in most files this will not be the only search term since alternative names and, particularly, the CAS Registry Number will be required. (Details of the procedures for searching for substances are given in Chapter 11, although this particular case is first considered in more detail in Section 7.1.3.)

The searcher now must add some scientific intuition. Required answers might come through treatment of the condition, or through research on cholesterol-lowering agents, so these concepts need to be checked in the various hardcopy index guides. (While index information can always be obtained online, those not familiar with searching, or with the databases, are well advised to do some research offline first.)

Indeed if this was done (see Section 7.1.1) it would be found that the condition usually is called hypercholesterolemia, while agents which lower cholesterol levels are called anticholesteremics. So the spreadsheet as originally outlined might be substantially revised and only two concepts might be searched (with a couple of different synonyms). Thus:

CONCEPT A	CONCEPT B	CONCEPT C	CONCEPT D
simvastatin	lowering	cholesterol	blood

becomes

CONCEPT A	CONCEPT B
simvastatin	hypercholesterolemia - treatment
	anticholesteremics

This exercise of first stating the search intent in "natural language" form, and then critically analyzing the concepts is extremely important. Too often inexperienced searchers confuse the science with indexing issues, and attempt, in the first instance, to use too many different concepts. There can be big differences between concepts and search terms, and in any case the latter can be very file-specific.

6.5 Search terms and fields

A natural language concept may be rather different from a search term! For example, while hypercholesterolemia is a concept, the search term at very least needs to include information on the search field. If the search is to be conducted in the Basic Index, then a single word concept might be identical to the search term but, in general, to "convert" a concept to a search term needs consideration of the search field, truncation, synonyms, and proximity operators. Search terms relate closely to search fields and this issue of search terms will be taken up again in Chapter 7.

6.6 Preliminary search; review of results

The next stage is to conduct a preliminary search and to look through some of the answers to determine whether or not they contain the information desired. Most files have free or inexpensive display formats (which are specified in the Database Summary Sheets) specifically for the purpose of assisting the searcher evaluate preliminary searches at minimum cost. These formats display some of the fields in the record, usually the index fields.

Sometimes, however, the search terms which caused retrieval of the answers are not seen in the free display format. This particularly occurs when searches are performed in Basic Indexes which contain abstracts, and when the abstract is not displayed in the free display format. However, these free display formats are designed only to help in the evaluation of the search, and since as many answers may be displayed here as desired, by the time a number are scanned then good assessments of the search effectiveness may be achieved.

It is very important when scanning through answers that the searcher asks:

• Is this a good answer, and why? or
• Why is this not a good answer?

In the former case the searcher should look for alternative terms in the record which might be included to increase the comprehensiveness of search, while in the latter case the searcher should think either of what additional terms in the search statement would give more precise answers, or which additional terms would exclude the record (without excluding other relevant answers). These alternatives may be achieved usually either by use of the AND or NOT operators respectively with the appropriate search terms.

Even if all the answers "look perfect" the searcher should reflect for a moment on what might be missing. Clearly it is hard to know about what is not seen, but sometimes it is worthwhile to slightly modify what appeared to be a very good initial search in order to see whether a different strategy might produce better results!

Important notes:
- An initial answer set can either be too large, appear right, or be too small.
- If it is too large, either by containing irrelevant answers or being a search on a subject which has extensive information, then techniques need to be employed to reduce the answer set.
- If initial answers "look perfect", it is still a good idea to vary the search a little and to evaluate the answers retrieved.
- If the answer set is too small, then techniques need to be employed to expand the search, for example to include alternative terms.

6.7 Revision of search profile

There are a number of ways in which a search profile may be revised. Some may increase, and some may decrease, the size of answer sets. A summary is given in Figure 6.3, while the application of these options is discussed in Section 7.3.2.

FACTOR	HOW TO DECREASE ANSWER SETS	HOW TO INCREASE ANSWER SETS
PROXIMITY OPERATORS	Use increasingly restrictive operators (e.g., (L) rather than AND)	Use decreasingly restrictive operators (e.g., AND rather than (L))
CONCEPTS and FIELDS	(a) Search more concepts in same fields	(a) Search fewer concepts in same fields
	(b) Search same concepts in less fields (e.g., exclude AB Field)	(b) Search same concepts in more fields (e.g., include AB Field)
	(c) Add concepts involving additional fields (e.g., include LA, DT Fields)	(c) Remove concepts involving additional fields
TERMS	(a) Use more precise synonyms	(a) Use more synonyms
	(b) Use narrower terms from the Thesaurus	(b) Use broader terms from the Thesaurus

Figure 6.3   Options to decrease or increase answer sets

6.8 Full search

Once the concepts finally have been "converted" into search terms with which the searcher is satisfied, the full search can be performed.

Actually the search may be developed in one of two ways, or using a combination of the two. For example, if there are three concepts, they may be searched in separate steps in which case three different answer sets (L-numbers) will be obtained. The final answer set then may be obtained by applying the requisite Boolean or proximity operators. That is:

         => S CONCEPT A   gives answer set L1
         => S CONCEPT B   gives answer set L2
         => S CONCEPT C   gives answer set L3
         then
         => S L1 AND L2 AND L3   gives answer set L4

Otherwise a single search query can be used throughout:

         => S CONCEPT A   AND   CONCEPT B   AND CONCEPT C

and this answer set would be identical to the one obtained in the stepwise manner.

The advantage of the former method is that commonly more synonyms are being identified and then added to each concept as the search is being investigated, and this method saves a little effort in actually typing in the entries. (To continually add synonyms for all the concepts to the whole search entry may be a lengthy process, even though most communications software allows an option which "scrolls back" through the lines entered whereupon the required ones may then be edited. Further, there normally is a limit on the number of characters which may be accepted at any one time by the host computer, and on STN the limit is 256 characters. Also, in files which have search term pricing, it is prudent not to repeat search terms in subsequent searches.)

However, there are two disadvantages of this procedure. First, it is valuable to see answer sets from combinations of concepts during the development stage and this disadvantage is overcome if the latter method is used. Second, systems allow a maximum number of answers (around 2 million) to be held during any one session and if many "intermediate" answer sets are obtained and if each have large numbers of answers then the answer-set system limit may be encountered.

In the event, it all depends on the nature of the query and often a combination of the two methods is used (keep some concepts separate but link others together), but in the meantime searchers should be aware of the two different possibilities.

6.9 Display of answers

Answers may be displayed through different delivery methods and in a number of formats.

6.9.1 Delivery methods

The principal method for display is online. All communications software have options for capture of online sessions and when such options are chosen the results may be browsed, edited, or printed offline. What appears on the terminal screen may be saved on the user's computer (in a file which is usually called a transcript) and the instructions which come with the software package detail how this is done. If needed, the transcripts may be transferred to other word-processing programs, although some re-formatting usually is required. The only restriction here at present is that structure diagrams and graphic images may not be easily transported into other programs, and generally may be printed only from the (graphics) software used in the online session.

Alternatively, answers may be delivered as offline prints, which are sent out by airmail, or by FAX. Each vendor has a slightly different procedure for this, but on STN it is achieved through the PRINT command. When the PRINT command is entered the searcher will be prompted with the subcommands which include the L-number to be printed, the number of answers and formats to be printed, and the address to which the prints are to be sent. After all instructions have been entered, the system will provide a print number which should be used in the event of any queries relating to the request.

There usually is a small additional charge for offline prints, but this is compensated for since local print expenses are not incurred, and since connect hour charges do not apply. The disadvantage with offline prints is that an electronic version of the results is not obtained, and electronic versions usually are easiest to use to establish personalized databases.

The third option is to have the answers sent through e-mail. Again there is a small additional charge, but there are savings in connect hour fees. The transcript comes in electronic format, and answers may easily be sent by e-mail to colleagues. However, presently most e-mail networks run with programs which handle text formats only, so the use of e-mail is limited when structure diagrams or graphics images are involved. (On STN, answers are sent by e-mail through one of the subcommand options under the PRINT command. When entering an INTERNET address, it is necessary to add **.internet** at the end of the (usual) e-mail address.)

6.9.2 Display formats

All, or any part, of the record in the database may be displayed, and the Database Summary Sheet for each file details all display formats available. Default display formats are file-specific and generally include the information necessary to retrieve the original article (title, authors, corporate source, source). If required, users may change the file default on some systems to establish their own default displays for individual files, and on STN this is done through the command: **SET DEFAULT DFIELDS**.

However, commonly additional information may be required. For example, if the searcher does not have ready access to the original articles then display of the abstract and indexing fields may be very useful.

Nearly all files have "hit term highlighting", in which the terms in the record which corresponded with the search terms are highlighted, and displays which additionally show hit terms can assist later with the analysis of records. On most systems and in most files, HIT terms are automatically highlighted in fields which are displayed. However, if the HIT terms are in the abstract field only they will not be displayed in the BIB format but will if BIB HIT display is requested.

Some common display formats used on STN are summarized in Table 6.1, although it must be stressed there are a large number of possible options and that individual users may have quite different preferences. Remember, however, that the display format is just one of the instructions required under the commands that display information, and that the answer set and answer number (or range) must be entered also (see Section 2.2).

Table 6.1   Examples of some common display formats used on STN

DISPLAY FORMAT	DISPLAY OUTCOME
Single fields. (Examples)	(Letter codes can be used to display fields)
TI	title field
AU	author field
AB	abstract field
Field groups	
BIB	bibliographic information with two letter field codes indicated (generally includes at least AN, TI, AU, CS, SO, DT, and LA Fields)
CBIB	bibliographic information in condensed format, that is, text of fields continue along the line without specifying field codes (this is often the quickest way to display bibliographic information)
IBIB	bibliographic information in indented format with full names of field codes
IND	all index entries
ALL	all information in the record with two letter field codes indicated
IALL	all information in the record in indented format with full names of field codes
HIT	all fields containing HIT terms
SCAN	free display format (generally includes title and index entries only)
Combinations	
BIB IND	all information in BIB and IND fields
BIB HIT	BIB information plus fields containing HIT terms
BIB ABS	BIB information plus abstract text
SCAN HIT	hit terms within the SCAN format options only

Summary

- There are a number of *principles* involved in setting up search queries.
- Whatever the *scope and intent* of the search, the searcher should aim to achieve a comprehensive search of the area chosen and to understand the full implications of the limitations set.
- *Concepts* should first be stated in *natural language* words, that is, the language used in the usual form of communication between scientists.
- *Search terms* may be file-specific and it is important to understand the database policies of the files to be searched.
- The "conversion" of *concepts to search terms* involves consideration of search fields, truncation, synonyms, and proximity operators.
- After a preliminary search, answers should be *scanned in the free or inexpensive display format for the file*, and, if necessary, the search should be revised as better search terms are identified.
- There are many techniques which may be used to increase or decrease answer sets; they mainly involve proximity operators, concepts and fields, and search terms (particularly synonyms). However, it is the *relevance and comprehensiveness*, and not the size, of the answer set which is most important.
- After the final search has been completed, answers may be displayed in a number of *formats* (full or parts of records), and through different delivery *methods* (online, offline, FAX, e-mail).

7

Bibliographic Databases: Search Terms

In this chapter we work through a search. We learn:

- *Different approaches to finding **initial** search terms.*
- *How to review results of an initial search.*
- *Options to revise an initial search including use of proximity operators, concepts and fields, and terms.*
- *How to obtain an unique answer set in a multifile search environment by removing duplicates.*

*The **principles** are worked through with a search to find information on how a substance, called simvastatin, affects blood cholesterol levels.*

Now that the searcher is familiar with the various bibliographic search fields, and in particular with the issues relating to index entries, the principles listed in Chapter 6 may be incorporated into actual search strategies.

So, having:

1. determined the scope and intent of the search;
2. determined the "natural language" concepts; and
3. selected the file,

it now is necessary to start listing the search terms under each of the concepts (Table 7.1).

Table 7.1 A typical search spreadsheet

CONCEPT A	CONCEPT B	CONCEPT C	CONCEPT D
search term A1	search term B1	search term C1	search term D1
search term A2	search term B2	search term C2	search term D2
search term A3		search term C3	

7.1 Choosing initial search terms

From the discussion in Chapters 4 and 5 it will be apparent that entries in the free text fields are quite different from entries in the index fields, and *initial* search terms may be based on one or other of these two somewhat different areas. Initial search terms may cross both areas, but what is important is that the two areas are not confused! This is particularly because some index headings are in inverted format, many headings are entered as bound phrases (note, however, that in some files it is possible to search for individual words in the index headings as well as to search for the index headings as bound phrases and this information is obtained from the Database Summary Sheets), and the text in index headings may be significantly different from normal scientific usage.

Generally scientists, from their knowledge of the discipline area, can identify possible "natural language" terms but unless the scientist is very familiar with online databases, these initial terms should be used cautiously and the searcher should remain flexible about their continued use as the search query is being developed.

While there is no single correct way to approach searches in bibliographic files, and in any case the techniques differ with the different types of problems and the databases searched, usually it is better to approach problems through index entries.[*] Certainly at some stage or other the searcher will need to gain some idea of how the subject has been indexed and this may either be done offline or online.

Accordingly, some *starting options* to identify index terms are:

1. Look up the print index guides;
2. Search for the record for a known article of particular relevance;
3. Perform a quick general (or casual) search; or
4. Expand in the index heading field, and, if possible, use the online thesaurus.

To illustrate these different approaches, consider their application to the problem of finding information on the effect of simvastatin on the lowering of blood cholesterol levels. In Chapter 6 two natural language concepts were identified (Figure 7.1).

CONCEPT A   **CONCEPT B**
simvastatin   hypercholesterolemia - treatment
                                 anticholesteremics

search terms   **search terms**
     ?   ?

Figure 7.1   Revision of initial concepts

---

[*]Note that this comment refers to bibliographic databases which have extensive indexing. Other types of databases like full text databases (Chapter 8), patent databases (Chapter 9) and substance-based databases (Chapter 16) are approached in quite different ways.

The four starting options listed above will now be discussed and examples will be taken from the BIOSIS, CAplus, EMBASE and MEDLINE Files. Each will be discussed as separate entities, because while only one of these options would be chosen as the starting point in an actual search, it is valuable here to work through each of them (since at various times one or other will be the preferred starting point).

7.1.1 Option 1: Look up the print index guides
(This option will be applied to the CAplus and EMBASE Files)

CAplus File
The Chemical Abstracts Index Guide contains the Index Headings and very quickly the searcher may find key areas. Even at this stage it is important to remember that Index Headings change with time, so the index guide(s) relevant to the period to be searched should be consulted.   The heading: **Hypocholesteremics**[*] appears with the note: *See Anticholesteremics and Hypolipemics* and under this latter heading appears:

Anticholesteremics and Hypolipemics
Studies of anticholesteremics and hypolipemics as a class as well as studies of new anticholesteremics and hypolipemics are indexed at this heading. Studies of known anticholesteremics and hypolipemics are indexed at those specific headings and at *Cholest-5-en-3-ol (3b)-* [57-88-5], *biological studies* or *Lipids, biological studies*

A similar entry occurs in the CA Headings List and this manual additionally indicates that the Index Heading **Anticholesteremics** was used prior to the 10th Collective Index.
In turn, simvastatin appears in the Guide as:

Simvastatin
See Butanoic acid, 2,2-dimethyl-, 1,2,3,7,8,8a-hexahydro-3,7-dimethyl-8-[2-(tetrahydro-4-hydroxy-6-oxo-2H-pyran-2-yl)ethyl]-1-naphthalenyl ester, [1S-[1a,3a,7b,8b(2S,4S*),8ab]]- [79902-63-9]*

From this it is clear that a preliminary search based on ANTICHOLESTEREMICS AND HYPOLIPEMICS and on SIMVASTATIN or its CAS Registry Number, 79902-63-9, should be performed. While *Cholest-5-en-3-ol (3b)-* [57-88-5], *biological studies* or *Lipids, biological studies* are index headings which are also readily found in the Index Guide, the searcher may or may not consider these a little too general even in the initial stages of the search. In any case it is advisable to start with the "safest" option first and then to vary the search in the light of the initial information retrieved.
While these headings have been identified through the index entries in print manuals, and while they may be searched in the CT Field, it is likely that they might be useful as "free text" search terms as well. So the procedure is to logon and then perform a number of expansions both in the Index Heading and non-index fields, and some expansions and searches are shown in Screen 7.1.
There are a number of points to note (Screen 7.1).   First, expansions on SIMVASTATIN and the CAS Registry Number 79902-63-9 were performed to verify their presence, but just the search is shown here. While there are similar numbers of entries for

---

[*]The heading **hypercholesteremics** does not appear (hypo = low; hyper = high).

the individual terms, the search on the two terms produces slightly more entries (284). This arises since the substance name appears in the "free text" entries in records which did not list the substance as its Registry Number perhaps because of editorial policies (remember not every substance in an article is indexed), or because derivatives of simvastatin and not the actual substance might have been reported.

Second, expansions on ANTICHOLESTEREMICS are shown in the Basic Index and in the CT Field, and searches on relevant terms afforded answer sets L2, L3, and L4.

Third, since Index Headings are entered as individual words in the Basic Index in this file, the search: => S ANTICHOLESTER? (which gives answer set L2) will pick up the terms in the Index Headings. However, if ANTICHOLESTEREMICS AND HYPOLIPEMICS is entered as an Index Heading (see the search which gives L3), it contains a reserved term (AND)[*] and so the entry must be masked in quotations: => S "ANTICHOLESTEREMICS AND HYPOLIPEMICS"/CT.

```
                     Screen 7.1ᵃ  Initial investigations in the CAplus File
=> FIL CAPLUS
=> S SIMVASTATIN OR 79902-63-9
         255           SIMVASTATIN
         251           79902-63-9
L1       284           SIMVASTATIN OR 79902-63-9
=> E ANTICHOLESTEREMICS 5
E1         3           ANTICHOLESTEREMIA/BI
E2      2061           ANTICHOLESTEREMIC/BI
E3      4816 -->       ANTICHOLESTEREMICS/BI
E4         1           ANTICHOLESTEREMICS3/BI
E5         1           ANTICHOLESTEREMMIC/BI
=> E ANTICHOLESTEREMICS/CT 5
E1         1           ANTICHARIS GLANDULOSA/CT
E2         1           ANTICHARIS LINEARIS/CT
E3       769 -->       ANTICHOLESTEREMICS/CT
E4      4013           ANTICHOLESTEREMICS AND HYPOLIPEMICS/CT
E5         1           ANTICHOLESTEREMUS AND HYPOLIPEMUS/CT

=> S ANTICHOLESTER?
L2      5128           ANTICHOLESTER?
=> S "ANTICHOLESTEREMICS AND HYPOLIPEMICS"/CT
L3      4013 "ANTICHOLESTEREMICS AND HYPOLIPEMICS"/CT
=> S ANTICHOLESTEREMICS/CT
L4       769           ANTICHOLESTEREMICS/CT

=> S L1 AND L2
L5        86           L1 AND L2
=> S L1 AND L3
L6        76           L1 AND L3
=> S L1 AND L4
L7         0           L1 AND L4
```

ᵃCopyright by the American Chemical Society and Reprinted with Permission

---

[*]Reserved terms are terms which have special meaning in the system; for example, AND is used as the Boolean operator. When reserved terms are used within search terms they must be entered in quotations.

Finally, searches linking the two concepts gave answer sets L5, L6, and L7. The reason why L7 has no answers is that the Index Heading, ANTICHOLESTEREMICS/CT was used prior to the 10th Collective Index (prior to 1977) which was before the time when the use of simvastatin as an anticholesteremic was realized. This illustrates the importance of using the right index heading for the time period involved!

The procedure now would be to review some of the answers in answer sets L5 and L6 and then to revise the search strategy in the light of entries seen in the records (see Section 7.2). In particular, it would need to be investigated why the search in the Basic Index gave 86 answers while that using the Index Heading gave only 76 answers; that is, the search: => **S L5 NOT L6** would give the unique answers and then they should be scanned for relevance.

In fact, from review of the initial answers, it would be found that HYPERCHOLESTEROLEMIA, HYPERCHOLESTEROLEMIC, HYPERLIPIDEMIA, and HYPERLIPIDEMIC were "free text" terms used and, when these terms were expanded, that their postings were 4051, 1733, 2926 and 1117 respectively, so the spreadsheet for possible terms in the CAplus File (Figure 7.2) would be prepared.

CONCEPT A	**CONCEPT B**
simvastatin	hypercholesterolemia - treatment
	anticholesteremics
Search terms	**Search terms**
simvastatin	"anticholesteremics and hypolipemics"/ct
79902-63-9	anticholesteremics/ct
	anticholesteremia
	anticholesteremic
	anticholesteremics
	hypercholesterolemia
	hypercholesterolemic
	hypercholesterolemics
	hyperlipidemia
	hyperlipidemic
	hyperlipidemics

Figure 7.2   List of possible search terms in the CAplus File

This list would then be considered carefully. Since single words from Index Headings are in the Basic Index in the CAplus File, then all the terms under CONCEPT B could be searched with three (truncated) search terms and one possible final search might be:[*]

=> S **(SIMVASTATIN OR 79902-63-9) AND (ANTICHOLESTER? OR HYPERCHOLESTEROL? OR HYPERLIPIDEM?)**

Of course, the searcher may wish to restrict searches to controlled terms in which case the search would be: => S **(SIMVASTATIN OR 79902-63-9) AND ANTICHOLESTEREMICS?/CT**, it being noted that truncation symbols may be used

---

[*]This search gave 129 answers.

in searches involving bound phrases and that this search would cover both of the controlled terms listed in Figure 7.2.

EMBASE File
The EMTREE thesaurus is printed in two volumes: Volume 1 contains an alphabetical list of EMTREE terms while Volume 2 contains the hierarchical tree structure. When these are consulted, the headings HYPERCHOLESTEROLEMIA and SIMVASTATIN are identified, and these may be investigated as initial search terms.

Some expansions and searches are shown in Screen 7.2 and again the points noted above (for the CAplus search) are relevant. It also is to be noted that the expansion on HYPERCHOLESTEROLEMIA/CT gave a display somewhat different from the expansion on ANTICHOLESTEREMICS/CT in the CAplus File, and from the expansion of HYPERCHOLESTEROLEMIA in the Basic Index; the first expansion listed FREQUENCY and AT (associated terms) and this indicated that this expansion was part of a thesaurus!

Screen 7.2[a] Initial investigations in the EMBASE File

```
=> FIL EMBASE
=> S (SIMVASTATIN  OR  79902-63-9)
          1287          SIMVASTATIN
          1258          79902-63-9
L1       1287          (SIMVASTATIN OR 79902-63-9)
=> E HYPERCHOLESTEROLEMIA  8
E1         1            HYPERCHOLESTEROLE/BI
E2         1            HYPERCHOLESTEROLEAEMIA/BI
E3       9838 -->       HYPERCHOLESTEROLEMIA/BI
E4         1            HYPERCHOLESTEROLEMIA1/BI
E5         1            HYPERCHOLESTEROLEMIAAND/BI
E6         1            HYPERCHOLESTEROLEMIANT/BI
E7        31            HYPERCHOLESTEROLEMIAS/BI
E8       1681           HYPERCHOLESTEROLEMIC/BI


=> E HYPERCHOLESTEROLEMIA/CT  5
E# FREQUENCY  AT  TERM
-- ---------  --  ----
E1    0        2    HYPERCHOLESTEROLAEMIC XANTHOMATOSIS/CT
E2    0        2    HYPERCHOLESTEROLAEMIC XANTHOMATOSIS,FAMILIAL/CT
E3  7461      22 -->  HYPERCHOLESTEROLEMIA/CT
E4    0        2    HYPERCHOLESTEROLEMIA, FAMILIAL/CT
E5    0        2    HYPERCHOLESTEROLEMIA,FAMILIAL/CT


=> S HYPERCHOLESTEROL?
L2    10753      HYPERCHOLESTER?
=> S HYPERCHOLESTEROLEMIA?/CT
L3     7461      HYPERCHOLESTEROLEMIA?/CT


=> S L1 AND L2
L4      741    L1 AND L2
=> S L1 AND L3
L5      631    L1 AND L3
```

[a]Copyright Elsevier Science and Reprinted with Permission

However, it now must really be questioned why the search in the Basic Index gives 110 more answers, and to check this the search: => **S L4 NOT L5** might be conducted and the answers reviewed (see Section 7.2). It would then become apparent that an additional index term is used by the database.

To check the details, the thesaurus is expanded further (Screen 7.3) and now the entry E21 indicates that FAMILIAL HYPERCHOLESTEROLEMIA/CT is a non-explosion term (NXT) for HYPERCHOLESTEROLEMIA/CT, and that it has 1020 postings.[*]

Screen 7.3[a] Expansion of HYPERCHOLESTEROLEMIA/CT

=> **E E3+ALL/CT**

E1	0	BT5	Physical diseases, disorders and abnormalities/CT
E2	1	BT4	physical disease by body function/CT
E3	2068	BT3	metabolic disorder/CT
....			
E10	3576	BT1	hyperlipidemia/CT
E11	7461	-->	hypercholesterolemia/CT
E12	8400	MN	C3.540.30.200.400./CT
E13	8400	MN	C3.540.30.400.400./CT
			HNTE Creation date 01 JUL 79
E14	0	UF	cholesteremia/CT
E15	0	UF	cholesterinemia/CT
E16	170	UF	cholesterolemia/CT
E17	0	UF	hypercholesteremia/CT
E18	0	UF	hypercholesterinaemia/CT
E19	0	UF	hypercholesterinemia/CT
E20	0	UF	hypercholesterolaemia/CT
E21	1020	NXT	familial hypercholesterolemia/CT
E22	63167	RMN	C4.20.10./CT

********* END***

[a]Copyright Elsevier Science and Reprinted with Permission

Accordingly, if searches including familial hypercholesterolemia (the genetically linked condition) also are required, this controlled term should additionally be used in the revised search statement and while the two controlled terms may be typed in separately, use may be made of the MN code which appears in E12 and E13 (Screen 7.3). This code includes the thesaurus terms and the non-explosion (but related) terms, so the searches:=> **S E11 OR E21** or => **S E12** give the same answer set (8400 answers).

So, depending on the intention of the search, any combinations of the terms listed in Figure 7.3 may be used as search terms in the EMBASE File.

---

[*]A non-explosion term means that it is not an associated term within the thesaurus being expanded.

CONCEPT A	CONCEPT B
simvastatin	hypercholesterolemia - treatment
	anticholesteremics

Search terms[a]	Search terms[a]
simvastatin	hypercholesterolemia/ct
79902-63-9	familial hypercholesterolemia/ct
simvastatin (l) dt	C3.540.30.200.400/ct
	hypercholesterolemia (l) dt
	hypercholesterol?
	hyperlipidem?

Figure 7.3   List of possible search terms in the EMBASE File
[a]Note that the terms would be identified by scanning through answers. In particular, it would be noted that "dt" is used for drug therapy

7.1.2   *Option 2: Search for the record for a known article of particular relevance (This option will be applied to the BIOSIS and CAplus Files)*

BIOSIS File
Independently the problem may be approached in a completely different way if a particularly relevant article already was known. For example, suppose it was known that the paper by Felgines *et al.* in *Life Sciences* (1994, volume 54, pages 361-7) titled: "Effect of simvastatin treatment on plasma apolipoproteins and hepatic apolipoprotein mRNA levels in the genetically hypercholesterolemic rat (RICO)", was one of particular relevance.

Probably the easiest way to find the online record is through a search of a few words in the Title Field. For example, the search: => S   (SIMVASTATIN TREATMENT AND APOLIPOPROTEIN AND HYPERCHOLESTEROLEMIC)/TI retrieves the record in the BIOSIS File (Screen 7.4).

Screen 7.4[a]   Finding the online record for a key article in the BIOSIS File

=> **FIL BIOSIS**
=> **S   (SIMVASTATIN TREATMENT AND APOLIPOPROTEIN**
     AND HYPERCHOLESTEROLEMIC)/TI
L1 1 (SIMVASTATIN.....
=> **D ALL**
AN 94:115273 BIOSIS
DN 97128273
TI   Effect of simvastatin treatment of plasma apolipoproteins and hepatic apolipoprotein
        mRNA levels in the genetically hypercholesterolemic rat (RICO).
AU   Felgines C; Serougne C; Mathe D; Mazur A; Lutton C
CS   Lab. Maladies Metaboliques, INRA, Theix, 63122 St Genes Champanelle, FRA
SO   Life Sciences 54 (5). 1994. 361-367. ISSN: 0024-3205
LA   English
AB   The effects of long-term treatment with simvastatin on plasma lipoproteins, plasma
        apolipoproteins, and on hepatic apolipoprotein gene expression were evaluated in
        genetically hypercholesterolemic (RICO) rats. Simvastatin administration caused a
        decrease in plasma triglyceride and ....

```
┌──────────────────────────────────────────────────────────────────────────┐
│ Screen 7.4 (continued)                                                     │
│ ST      RESEARCH ARTICLE; SIMVASTATIN; METABOLIC-DRUG; TRIGLYCERIDES;      │
│         APOLIPOPROTEIN-B; APOLIPOPROTEIN-A-I; APOLIPOPROTEIN-IV;           │
│         APOLIPOPROTEIN-E; PRETRANSCRIPTIONAL LEVEL; POSTTRANSCRIPTIONAL    │
│         LEVEL                                                              │
│ RN      79902-63-9 (SIMVASTATIN)                                          │
│ CC      Genetics and Cytogenetics-Animal  *03506                          │
│         Biochemical Studies-Nucleic Acids, Purines and Pyrimidines  10062 │
│         Biochemical Studies-Proteins, Peptides and Amino Acids  10064     │
│         Biochemical Studies-Lipids  10066                                 │
│         Biochemical Studies-Sterols and Steroids  10067                   │
│         Replication, Transcription, Translation  10300                    │
│         Pathology, General and Miscellaneous-Therapy  *12512              │
│         Metabolism-Lipids  *13006                                         │
│         Metabolism-Sterols and Steroids  *13008                           │
│         Metabolism-Proteins, Peptides and Amino Acids  *13012             │
│         Metabolism-Nucleic Acids, Purines and Pyrimidines  *13014         │
│         Metabolism-Metabolic Disorders  *13020                            │
│         Digestive System-Physiology and Biochemistry  *14004              │
│         Pharmacology-Drug Metabolism; Metabolic Stimulators  *22003       │
│         Pharmacology-Clinical Pharmacology  22005                         │
│         Laboratory Animals-General  28002                                 │
│ BC      Muridae  86375                                                    │
└──────────────────────────────────────────────────────────────────────────┘
```
[a]Copyright by BIOSIS and Reprinted with Permission

The indexing in this record for the two concepts in this File is then apparent: the CAS Registry Number 79902-63-9 for simvastatin appears in the RN Field; and any one of the index headings the searcher feels is particularly relevant, for example "Pharmacology-Drug Metabolism; Metabolic Stimulators".

However, what are the search terms which this record indicates might be used to search for other records in the File? They are shown in Figure 7.4!

CONCEPT A	CONCEPT B
simvastatin	hypercholesterolemia - treatment
	anticholesteremics
Search terms	**Search terms**
simvastatin[a]	"Pharmacology-Drug Metabolism; Metabolic Stimulators"/CC[b]
79902-63-9[a]	22003/CC[b]

Figure 7.4 Initial search terms identified in the BIOSIS File

[a]The Basic Index for the BIOSIS File contains single words from titles, supplementary terms and abstracts, and CAS Registry Numbers, so no field codes are required for these search terms
[b]The code 22003 may be used instead of the full title; indeed in many files use of the code is easier and may give better retrieval

At this point the searcher may possibly be a little disappointed that a more specific index heading relating to hypercholesterolemia had not been identified in this record in the File, but after all, this is only an initial search and so a search using some of the index terms found in Screen 7.4 might next be attempted. This immediately retrieves a relevant term, antiatherogenic agent (Screen 7.5), which, for example, may then need to be added as a synonym for CONCEPT B in a full search. Displays of further answers would indicate that HYPERCHOLESTEROLEMIA (7608 postings in the Basic Index), HYPERCHOLESTEROLAEMIA (596 postings), HYPERCHOLESTEROLEMIC (2078 postings) and ANTIATHEROGENIC (2215 postings) are terms commonly used, but it would be noted that these appear only in the free text fields and not in the index fields. It will be apparent from this discussion that general index headings like those in the BIOSIS File are very preliminary entry points and that they are used mainly to restrict answers to very general areas, or to identify relevant free text terms which then may be used as additional terms in the search.

Screen 7.5[a] Initial search in the BIOSIS File
```
=> S (SIMVASTATIN OR 79902-63-9) AND 22003/CC b
            614   SIMVASTATIN
            593   79902-63-9
         647261   22003/CC
L2          510   (SIMVASTATIN OR 79902-63-9) AND 22003/CC
=> D SCAN c
TI    A comparison of the effects of simvastatin and pravastatin monotherapy on muscle
      histology and permeability in hypercholesterolaemic patients.
ST    RESEARCH ARTICLE; HUMAN; SIMVASTATIN; METABOLIC AGENT;
      ANTIATHEROGENIC AGENT; PRAVASTATIN; METABOLIC AGENT; ANTIATHEROGENIC
      AGENT; LOW DENSITY LIPOPROTEIN CHOLESTEROL LEVEL; NO MUSCLE DAMAGE
```

[a]Copyright by BIOSIS and Reprinted with Permission
[b]Note that is is sufficient to enter only the numeric classification code and it is not necessary to add the full index heading
[c]The search gave 510 answers but these would not be displayed in full now since at this stage the best search terms are merely be explored. So the inexpensive display format, D SCAN, is used (see Section 7.2)

So, and again depending on the search intentions, a final search in the BIOSIS File may involve the entry: **=> S (SIMVASTATIN OR 79902-63-9) AND (22003/CC OR HYPERCHOLESTEROL? OR ANTIATHEROGEN?).**

CAplus File
Alternatively the searcher may wish to retrieve the record in another file, in which case, since the search terms used to retrieve answer set L1 are in the Title Field, and since entries in the different files are very similar in this field, then it is sufficient (on STN) simply to enter the next file and search: => S L1. This feature of being able to use an L-number search query across a number of files saves considerable effort, and is particularly valuable when the same search terms can be used in the different files.

The search in the CAplus File is shown in Screen 7.6, and specific index entries for both simvastatin and "Anticholesteremics and Hypolipemics" are immediately apparent.

Screen 7.6[a] Finding the online record for a key article in the CAplus File

=> **FIL CAplus**
=> **S L1**
...
=> **D SCAN**
CC 1-10 (Pharmacology)
ST simvastatin hypolipidemic apolipoprotein liver
TI Effect of simvastatin treatment of plasma apolipoproteins and hepatic apolipoprotein
    mRNA levels in the genetically hypercholesterolemic rat (RICO).
IT Anticholesteremics and Hypolipemics
       (simvastatin as, hepatic apolipoprotein formation modulation by)
IT Liver, metabolism
       (simvastatin effect on apolipoprotein formation in, hypolipidemic
    activity in relation to)
IT Lipoproteins
    RL: BIOL (Biological study)
       (apo-, simvastatin effect on formation of, in liver, hypolipidemic activity in relation to)
IT 79902-63-9, Simvastatin
    RL: BAC (Biological activity or effector, except adverse); BIOL (Biological study)
       (hypolipidemic activity of, hepatic apolipoprotein modulation in)
IT 9028-35-7, HMG-CoA reductase
    RL: BSU (Biological study, unclassified); BIOL (Biological study)
       (inhibitor, simvastatin as, hepatic apolipoprotein formation modulation by)

---

[a]Copyright by the American Chemical Society and Reprinted with Permission

From this point a search: => **S (SIMVASTATIN OR 79902-63-9) AND "ANTICHOLESTEREMICS AND HYPOLIPEMICS"/CT** may be conducted and the search is at the same point as described in Screen 7.1 and Figure 7.2. It is just that this point was reached by a different process - that of working first from a known document.

Remember that, at this stage, only the initial search terms are being identified. Once the preliminary search is performed, the answers are scanned for further important terms, and finally the complete search statement is made.

This approach of finding a particularly relevant known record may also have been done in the other targeted files (EMBASE and MEDLINE). It is not necessary here to explore all files in this way as it is sufficient to illustrate the principles in the BIOSIS and CAplus File.

7.1.3   Option 3. Perform a quick general (or casual) search
(This option will be applied to the EMBASE File)

EMBASE File
However, if the print Index Guides are not readily available and if an initial, relevant article is not known, a quick general (or casual) search needs to be performed in order to identify

possible search terms. It is best to explore the "safest" option first, that is, the concept which is most likely to be one for which search terms may be conceived with the greatest certainty, and then to scan through a number of the records.

Of the two concepts in the query being investigated, search terms for the first (simvastatin) may be identified most easily since in many files substances are indexed as their CAS Registry Numbers. Indeed, as discussed in Chapters 11 and 16, the recommended procedure to search for information on substances is to locate the record in the REGISTRY File (which is the authorative database for chemical substances, and is discussed in detail in Chapter 11 *ff*) and then to scan, in this record, the list of files in which information on the substance is present.

(The reader might ask: Why choose this procedure for simvastatin, but not cholesterol, since after all isn't cholesterol also a chemical substance? The answer comes only through knowledge of the subject in which "blood cholesterol levels" refer to that generic group of substances comprising cholesterol and other related steroids, including high density lipoproteins (HDLs) and low density lipoproteins (LDLs). Actually it is interesting to note that only the EMBASE File *indexed* the Felgines *et al.* article with the substance cholesterol (and its CAS Registry Number, 57-88-5). It happened that "cholesterol" was mentioned by the authors in the abstract so once again the lessons for the author and the searcher are apparent. Authors should take great care in writing titles and abstracts, and searchers should take great care in choosing concepts and then search terms.)

The record in the REGISTRY File for simvastatin is easily found on a name based search term (specifically with the search: => **S SIMVASTATIN/CN** - see Section 12.8), and is shown in Screen 7.7. Of particular note here is the Locator Field (LC) which lists the files in which the CAS Registry Number for simvastatin appears. (If the searcher is not aware of the content of the files, then the Database Catalogues or Summary Sheets should be consulted.)

The Locator Field indicates that the CAS Registry Number appears in at least some records in the files listed, but the actual number of records is shown (below the structure diagram) only for the CAplus, CAPREVIEWS and CA Files.

Independent searches on the CAS Registry Number (79902-63-9) in each of the other files may easily be done[*] and while in the initial stages of the search this information is not really needed, it nevertheless is of interest here to note how many actual records there are (Table 7.2).

---

[*]This is done by searching the L-number for the REGISTRY File answer set in the files of interest. Indeed this has the added advantage in that the deleted CAS Registry Numbers are searched in the files also.

Screen 7.7[a] Record for simvastatin in the REGISTRY File

RN   79902-63-9 REGISTRY
CN   Butanoic acid, 2,2-dimethyl-, 1,2,3,7,8,8a-hexahydro-3,7-dimethyl-8-[2-
      (tetrahydro-4-hydroxy-6-oxo-2H-pyran-2-yl)ethyl]-1-naphthalenyl ester, [1S-
      [1.alpha.,3.alpha.,7.beta.,8.beta.(2S*,4S*),8a.beta.]](9CI) (CA INDEX NAME)
OTHER NAMES:
CN   L 644128-000U   CN   MK 733
CN   Simvastatin   CN   Synvinolin
CN   Velostatin   CN   Zocor
FS   STEREOSEARCH
DR   118607-03-7, 98609-43-9   MF   C25 H38 O5 ....
LC   STN Files:ANABSTR, BEILSTEIN*, BIOBUSINESS, BIOSIS, CA, CANCERLIT,
      CAPLUS,CAPREVIEWS, CASREACT, CEN, CHEMLIST, CBNB, CIN, CJACS, DDFU,
      DRUGNL, DRUGU, DRUGUPDATES, EMBASE, IPA, MEDLINE, MRCK*,
      NAPRALERT, PHAR, PNI, PROMT, RTECS*, TOXLINE, TOXLIT, USAN, USPATFULL
                (*File contains numerically searchable property data)
      Other Sources: WHO
DES *
Absolute stereochemistry.

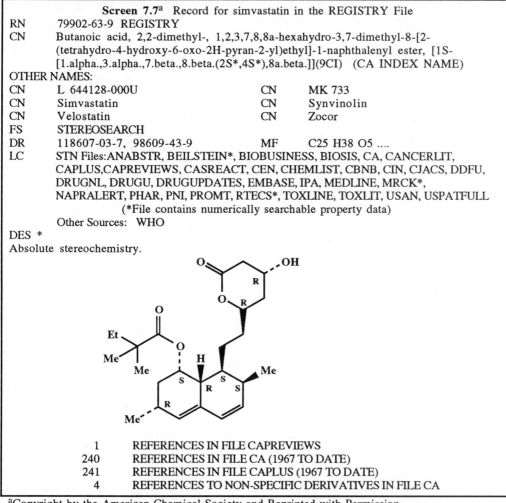

      1   REFERENCES IN FILE CAPREVIEWS
    240   REFERENCES IN FILE CA (1967 TO DATE)
    241   REFERENCES IN FILE CAPLUS (1967 TO DATE)
      4   REFERENCES TO NON-SPECIFIC DERIVATIVES IN FILE CA

[a]Copyright by the American Chemical Society and Reprinted with Permission

Table 7.2 Numbers of postings for the CAS Registry Number for simvastatin in selected files[a]

ANABSTR	4	BEILSTEIN	1	BIOBUSINESS	65
BIOSIS	598	CAplus	251	CANCERLIT	17
CAPREVIEWS	1	CASREACT	4	CEN	1
CHEMLIST	1	CBNB	42	CIN	23
CJACS	3	DDFU	1	DRUGNL	2
DRUGU	1	DRUGUPDATES	1	EMBASE	1254
IPA	89	MEDLINE	493	MRCK*	1
NAPRALERT	1	PHAR	1	PNI	385
PROMT	185	RTECS	1	TOXLINE	236
TOXLIT	194	USAN	1	USPATFULL	39

[a]Note that the postings refer to the number of records in which the CAS Registry Number appears. The relative number of postings in the EMBASE, BIOSIS, MEDLINE, and CAplus Files, that is, the files mentioned in Section 7.1, is worth noting. Note also that those files which have only a single record are substance-based files (see Chapter 16).

It should also be mentioned here that the CAS Registry Numbers were not entered in many of the databases at the time of their initial preparation, but were entered subsequently through a procedure which involved a computerized match of names in the REGISTRY File with names in the electronic records for the databases. This matching process is reliable, and excellent correlations were obtained, although the limitations mentioned at the end of Section 5.5 should be noted. However, for files which do not have CAS Registry Numbers this procedure of searching by names needs to be done online by the searcher, and the actual process is outlined in Section 10.2.

While any of the files listed could now have been selected, Screen 7.8 shows the procedure for crossover of the CAS Registry Number to the EMBASE File. That is, once the EMBASE File has been entered it is sufficient merely to search the L-number of the answer set from the REGISTRY File. When this procedure is used, the system always automatically searches the CAS Registry Numbers from the REGISTRY File answer set in the new file. So the search: **S L1**, is equivalent to the search: **S (79902-63-9 OR 118607-03-7 OR 98609-43-9)**, the latter two being the deleted CAS Registry Numbers seen in Screen 7.7.

Screen 7.8[a]   Record in the EMBASE File[b]

```
=> FIL EMBASE
=> S L1[b];D ALL
AN    94037035 EMBASE
TI    Effect of simvastatin treatment on plasma apolipoproteins and hepatic apolipoprotein
      mRNA levels in the genetically hypercholesterolemic rat (RICO).
AU    Felgines C.; Serougne C.; Mathe D.; Mazur A.; Lutton C.
CS    Lab. des Maladies Metaboliques, INRA, 63122 St Genes Champanelle, France
SO    LIFE SCI., (1994) 54/5 (361-367). ISSN: 0024-3205  CODEN: LIFSAK
CY    United States
DT    Journal
FS    005    General Pathology and Pathological Anatomy
      022    Human Genetics                029    Clinical Biochemistry
      030    Pharmacology                  037    Drug Literature Index
LA    English
AB    ....same as in Screen 7.4
CT    EMTAGS: therapy (0160); digestive system (0935); liver (0946); nonhuman (0777); rat
      (0733); mammal (0738); controlled study (0197); animal experiment (0112); animal model
      (0106); biological model (0502); animal tissue, cells or cell components (0105); male
      (0041); oral drug administration (0181); article (0060)
```

Medical Descriptors:

*hypercholesterolemia: DT, drug therapy	*lipoprotein metabolism
genetic disorder	lipoprotein blood level
gene expression	tissue level
liver	nonhuman
rat	controlled study
animal experiment	animal model
animal tissue	male
oral drug administration	article

Screen 7.8 (continued)
Drug Descriptors:
*simvastatin: DT, drug therapy   *lipoprotein: EC, endogenous compound
*apolipoprotein: EC, endogenous compound   *messenger rna: EC, endogenous compound
cholesterol: EC, endogenous compound   triacylglycerol: EC, endogenous compound
phospholipid: EC, endogenous compound   apolipoprotein a1: EC, endogenous compound
apolipoprotein a4: EC, endogenous compound   apolipoprotein b: EC, endogenous compound
apolipoprotein e: EC, endogenous compound
RN   79902-63-9; 57-88-5

---

[a]Copyright by Elsevier Science and Reprinted with Permission
[b]For comparison purposes the record shown is the one for the article on which this discussion is
being focussed, but of course any of the 1254 answers may have been illustrated

Once again, by checking the index entries, the initial search terms for the EMBASE File
may be identified, and then the database may be searched. After some of these answers are
scanned for further relevant search terms, the final search may be performed. That is, the
search now follows the lines discussed in Section 7.1.1.

7.1.4   Option 4: Expand in the index heading field, and, if possible, use the online thesaurus
(This option will be applied to the MEDLINE File)

MEDLINE File
Whether or not the file has an online thesaurus (see Section 5.3.1) it first is necessary to
expand on a term in the index heading field, and the searcher's knowledge of the science
involved is crucial. Even if the initial term used is not present, generally the expanded list
will indicate a relevant index heading.

If there is an online thesaurus, then it will indicate all broader and narrower terms and
this makes the task of finding relevant index headings so much easier. For example, the
MEDLINE File has an online thesaurus (in the CT Field) and an expansion on any
appropriate term puts the searcher into the right ball park. In Screen 7.9 the expansion was
performed on the term HYPERCHOLESTEROL/CT and even though it was not in the
thesaurus, other terms readily became apparent.

Screen 7.9[a]   Initial expand in index heading field in the MEDLINE File
=> **E HYPERCHOLESTEROL/CT**

E#	FREQUENCY	AT	TERM
E1	0	2	HYPERCHOLESTEREMIA/CT
E2	0	2	HYPERCHOLESTEREMIAS/CT
E3	0	-->	HYPERCHOLESTEROL/CT
E4	8033	14	HYPERCHOLESTEROLEMIA/CT
E5	0	2	HYPERCHOLESTEROLEMIA, ESSENTIAL/CT
E6	2537	43	HYPERCHOLESTEROLEMIA, FAMILIAL/CT
E7	998		HYPERCHOLESTEROLEMIA, FAMILIAL: BL, BLOOD/CT
E8	1		HYPERCHOLESTEROLEMIA, FAMILIAL: CI, CHEMICALLY INDUCED/CT
E9	4		HYPERCHOLESTEROLEMIA, FAMILIAL: CL, CLASSIFICATION/CT
E10	1		HYPERCHOLESTEROLEMIA, FAMILIAL: CN, CONGENITAL/CT
E11	350		HYPERCHOLESTEROLEMIA, FAMILIAL: CO, COMPLICATIONS/CT
E12	122		HYPERCHOLESTEROLEMIA, FAMILIAL: DH, DIET THERAPY/CT

[a]Copyright by the National Library of Medicine and Reprinted with Permission

It may be necessary now for the searcher to expand on a few of those headings with associated terms (AT) in order to be assured that the best index headings to answer the search question are used, and an example is given in Screen 7.10. However, before this screen is discussed it is necessary to comment here that index headings are searched in the CT Field as bound phrases, and that if all index headings mentioning HYPERCHOLESTEROLEMIA are to be searched in this field then the search term needs to include truncation: => S **HYPERCHOLESTEROLEMIA?/CT.** (Note that truncation symbols, but not proximity operators, are acceptable for searches involving bound phrases.) When this search is done 10,324 records (rather than 7902) are retrieved, but of course the searcher would need to assess whether these additional records were relevant.

Screen 7.10[a]　　Explosion of a thesaurus term in the MEDLINE File

```
=> E  E4+ALL/CT
E1       0        BT4     C Diseases/CT
E2       0        BT3      Nutritional and Metabolic Diseases (Non MeSH)/CT
E3     3698       BT2        Metabolic Diseases/CT
E4    10523       BT1    Hyperlipidemia/CT
E5     8033      -->            Hypercholesterolemia/CT
E6     8033              MN      C18.452.494.396./CT
                        DC    an INDEX MEDICUS major descriptor
                        NOTE  Abnormally high levels of cholesterol in the blood.
                        INDX  high blood cholesterol levels
                        AQ      BL CF CI CL CN CO DH DI DT EC EH EM EN EP ET
                                GE HI IM ME MI MO NU PA PC PPPS PX RA RH RI
                                RT SU TH UR US VE VI
                        HNTE    80; was HYPERCHOLESTEREMIA 1963-79;
                                HYPERLIPEMIA, ESSENTIAL FAMILIAL was heading
                                1963-79 (see note under HYPERLIPIDEMIA for
                                former cross refs  to it)
                        ONTE    use HYPERCHOLESTEROLEMIA to search
                                HYPERCHOLESTEREMIA 1966-79; search
                                HYPERLIPEMIA, ESSENTIAL FAMILIAL under
                        HYPERLIPIDEMIA/genetics 1966-79
E7       0              UF      Hypercholesteremia/CT
E8       0              UF      Hypercholesteremias/CT
E9       0              UF      Hypercholesterolemias/CT
********* END***
```

[a]Copyright by the National Library of Medicine and Reprinted with Permission

Screens 7.9 and 7.10 contain a lot of important information! For example, Screen 7.9 indicates that the two main thesaurus entries are HYPERCHOLESTEROLEMIA (14 associated terms; 8033 records) and HYPERCHOLESTEROLEMIA, FAMILIAL (43 associated terms; 2537 records). While Screen 7.10 shows the explosion on the first term, it would also be necessary to explode the second term in order to check on the most appropriate entries. Meanwhile the NOTE, HNTE (historical note) and ONTE (other note) provide information on thesaurus terms, while all the two letter entries in the AQ Field are the descriptive codes used in association with the heading (BL= blood, DT = drug therapy, TU = therapeutic use, etc.).

Accordingly an initial search might be: => S **(SIMVASTATIN OR 79902-63-9) AND HYPERCHOLESTEROLEMIA?/CT** and when some of the answers were reviewed they quickly show up another thesaurus term, ANTICHOLESTEREMIC AGENTS/CT. In turn this term would be exploded and further useful terms would be uncovered. (It would be found that while a number of anticholesteremic substances, for example, cholestyramine, doxazosin, halofenate, lovastatin, and probucol are listed in the thesaurus, there is presently no thesaurus listing for simvastatin.)

Finally, Figure 7.5 shows a list of search terms, which were found through this process, and from which the final search may be constructed.

CONCEPT A	**CONCEPT B**
simvastatin	hypercholesterolemia - treatment
	anticholesteremics
Search terms	**Search terms**
simvastatin	hypercholesterolemia?/ct[a]
79902-63-9	anticholesteremic agents/ct[a]
	hypercholesterol?
	anticholester?

Figure 7.5 List of possible search terms in the MEDLINE File
[a]These controlled terms could be linked ((L) operator) to qualifiers like BL, DT, TU, etc. for more precise searches

In summary, these four options have merely shown alternative ways in which initial search terms based on index headings may be retrieved. An extremely important but somewhat advanced variation on these options uses the SmartSELECT feature and is discussed in Section 10.1.3 and searchers are urged to consider this possibility. (Indeed it can be one of the most useful ways of finding key index entries!) Ultimately, all methods eventually lead to a similar result and a comprehensive search (using whatever planned limitations the searcher requires) on the effects of simvastatin on lowering blood cholesterol levels is obtained. However, it will be appreciated from the above discussions on how initially to find index entries, that a variety of techniques are possible and the searcher should remain alert at all times and pick up clues which will lead to better answer sets.

Alternatively, initial search terms may always be based on free text fields (indeed this often represents the only option when very specific information, which may not have been picked up in index fields, is required), and here the searcher must rely on knowledge of the field of research. However, before a search is attempted it is advisable to expand on possible terms, either in the Basic Index, or in the Title or Abstract Fields.

Any one of the index term approaches, or free text options, or combinations of them all, may be used and ultimately the exact method of choice does not matter greatly. What is important is to get into the right ball park, to understand the rules, and then to investigate the details of the game.

Important notes:
- There are a number of ways in which initial search terms may be determined.
- Hardcopy index guides can be a valuable indicator of initial search terms.
- Or if you know a particularly relevant article, find its record and examine the index entries.
- Otherwise do a casual search, starting with the "safest" concept first.
- Or work your way through an online thesaurus.
- Or use the SmartSELECT feature (see later, Section 10.1.3).
- Eventually searches should be attempted both in the free text and index entries, and the results compared.
- Revised search profiles may then be formulated.

7.2   Preliminary search and review of results

In this step, the searcher should take maximum advantage of the free or inexpensive search and display options. These vary with files and systems, but some suggestions to be considered on STN are:

- use learning files if unfamiliar with the full file (a number of the major files have learning files which have very low connect hour rates and which do not have search and display charges. Learning files are subsets of the full files and often may be of considerable use in the development of search queries at minimum cost - see Section 10.6.4);
- use the EXPAND command to identify potential search terms;
- use the INDEX command (see Section 10.1.2); and
- use the free or inexpensive display formats DISPLAY SCAN or DISPLAY TRIAL.

As mentioned in Section 6.6, after the preliminary answer set has been obtained the searcher should display at least some of the answers in the free or inexpensive display format, and should look for alternative terms in the records which may be included to increase the comprehensiveness of the search, or should think of what additional terms in the search statement may exclude unwanted records (without excluding other relevant answers) in order to increase the efficiency of the search.

The display options, SCAN and TRIAL, on STN may display different fields in different files, but essentially they provide sufficient information, either free or inexpensively, upon which the searcher may operate to obtain better search results. The TRIAL option operates in the usual manner for the DISPLAY command (answers in reverse chronological order, and ranges of answers possible); it is just that only a system-defined subset of the record is displayed. However, the SCAN option first displays one answer and then prompts for the number of answers to be displayed subsequently (Screen 7.11).

```
                    Screen 7.11ᵃ  Example of use of D SCAN in the CAplus File

=> S (SIMVASTATIN  OR  79902-63-9)    AND  "ANTICHOLESTEREMICS
       AND  HYPOLIPEMICS"/CT
           254   SIMVASTATIN
           249   79902-63-9
          4013   "ANTICHOLESTEREMICS AND HYPOLIPEMICS"/CT
L1          76   (SIMVASTATIN OR 79902-63-9) AND "ANTICHOLESTEREMICS AND
                 HYPOLIPEMICS"/CT


=> D SCAN
L1   76 ANSWERS  CAPLUS COPYRIGHT 1995 ACS
CC   1-10 (Pharmacology)
TI   Effects of inhibition of cholesterol biosynthesis by simvastatin on the adrenal and
     testicular function
ST   simvastatin adrenal testes cholesterol biosynthesis inhibition
IT   Adrenal gland
     Testis
       (simvastatin effect on, in men)
IT   Anticholesteremics and Hypolipemics
     (simvastatin, cholesterol biosynthesis and adrenal and testis function in men response to)
IT   57-88-5
     (anticholesteremics and Hypolipemics, simvastatin, cholesterol biosynthesis and adrenal
     and testis function in men response to)
IT   79902-63-9, Simvastatin
     (cholesterol biosynthesis and adrenal and testis function in men response to)
IT   57-88-5, Cholest-5-en-3-ol (3.beta.)-, biological studies
     (simvastatin effect on biosynthesis of, immune, adrenal and testis function response to)
HOW MANY MORE ANSWERS DO YOU WISH TO SCAN? (1):0
```
ᵃCopyright by the American Chemical Society and Reprinted with Permission

If required, all answers may be displayed in this format, although at any subcommand prompt the display may be terminated (and the user returned to the command prompt) by entering either END or 0 (that is, zero answers).

In the DISPLAY SCAN option the answers are selected randomly, and, of course, the maximum information to be displayed in this format is limited by the system. However, the searcher may specify any lesser amount of the system-allowed information by entering the instruction after the command. For example:=> D SCAN TI or D SCAN HIT, will display only the Title Field or the HIT terms respectively (but in the latter case only if they are contained within the allowed SCAN options).

The only problem encountered with the use of these options is that sometimes the HIT terms are not in that part of the record displayed. This particularly occurs when searches are performed in Basic Indexes which contain abstracts, and when the abstract is not displayed in the free format. However, these free display formats are simply designed to help in the evaluation of the search, and since as many answers can be displayed here as desired, by the time a number are scanned then good assessments of the search effectiveness can be achieved.

7.3   Revise search profile

There are a number of ways in which a search profile might be revised. Some may decrease, and some may increase, the size of answer sets. These were summarized in Figure 6.3, and now are discussed more fully. Of course, it should always be remembered that it is the relevance of the answers rather than the size of the answer set which is important, so techniques to decrease or to increase sizes of answer sets are merely used to increase their relevance!

7.3.1 Proximity operators
Use more restrictive proximity operators to decrease the size of answer sets and fewer restrictive operators to increase their size
The operators available on STN are listed in Table 2.3 in order of increasing restriction, that is: AND > (L) > (P) > (S) > (nA) > (nW).

However, the content of the database should be considered carefully before the use of operators is attempted. For example, if free text and index entries are to be linked, the AND operator must be used in those databases in which index entries contain index headings alone.

Indeed, the records from the BIOSIS, CAplus, and EMBASE Files in Screens 7.4, 7.6, and 7.8 should be studied carefully. The key entries which appear in the records are:

        simvastatin   hypercholesterolemic
        79902-63-9   hypercholesterolemia
                         anticholesteremics.

Because both SIMVASTATIN and HYPERCHOLESTEROLEMIC appear in the title and in the abstract, then *in this case* a search: => S SIMVASTATIN (L) HYPERCHOLESTEROLEMIC would retrieve the records shown, but only because of the author terminology. A search which used this (L) operator in the index fields would not have produced a hit in any of the files, while it should be noted that in the CAplus File a search: => S SIMVASTATIN (L) ANTICHOLESTEREMICS, but *not* a search: => S 79902-63-9 (L) ANTICHOLESTEREMICS, would have produced a hit. The point here is that CAS Registry Numbers appear only in certain parts of records and care should be exercised to ensure the correct promixity operators are used.

Accordingly, care should be taken when more restrictive operators are used to narrow answer sets lest wanted answers are removed! The corollary is that, if a search which used a more restrictive operator in the first instance produces unexpectedly few answers, then the AND operator should be tried.

Each of these points may be illustrated with an example (Screen 7.12) in which the (L) operator is used in the first, and the AND operator in the second, instance. The latter search gives a further 134 answers, but are they relevant? This is answered only by looking at what is contained uniquely in the second answer set (the search: S L2 NOT L1 gives the unique answers) but the point is that the searcher should always take care in using proximity operators and, in any event, perhaps check the answer sets obtained when less restrictive operators are used.

```
┌─────────────────────────────────────────────────────────────────────────┐
│      Screen 7.12ª  Comparison between use of operators for searches in the EMBASE File
│
│  => S SIMVASTATIN (L) DT AND HYPERCHOLESTEROLEMIA (L) DT
│          1283      SIMVASTATIN
│        377301      DT
│           872      SIMVASTATIN (L) DT
│          9821      HYPERCHOLESTEROLEMIA
│        377301      DT
│          2148      HYPERCHOLESTEROLEMIA (L) DT
│  L1       557      SIMVASTATIN (L) DT AND HYPERCHOLESTEROLEMIA (L) DT
│
│  => S SIMVASTATIN AND HYPERCHOLESTEROLEMIA AND DT
│          1283      SIMVASTATIN
│          9821      HYPERCHOLESTEROLEMIA
│        377301      DT
│  L2       691      SIMVASTATIN AND HYPERCHOLESTEROLEMIA AND DT
└─────────────────────────────────────────────────────────────────────────┘
```
ªCopyright by Elsevier Science and Reprinted with Permission

7.3.2   Concepts and fields

As each additional concept is added the demands on specific matches in the record are increased. However, it must be recognized that the demands are on what actually appears in the database record and this does not necessarily correspond with all the information in the original article. All the concepts requested might be in the original article but not in the online record, so once again knowledge of the content, particularly of the abstract and index fields, is essential.

In the initial discussion in Chapter 6 on the effect of simvastatin in lowering cholesterol levels in blood, the "natural language" concept BLOOD was omitted from the list of concepts and the value of this may now be seen. Thus, in the four records for the feature article by Felgines et al., the term BLOOD appears in the EMBASE and MEDLINE records, but not in the BIOSIS and CAplus records.[*] Specifically which records may have contained this term would have been difficult to predict at the outset, so the addition of more concepts in the same search fields should be treated cautiously.

However, the outcome of adding more concepts in some specialized fields may be predicted with certainty, and Table 7.3 summarizes a number of such commonly used restrictions.

---

[*]Three of the records are shown in Screens 7.4, 7.6, and 7.8. The actual record for the MEDLINE File is not presented here, but it did contain the qualifier BL in the index entries.

Table 7.3 Some ways to restrict the number of answers by adding concepts in additional fields[a]

FIELD	USE	EXAMPLE[b]
CC or	to restrict answers to index headings or section codes	**S L1 AND ME/CT**[c]
CT		**S L1 AND 22003/CC**[d]
DT	to restrict answers to specific document types	**S L1 AND P/DT**[e]
LA	to restrict answers to specific languages	**S L1 AND EN/LA**
PY	to restrict answers to publication year(s)	**S L1 AND 1995/PY**[f]
REVIEW[g]	to restrict answers to review articles	**S L1 AND REVIEW**

[a]These fields generally apply to bibliographic databases but Database Summary Sheets should be consulted for each file to ensure that the various search fields are available
[b]Searches would be conducted in conjunction with other terms, for example with an answer set, L1
[c]ME = metabolism (MEDLINE FILE index entry)
[d]22003 = Pharmacology-Drug Metabolism; Metabolic Stimulators (BIOSIS File index entry)
[e]P = patent document type (in most files)
[f]See also Table 4.2
[g]Review articles are mainly searched in the Basic Index but see also Section 4.3.5

7.3.3   *Terms*

Synonyms

Many terms are true synonyms and may be full alternative terms (for example: 79902-63-9 or simvastatin; ENGLISH/LA or EN/LA; 22003/CT or "Pharmacology-Drug Metabolism; Metabolic Stimulators"/CT), variations in spelling (sulphur or sulfur), singulars and plurals (hypercholesterolemic or hypercholesterolemics), acronyms (IR or infra-red), or standard abbreviations used by the database (oxidation or oxidn).

In these cases it may be sufficient to use just one of the synonyms. This particularly applies to abbreviations or codes in controlled terms (DT and drug therapy in the EMBASE File - see Screen 7.8). In other cases both must be used. For example, in Screen 7.6 it is noted that use of both 79902-63-9 and simvastatin might be important in certain situations, while, particularly in the CAS bibliographic files, the use of the standard abbreviation is most desirable (although searches on the full word will generally produce a few additional answers usually because full words, and not standard abbreviations, always appear in the titles).

However, other terms may not be true synonyms, that is, they have slightly different meanings, and the use of more specific terms may give more relevant answer sets. For example, there are differences between ANALYSIS, DETERMINATION, DETECTION, ESTIMATION, ASSAY, IDENTIFICATION, QUANTIFICATION, etc. In a broad search all of these terms may be considered, but if too many answers are retrieved then only those terms which best satisfy the requirement should be used.

Finding synonyms can be extremely important in online searching - and also quite difficult. Again, knowledge of the database(s) used, and thorough investigation of answers obtained in the preliminary search, are crucial.

Thesaurus

When a thesaurus is available related terms are readily identified and clearly may be used to restrict answer sets (if narrower terms are used), or to broaden answer sets (if broader terms are used).

7.4   Full search

So, what research has been reported on simvastatin for lowering blood cholesterol levels and how may it be found in the BIOSIS, CAplus, EMBASE and MEDLINE Files?

The *principles* involved in the search are demonstrated in Screen 7.13. Clearly very considerable research has been conducted in this area, and the term REVIEW has been added to each of the searches not only to obtain a workable answer set but also to illustrate an application of one of the concepts shown in Table 7.3. (Note that it is well beyond the scope of this text to investigate the best search terms in all of the files. To do this, many of the answers from the initial search would have to be displayed, and then relevant terms would be determined. Indeed, if this was an actual search, precisely this would need to be done and the final search might be a little different from the one demonstrated here.)

```
             Screen 7.13ᵃ  Search for reviews on   simvastatin as an anticholesteremic
=> FIL BIOSIS
=> S      (SIMVASTATIN OR 79902-63-9) AND (22003/CC OR
          ANTIATHEROGEN? OR HYPERCHOLESTEROL?) AND REVIEW
          619    SIMVASTATIN              598        79902-63-9
       648419    22003/CC                2226        ANTIATHEROGEN?
         9045    HYPERCHOLESTEROL?     251035        REVIEW
L1        24     (SIMVASTATIN OR 79902-63-9) AND (22003/CC OR ANTIATHEROGEN? OR
                 HYPERCHOLESTEROL?) AND REVIEW
=> FIL CAPLUS
=> S  (SIMVASTATIN OR 79902-63-9) AND  (ANTICHOLESTEREM? OR
      HYPERCHOLESTER?) AND  REVIEW
          255    SIMVASTATIN             251    79902-63-9
         4985    ANTICHOLESTEREM?       5165    HYPERCHOLESTER?
      1036184    REVIEW
L2        10     (SIMVASTATIN OR 79902-63-9) AND (ANTICHOLESTEREM?
                 OR HYPERCHOLESTER?) AND REVIEW
=> FIL EMBASE
=> S  SIMVASTATIN (L) DT AND HYPERCHOLESTEROL? AND REVIEW
         1287    SIMVASTATIN          378535 DT
          875    SIMVASTATIN (L) DT    10658 HYPERCHOLESTEROL?
       339242    REVIEW
L3        79     SIMVASTATIN (L) DT AND HYPERCHOLESTEROL? AND REVIEW
=> FIL MEDLINE
=> S  (SIMVASTATIN OR 79902-63-9) AND  HYPERCHOLESTEROL? AND
      REVIEW
          534    SIMVASTATIN               493 79902-63-9
        12854    HYPERCHOLESTEROL?      140692 REVIEW
L4         7     (SIMVASTATIN OR 79902-63-9) AND HYPERCHOLESTEROL? AND REVIEW
```
ᵃCopyright by BIOSIS, the American Chemical Society, Elsevier Science and National Library of Medicine and Reprinted with Permission

It is to be noted that a total of 120 records are retrieved but these would not be displayed at this stage, since some at least would be duplicated and there is little point in paying to display duplicate answers.

7.5   Display of answers

It now is necessary to obtain an unique answer set and most systems support a feature which allows the removal of duplicate records obtained from searching of multiple files. On STN this is done with the DUPLICATE command. When this command is implemented, the system looks through the various answers in the different files and identifies duplicates through matching terms in the bibliographic fields (particularly in the Title, Author, Corporate Source and Source Fields). Since entries in these fields in the different files may not be identical, the system sets a threshold value and all those records which exceed this value are deemed to be duplicates.

   In the normal execution of the command the final answer set is one based on chronological order, but this may not always be the most convenient. For example, the searcher may wish to use file-specific display formats and this may be done most easily if the answers in the final set are sorted by files.

   So, if required, the system may be instructed to sort the answers by files and on STN this is done with the **SET DUPORDER FILE** command (Screen 7.14).

Screen 7.14[a]   Obtaining an unique answer set with the DUPLICATE command,
with answers sorted into files

=> **SET DUPORDER FILE**
SET COMMAND COMPLETED

=> **DUPLICATE**
ENTER REMOVE, IDENTIFY, ONLY, OR (?):**REMOVE**
ENTER L# LIST OR (END):**L1 L2 L3 L4**
DUPLICATE PREFERENCE IS 'BIOSIS, CAPLUS, EMBASE, MEDLINE'
KEEP DUPLICATES FROM MORE THAN ONE FILE? Y/(N):.
. . . .
PROCESSING COMPLETED FOR L1
PROCESSING COMPLETED FOR L2
PROCESSING COMPLETED FOR L3
PROCESSING COMPLETED FOR L4
L5   99 DUPLICATE REMOVE L1 L2 L3 L4 (21 DUPLICATES REMOVED)
          ANSWERS '1-24' FROM FILE BIOSIS
          ANSWERS '25-31' FROM FILE CAPLUS
          ANSWERS '32-98' FROM FILE EMBASE
          ANSWER '99' FROM FILE MEDLINE

---

[a]Copyright by STN and Reprinted with Permission

   Screen 7.14 illustrates that 21 duplicates are removed, that is, that there are now 99 unique records, and the various answer numbers are indicated. The answers may now be displayed in any way desired and Screen 7.15 shows a few of the answers, from the different files, and, by way of illustration, in different formats.

   It is perhaps a little surprising that there are so few duplicates since these four files do index extensively in this area of research. However, probably, many of the records for these 99 articles *are* in each of the files, but it is just that the search terms used did not retrieve them!

Screen 7.15[a] Display of some of the answers in different formats for the different files
BIOSIS File
=> **D 1 BIB HIT**
L5 ANSWER 1 OF 99 BIOSIS COPYRIGHT 1995 BIOSIS   DUPLICATE 1
AN   95:183264 BIOSIS
DN   98197564
TI   An update on lipid-lowering therapy.
AU   Barth J D; Mancini G B J
CS   Cardiovasc. Dis. Prev., Div. Cardiol., Dep. Med., S212-2211 Wesbrook Mall, Vancouver
          Hosp. Health Sci. Cent., Univ. B.C., Vancouver, BC V6T 2B5, Canada
SO   Current Opinion in Lipidology 6 (1). 1995. 32-37. ISSN: 0957-9672
LA   English
ST   LITERATURE **REVIEW**; HUMAN; LOVASTATIN; METABOLIC-DRUG;
          CARDIOVASCULAR-DRUG; **SIMVASTATIN**; METABOLIC-DRUG;....
RN   75330-75-5 (LOVASTATIN)   **79902-63-9 (SIMVASTATIN)**
          81093-37-0 (PRAVASTATIN)   93957-54-1 (FLUVASTATIN)....
CC   ....
          Pharmacology-Drug Metabolism; Metabolic Stimulators *22003
          Pharmacology-Clinical Pharmacology *22005
          Pharmacology-Cardiovascular System *22010

CAplus File
=> **D 25 CBIB**
L5 ANSWER 25 OF 99 CAPLUS COPYRIGHT 1995 ACS
1994:498901   Document No. 121:98901 Antiatherosclerotic drugs: A critical assessment.
Raiteri, M.; Corsini, A.; Soma, M. R.; Donetti, E.; Bernini, F.; Fumagalli, R.; Paoletti, R. (Ist. di
Sci.Farmacol., Univ. di Milano, Milan, I-20133, Italy). Med. Sci. Symp. Ser., 2(DRUGS
AFFECTING LIPID METABOLISM), 317-31 (English) 1993. CODEN: MSSYEI. ISSN: 0928-
9550.

EMBASE File
=> **D 32 TI**
L5 ANSWER 32 OF 99 EMBASE COPYRIGHT 1995 ELSEVIER SCI. B.V.DUPLICATE   12
TI Pravastatin. A **review** of its pharmacological properties and therapeutic potential in
hypercholesterolaemia.

MEDLINE File
=> **D 99 TI IND**
L5 ANSWER 99 OF 99 MEDLINE
TITLE: [**Simvastatin** in the treatment of hypercholesterolemia in the aged. An
           epidemiological and clinical study].
           La simvastatina nel trattamento dell'ipercolesterolemia dell'anziano. Studio
           epidemiologico e clinico.
CONTROLLED TERM: ....
           Hypercholesterolemia: BL, blood
           ***Hypercholesterolemia: DT, drug therapy**
           Lipoproteins, HDL Cholesterol: BL, blood
           Lipoproteins, LDL Cholesterol: BL, blood ....
CAS REGISTRY NO.:   57-88-5 (Cholesterol); 75330-75-5 (Lovastatin);
                       79902-63-9   (simvastatin)
CHEMICAL NAME: EC 1.1.1.88 (Hydroxymethylglutaryl CoA Reductases); ....

[a]Copyright by BIOSIS, the American Chemical Society, Elsevier Science and National Library of
Medicine and Reprinted with Permission

Chapter 6 commenced with the statement: "There are a number of *principles* involved in setting up the search query through to the retrieval of the final answer set", and from the sections which have followed it is obvious that there is a real challenge in doing online searching *properly*. However, it is just as important to do the searching properly as it is to do proper research! There is little point in doing something which already has been reported before, while the knowledge of related research in the literature may considerably help progress in research on an original project.

Every time a search is performed all the principles listed in Figure 6.1 should be addressed. While it is difficult in a text to cover the details, since every search is different and the searcher might explore any number of directions after the preliminary search results are obtained, it is essential that the principles are understood.

Perhaps even the principles in Figure 6.1 may be summarized further and the most fundamental steps in searching bibliographic files may be listed:

Fundamental steps in
searching bibliographic files

Step 1   Think carefully about the *concepts*. In the first instance it is better to include too few than too many and to use search terms for the "safest" concepts first. Remember that concepts should be stated in the scientist's/searcher's "natural language" and should not be confused with search considerations.

Step 2   Think carefully about the *files* and the *search terms*. Search terms based on indexing entries can be very file-specific, while search terms based on free text can be very valuable where authors take particular care in writing titles and abstracts.

Step 3   Conduct preliminary searches and review results using free or inexpensive display formats. Critically analyse records and seek terms which can improve the search question (this particularly relates to the identification of synonymous terms). While there are a number of ways to increase or decrease the size of the answer set, always aim to achieve the *most relevant answers using whatever planned restrictions necessary*.

In these preliminary searches (in bibliographic files which have extensive indexing) it often is better to work initially through the index entries, and later to expand the search to include free text terms.

Step 4   Conduct the final search and display answers using either online, offline or e-mail methods. If searches are done across a few files it is necessary to obtain the unique answer set before the final display.

Summary

- *Initial search terms* may be based on index or free text fields, or combinations of them both and it is important to realize how they differ.
- *Final search terms* may use combinations of index and free text fields.
- Index entries may be obtained from:
  - print index guides;
  - finding the record for a known, relevant article;
  - a quick or casual search;
  - expanding in the index heading field (including additional expansions if an online thesaurus exists); or
  - using the SmartSELECT feature to tabulate index headings from an initial answer set.
- After a preliminary search, the *free or inexpensive display formats* are used to help identify relevance of the articles and/or alternative search terms.
- A number of options exist for increasing the answer set, or to narrowing it to more specific areas and they use different:
  - proximity operators;
  - concepts and/or fields;
  - terms (particularly involving widening or narrowing of synonyms).
- When full searches are performed across files, it is usual to eliminate duplicate records prior to display.

SUMMARY OF COMMANDS COMMONLY USED
IN BIBLIOGRAPHIC FILE SEARCHES ON STN

ENTER FILE
=> **FIL <FILENAME>**
Hint: If you are unsure of the file to enter try a quick search across a cluster using the INDEX command (Section 10.1.2). However, use only very general search terms otherwise you may get a false impression of the number of hits in the various files.

USE THE EXPAND COMMAND
=> **E <TERM>/FIELD**   (in many cases the Basic Index is
    (gives E-number list)   used so no field code is
                                 required)
Hint: In bibliographic databases try searching first on index terms, which may be found in print index guides, through finding index entries from articles which are known to be relevant, through a quick (casual) search (additionally using the SmartSELECT feature to identify index headings) or through thesaurus entries.

SEARCH
=> **S <TERMS>/FIELD**   (or => **S <E-NUMBERS>**)
    (gives L-number answer set)

DISPLAY
=> **D SCAN**   (or => **D TRI**)
    (gives answer then subcommand   *(used in those files which*
    prompt at which either the   *do not have D SCAN option.*
    number of additional answers   *TRI is a display format so*
    required is entered, or END is   *answer numbers must be*
    entered to return to command prompt)   *entered:* **D TRI L1 1-5)**

REVISE SEARCH
                 REVISE SEARCH IF NEEDED CONSIDERING
                           FIELDS
            BOOLEAN AND PROMIXITY OPERATORS
                     SYNONYMS
                     TRUNCATION

=> **S <NEW TERMS>/FIELD**
    (gives new L-number set)

=> **D SCAN**   (or => **D TRI**)
    (if needed)

FINAL DISPLAY OF ANSWERS
=> **D <L-NUMBER> <ANSWER NUMBERS> <ANSWER FORMAT>**
    (example: **D L2 1- BIB)**

EXIT SYSTEM
=> **LOG Y**

8

Full Text Files

In this chapter we learn:

- *Full text files contain the text information of the print versions and, in some cases, the graphic and tabular information additionally can be displayed (but not searched).*
- *Searching in full text files circumvents the problems associated with searching index terms and abstracts in bibliographic databases, and almost invariably additional relevant answers are retrieved.*
- *Special options are available for the display of fields in full text files.*
- *Full text files are available for some scientific journals and some business and news publications, and slightly different techniques are used to search the two different types.*

8.1 The primary and the secondary literature

The chapters up to this point have considered information in the secondary literature only, that is, the information assembled by the database producers. This secondary literature is exceptionally valuable as the first point of entry, and, in particular, it assembles a very large literature resource which otherwise would be beyond the reach of the usual library or end user. Further, it brings together the literature in an organised way through its structure, and through the indexing of the various database producers.

The producers of the secondary literature also enhance the original product significantly, for example, structure, chemical reaction and numeric searches are possible only because various database producers have carefully collated the literature and then provided a product well beyond that of the original documents.

However, the secondary literature does have a major limitation in that what appears in the indexed record is very much an outcome of the policies of the database producers. An original document of perhaps 6,000 words may be indexed in a mere few hundred words. Provided that these policies fully meet the searcher's requirements, and the words entered in the records are exactly those the searcher expects and needs to retrieve records, then there are no problems. However, this is very rarely the case, so direct access to the primary literature will always be valuable in order to retrieve documents which may be missed even in the most carefully constructed search (for example, because of the way the document was indexed or because of the terminology used by the author in the "free text" section of the database).

Some of the primary literature now is available additionally in electronic form, and this chapter is concerned with the electronic forms of the primary literature, particularly those available through online networks.

8.2 Full text: electronic versus hardcopy

The main advantages of the electronic versions over the hardcopy versions are that they are directly accessible from the laboratory or office, and that the electronic versions are fully searchable by individual words. This latter aspect is important since effectively the whole document, rather than just the abstracted form, may be searched and the many terms and concepts which are not indexed may be retrieved.

On the other hand, full text files have their disadvantages. The first is that they are not indexed! That is, they are not written with reference to subject areas, or even to more specific topics within a given area. Neither should they be, since it is the primary responsibility of the authors to present in the main body of the article their specific scientific results. As noted earlier, perhaps only in the title, or more particularly in the abstract, should the authors make reference to the more general aspects of their work in a way which will facilitate its retrieval through an online system. After all, if the most brilliant work is written in such a way that few will find ways to retrieve it, then its ultimate value to the science will be greatly diminished.

The second main disadvantage is that the database can become overwhelmingly large and when every word in the original document is searchable many hits may occur. So special techniques must be used not only to search, but also to display full text records.

8.3   Full text databases

Many of the full text files currently on STN are indicated in Table 8.1. Some of these files are full text versions of scientific journals, while others are full text versions of news and business files, taken from a variety of sources including daily newspapers and weekly magazines which deal with business, management, and marketing issues worldwide. Scientific journal, and news and business, articles have different functions. As their presentations differ, they will be discussed separately.

Table 8.1 Full text files on STN

FILE	CONTENT	YEARS
ABI-INFORM	Business and management	1971-
CEN	Chemical and Engineeering News	1991-
CJACS	23 American Chemical Society journals	1982-
CJAOAC	Analytical Chemical Journal	1987-
CJELSEVIER	4 Elsevier journals	1990-
CJRSC	14 Royal Society of Chemistry journals	1987-
CJVCH	Angew. Chem. Int. Ed	1988-
CJWILEY	8 John Wiley journals	1987-
DRUGNL	Pharmaceutical News (IMSWORLD)	1991-
INVESTEXT	Business News (Thomson Financial Services)	1982-
JPNEWS	Science news from Japan (COMLINE)	1986-
NLDB	Business and Industry News (Information Access Co)	1988-
PHIC	Pharmaceutical News (PJB)	current
PHIN	Pharmaceutical News (PJB)	1980-
PROMT	Business and Industry News (Information Access Co)	1978-
USPATFULL	US Patents	1971-

8.4   Online records of full text scientific databases

In full text databases, the complete original article appears, although diagrams and tables may not be included in some cases. As the technologies of storage and transmission of electronic data develop, the online records will become increasingly closer to the presentation in the original article. Already, some of the diagrams present in the print versions of the ACS journals, the diagrams in some of the Derwent patent files, and the diagrams in the USPATFULL File may be displayed online. For example, the CJACSplus database contains images from the 23 ACS journals from 1992, the World Patent Index Files contain over 1.5 million drawings since 1988, and the USPATFULL File has images for patents from 1993 onwards. The images may be received online as Tiff files through the STN Express software. (For information on how to display images in the CJACSplus File see Table 8.4; display options for images in the WPI Files have the letter G as suffix, for example **D ALLG** displays all the record including the graphic image.)

However, while the diagrams and tables are important, mostly it is the text of the files which is of particular interest for search purposes, and, in general, the text in the online record is identical to the text in the print version. However, it is organised a little differently and this is best illustrated by examining a typical record.

Accordingly, Screen 8.1 shows the bibliographic section of a record from the CJACS File. The Document Number Field (DN) is merely an additional reference point since the CJACS database identifies, through the DN, the journal in which the original article appears. Other fields are similar to those in bibliographic databases although information on the process of publication of the manuscript appears in the Manuscript Field (MS).

Screen 8.1[a]   Bibliographic section of a record from the CJACS File

AN	95:2416 CJACS
DN	ES940419N
SO	Environmental Science & Technology, (1995), 29(3), 740-750. CODEN: ESTHAG. ISSN: 0013-936X
TI	Synchronous Response of Hydrophobic Chemicals in Herring Gull Eggs from the Great Lakes
AU	(1) Smith, Daniel W.
CS	(1) BCM Engineers, Inc., One Plymouth Meeting, Plymouth Meeting, Pennsylvania 19462
PD	MAR 1995
MS	Received date: 7 JUL 1994
	Revised manuscript received date: 28 NOV 1994
	Accepted for publication date: 12 DEC 1994
DT	Articles

[a]Copyright by the American Chemical Society and Reprinted with Permission

---

The abstract then follows in the Abstract Field and it is identical to the record for the abstract which is in the bibliographic files (see Section 4.3.6) in which the article is indexed (Screen 8.2).

Screen 8.2[a]   Abstract in the CJACS File

AB Herring gull eggs from Great Lakes nesting sites exhibit short-term changes in hydrophobic
chemical concentrations that are synchronized within and between Great Lakes. At one Lake
Ontario site, for example, short-term deviations from long-term trends for PCBs, DDE, mirex,
hexachlorobenzene, and dieldrin in gull eggs tend to correlate significantly with each other,
with these chemicals at another site in Lake Ontario, and with gull egg chemicals from Lakes
Superior, Huron, and Erie. Similar comparisons made for other Great Lakes are also
significantly....

The text of the original article then appears and each paragraph is numbered separately. For
the article shown in Screen 8.1 there are 46 different paragraphs and the text from a few
representative paragraphs is shown in Screen 8.3.

Screen 8.3[a]   Examples of text entries from main section of the record (CJACS File)

TX TX(1) of 46. Introduction. Discussions of recent chemical trends in the Great Lakes often
observe that the rate of decline of certain organic chemicals has slowed or even reversed
during the last half-decade (1-7). For example, the declines of mirex, TCDD, DDE, and PCBs
in Lake Ontario have reportedly slowed or ceased, and current levels are assumed to be
maintained by external sources (8). Similarly, the decline of PCBs and DDT in Great Lakes
salmonids is reported by some authors (1, 5) to have stalled across the Great Lakes. Also of
concern were recent data for hexachlorobenzene (HCB) in herring gull eggs, which increased
at 9 of 10 Great Lakes sites in 1992 (9).....
TX(6) of 46. Methods. Gull egg data were taken from published reports of the Canadian Wildlife
Service (9, 13). Information and references on analytical methods and sampling can be found
in these reports. My analysis considers data for five hydrophobic organic chemicals (PCBs,
DDE, HCB, dieldrin, mirex) from two sampling sites for each Great Lake. The sites are
depicted in Figure 1. Data from Muggs Island and Leslie St. Spit, two small islands in
Toronto Harbor, were combined to make one long-term data set for Toronto Harbor.....
TX(13) of 46. Results and Discussion. Same lake/different chemical concentrations were almost
as highly correlated as same lake/same chemical.Figure. .Figure. comparisons. For example,
HCB, PCB, DDE, dieldrin, and mirex behaved synchronously over the short-term at both sites
from Lake Ontario; more specifically, out of 40 pairwise comparisons of normalized
deviations for different chemicals in Lake Ontario, 36 were significant at the 0.10 probability
level (Figure 5). Short-term dynamics of.Figure. .Figure. hydrophobic chemicals were less
orderly in the other Great Lakes, although these comparisons were still highly ....

Finally the cited references and the figure captions are presented and some representative
entries are given in Screen 8.4.

Screen 8.4[a] References and captions from a full text scientific database (here CJACS File)

RE	
RE(1) of 38.	.crsprod.. Abstract published in Advance ACS Abstracts, January 15, 1995.
RE(2) of 38.	Baumann, P. C.; Whittle, D. M. Aquat. Toxicol. 1989, 11, 241-257.
RE(3) of 38.	Baker, J. E.; Eisenreich, S. J. Environ. Sci. Technol. 1990, 24, 342-352.
RE(4) of 38.	Mackay, D.; Gilbertson M. Environ. Toxicol. Chem. 1991, 10, 559-561.
RE(5) of 38.	IJC. Virtual Elimination Tast Force: Draft Final Report; International Joint Commission: Windsor, Ontario, 1993.
....	
CP CP(1) of 11.	Figure 1. Sites of herring gull colonies from which eggs were taken.
CP(2) of 11.	Figure 2. PCBs in herring gull eggs from two sites in Lake Superior over time.
CP(3) of 11.	Figure 3. PCBs in herring gull eggs from Lake Superior with best-fit regression lines. Data are the same as those depicted in Figure 1 from 1978 onward.
CP(4) of 11.	Figure 4. Percent deviation from prediction of the best-fit log-linear regression for PCBs in eggs from Lake Superior.

[a]Copyright by the American Chemical Society and Reprinted with Permission

So the major differences between full text databases and bibliographic databases are immediately apparent. While both contain the same abstracts, the latter contain more extensive bibliographic details and much more extensive indexing. On the other hand, the full text databases contain the full text. That is, the databases feature author terminology rather than indexing! Accordingly searches in full text databases focus on "free text" terms rather than on index entries.

Important notes:
- **The text in full text files is identical to the text in the original document except for special keyboard characters (Greek letters, numeric symbols, etc. which are spelt out).**
- **Bibliographic information and abstracts are presented similarly to the presentation in bibliographic databases.**
- **The text of the original article, cited references, and text of captions are entered in the TX, RE, and CP Fields all of which are individually numbered.**
- **Presently graphic and tabular data may be obtained only from some of the database records.**
- **Full text databases feature "free text" (author terminology) and have limited indexing.**

8.5   When to search full text databases

Of course, if the print materials are not readily available then the online networks offer immediate access to the original articles and this constitutes an obvious reason why full text databases might be searched. However, if the scientist has the print versions of the journals, and has access to bibliographic databases through online networks, the key question is: "When would I want to search the full text, electronic version?"

The two main answers are when searches in bibliographic databases are not producing the necessary answers (perhaps because their indexing is not sufficiently covering the aspects of the original literature of special interest, or when the abstracts are either not available or are lacking in sufficient details), and when searches across a number of different databases are required, that is, when special features of several databases, one of which is a full text database, are needed to fully answer the search question.

In short, the first answer addresses the issues that the bibliographic databases contain only a fraction of the information in the original article and that their indexing policies may not match those of the searcher, while the second answer addresses the issue that print materials do not have anywhere near the cross-linking that is so readily available between different databases in electronic networks.

8.6   Comparing full text records with indexed records

The first answer given above is illustrated by comparing entries in full text and indexed databases. Thus the article shown in Screens 8.1, 8.2, 8.3, and 8.4 was indexed in 7 other databases on the STN network including BIOSIS, CAplus, CONFSCI, EMBASE, PROMT, SCISEARCH and TOXLIT.[*] Of interest here is the indexing applied by the different databases (Screen 8.5).

Screen 8.5[a] Index entries for records in bibliographic databases for the article shown in Screen 8.1

BIOSIS   File
ST   RESEARCH ARTICLE; PHYTOPLANKTON DIET; POLYCHLORINATED BIPHENYLS; DDE;
       MIREX; HEXACHLOROBENZENE; DIELDRIN; LAKE ONTARIO; LAKE SUPERIOR; LAKE
       HURON; LAKE ERIE; WEATHER PATTERNS
RN   60-57-1 (DIELDRIN)   72-55-9 (DDE)   92-52-4D (BIPHENYLS)
       118-74-1 (HEXACHLOROBENZENE)   2385-85-5 (MIREX)
CC   Ecology; Environmental Biology-Plant *07506
       Ecology; Environmental Biology-Limnology *07514
       Ecology; Environmental Biology-Wildlife Management-Terrestrial *07518
       Biochemical Studies-General 10060
       Nutrition-General Dietary Studies *13214
       Reproductive System-Physiology and Biochemistry *16504
       Toxicology-Environmental and Industrial Toxicology *22506
       Public Health: Environmental Health-Air, Water and Soil Pollution*37015
       Pest Control, General; Pesticides; Herbicides *54600
BC   Charadriiformes 85518

---

[*]Brief comments on some of these files appear in Section 3.3. The CONFSCI File provides information on research papers presented at scientific conferences around the world, while the PROMT File provides sci-tech business information.

Screen 8.5 (continued)
CAplus File
ST chlorobiphenyl gull egg Great Lakes; DDE gull egg Great Lakes; mirex gull egg Great Lakes; hexachlorobenzene gull egg Great Lakes; dieldrin gull egg Great Lakes
IT Egg
    (herring gull; synchronous response of hydrophobic chems. in herring gull eggs from Great Lakes)
IT Environmental pollution
    Larus argentatus
    Water pollution
    (synchronous response of hydrophobic chems. in herring gull eggs from Great Lakes)
IT 50-29-3, DDT, occurrence 60-57-1, Dieldrin 72-55-9, DDE, occurrence 92-52-4D, Biphenyl, chloro derivs. 118-74-1, Hexachlorobenzene 2385-85-5, Mirex
    (in herring gull eggs from Great Lakes)
CONFSCI File
CC 4300; 7500 PHARMACOLOGY
EMBASE File
CT EMTAGS: north america (0405); algae, lichens, mosses and ferns (0698); plant (0699); epidemiology (0400); article (0060)
    Medical Descriptors:

*egg	*water contamination	canada
lake	egg yolk	phytoplankton
food chain	weather	geographic distribution
water sampling	water quality	hydrophobicity
ecotoxicity	article	

    Drug Descriptors:
    *polychlorinated biphenyl: TO, drug toxicity
    *1,1 dichloro 2,2 bis(4 chlorophenyl)ethylene: TO, drug toxicity
    *mirex: TO, drug toxicity
    *hexachlorobenzene: TO, drug toxicity
    *dieldrin: TO, drug toxicity
RN 72-55-9; 2385-85-5; 118-74-1; 55600-34-5; 60-57-1; 13366-73-9
PROMT File
CT *PC8519190 Pollution R&D NEC
CC *EC31 Science & Research
GT *CC2CAN Canada
RN 60-57-1 (DIELDRIN)
SCISEARCH File
CC ENVIRONMENTAL SCIENCES; ENGINEERING, ENVIRONMENTAL
STP KeyWords Plus (R): POLYCYCLIC AROMATIC-HYDROCARBONS; BIOACCUMULATION; SUPERIOR; FLUXES; FISH; PCBS
TOXLIT File
ST Chlorobiphenyl gull egg Great Lakes; DDE gull egg Great Lakes; Mirex gull egg Great Lakes; Hexachlorobenzene gull egg Great Lakes; Dieldrin gull egg Great Lakes; Egg Herring gull; synchronous response of hydrophobic chems. in herring gull eggs from Great Lakes; Environmental pollution Synchronous response of hydrophobic chems. in herring gull eggs from Great Lakes; Larus argentatus Synchronous response of hydrophobic chems. in herring gull eggs from Great Lakes; Water pollution Synchronous response of hydrophobic chems. in herring gull eggs from Great Lakes
RN 50-29-3; 60-57-1; 72-55-9; 92-52-4; 118-74-1; 2385-85-5

As was discussed in some detail in Chapter 3 the indexing in the files is quite different, and the searcher always has to consider what search terms are required in the free-text or index entries. However, the ability to search the full text of the original article overcomes the limitations of searches in the abstract and index fields.

While Screens 8.1, 8.2, 8.3 and 8.5 present the problems in a specific case, of course the searcher would approach the issue from the opposite side. That is, the effectiveness of the indexing and the information in worthwhile records are not known, since the object of the search is to find such records! So in order really to assess the merits of searching full text files it is necessary to compare the searches (rather than the displays) in bibliographic files with those in full text files. (Note that this text has focused first on database content since it is felt the searcher must have familiarity with actual database records. Even though only very few records have been displayed, nevertheless they give a general indication of the content and of the issues involved. However, the point being made here is that the searcher does not know the detailed content of the records required from the search, and so other issues arise which need to be addressed in a different way.)

Accordingly, Table 8.2 shows the number of hits obtained in some different databases using the search: => **S (PCB# OR CHLOR? BIPHENYL#) AND (GULL# OR LARUS),**[*] that is, searches on information on how PCBs or chlorinated biphenyls may effect gulls. All of the databases listed have information in the biosciences, and the list gives an interesting comparison of the databases even after allowing for the limitation that the search involved some general search terms and did not address file-specific terminologies.

Table 8.2 Number of hits in different databases in the biosciences for the search: S (PCB# OR CHLOR? BIPHENYL#) AND (GULL# OR LARUS)

ANABSTR	3	AQUASCI	54	BIOBUSINESS	4
BIOSIS	76	CABA	17	CAPLUS	101
CEN	6	CJACS	11	FSTA	10
HEALSAFE	12	LIFESCI	32	MEDLINE	13
NTIS	4	OCEAN	17	PROMT	29
SCISEARCH	51	TOXLINE	98	TOXLIT	43

However, when the *indexing* shown in the representative cases (Screen 8.5) is considered, very little file-specific terminology might have been applicable! Further, the results in Table 8.2 were obtained with the search as indicated in the BIOSCIENCE cluster using the INDEX command (see Section 10.1.2). Besides the limitation of file-specific terminologies, there is the additional limitation of file-specific features on this broad search. As some files do not allow left-hand truncation, the term ?CHLOR? could not be included anywhere in the search query as zero answers would have been retrieved in those files in which such truncation is not allowed. (Unfortunately, a single incorrect entry effectively aborts the whole search even if it is one of a number of synonyms.)

---

[*]These search terms cover most of the file-specific terminologies, however searches in individual files could be improved. For example, CAS Registry Numbers could be used as further synonyms (although PCBs are often considered as non-specific derivatives and are searched reasonably comprehensively using text terms), while some of the files allow left-hand truncation in which case ?CHLOR? would allow for terms like POLYCHLORINATED. Note that the term LARUS is the generic scientific name for the gull family.

Of interest, on the one hand, are the numbers of hits in the TOXLINE File (98 hits from a file which covers from the 1940s onwards) and of the other major bibliographic databases, CAplus File (101 hits, 1967 onwards) and BIOSIS File (76 hits, 1969 onwards). On the other hand, the full text CJACS database gave 11 hits and this database really contains only two journals in the biosciences (*Environmental Science & Technology* and *Journal of Agricultural & Food Chemistry*) and records for these date back only to 1982. In view of the fact that the major bibliographic databases listed cover several thousands of journals over a much longer time period (of course, in some instances the most recent research is the most relevant and indeed the research area may be a very new one, so the time period covered is of lesser importance), it is obvious that the CJACS File affords proportionately a very large number of hits! The only moderating aspect is that the AND operator was used to connect the two concepts in the search, and that use of this operator in full text files may give answers in which the two concepts, while present in the article, are not really connected. (The effect of the (P) and (S) operators are addressed in Section 8.7.)

This situation is repeated in almost any comparison between searches in bibliographic and full text files, and of course it is not surprising. Because full text files have all the words of the original article, there will be a much higher proportion of hits than searches in bibliographic databases. As mentioned in Section 6.2, there is a difference between searching the literature and searching bibliographic databases!

The lesson here for authors is to include as many important terms as possible in the abstract of the article. The lesson for the searcher is to be aware that searching full text articles is likely to retrieve a number of answers which will not be retrieved in a search of bibliographic databases and this applies particularly to those instances where abstracts do not cover all the key points of the article and where key concepts are not routinely indexed.

8.7   Searching full text databases

Bibliographic search fields (for example, AN, AU, CS, DT, SO,[*] TI) in full text databases are searched in the same way as they are searched in bibliographic databases, although it should be noted that these fields are available only in those full text databases which are the electronic versions of scientific journals. News and business databases generally do not have these fields; journalistic reporting is quite different from reporting scientific information and, for example, authors' names do not appear.

Most searches are conducted in the Basic Index which contains individual words from the title, text, captions, and table titles. The individual words are connected with Boolean or proximity operators, and extensive use is made of the (P) and (S) operators which limit terms to paragraphs and sentences respectively.

The usual care with the use of more restrictive operators should be exercised, and Table 8.3 lists the number of hits in some representative files when the concept (PCB# OR CHLOR? BIPHENYL#) was linked with (GULL# OR LARUS).

---

[*]Fields within the SO Field (for example, JT, PY, IS, VL) are searched in the normal manner.

Table 8.3 Comparison of numbers of hits obtained when different operators are used. Concepts linked are (PCB# OR CHLOR? BIPHENYL#) and (GULL# OR LARUS)

FILE	OPERATOR	AND	(L)	(P)	(S)
Bibliographic					
CAPLUS		101	79	79	58
TOXLINE		98	89	89	89
BIOSIS		76	71	76[a]	71
AQUASCI		54	47	47	47
SCISEARCH		51	38	37	29
LIFESCI		32	32	32	30
CABA		17	15	15	15
MEDLINE		13	13	13	13
Full text					
CJACS		11	11	8	6

[a](P) operator is not available in the BIOSIS File, so the AND operator was assumed in the search.

Note that in some of the files the application of the different proximity operators produces identical results. For example, a single information unit, a paragraph and a sentence have the same meanings in some of the files and hence the (L), (P), and (S) operators give the same numbers of hits. Again this illustrates the point that there are many file-specific features even within a single system, and most commonly this arises because of the different forms in which the electronic versions are received by the vendors from the various database producers.

Finally, even when the (S) operator is used to link the concepts in the CJACS File there are 6 answers which is almost one tenth of the number of answers retrieved in the broadest possible search in the BIOSIS File.

When the results in Tables 8.2 and 8.3 are analysed, the full impact of searching for text information is realized. The principles involved with choice of database (including bibliographic or full text), determination of search terms, use of proximity operators and indexing policies, surely make online searching an intellectual challenge!

Important note:
- **Almost invariably, searches in full text databases will retrieve answers not retrieved by searches in bibliographic databases, so searches in full text databases should always be considered, particularly when electronic versions of *key journals* are available.**

8.8   Displays in full text databases

Individual fields may be displayed in the usual way, although there are some display options which apply particularly to full text databases (Table 8.4).

Table 8.4 Special display options in full text databases

FIELD	USED TO DISPLAY	EXAMPLE	
CP	all captions	D	CP
CP(n)	caption n	D	CP(1-5)
GI	journal page image availability	D	GI
RE	all references	D	RE
RE(n)	reference n	D	RE(1)
TT	all table titles	D	TT
TX	all text fields	D	TX
TX(n)	text field n	D	TX(6)
PAGE.FIRST	image of first page	D	PAGE.FIRST[a]
PAGE.CONT	images of remaining pages	D	PAGE.CONT
PAGE.ALL	images of all pages	D	PAGE.ALL
KWIC	key words in context (hit terms plus 20 words on either side	D	KWIC
OCC	fields containing hit words and the number of times they appear	D	OCC

[a]D PAGE1 or D PAGE2 etc. can also be used. Any software which handles Tiff images compressed in Group 4 fax format may be used to capture images under this display option.

However, a display option frequently used in full text files on STN is DISPLAY BROWSE, which, *inter alia*, permits the searcher to scroll through the record, and to perform additional searches within specific records. The entry into this option is: => D BRO L# whereupon the subcommand prompt is presented. Some of the more common options for this subcommand prompt are given, along with comments, in Table 8.5.

It is important to recognize that DISPLAY BROWSE operates on an answer set, and that two different levels of operation are possible. At the first level it operates on the records in the whole answer set very much in the same way as the DISPLAY command usually works.[*] For example: => **D 1-5 TI** displays titles as usual, and the corresponding entry within DISPLAY BROWSE merely leaves out the command, D. Meanwhile, at the second level it operates within a single record whereupon the display options shown in Table 8.4, and the F, B, and S options in Table 8.5 are used. At this level the answer number is not entered, since the system automatically defaults to the last answer number browsed. (Generally options within Table 8.4 are chosen for single records at a time, since it makes little sense, for example, to display TX(6) for a number of different records!)

---

[*]Provided that the options are available in the records under investigation (note, for example, that **D IND** is not acceptable in most full text files which don't have index entries), the entries at the subcommand level within **D BRO** are identical to those in the DISPLAY command (Figure 2.2) except that the command D is omitted. However, searches can continue through to later records (see below).

Table 8.5   Options within DISPLAY BROWSE

OPTION	COMMENTS
:1-3	displays answers 1,2, and 3 in the default format (for example, in the bibliographic format)
:4 OCC	displays the field codes which have hits and the number of hits in the individual fields for answer 4
:5 KWIC	displays the hit words in context[a] in answer number 5
:*KWIC	the asterisk requests the default format be changed to the format indicated (:*TI would change the default to TI Field, while :* changes back to the initial file default)
:TX(6)	displays text field 6 for the last answer number being browsed (for example, if :TX(6) followed the last subcommand entry :4 OCC, the 6th text field of answer number 4 would be displayed)
:F	scrolls forward to the next field within a single record
:F4	scrolls forward 4 fields within a single record
:B	scrolls back one field within a single record
:B2	scrolls back 2 fields
:S TERM	searches forward within record for "TERM"
:S- TERM	searches backward within record for "TERM"
:END	leaves display browse and returns to command prompt[b]

[a]KWIC is set by the system as 20 words on either side of the hit terms, but users may reset the requirement to any number of words between 0 and 50
[b]Remember that END terminates *any* subcommand!

The extent to which a full text record is displayed online depends on the user's requirements. Generally, once the initial answer set has been obtained, DISPLAY BROWSE is implemented and OCC is entered. If :OCC is entered the system defaults to answer number 1, but other answer numbers may be entered as desired. (Note that it is important to display occurrences first, since single records may be very lengthy and the searcher needs to evaluate the size of the record, and the number of hits within it, before extensive displays are implemented.) It is usual then to implement the subcommand KWIC, or to display a few text fields with hits, and to evaluate the answers in turn. Following initial evaluation, the search may be modified if needed.

Eventually, the answers need to be displayed and either the bibliographic information, the full online record, or the page images are captured. In turn, the choice between these depends on whether the original document is readily available in print form, or whether the graphic and tabular information (which is not available in the normal display of the online record, but is available in the page images) is needed. Naturally the other consideration is the cost factor. This text does not consider specific costs since they vary greatly with files and in any case change with time. However, searchers should always be cautious in interpreting costs (see, for example, Section 1.4.4) since there is a real cost associated when the searcher spends time in the library looking up print materials! In any event the potential online costs may always be displayed using the command: **HELP COST** at any prompt in the File on STN, while the costs incurred at any time may be displayed using the command: **D COST.**

The process of search and display in full text databases is illustrated in Screen 8.6 which works through part of a search in the CJACS File.

As usual there are a number of points to note. First, the CJACS File allows left-hand truncation in the Basic Index so this additional option was implemented here to retrieve, *inter alia*, the term POLYCHLORINATED.

Screen 8.6[a] Illustration of the process of search and display in full text databases (CJACS File)
```
=> S (PCB# OR ?CHLOR? BIPHENYL#) AND (GULL# OR LARUS)
        886     PCB#
      91817     ?CHLOR?
       3564     BIPHENYL#
        672     ?CHLOR? BIPHENYL#
                  (?CHLOR?(W)BIPHENYL#)
         56     GULL#
          9     LARUS
L1       11     (PCB# OR ?CHLOR? BIPHENYL#) AND (GULL# OR LARUS)
=> D BRO L1
:2
```
L1   ANSWER 2 of 11 COPYRIGHT 1995 ACS
AN   95:2400 CJACS
SO   Environmental Science & Technology, (1995), 29(3), 604-612. CODEN: ESTHAG. ISSN:
     0013-936X
TI   Bioenergetics-Based Model for Accumulation of **Polychlorinated Biphenyls** by
     Nestling Tree Swallows, Tachycineta bicolor
AU   (1) Nichols, John W. (*); (2) Larsen, Christen P.; (3) McDonald, Michael E.; (4) Niemi,
     Gerald J.; (5) Ankley, Gerald T.
CS   (1,2,3,4,5) U.S. Environmental Protection Agency, Environmental Research Laboratory-
     Duluth, 6201 Congdon Boulevard, Duluth, Minnesota 55804, and Natural Resources
     Research Institute, University of Minnesota-Duluth, 5013 Miller Trunk Highway, Duluth,
     Minnesota 55811
:OCC
L1 ANSWER 2 of 11 COPYRIGHT 1995 ACS

field	count	field	count	field	count
TI	2	TX(1)	4	TX(2)	3
TX(3)	1	TX(6)	4		
....					
CP(7)	5	CP(8)	2	TT(1)	1

:TX(1)
L1 ANSWER 2 of 11 COPYRIGHT 1995 ACS
TX   TX(1) of 66. Introduction. Concern about adverse effects of environmental contaminants on
     wild birds increased during the 1960s with the demonstration that DDT and related
     compounds in raptorial and piscivorous birds had caused widespread population declines due
     to eggshell thinning and resulting reproductive failure (1, 2). More recently, it has been
     suggested that persistent polychlorinated aromatic hydrocarbons (PCHs, including
     polychlorinated biphenyls (PCBs), dibenzofurans (PCDFs), and dibenzo-p-dioxins
     (PCDDs)) have adversely affected several nonraptorial piscivorous species including
     Forster's terns, common terns, black-crowned night herons, double-crested cormorants, and
     herring **gulls** (3-9)....
:S MICHIGAN
.ANSWER 4 COMPLETED - SEARCHING 'MICHIGAN'
L1 ANSWER 5 of 11 COPYRIGHT 1995 ACS
TX   TX(19) of 25. Results and Discussion. Pattern Recognition in Herring **Gulls**. Hierarchical
     cluster analysis separated the egg samples, collected from 1984 to 1991, into two classes
     (Figure 3.Figure.). Class 1 consisted primarily of eggs from Lake Ontario, St. Lawrence
     River, Niagara River, and Saginaw Bay (Channel/Shelter Island). Class 2 contained eggs
     from Lakes Superior, **Michigan**, Huron, and Erie and the Detroit River. In class 1, there
     was a 16% misclassification rate, that is, 16% of the samples included in class 1 were
     collected from ....
:END

Second, DISPLAY BROWSE was chosen to review some of the answers. There is no specific cost associated with DISPLAY BROWSE, but instead costs are associated with the fields displayed within this command: display of OCC is free; there is no D SCAN option; and within D BRO display costs are associated per answer. That is, all TX fields in a single answer may be displayed one after another and only a single TX field charge is incurred. However, if the searcher later returns to the answer, then a new TX field display charge is incurred.

Third, the entry, **2**, asks for the default display format for answer number 2 but, of course, any answer may be specified.

Fourth, **OCC** asks for the listing of occurrences and only some of the list is illustrated here (note the list extended into the captions and table title fields). Once a single record (here answer 2) has been chosen the display options default to this record until another answer number is entered.

Finally, it is noted that 4 postings occurred in text field 1, and this paragraph is displayed as a check of the answers retrieved.

This clearly is an answer which satisfies the search query, and so it, or indeed all the other answers may now be browsed or displayed online either in full or, for example, in the CBIB format if the searcher now preferred to locate the original print article.

However, another feature within the DISPLAY BROWSE format is that further terms may be searched, and if the new search term is not present in the current record under display, the system then continues to search in subsequent records until a hit is obtained. For example, if all the 11 original answers were suitable, but if instead it was of special interest to see whether any referred specifically to studies in Lake Michigan, then MICHIGAN is searched (Screen 8.6). The system continues searching until it finds a hit, which in this case first occurs in answer 5. Searches of this type may be very valuable in finding more specific answers within a larger answer set, which also, nevertheless, is considered to be of value and worth further investigation.

8.9   Linking with other databases

While it may be sufficient merely to display the answer set obtained from a full text database, commonly searches in these databases are components of other searches on the system and it is necessary to establish links between the various answer sets obtained.

In particular, this chapter has emphasised that additional answers will be obtained when searches are conducted in full text databases and the question is how to identify these additional answers, or, indeed, how to obtain a single answer set which does not have duplicate records.

Unfortunately currently there is no general and simple solution to this problem, except for those files which are linked by the system. Such links are normally indicated through the Other Sources Field (OS). For example, the CJACS and CAplus Files are linked through the Other Sources Field (which appears only in the latter file). The process of elimination involves separate searches in the two files, and then to add the term NOT CJACS/OS to the CAplus answer set.

Thus, when the search terms used in Screen 8.6 (which gave 11 answers in the CJACS File) were used instead in the CAplus File, 114 CAplus File records were retrieved and only two of these were eliminated when the term NOT CJACS/OS was added.* This means that 9 of the answers retrieved from the CJACS File were not retrieved by the search in the CAplus File, even though all of these 9 articles indeed had records in the latter file! It was just that the CAplus File records did not contain any mention of GULL# or LARUS, that is, of the second concept used in the search. This reinforces the point, made repeatedly in this text, that index and abstract entries are chosen by indexers and authors respectively, and they may not be in full accord with the terms used by the searcher. It also reinforces the point made in Section 6.4 that concepts may be present in the original article but not in the database record!

While this example illustrates one of the important aspects of being able to link full text and bibliographic databases, the other main aspect is that the links enable immediate access to the original literature. For example, if an answer set has been obtained in the CAplus File, those records which also appear in any one of the full text scientific databases on STN may be retrieved; in many cases this is useful since experimental details can be found immediately. (Currently the CAplus file is linked, through the OS Field, with all the full text scientific databases, and with the CASREACT and MARPAT Files.)

8.10 Business and news databases

Full text business and news databases are written in the very familiar journalistic or conversational language, and this makes text entries so easy to search. Meanwhile, the indexing in business and news databases is limited to general areas and so like with searches in the full text scientific databases, searches in full text business and news databases also are focused initially on the free text entries.

So the procedure is to identify the key concepts, but in this case the concepts are usually identical to the search terms (searches are conducted in the Basic Index so no field qualification is needed) and it is merely necessary to use the most appropriate proximity operators to connect them.

The only problem is that, for example, there are so many business and news aspects related to the effects of PCBs on gulls - including research reports, and environmental and regulatory information to name just three. A general solution to the problem is to look first for the scientific aspects of the question, then to scan the records and to add indexing terms to narrow the answers to those required.

> **A general strategy for searching business and news information in full text databases:**
> - **select the concepts;**
> - **determine all synonyms which may be in natural language or journalistic usage;**
> - **search the concepts/synonyms;**
> - **SCAN the records and determine appropriate index entries to narrow the answer set to required areas;**
> - **add index-derived search terms; and**
> - **display answers.**

---

*That is, the search in the CJACS File gave 11 answers (L1). The search in the CAplus File gave 114 answers (L2). The search: **S L2 NOT CJACS/OS** gave 112 answers (L3).

Screen 8.7 shows the procedure in the News Letter Database (NLDB File), which contains the full text of more than 600 of the most important business and industry newsletters published almost worldwide in areas right across the sciences.

Screen 8.7[a] Example of search in NLDB File

=> **FIL NLDB**
=> **S (PCB# OR (POLYCHLOR? OR CHLOR?) (W) BIPHENYL#) AND (GULL# OR**
LARUS)
L1   16   (PCB# OR (POLYCHLOR? OR CHLOR?) (W) BIPHENYL#) AND...
=>   **D SCAN**

TI   FOOD CHAIN POLLUTANTS THREATEN PLANETS SURVIVAL: NWF REPORT
CT   CH Chemical; GV Government and Regulatory

HOW MANY MORE ANSWERS DO YOU WISH TO SCAN? (1):**3**

TI   NO ANSWERS YET ON ENVIRONMENTAL RISKS OF ESTROGEN
CT   EV Environment; CH Chemical; GV Government and Regulatory

TI   CHINESE FOOD CLASS I RECALL DUE TO BOTULINUM POTENTIAL
CT   CH Chemical; GV Government and Regulatory

TI   ENVIRONMENT: POLITICIANS TO DISCUSS POLLUTION THREATENED ARCTIC
CT   LA Latin America; GN General News; AF Africa; PC Pacific Rim

HOW MANY MORE ANSWERS DO YOU WISH TO SCAN? (1):**END**

---

[a]Copyright by the Information Access Company and Reprinted with Permission

Notes (Screen 8.7):

- The NLDB File does not allow left-hand truncation, so POLYCHLOR? was added to the search in order to improve recall.
- POLYCHLOR? AND CHLOR? are included in parentheses since both need to be connected with BIPHENYL#, and the (W) operator now must be used (implied proximity operates only between single words and not nested words);
- D SCAN (free display format) displays Title and Controlled Term Fields in the NLDB File (as usual the Database Summary Sheet for the File details the search and display fields, including fields displayed in the D SCAN format); and
- indexing in the File appears only in the CT Field and is restricted to general headings.

Depending on the intent of the search, the answer set L1 may now be restricted using terms in the CT Field. For example, if Government and Regulatory information is required, the search: => **S L1 AND GV/CT** will narrow the answer set, and the final answers may be displayed in full.

Two other important international business and news databases are the INVESTEXT and PROMT Files. As with all databases, it is necessary to know from the outset their general subject coverage and content, and the Database Summary Sheets supply basic information. There still are, however, a number of general principles which need to be followed, and, for example, if information on the commercial aspects of the substance taxol is required, it is advisable to start first with the "safest" search concept and then to build the specific search after some initial answers are scanned.

For this question, the "safest" search concept relates to taxol and immediately the searcher needs to consider the appropriate search terms. In business and news databases generally only simple or trade names are reported, so the procedure is to first check the listed names in the entry for the substance in the REGISTRY File. While the PROMT File contains CAS Registry Numbers, the INVESTEXT currently does not so a decision has to be made as to which names to search in the latter file. In this case, taxol has only two simple synonyms (taxol A and paclitaxel) and when these were searched 925 records were retrieved in the INVESTEXT File. The D SCAN format is now used, and representative displays are shown in Screen 8.8. From these records it may then be decided as to which are the preferred additional terms to use and, for example if information relating to anticancer agents is required then the search term ANTICANCER AGENTS/DP may be added.

Screen 8.8[a] Two answers scanned in the INVESTEXT File

Answer 1

TI	Rx Scrips - Industry Report
SH	Bristol-Myers Squibb - Strategic Issues
CT	COMPANY ANALYSES; SALES BY PRODUCT/SALES BY PRODUCT LINE;COMPETITION; SALES/EARNINGS; MERGERS/ACQUISITIONS; MARKETING STRATEGY/ACTIVITY; PROJECTIONS
CO	BRISTOL-MYERS SQUIBB CO. (Ticker Symbol: BMY; Other Codes: 101200)
CA	NEW YORK (STATE OF)
COR	MID-ATLANTIC/MIDDLE ATLANTIC REGION; UNITED STATES OF AMERICA; NORTH AMERICA

Answer 2

TI	Health Care Worldwide: Weeks End 5/5,5/12 - Industry Report
SH	Liposome Technology - 1Q Results & Rating
TT	Liposome Technology Earnings Estimates 1994-95
CT	COMPANY ANALYSES; EARNINGS PER SHARE; PROJECTIONS; INVESTMENT RECOMMENDATION; SALES/EARNINGS; QUARTERLY/INTERIM RESULTS; NEW PRODUCTS/SERVICES; SALES BY PRODUCT/SALES BY PRODUCT LINE; RESEARCH AND DEVELOPMENT
CO	LIPOSOME TECHNOLOGY, INC. (Ticker Symbol: LTIZ; Other Codes: 476700)
CA	CALIFORNIA (STATE OF)
COR	PACIFIC STATES REGION; UNITED STATES OF AMERICA; NORTH AMERICA
DP	DRUGS
SIC	2830
CC	PHARMS PHARMACEUTICALS
DP	ANTICANCER AGENTS
SIC	2834
CC	BIOTEC BIOTECHNOLOGY; PHARMS PHARMACEUTICALS

[a]Copyright by Thomson Financial Services and Reprinted with Permission

---

Since the PROMT File contains CAS Registry Numbers, the search: **S TAXOL OR 33069-62-4** is conducted. In this case 756 records were retrieved and D SCAN is used (Screen 8.9).

Screen 8.9[a] Answers scanned in the PROMT File

Answer 1
TI	Clinton unveils plans for FDA
WC	712 *FULL TEXT IS AVAILABLE IN THE ALL FORMAT*
CT	*PC2830000 Drugs & Pharmaceuticals
CC	*EC94 Government Regulation (cont)
GT	*CC1USA United States

Answer 2
TI	Taxol shows impressive survival benefit	
WC	355 *FULL TEXT IS AVAILABLE IN THE ALL FORMAT*	
CT	*PC2834140 Anticancer Drugs	
CC	*EC34 Product Specifications	
CO	*Bristol-Myers Squibb	
GT	*CC1USA United States	
RN	50-18-0 (CYCLOPHOSPHAMIDE)	7440-06-4 (PLATINUM)
	15663-27-1 (CISPLATIN)	33069-62-4 (PACLITAXEL)
	33069-62-4 (TAXOL)	41575-94-4 (CARBOPLATIN)

Answer 3
TI	Drug plan for breast cancer patients
CT	*PC2834140 Anticancer Drugs
CC	*EC31 Science & Research
GT	*CC9AUS Australia
RN	33069-62-4 (TAXOL)

Answer 4
TI	ASCO 1994 Offers Scattered Promise Summary --	
WC	305 *FULL TEXT IS AVAILABLE IN THE ALL FORMAT*	
CT	*PC8000221 Cancer R&D	
CC	*EC31 Science & Research	
GT	*CC1USA United States	
RN	33069-62-4 (PACLITAXEL)	33069-62-4 (TAXOL)
	114977-28-5 (DOCETAXEL)	114977-28-5 (TAXOTERE)

[a]Copyright by the Information Access Company and Reprinted with Permission

It should be noted that the PROMT File focuses on business, with Product, Event and Geographic indexing. It covers the business news on over 65 industries, including significant technological events. However, because it is primarily a business database it does not focus on specific scientific or technical details, and for this reason the general strategy outlined above (that is, look for the "safest" option and then SCAN answers) often achieves the required result most effectively.

However, other strategies may be used. For example, problems may be approached from indexing entries, in which case the files are entered and possible terms are expanded in controlled term fields. Once likely terms have been identified, initial searches may be conducted and the answers scanned. As with all text based searches, various methods may be used as long as the principal focus of the file searched is appreciated. In the case of searches in business and news databases, the principal focus is the full text which in turn is written in journalistic style; the secondary focus, which becomes very important in targeting key articles of interest, is the indexing.

Summary

- *Full text files* are increasingly becoming available, and can be broadly grouped into the electronic versions of scientific journals, and business and news articles.
- In the electronic version of full text files the *complete text may be searched* (including, if available, the citations and experimental details). This has advantages in that the full original literature is being searched, but the main disadvantage is that full text files often have very limited indexing.
- Because of the amount of information in a single record, the paragraph and sentence operators ((P) and (S) on STN) are commonly used to link search terms.
- Special options exist for the display of the records. Generally D BROWSE is used, and individual fields and text paragraphs are displayed. D OCC and D KWIC are commonly used to identify where the search terms occur and to display them in context respectively.

9

Patent Information

In this chapter we learn:

- *Patent articles contain extensive scientific and technical information not reported elsewhere.*
- *Patent information may be found in specialist patent databases and in bibliographic files which index patents.*
- *Key aspects of patent records (which are not in journal records) are fields involving patent families and legal status information.*
- *Titles, abstracts, and indexing in patent records all vary considerably between the different databases.*
- *Searches on subjects in patent articles may be complicated by the different types of information in the databases.*
- *Major patent index classifications are those produced by the WIPO (IPC codes) and the USPTO (NCL codes), although other countries and patent organizations also have independent classifications.*
- *There are a number of special techniques for searching legal aspects of patent records, and for finding information on patent families.*

9.1   The importance of patent databases

The patent literature is important from many viewpoints. First, patents offer industry the economic protection for its inventions. In effect patents give the organization the monopoly to exploit the invention for commercial purposes, and without this there would be little incentive for the company to make the investment in the research, development and marketing.

All the major developed countries have their own patent organizations, or have agreements with the patent or intellectual property offices of their trading partners. Unfortunately the rules under which these different offices work are not uniform although luckily there are many common aspects.

In some countries the inventor's first step is to make a provisional or priority patent application to the patent office, and this gives protection for a very limited period during which the inventor may develop the invention towards a commercial product. Priority patent applications are checked by the patent examiners in the intellectual property offices and may be granted provided they meet certain criteria, which generally relate to the originality and novelty of the invention. Any previous report, be it in the actual literature or through a conference presentation or even in a casual conversation between scientists who have not jointly signed confidentiality agreements, may constitute a prior disclosure, in which case, in some countries, the invention may be deemed "public knowledge" and not patentable.

As soon as possible, the inventor (or the patent assignee) needs to make a full patent application which must detail the specific claims and be fully supported by the technical information. (However, not always are precise details required; the information may be 'prophetic' and this applies particularly to chemical substances (see Section 15.10.1).) Further, the inventor needs to prove that the work is original, and that there are no prior claims. The patent or intellectual property office notes the date of the application (this is the patent application date) and then proceeds to examine the information in detail.

During this time other interested parties may challenge the application on any one of a number of technical or legal grounds. If not challenged, or if any challenge is dismissed by the patenting organization, and if the patent office is satisfied on the technical and legal aspects, the document eventually becomes a fully granted patent. Once the patent is granted the inventor has exclusive rights to develop and market the product normally for a period of up to 20 years.

As the processes and rules applying to patents vary slightly between countries, a single patent may need to be taken out in a number of countries. The various applications granted then become part of a patent family. However, many countries have signed a Patent Cooperation Treaty (PCT), which is an agreement for international cooperation on patent documents, and it is up to the inventor to determine whether specific patent applications in the various countries need to be made.

It follows that not only is the originality of the technical information important, but also the legal aspects, which generally relate to the dates on which the various stages of the patenting process occurred, and the countries (states) in which the patent was registered. The ways in which these are covered by database producers vary, but the major issues will be presented in this chapter.

A final general point to be noted is that much of the technical information in patents is never published elsewhere. Generally the patent assignees consider the information now has been made public, and they do not seek to publish it in the alternative scientific literature (for example, in scientific journals). Indeed it is estimated that about 80% of the technical information in patents is published in patent documents alone, so the patent literature constitutes a very important and extensive literature resource!

Important notes:
- **Patent databases contain very extensive scientific and technical information which is not published in other sources; hence**

- **patent databases must be searched if comprehensive searches are required; and**
- **comprehensive searches are needed particularly to establish prior art since in turn new patents will be approved only, *inter alia,* if their claims are novel.**

9.2   Patent databases

The major *specialist patent databases* are summarized in Table 9.1, together with their subject coverage and starting years. While some cover the world's patent literature, others cover the patent literature either in a specified area (for example, the APIPAT File covers only the petroleum and petrochemical industry), or from specific countries or continents (particularly Germany, Japan, the USA, and Europe). Currently the majority are bibliographic databases, although the USPATFULL File is a full text file, and the Derwent databases (WPI Files) and PATDPA Files additionally contain patent drawings.

Table 9.1   Specialist patent databases

PRODUCER	STN FILES	COVERAGE	STARTING YEAR	PATENT RECORDS (million)
American Petroleum Institute	APIPAT	petroleum and petro- chemical industry	1964	0.3
IFI Plenum	IFIPAT,IFIUDB IFICDB,IFIREF, IFIRXA[a]	US Patents; covers all areas	1950	3.0
European Patent Office	INPADOC	57 patent issuing organizations including European Patent Office and World Intellectual Property Organization; covers all areas	1968	25
	INPAMONITOR	Same areas as INPADOC but covers last 4 weeks only		
Japanese Patent Information Organization	JAPIO	Complete unexamined Japanese patent applications; covers all areas	1976	4.6
German Patent Office	PATDD, PATDPA, PATGRAPH	Patents filed in Germany; covers all areas	1968	2.4
Wila-Verlag	PATOSDE, PATOSEP, PATOSWO	German patents European patents World patents; cover all areas	1968 (Ger) 1978 (Eur) 1983 (World)	1.5 0.6 0.2
US Patent and Trademark Office	USPATFULL	Full text, US Patents; covers all areas	1971	2.0
Derwent Publications	WPIDS,[a] WPINDEX[a]	Patents from 31 countries and from European Patent Office and World Intellectual Property Organization; covers all areas	1963 (Pharmacy) 1965 (Ag. and Vet.) 1966 (Plastics/Polymers) 1970 (all other Chem.) 1974 (all other areas)	6.6

[a]See text below for notes on these files.

Notes (specialist patent databases, Table 9.1):

- The IFIPAT File contains records for all granted US utility patents, reissue patents, and defensive publications related to chemistry from 1950, related to mechanical and electrical patents from 1963, and related to design patents from 1980.
- The IFIUDB File contains the information in the IFIPAT File plus indepth indexing (by Uniterms) for all chemical patents. The Uniterms involve either General Uniterms (like Index Terms), or Fragment Uniterms (relating to chemical structure fragments).
- The IFICDB File contains all the information in the IFIPAT and IFIUDB Files, but also contains an added level of indexing with the Fragment Codes. Substructure searching of chemical substances (using only these codes) and role indicators (which show the role of the substance within the scope of the patent) are available in this File which is accessible only to IFI subscribers.
- The IFIREF File is a special reference file for the other IFI Files and contains USPTO Classification Codes plus data for General, Fragment and Compound Uniterms.
- The IFIRXA contains records since 1975 for those US patents which have been reassigned, reissued, extended or reexamined, and indicates the present owners of the patent.
- The INPAMONITOR File contains the most current citations on patent and utility models (published during the last four weeks).
- The WPIDS File, which is available only to Derwent subscribers, contains the information in the WPINDEX File plus some enhanced indexing.

On the other hand, many general bibliographic databases have extensive information from the patent literature, and these databases are listed in Table 9.2. The major difference here is that these databases mainly cover specific subject areas, and generally the indexing emphasizes the technical rather than the legal aspects of the original document.

Table 9.2 Some bibliographic databases with patent information

FILE	AREA COVERED	STARTING YEAR	NUMBER PATENT RECORDS
BIOSIS	life sciences	1969	37,000
BIOBUSINESS	life sciences	1985	96,000
BIOTECHABS, BIOTECHDS	biotechnology	1982	55,000
CAplus, CA, CAOLD, CApreviews	chemistry and chemical engineering	1967 1957-66 current only	2,000,000
CERAB	ceramics	1976	43,000
EMA	engineered materials	1986	26,000
ENERGY	energy research/technology	1974	140,000
FSTA	food science/technology	1981	35,000
INIS	nuclear research/technology	1970	43,000
METADEX	metallurgy/materials science	1966	8,000
RAPRA	rubber/plastics	1972	23,000

9.3   Indexing of patents

The information in patent databases differs from one database to another. In general, those databases produced by the specialist patent databases listed in Table 9.1 will have more comprehensive legal data, while those listed in Table 9.2 will have more comprehensive technical and scientific information. However, databases in the former group which list the patent claims (for example, the IFIPAT, PATOSDE, PATOSEP Files), and, of course, the USPATFULL File which contains the full patent documents, provide very extensive technical information.

The legal and technical aspects will now be compared for some of these databases, and, in particular, the US patent: US 4937259 will be discussed. The title page of the actual patent is shown in Figure 9.1, but the actual patent extends to a further 9 pages which contain the technical information, examples of experimental procedures, patent claims and prophetic substances covered within the patent.

United States Patent [19]

Lee

[11]   Patent Number: 4,937,259
[45]   Date of Patent: June 26, 1990

[54] **ANTIHYPERCHOLESTEROLEMIC COMPOUNDS**

[75] Inventor: Ta JYH, Lee, Lansdale, Pa

[73] Assignee: Merck & Co., Inc., Rahway, N.J.

[21] Appl. No.: 363,816

[22] Filed: Jun. 9, 1989

[51] Int. Cl. A61K 31/365; C07D 309/30
[52] U.S. Cl. 514/460; 549/292
      ....514/459; 514/252; 514/255; 514/325;
      ....514/423; 546/204; 546/196; 548/525;
      ....544/374; 544/375
[58] Field of Search.......549/292; 514/459,
            460, 514/824, 252, 255, 325, 423;
            544/374,375;546/196,204; 548/525

[56]   References Cited

        U.S. PATENT DOCUMENTS

    4,448,979 5/1984 Terahara et al..549/292
    4,517,373 5/1985 Terahara et al..549/292
    4,537,859 8/1985 Terahara et al..435/136
    4,604,472 8/1986 Ide et al. 549/292
    4,733,003 3/1988 Ide et al. 560/119
    4,855,456 8/1989 Lee et al. 549/292

        FOREIGN PATENT DOCUMENTS

    2075013 11/1981 United Kingdom 549/292

Primary Examiner- Glennon H. Hollrah
Assistant Examiner-Mark W. Russell
Attorney, Agent, or Firm - Melvin Winokur; Joseph F.DiPrima

[57] **ABSTRACT**
Compounds of Formula (I) and (II):

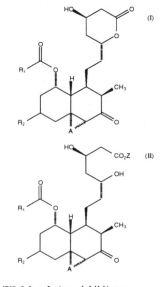

are HMG-CoA reductase inhibitors.
    8 Claims, No Drawings

Figure   9.1   Title page of patent: US 4937259

9.3.1   Indexing of the legal aspects

The major fields in which the legal aspects appear are shown in Table 9.3. The key dates are, in chronological order:

- **priority application date**, that is, the date on which the initial (provisional) application was made with the first (and usually regional) patent office;
- **patent application date**, that is, the date on which the full patent was filed with the patent office; and
- **patent date**, that is, the date on which the full patent was granted by the patent office.

However, different patent organizations may include additional information like equivalent application dates, dates of public inspection and dates of expiration of the patent, and these dates may appear in some of the specialist patent databases.

Table 9.3 Fields with legal information

FIELD	FIELD NAME	CONTENTS
AI	Application Information followed by the Application Date[a]	Country Code followed by the Application Number
AU	AUthor	Names of authors (inventors)
CS	Patent Assignees	Organization that applied for the patent
DS	Designated States	Names of states (countries) in which patent has been filed
IN	INventor	Synonymous with AU
LO	LOcation	Address of organization
PA	Patent Assignees	Synonymous with CS
PI	Patent Information	Country Code followed by Patent Number followed by Patent Kind Code[b] followed by Patent Date[a]
PN	Patent Number	The Patent Number from the PI[c]
PRAI	PRiority Information	Priority Country Code followed by Priority Application Number followed by Priority Application Date[a]

[a]Dates are usually represented in the format Year Month Day, that is, YYMMDD.
[b]Patent Kind Codes vary from country to country. The full lists are published in a variety of sources, for example, in the manual: *Patent Information from CAS* available from the Chemical Abstracts Service.
[c]This is the key number for identification of the actual patent grant.

Comparisons between the ways in which the *legal status* and the *basic bibliographic information* relating to the inventors, assignees and work locations are presented in some representative databases are shown in Screen 9.1 (CAplus File), Screen 9.2 (INPADOC File), Screen 9.3 (IFIPAT File), and Screen 9.4 (WPI File). Where available the indented display format has been used, since patent field codes can be extensive and the indented format allows easier identification of the fields. In this particular case, there was no prior (provisional) patent application and so the important dates and patent number details, all of which appear in all records, are:

patent application date:	9 June 1989
patent application number:	US 89-363816
(final) patent grant date:	26 June 1990
(final) patent number:	US 4937259

The WPI File additionally contains the patent family data (patent numbers and dates in Europe, Canada and Japan), and the country codes for the 7 states (CH DE FR GB IT LI NL) designated under the European filing.

It should be noted that the entries in the Title Field differ considerably. This is because, for patents, the titles are often written by the database producer and this must be kept in mind in searching technical information in a multifile environment.

Screen 9.1[a] Bibliographic and legal status information in the CAplus File

TITLE:	Preparation of pyranone derivatives as antihypercholesterolemic compounds
INVENTOR(S):	Lee, Ta Jyh
PATENT ASSIGNEE(S):	Merck and Co., Inc., USA
SOURCE:	U.S., 10 pp. CODEN: USXXAM

	NUMBER	DATE
	--------------	------
PATENT INFORMATION:	US4937259 A	900626
APPLICATION INFORMATION:	89US-0363816	890609
DOCUMENT TYPE:	Patent	
OTHER SOURCE	MARPAT 113:204821	

[a]Copyright by the American Chemical Society and Reprinted with Permission

---

Screen 9.2[a] Bibliographic and legal status information in the INPADOC File

AN:	17445826 INPADOC EW 9050 UP 901222
TITLE:	ANTIHYPERCHOLESTEROLEMIC COMPOUNDS.
INVENTOR(S):	
ORIGINAL:	LEE; TA JYH
STANDARDIZED:	LEE TA JYH
LOCATION:	US
PATENT ASSIGNEE(S):	
ORIGINAL:	MERCK & CO., INC.
STANDARDIZED:	MERCK & CO INC
LOCATION:	US
DOCUMENT TYPE:	Patent
PATENT INFO. TYPE:	USA UNITED STATES PATENT

	NUMBER		DATE
PATENT INFORMATION:	US4937259	A	900626
APPLICATION INFORMATION:	89US-0363816	A	890609
PRIORITY APPLN. INFO.:	89US-0363816	A	890609

[a]Copyright by the European Patent Office and Reprinted with Permission

---

Screen 9.3[a] Bibliographic and legal status information in the IFIPAT File

AN	2058252 IFIPAT;IFIUDB;IFICDB
TITLE:	ANTIHYPERCHOLESTEROLEMIC COMPOUNDS; HYDROXYMETHYLGLUTARYL-COENZYME A REDUCTASE INHIBITORS
INVENTOR(S):	Lee, Ta Jyh, Lansdale, PA
PATENT ASSIGNEE(S):	Merck & Co, Inc, Rahway, NJ
PRIMARY EXAMINER:	Hollrah, Glennon H
ASSISTANT EXAMINER:	Russell, Mark W
AGENT:	DiPrima, Joseph F
	Winokur, Melvin

```
                               NUMBER       DATE
                               -------------   -----------
PATENT INFORMATION:            US4937259      900626
                               (CITED IN 001 LATER PATENTS)
APPLICATION INFORMATION:       89US-0363816   890609
FAMILY INFORMATION:            US4937259      900626
DOCUMENT TYPE:                 UTILITY
FILE SEGMENT:                  CHEMICAL
```

[a]Copyright by IFI/Plenum Data Corporation and Reprinted with Permission

---

Screen 9.4[a] Bibliographic and legal status information in the WPI File

ACCESSION NUMBER:	90-216853 [28] WPINDEX
DOC. NO. CPI:	C90-093709
TITLE:	New 2-methyl-3-oxo-8-acyloxy 1-substd. decahydro-naphthalene derivs. - having HMG- COA reductase inhibiting activity, useful as antihypercholesterolaemic.
DERWENT CLASS:	B03
INVENTOR(S):	LEE, T J Y
PATENT ASSIGNEE(S):	(MERI) MERCK & CO INC
COUNTRY COUNT:	10

PATENT INFORMATION:

```
       PATENT NO KIND DATE  WEEK  LA  PG MAIN IPC
       ---------------------------------------------------------------
       US4937259      A     900626 (9028)*                    <--
       EP-402154      A     901212 (9050)
          R: CH DE FR GB IT LI NL
       CA2018478      A     901209 (9110)
       JP03068537     A     910325 (9118)
```

APPLICATION DETAILS:

```
       PATENT NO  KIND              APPLICATION   DATE
       ---------------------------------------------------------------
       US4937259 A                  89US-0363816  890609
       EP-402154 A                  90EP-0306240  900608
       JP03068537 A                 90JP-0152495  900611
```

PRIORITY APPLN. INFO:	89US-0363816 890609
REFERENCE PATENTS:	3.Jnl.Ref ; EP--65843; EP--74222; JP59048418

[a]Copyright by Derwent Publications Ltd and Reprinted with Permission

9.3.2   Indexing of the technical aspects

Two different basic levels of indexing are applied to the technical aspects of the patent. The first level relates to the International Patent Classifications (IPC), or classifications produced by national organizations (for example, the USPTO's manual of classifications); the second level is the indexing of the specific database.

The full International Patent Classification is published by the World Industrial Property Organization (WIPO) and is available in both print and CD-ROM versions. It is important to note that it is updated every 5 years in order to take into account new technologies. Accordingly, if information is required over a wide time period all codes covering the time period of interest must be used.

The IPC is an hierarchical system consisting of five levels. The classification is presented linearly with an hyphen before the subgroup, so the IPC A61K031-365 represents:

LEVEL	REPRESENTED BY		EXAMPLE
SECTION	single letter code	A	Human Necessities
CLASS	two digit code	61	Medical or Veterinary Science; Hygiene
SUBCLASS	single letter code	K	Preparations for Medical, Dental, or Toilet Purposes
MAIN GROUP	three digit code	031	Medicinal preparations containing organic active ingredients
SUBGROUP	two or three digit code	365	Lactones.

A thesaurus is available for the IPC codes, and it may be displayed in the USPATFULL File. Indeed, on STN this File has the thesaurus for both the IPC and NCL (US National Codes) Fields (and the various subfields, for example the ICM and ICS Fields), and terms may be exploded through a number of relationship codes which include ALL (All associated terms), HIE (Hierarchy terms), TI (Complete title of the SELF term), BT (Broader Term), NT (Narrower Term), NEXT (Next Classification), NEXT(n) (Next n number of classifications), PREV and PREV(n) (Previous Classifications), BRO (Complete Class), BRO(n) (Next n number of classes), and RT (Related Term). For example, Screen 9.5 shows the explosion that lists the "Complete title of the SELF term".

Screen 9.5[a] Explosion of IPC thesaurus in USPATFULL File

```
=> E   A61K031-365+TI/IC
E1              0   BT7  A/IC
                    SECTION A - HUMAN NECESSITIES
E2              0   BT6  A6/IC
                    HEALTH; AMUSEMENT
E3              0   BT5  A61/IC
                    MEDICAL OR VETERINARY SCIENCE; HYGIENE
E4          50121   BT4  A61K/IC
                    PREPARATIONS FOR MEDICAL, DENTAL, OR TOILET PURPOSES (bringing
                    into special physical form  A61J; chemical aspects of, or use of materials for,
                    bandages, dressings, absorbent pads or  surgical articles A61L; compounds per
                    se C01, C07, C08, C12N; soap compositions C11D;  micro-organisms per se
                    C12N)
E5            185   BT3  A61K031-00/IC
                    Medicinal preparations containing organic active ingredients (2)
                        ( IPC EDITION: 2-6 )
```

```
Screen 9.5 (continued)
E6          245    BT2  A61K031-33/IC
                   . Heterocyclic compounds (2)
                        ( IPC EDITION:  2-6 )
E7          444    BT1  A61K031-335/IC
                   .. having oxygen as the only ring hetero atom (2)
                        ( IPC EDITION:  2-6 )
E8          242    -->  A61K031-365/IC
                   ... Lactones (2)
                        ( IPC EDITION:  2-6 )
```

[a]Copyright the World Intellectual Patent Office and Reprinted with Permission

As with most indexing systems, there is often a fine dividing line between whether a document should be indexed under one or other section. So as a further aid, one or more IPCs may be listed under a main or secondary class (ICM or ICS respectively) depending on whether the indexer considers the IPCs relate to a primary or secondary aspect of the document.

Meanwhile, the main US classification for the patent shown in Figure 9.1 is NCL code 514/460, and this can also be exploded in the thesaurus (Screen 9.6).

Screens 9.5 and 9.6 thus show the main classifications (IPC and NCL) for the patent given in Figure 9.1 and from a quick comparison, it is immediately apparent that the index classifications, for the same document, refer to quite different aspects.

Additional indexing often is applied by the database producer. Those bibliographic databases (listed in Table 9.2) which have patent information apply the same indexing rules irrespective of the source of the original document (that is, irrespective of whether it was a journal article or patent document), while a summary of some enhanced indexing used by some specialist patent databases is given in Table 9.4.

```
                  Screen 9.6[a]  NCL explosion in the USPATFULL File

=> E   514/460.000+TI/NCL
E1          0      BT5  514000000/NCL
                   DRUG, BIO-AFFECTING AND BODY TREATING COMPOSITIONS
E2          0      BT4  514002*00/NCL
                   *ing to subclasses 1-21. ....*
                   (COLLECTION TERM, NO PATENT POSTINGS.)
E3          462    BT3  514183000/NCL
                   .Heterocyclic carbon compounds containing a hetero ring having chalcogen
                   (i.e., O,S,Se or Te) or nitrogen as the only ring hetero atoms DOAI
E4          86     BT2  514449000/NCL
                   .Oxygen containing hetero ring
E5          87     BT1  514451000/NCL
                   ...The hetero ring is six-membered
E6          304 -->     514460000/NCL
                   ....Chalcogen bonded directly to ring carbon of the hetero ring
********* END***
```

[a]Reprinted with the Permission of the US Patent and Trademark Office

It is beyond the scope of this text to discuss all the various types of indexing, but, as usual, the searcher should consult the Database Summary Sheets, the index guides, or the database producers.

Table 9.4 Additional indexing in specialized patent databases

FILE	ADDITIONAL INDEXING
APIPAT	controlled terms according to the API thesaurus, CAS Registry Numbers
IFIUDB	IFI UNITERM codes, CAS Registry Numbers
IFICDB	further in-depth indexing of chemical-related patents by fragmentation codes and role indicators, CAS Registry Numbers, NCL codes
IFIREF	125,000 US Patent Classification Codes and 40,000 general, fragment and compound Uniterms
JAPIO	JAPIO classifications and keywords
PATDD	keywords
PATDPA	PASSAT terms
USPATFULL	Thesaurus for USPTO Manual of Classifications and IPC, CAS Indexing and CAS Registry Numbers
WPIDS	Derwent File Segment and Manual Codes, Chem. and polymer indexing codes
WPINDEX	Derwent File Segment and Manual Codes

The indexing for the document shown in Screens 9.1, 9.2, 9.3, and 9.4 for the different databases is shown in Screen 9.7. The indexing in the CAplus File follows the usual indexing for the file and has substantial technical information, while the indexing in the other files shown relates mainly to either the International Patent Classification (IPC) or National Patent Classification.

Screen 9.7[a] Indexing of patent documents

CAplus   File
INT. PATENT CLASSIF.:
     MAIN: A61K-031/365
   SECONDARY: C07D-309/30
US PATENT CLASSIF.:   514460000
CLASSIFICATION: 1-8 (Pharmacology)
                     Section cross-reference(s): 27
OTHER SOURCE(S):   MARPAT 113:204821
SUPPL. TERM: pyranone deriv prepn anticholesteremic hypolipemic;
                hydroxymethylglutarylCoA reductase inhibitor pyranone deriv
INDEX TERM: Anticholesteremics and Hypolipemics
                (pyranone derivs., as hydroxymethylglutaryl-CoA
                reductase inhibitors)
INDEX TERM: 75-11-6, Diiodomethane
              ROLE: RCT (Reactant)
              (cyclization by, of octahydronaphthyl deriv.)
INDEX TERM: 37250-24-1, Hydroxymethylglutaryl-COA reductase
              ROLE: BIOL (Biological study)
              (inhibitors of, pyranone derivs. as)
INDEX TERM: 130099-84-2P....

Screen 9.7 (continued)

INDEX TERM: 130099-83-1P

    ROLE: SPN (Synthetic preparation); PREP (Preparation)

    (prepn. of, as anticholesteremic and hypolipemic agent)

INDEX TERM: 18162-48-6, Tert-Butyldimethylsilyl chloride

    ROLE: RCT (Reactant)

    (reaction of, with pyranone deriv.)

INDEX TERM: 79902-63-9

    ROLE: RCT (Reactant)

    (reaction of, with tert-butyldimethylsilyl chloride)

INPADOC File

OTHER SOURCE	CA 113:204821
INT. PATENT CLASSIF.:	
MAIN:	(5) A61K-031-365
SECONDARY:	(5) C07D-309-30
NAT. PATENT CLASSIF.:	514460; X549292; X514459; X514252; X514255; X514325;
	X514423; X546204; X546196; X548525; X544374; X544375[b]
STATUS:	T

IFIPAT File

FILE SEGMENT	CHEMICAL
OTHER SOURCE	CA 113:204821

CITED US REFERENCES:

US 4448979	May 1984	549292000	Terahara et al.
US 4517373	May 1985	549292000	Terahara et al.
US 4537859	Aug 1985	435136000	Terahara et al.
US 4604472	Aug 1986	549292000	Ide et al.
US 4733003	Mar 1988	560119000	Ide et al.
US 4855456	Aug 1989	549292000	Lee et al.

FOREIGN REFERENCES:	GB 2075013	Nov 1981	54929

U.S. PATENT CLASSIF.:

MAIN:	514460000
SECONDARY:	514252000; 514255000; 514325000; 514423000;
	514459000; 544374000; 544375000; 546196000;
	546204000; 548525000; 549292000

INT. PATENT CLASSIF.:

MAIN:	A61K-031/365
SECONDARY:	C07D-309/30
FIELD OF SEARCH:	514252000; 514255000; 514325000; 514423000;
	514459000; 514460000; 514824000; 544374000;
	544375000; 546196000; 546204000; 548525000;
	549292000
ART UNIT:	129

WPINDEX File

INT. PATENT CLASSIF.:	A61K-031-36; C07C-069-73; C07C-255-19; C07C-323-51;
	C07D-309-30; C07D-405-12; C07D-407-08
FILE SEGMENT:	CPI
FIELD AVAILABILITY:	AB; DCN
MANUAL CODES:	CPI: B06-A03; B07-A02; B12-G01B1; B12-H03

[a]Copyright by the American Chemical Society, the European Patent Office, IFI/Plenum Data Corporation, and Derwent Publications Ltd and Reprinted with Permission

[b]The X preceding the Classification Number indicates the codes which the examiners searched (that is, checked for prior knowledge).

While the indexing for the IFIPAT File is shown in Screen 9.7, it should be noted that the IFICDB (IFIUDB) File contains additional indexing including "General Uniterms", and "Fragment Uniterms". (The General Uniterms in the File were: ADMINISTERING 00097; ANTICHOLESTEROL AGENTS 00293; ANTILIPEMIC AGENTS 00324; ARTERIOSCLEROSIS 00423; CARRIERS 00874; ENZYME INHIBITORS 01987; PROCESS 06232; ENZYMES/CT/ 10003; DRUGS/CT/ 10030; COMPOSITION 21450; ENZYMES/OXIDOREDUCTASES/ 01992-10. The Fragment Uniterms relate to Markush structure fragments.)

9.3.3   Abstracts and claims

Screen 9.8 shows the actual abstracts in the CAplus, IFIPAT, and WPIDS/WPINDEX Files for the records shown in Screens 9.1, 9.3, and 9.4 respectively (abstracts do not appear in the INPADOC File).

Screen 9.8[a]   Abstracts of patent documents in CAplus, IFIPAT, and WPI Files

CAplus File[b]

AB   The title compds. I and II [R1 = (un)substituted alkyl, cycloalkyl or Ph, etc.; R2 = H, Me; A = CH2, O; Z = H, (un)substituted alkyl, etc.] are prepd. as hydroxymethylglutaryl-CoA reductase inhibitors, useful as anticholesteremic and hypolipemic agents (no data). 6(R)-[2-[2(R),6(S)-Dimethyl-8(S)-2,2-dimethylbutyryloxy)-.alpha.4,4a-methyleno-1,2,3,4,4a,5,6,7,8,8a(R)-decahydro-3-oxonaphthyl1(S)ethyl]-4(R)-hydroxy-3,4,5,6-tetrahydro-2H-pyran-2-one (III) was prepd. in 8 steps. In the last step, a soln. of 6(R)-[2-[2(R),6(S)-dimethyl-8(S)-(2,2-dimethylbutyryloxy)-.alpha.4,4a-methyleno-1,2,3,4,4a,5,6,7,8,8a(R)-decahydro-3-oxonaphthyl1(S)ethyl]-4(R)-(tert-butyldimethylsilyloxy)-3,4,5,6-tetrahydro-2Hpyran-2-one and HOAc in THF was treated with Bu4NF to give III. III was 86% more inhibitory in vitro of hydroxymethylglutaryl-CoA reductase, than the std. mevastatin.

IFIPAT File

AB   Compounds of Formula (I) and (II):
                                        D R A W I N G[c]
                          are HMG-CoA reductase inhibitors.

WPI File

AB   US 4937259 A   UPAB: 930928
     Octahydronaphthalene derivs. of formula (I) are new. Q = a gp. of formula (a). R1=1-10C alkyl (opt. substd. by 1 or more of halo, OH, 1-10C alkoxy, 2-6C alkoxycarbonyl. 1-5C acyloxy, 3-8C cycloalkyl, Ar, Q1S(O)n, OXO, CN, NR3R4 or CONR3R4), 1-10C alkoxy, 2-10C alkenyl, 3-8C cycloalkyl (opt. substd. by 1-10C alkyl (opt. substd. by halo, OH, 1-10C alkoxy, 2-6C alkoxycarbonyl, 1-5C acyloxy, Ar, Q1S(O)n or OXO), QS(O)n, halo, OH, 1-10C alkoxy, 2-6C alkoxycarbonyl, 1-5C acyloxy or Ar), Ar, NH2, mono- or dip (1-5C alkyl)amino, ArNH, ArQ2N or piperidinyl, pyrrolidinyl or piperazinyl; Ar = phenylsubstd. by X and Y; Q1=1-10C alkyl, 3-8C cycloalkyl or Ar; Q2=1-10C alkyl; R2=H or Me; R3 and R4=1-5C alkyl or Ar; A=CH2; X and Y=H, OH, halo, CF3, 1-3C alkoxy, 2-4C alkoxycarbonyloxy, benzoyloxy, 2-4C alkoxycarbonyl, phenoxycarbonyl or 1-5C alkyl; n is not defined on the claims but is 0-2 in the disclosure.

USE - (I) have HMG-COA reductase inhibiting activity and so are useful as antihypercholesterolaemic agents for treating arteriosclerosis, hyperlipidaemia, familiar hypercholesterolaemia etc. Dose is 10-2000 (pref. 10-100) mg/day.

---

[a]Copyright by the American Chemical Society, IFI/Plenum Data Corporation and Derwent Publications Ltd and Reprinted with Permission
[b]The structure diagrams appeared in the CAplus File record
[c]As in Figure 9.1

The major point to note once again is that the abstracts are very different! The database producers have their own policies regarding the writing of abstracts, for example in general CAS will focus on the chemical abstracts, although Derwent tends to focus on the legal boundaries of the patent applications and the specific novelty.

Finally, the IFIPAT File contains the text for the patent claims (Screen 9.9). The full patent document also appears in the USPATFULL File, and the online record contains all the text, including the background to the invention, the discussion, the experimental details, and the claims. Currently the cost of a full display of a record in the USPATFULL File is $3.50, so this is one of the cheapest and quickest ways to obtain the full document, although it should be noted that the online record will not generally contain graphics and tabular information.

Screen 9.9[a]   Claims in the IFIPAT File
(Note only the first parts of the first two claims are shown here)

CLMN   8
ECLM 1. A compound represented by the structural formulae (I) or (II): 1-((4-(HO-),6-
          (O=)TETRAHYDROPYRAN-2-YL)-CH2-CH2-),2-(CH3-),3-(O=),4,4a-(-A-),6-R2,8-
          (R1-COO-)DECALIN (I) wherein: R1 is: (1) C1-10 alkyl; (2) substituted C1-10 alkyl
          in which one or more substituent(s) is (a) halogen, (b) hydroxy, (c) C1-10 alkoxy, (d)
          C1-5 alkoxycarbonyl, (e) C1-5 ....
ACLM 2. A compound of claim 1 wherein: R1 is selected from: (1) C1-10 alkyl; (2) substituted
          C1-10 alkyl in which one or more substituent(s) is selected from (a) halogen, (b)
          hydroxy, (c) C1-10 alkoxy, (d) C1-5 alkoxycarbonyl, (e) C1-5 acyloxy, (f) C3-8
          cycloalkyl, (g) phenyl, (h) substituted phenyl in which the substituents are X and Y,
          (i) C1-10alkyl S(O)n, (j) nitrile, (k) NR3R4, (l) ...

[a]Copyright by IFI/Plenum Data Corporation and Reprinted with Permission

---

9.4   Searching of the patent databases

All the screens shown above relating to the records for the original document in Figure 9.1 should be carefully studied. After all, this is representative of the actual material which is available to be searched, and it certainly comes in very different forms in the different files!

> **Important notes:**
> - **The key patent databases have information which is common to them all, but individual databases have *special features*. The major consideration in the choice of database is the *specific type* of information you require.**
> - **Accordingly, you need to know the content of the databases. While the figures in this chapter give a representative overview, you should seek further information from the database producers.**

While the principles outlined in Chapter 6 for searching bibliographic databases (that is, those listed in Table 9.2) still apply for searching for patents in those databases, it is apparent that special consideration needs to be given to searching for records in the specialist patent databases (that is, those listed in Table 9.1).

Further, since the USPATFULL File is a full text file, the comments made in Chapter 8 apply. However, unlike those files considered in Chapter 8, some records in the USPATFULL File also contain the full indexing from the CAplus File so all the suggestions relating to searching index entries (Chapters 6 and 7) need additionally to be considered. Indeed the USPATFULL File is a very special source of information on patents and the only limitation is that it contains only patents issued by the U.S. Patent and Trademark Office (and from 1971 onwards).

Note that CA indexing in the USPATFULL File is added to all chemistry patents covered by CAS. However, the USPTO labels an additional 50% as chemistry patents but these are not indexed by CAS since CAS does not consider them to fall within their definitions of chemistry. This again emphasises the point that what appears in any database is very much dependent upon the policies of the database producers!

9.4.1   Subject searching (general)

Text searching is conducted in the same way as it is in bibliographic and, in the case of the USPATFULL File, in full text files, and the only additional initial consideration is whether information from the whole literature or just information from the patent literature is required.

Thus, if the intention is to retrieve all prior art on a subject, either to verify the novelty of the intended research (and hence the ability to patent successful outcomes) or simply to find background information which will assist with the research program, then it is necessary to search the whole literature and the process is exactly the same as the process discussed in Chapter 7, although, of course, the limited text-based indexing in some of the specialist patent databases needs to be considered.

On the other hand, sometimes the intention is to retrieve information from patent documents only. For example, the searcher might be interested in other companies who have patented information in the general field since answers retrieved here may indicate current or potential competitors in the marketplace.

Accordingly, if information from patents only is required then searches are conducted in those specialist databases (Table 9.1), and in those databases (Table 9.2) which contain patent information. In the latter group of searches it is necessary to add a search term AND P/DT in order to retrieve documents which relate to patents only.

> **Important notes:**
> * When "searching for patents" on subjects, you need to consider carefully why you are doing the search.
> * If you are looking for subjects which have been patented then you look in the specialist patent databases *and* in the bibliographic files which index patents. In the latter files you add the search term P/DT to restrict answers to patents.
> * If the intention of your search is to find "prior knowledge" independent of whether it has been patented or not, then you need to perform comprehensive searches both in bibliographic databases and patent databases. It is important to include the

latter since around 80% of the technical information reported in patents is not published elsewhere.

- Searching in the bibliographic files for patented information is conducted in the same way as normal keyword searches in the files; you search in one, or all, of the title, abstract and index fields.

- Searching in the specialist patent files is conducted in a similar way, although the presentation of the data in these files *is very different and you have to have a very good knowledge of the content of all the fields and of the indexing.*

9.4.2 Searches based on classification codes

International Patent Classification codes may be searched in a number of fields (see below), and here it is necessary to consult the WIPO, USPTO or Derwent publications to determine the appropriate code details (see Section 9.3.2). It must be remembered that these classifications change with time, and so the codes appropriate to the time period to be searched must be used.

It should also be remembered that the various codes are index codes, and the classification given very much depends on the way the inventors wrote the original patent and on how the indexer interpreted it. It certainly is not without precedent that relevant patents have been missed through searches based on patent codes alone. (Indeed the contents of Screens 9.5 and 9.6 need to be considered very carefully. They show the primary classifications, IPC and NCL, for the same patent and they are totally different. The specialist Derwent indexing is different again! So, in general, searching for subject information by patent index codes is not considered to be the preferred approach, but if it is attempted then great care should be taken to ensure all the correct codes for the databases and for the time periods required are used.)

The different databases enter the IPC codes in one, or a number, of fields including IPM (main), IPS (secondary), ICA (additional) or ICI (index), and the Database Summary Sheets contain details of the fields in the different files. However, very often it is not particularly important as to the exact field in which the code appears, and when the classification code is searched in the IPC field the search actually is conducted in whichever of the four fields are present in the file. In other words, the IPC Field is a "superfield" - and searches in this field may be performed in all of the files to retrieve all IPC codes listed in the record.

9.4.3 Patent superfields

In addition to the IPC superfield, three other "superfields" have been defined and they each relate to the key legal aspects of the patent. They are very useful search fields since they overcome the need to search in a number of related subfields.

The APPS superfield relates to the application number or priority application number, that is, to the application numbers given either at the stage of the priority (or provisional) application, or at the stage when the actual full application was made.

The PCS superfield relates to the countries in which the patent is granted (this also includes the designated states).

The PATS superfield relates to all those fields which contain actual patent numbers including the Patent Number Field (PN), the Filing Details Field (FDT), and the various additional fields in the different files which contain actual patent numbers.

Important notes:
- **You search in the APPS superfield to find all records with specific *application numbers*.**
- **You search in the IPC superfield to find all records with *IPC codes*.**
- **You search in the PCS superfield to find all records relating to *countries* covered by the patent.**
- **You search in the PATS superfield to find all records relating to *patent numbers*.**

9.4.4   Crossfile searching; patent families

In most cases the bibliographic databases in Table 9.2 index only the first patent document received by the database producer. (Interestingly, for example, the Japanese Patent Office completes the patent processing very quickly and the first patent document received is often that from the Japanese Patent Office. So, over 50% of the patents processed by the Chemical Abstracts Service are from the Japanese Patent Office.)

When patents taken out in other countries are received they are not indexed, so information on the family of patents may not be entered in the database. However, as with so many aspects of database construction, database producers respond over time to user requests. Accordingly, more and more information appears in the electronic records and it is necessary often to determine from the database producers when new features were implemented. For example, Table 9.1 shows time periods from which the Wila-Verlag and Derwent organizations added different types of information, while CAS started adding information on Designated States in the 1990s.

However, the WPI Files have long contained extensive family patent information and they constitute one source of patent families. Another source of extensive family information is the INPADOC File. It covers an even wider range of patents and the procedure for finding family and legal status information in this file is discussed in Section 9.4.6.

Patent family information is commonly needed for three reasons. It is needed to assist with the determination of countries covered by the patent, to assist with location of records when a patent number from a single country is known (which may not be the country of origin or indeed not the country from which the initial patent was received), or to determine patent details relating to other countries from which the original document might more easily be obtained.

To achieve patent family information the known patent number may be searched in the WPI Files (in the APPS or PATS superfields, or in one of the more specific fields, for example the PN Field). If the number is known independently, this may be done simply by searching the patent number in the File. However, commonly the patent is retrieved from another file on the network and it is necessary to "crossover" the number to the WPI File. This is most readily done by:

1. locating the patent in the first file (answer set L1);
2. entering the WPI File;
3. searching the patent number from the first file using the SmartSELECT feature (for example; => S L1 <PN,APPS>); and
4. displaying the answer.

The process, shown in Screen 9.10, uses the SmartSELECT feature (see Section 10.1.3).

Screen 9.10ª Locating patent families in the WPI Files

(L1 is an answer set obtained in the CAplus File using the appropriate search term(s). In this case L1 contained the CAplus File record for the patent shown in Figure 9.1.)
=> **FIL WPINDEX**
=> **S L1 <PN>**
SmartSELECT INITIATED
FILE 'CAPLUS' ENTERED ....
SEL L1 1- PN
L2   SEL L1 1- PN :   1 TERM
FILE 'WPINDEX' ENTERED ....
S L2
L3   1 L2
=> **D IBIB**
 ACCESSION NUMBER: 90-216853 [28]   WPINDEX
DOC. NO. CPI: C90-093709
TITLE: New 2-methyl-3-oxo-8-acyloxy 1-substd. decahydro-naphthalene
                         derivs. - having HMG-COA reductase inhibiting activity, useful as anti
                         hypercholesterolaemic.
(for the remainder of the BIB display see Screen 9.4)

In this case only a single patent number is crossed over (and since it was known the CAplus File entry had the patent number in the PN Field it was sufficient to search only for **<PN>**), but the same exercise may be conducted with any number of patents. For example, if patent families for all patents granted on anticholesterolemics are required then the answer set is first obtained in the CAplus File. In fact a search: => **S ANTICHOLESTEROL? AND P/DT** in the CAplus File gives an answer set, L1, which contains 135 records. Since all of these are records of patents, and since the CAplus file has entries in the PN Field for all patents, then the required search in the WPINDEX File is: => **S L1 <PN>.** This answer set contains 132 records.

However, within the SmartSELECT feature the search conducted in the second file need not be in the same search field as that from which the items are selected, and the search field may easily be changed. For example, the search in the WPINDEX File: => **S L1 <PN>/PATS** searches the Patent Numbers obtained in the CAplus File in the PATS superfield in the WPINDEX File (and this includes the PN, FDT, and REP Fields, that is, it additionally includes Patent Numbers in the Filing Details and Referenced Patents Fields). This second search gives 204 answers.

There are a number of points to note here. First, the search: => **S ANTICHOLESTEROL?** could have been conducted in the WPI Files, but only 113 records were retrieved (compared with 135 from the CAplus File). Remember that the titles and abstracts are written by the database producer, and there is different indexing in the WPI Files. (More extensive indexing is available in the WPIDS File which is available to those who are Derwent subscribers.) Note also that the search is a rather restrictive one and that other terms could have been used (however, the intent here is to illustrate the principles involved with family searching and a comprehensive search was not attempted).

Second, the search: => **S L1 <PN>** defaults to the PN Field in the second file (132 records). There are 3 less records here possibly because CAplus is more current, or because the CA database covers countries (like Poland) which are not in the WPI database.

Finally, the search: => **S L1 <PN>/PATS** includes the Referenced Patent Field (204 records). Often it is valuable to retrieve cited references particularly since the author determined that they contained related information. Note also that this search does not retrieve patent families in the same sense as the search: => **S L1 <PN>** since the additional answers now include patents which have been cited, and these may not be in the patent family.

The searches gave substantially different numbers of answers, and it would be necessary to determine whether the additional answers are relevant or not. For example, some of the answers in the final search may not be relevant since they may have referenced, for example patents relating to synthetic procedures. However, other answers might have been highly relevant and they now appeared because the free text and index entries did not contain the specific term stem ANTICHOLESTEROL.

Another method of finding patent families on STN is to use the FSEARCH command, which gathers in one answer set all the records that cover the same invention. The command may be followed by search terms including patent or application numbers, or most E-number or L-number terms. The SmartSELECT feature (see Section 10.1.3) may be used, and an example is given in Screen 9.11.

Screen 9.11[a] Use of FSEARCH to select the complete patent portfolio
```
=> FIL CAPLUS
=> S ANTICHOLESTEROL? AND P/DT
L1      135 ANTICHOLESTEROL? AND P/DT
=> FIL WPINDEX
=> FSEARCH L1 <PN>
SEA L1 <PN>
SmartSELECT INITIATED
L2      SEL L1 1- PN :   135 TERMS
FSE
*** ITERATION 1 ***
SEL L5 1- PN,APPS
L6      SEL L5 1- PN APPS :   830 TERMS
SEA L6
L7      181 L6
*** ITERATION 2 ***
....
*** ITERATION 4 ***
L7      205 L6
FSORT L7
L9      205 FSO L7
            31 Multi-record Families     Answers 1-110
               Family 1                  Answers 1-4
               Family 2                  Answers 5-6
....
               Family 31                 Answers 109-110
            95 Individual Records        Answers 111-205
```

[a]Copyright by the American Chemical Society and Derwent Publications Ltd and Reprinted with Permission

This screen is much truncated from the full screen display, but the essential features are shown. That is, in the first instance the search is conducted in the CAplus File and then the SmartSELECT feature is used in the WPINDEX File. This feature operates in the usual way namely that it instructs the system to:

> "go back to the original file, select the patent numbers, then obtain the full patent families for all the patents and to sort them so each family is collected together".

The final outcome is an answer set of 205 records,[*] some of which are multiple listings of a single patent family (31 families) and some of which are individual records (which still may have patent family information).

It will be noted in Screen 9.11 that the final answer set is obtained through an iterative process, and this is because the original search finds all the patent numbers from the CAplus File answer set in the PN and APPS Fields in the WPINDEX File. This new answer set will have identified some new patents and their patent numbers now are searched as well. The process continues by successive iterations until no new answers are retrieved. Notwithstanding the technicalities of the FSEARCH command, it is important to understand that all it is doing is finding the comprehensive patent family information within the parameters set, that is, in the WPINDEX File for the original search conducted in the CAplus File.

While the example in Screen 9.11 used the SmartSELECT feature, and while only one file (WPINDEX) was used, the FSEARCH command may be used in a multifile environment. In such cases it is usual to search only on a single patent number.

As usual, there are a number of issues relating to online searching; this text attempts to alert the searcher to the principles and the different types of answers the different procedures give, and it is up to the searcher to evaluate the best technique to retrieve the best answers to the specific problem posed!

9.4.5   Determining patent competition

Sometimes the intent of the search is to identify other companies who are active in the area, and the procedure here is to obtain the relevant records and then to extract information relating to the companies. The relevant records may be obtained in any way required, for example, by keyword search or by IPC or NCL codes. It doesn't matter, but what needs to be obtained first is an answer set in whatever file or files are appropriate.

For example, Screen 9.12 shows how information about companies may be extracted from an answer set.

Notes (Screen 9.12):

• The answer set, L1, has not been obtained by a comprehensive search! The principle being illustrated here is the selection of company information and this answer set suffices, but of course a comprehensive search would be constructed in the usual manner through the rigorous identification of the most appropriate search terms.

---

[*]It is coincidental that this result is so similar to the earlier search described, **S L1 <PN>/PATS,** which gives 204 answers. The answer sets are somewhat different since the earlier search retrieved referenced patents.

- The SmartSELECT feature needs to be used in order to obtain statistical analyses of results. (The SELECT command could be used to extract names of companies but options for statistical analyses of the selected items do not exist within this command.)
- There are a number of ways in which the SmartSELECT feature can be activated. The way shown here uses the entry: **SET TERM L#**, but one alternative includes the entry: **SET SMART ON.** (Other comments about the feature are given in Section 10.1.3.)

Screen 9.12[a]   Finding   information   on   companies   (WPI   File)

```
=> S ANTICHOLESTEROL?
L1     113 ANTICHOLESTEROL?
=> SET TERM L#
SET COMMAND COMPLETED
=> SELECT
SmartSELECT  INITIATED
ENTER ANSWER SET L# OR (L1):L1
ENTER ANSWER NUMBER OR RANGE (1):1-
ENTER DISPLAY CODE (TI) OR ?:PA
=> D
L2      SEL L1 1- PA :    85 TERMS
```

TERM #	# OCC	# DOC	% DOC	PA
1	7	7	6.19	TANABE SEIYAKU CO
2	6	6	5.31	SUMITOMO CHEM CO LTD
3	5	5	4.42	ROUSSEL-UCLAF
4	4	4	3.54	MERCK & CO INC
5	4	4	3.54	SHIONOGI & CO LTD
6	3	3	2.65	AMERICAN CYANAMID CO
7	3	3	2.65	AMERICAN HOME PROD CORP
8	3	3	2.65	ORMONOTERAPIA RICHTER SPA ....

[a]Copyright by Derwent Publications Ltd and Reprinted with Permission

---

- The full command, SELECT, has then been entered for illustrative purposes only. The alternative is to use the abbreviated form and to anticipate the subcommands: **SEL L1 1- PA**. Remember that PA (Patent Assignee) is the field in which company information is presented, and note that entering the SELECT command within the SmartSELECT feature automatically activates the SmartSELECT feature.
- There are 20 different companies listed in the answer set L1 and the top 8 are shown in Screen 9.12. It also is possible to display the items in alphabetical order. In this case, **D L2 1- ALPHA** would be entered (see Table 10.4).
- While this example illustrates how company information may be extracted from the answer set, L1, information from any other fields may be extracted also. For example, if patent countries need to be analysed, then the entry (within SmartSELECT) is: => **SEL L1 1- PC,DS** it being necessary to include the Designated States in order to list the countries within the European region. (If PC is selected, then only EP (Europe) would be listed.)

• Alternatively, if patents from specific countries are of interest only, then (within the SmartSELECT feature) the entry is: => **SEL L1 1- PN WITH "US"**. The selected items then are US patent numbers only.

The points noted here summarize the features of the SELECT command, but further details may be obtained either from manuals available from STN, or online with the HELP SELECT command.

9.4.6   Legal status information

The INPADOC File has the most complete patent family information on STN, in that it covers 57 patent issuing organizations and contains legal status information for patents from most European countries plus the US, EPO and WIPO. However, as seen in Screens 9.2 and 9.7, it contains very little subject information so it is not a good starting point for subject searches.

Important notes:
• **It is important to identify the strength of each file and to exploit this strength accordingly.**
• **The strength of the INPADOC File is its comprehensiveness with respect to family and legal information, and it is the file of choice when questions relating to identifying countries in which patent protection has been obtained, and to the current legal status of these patents.**

In order to locate complete family and legal status information, including the current publication status (for example, unexamined or granted) probably the best way is to search for the patent in the INPADOC File and then to browse the record. Note that, unlike other specialist patent files, each record in the INPADOC File represents a single member of the patent family, and all the family information is contained within each record.

The procedure is to search the patent number in the INPADOC File, and then to display the family and legal status information as required. The display command here is: => **D FAMS**, however, a D BROWSE option exists within the File. This enables a number of fields within the record to be displayed and only one display charge is incurred. (Note that DISPLAY FAMS is a display format in the INPADOC File which shows the full family and legal status information. It is not only important to know the correct search terms, but also it is important to know the appropriate display fields, which are listed in the Database Summary Sheets!)

For the patent given in Figure 9.1, the family and legal status information in the INPADOC File is shown in Screen 9.13 and the information in this screen should be compared with the corresponding information from the WPI File (Screen 9.4). In particular it should be noted that the legal status information and the current publication status is much more extensive!

Screen 9.13[a] Family and legal status information in the INPADOC File

```
=>  S  US4937259/PN
L1      1 US4937259/PN
        (US4937259/PN)

=> D BRO
:FAMS
PRAI 1: 89US-0363816    890609
 (1) PI US4937259    A 900626
   LS P PUBLICATION NUMBER
      890609 AE  A APPLICATION DATA (PATENT)
             US 89 363816 890609
      900626 A    PATENT
      940906 FP    - EXPIRED DUE TO FAILURE TO PAY MAINTENANCE FEE
             940629
 (2) PI EP-402154    A1 901212
   LS P PUBLICATION NUMBER
             US 89 363816 890609
      900608 AE  A EP-APPLICATION
             EP 90 90306240 900608
      901212 AK  A1 + DESIGNATED CONTRACTING STATES IN AN APPLICATION
             WITH SEARCH REPORT
             CH DE FR GB IT LI NL
      901212 A1    + PUBLICATION OF APPLICATION WITH SEARCH REPORT
      910710 17P   + REQUEST FOR EXAMINATION FILED
             910515
      930714 17Q   + FIRST EXAMINATION REPORT
             930601
      930728 18W   - WITHDRAWN
             930524
 (3) PI  CA2018478     AA 901209
 (4) PI  JP03068537    A2 910325
 (5) PI  US5010105     A  910423
   LS P PUBLICATION NUMBER
      890609 AA  A2 NO TEXT AVAILABLE
             US 89 363816 890609
      900509 AE  A APPLICATION DATA (PATENT)
             US 90 520899 900509
      910423 A    PATENT

PRAI 2: 90US-0520899    900509
   PI US5010105    A 910423 PRAI 1

5 members, 2 priorities, 4 countries
:END
```

Summary

- There are a number of databases which specialize in patent information, and there are other (bibliographic) databases which index patent documents.
- The ways in which the original patents are represented in all of these databases are very different: even titles and abstracts are different since in many cases these are *written by the database producers.*
- *Legal status information* relates mainly to dates for the various stages in which the patenting process was conducted.
- The original patent documents have index classifications, and the two main systems are the International Patent Codes, and the US National Codes (for which online thesauri are available in some files).
- A variety of additional indexing is applied by the database producers, and the searcher should know and take full advantage of the file-specific index entries.
- When searching for patent information it is *important to define the intent of the search,* and most commonly searches relate to subjects, classification codes, patent families, and legal status information.

10

Special Topics

In this chapter we learn:

- *Applications of the HELP, FILE, INDEX, and SELECT commands on STN.*
- *The different ways in which the SELECT command and the SmartSELECT feature operate.*
- *About some special topics including*
  - *current awareness searching;*
  - *citation searching;*
  - *searching for numeric properties; and*
  - *costs!*

The opportunities in online searching are almost as endless as the nature of science, the types of questions that needed to be solved, and the imagination of the searcher. Creative searching may be done in so many areas, but only when the content of the databases, and the mechanics of searching, are understood. This text deals primarily with basic principles from where searchers may expand their thinking and truly obtain value from online searching. While many topics have been addressed in the earlier chapters, there are a number of other basic issues which searchers need to know, and this chapter deals with some of them.

10.1 The commands on STN

A list of the commands on STN is given in Table 10.1. Details of the use of these commands may be obtained from the manual: *STN Guide to Commands* which is available from any STN Service Center. It should also be noted that within each command there are often a number of subcommand options, and that usually there are default options for these subcommands (Section 2.2). However, there are numerous online help messages which are there to assist the searcher, and the applications of some of these help messages are considered first.

Table 10.1 Commands on STN

COMMAND	FUNCTION
ACTIVATE	to recall a copy of a saved item from long-term storage
BATCH	to create a structure search to be run overnight
DELETE	to delete saved items, offline print requests, items in session etc.
DISPLAY	to display answers, queries, saved items, costs etc.
DOWNLOAD	to transfer information from a session directly to files on local computer
DUPLICATE	to identify or remove duplicate answers
EDIT	to change a field code created by a term EXPAND or SELECT
EXPAND	to display an alphabetical list of terms in an index
FILE	to change files
HELP	to request online help
INDEX	to specify and enter files to be used in STNindex
LOGOFF	to disconnect from STN International
NEWS	to view the STN news items
ORDER	to order documents from STN document delivery services
PRINT	to print answers at an STN Service Center and mail them
QUERY	to create a search profile without executing it
READ	to read and manipulate mail in the STNmail File
RUN	to execute software packages
SAVE	to save queries and/or answer sets under your loginid
SCREEN	to create a screen number for a structure search
SDI	to create an automatic update search
SEARCH	to search for text terms or chemical structures in a file
SELECT	to create search terms from an answer display field
SEND	to send a message to the STN Service Center
SET	to modify terminal parameters
SORT	to rearrange the order of the records in an answer set, by field
STRUCTURE	to create a chemical structure to be searched

10.1.1 The HELP command

At any prompt, online help messages always are available and on STN it is necessary to enter either the command HELP or the ? mark to display the information available. However, usually help in a specific area is needed and the area required should be added after the command. The options which are needed to start off in the right direction are given in Table 10.2, and an example of a general help entry is shown in Screen 10.1 for the RTECS File.

Table 10.2 General areas in which HELP is available on STN

AREA	FUNCTION
HELP MESSAGES	to list general help messages (for example, for files in, and features of, the system)
HELP FILE NAMES	to list files and a brief description of each file
HELP CLUSTER NAMES	to list all clusters
HELP COMMANDS	to list the commands available in the current file
HELP DIRECTORY	to list HELP messages for the current file
HELP CONTENT	to display a description of the content of the current file

The help messages relate to the file construction, and the mechanics of some specific aspects of searching the File. (Note, for example, that there are separate help messages to explain the use of the proximity operators in the File.) Thus, throughout this text there have been many references to "file-specific" issues, and help messages in each file may be displayed to explain the special applications. Other file-specific issues, for example STOPWORDS, may be displayed under the HELP CONTENT option. The important point is that all file-specific issues may easily be identified!

Screen 10.1[a] HELP DIRECTORY in the RTECS File

=> **HELP DIRECTORY**
The following HELP messages are available to obtain information on the RTECS File:

HELP ABBREV	- key to abbreviations used in RTECS
HELP ACCESSION	- RTECS accession number format
HELP CONTENT	- general RTECS File description
HELP COST	- price schedule for the RTECS File
HELP CROSSOVER	- file crossover searching in RTECS
HELP DESK	- RTECS File user assistance
HELP DFIELDS	- list of display field codes
HELP DUNITS	- specifying units for display fields
HELP EFFCODE	- RTECS Toxic Effects Codes
HELP EFIELDS	- SELECT command and E-number lists
HELP FA	- search and display field availability
HELP FORMAT	- predefined formats for display and print
HELP HIGHLIGHT	- Highlighting in RTECS
HELP (L)	- (L) operator use in the RTECS File
HELP MOLFORM	- molecular formulas in the RTECS File
HELP (P)	- (P) operator use in the RTECS File
HELP PROPERTIES	- Properties tabulated in the RTECS File
HELP QRD	- Query-Related Data in displays and prints
HELP RANGE	- RANGE parameters for the RTECS File
HELP (S)	- (S) operator use in the RTECS File
HELP SFIELDS	- list of search field codes
HELP SUNITS	- specifying units for search fields
HELP SURV	- list of meanings for codes found in SURV field
HELP UNITS	- default units for properties in the RTECS File
HELP USAGETERM	- use and distribution restrictions applicable to the RTECS File

For a list of more general help topics such as command usage, enter HELP MESSAGES at an arrow prompt (=>).

---

[a]Copyright by the National Institute for Occupational Health and Safety and Reprinted with Permission

While HELP CONTENT gives a general file description, the only additional information required is the detailed knowledge of the content of the database, an aspect which has been addressed at least in brief for a few files in this text. Particularly once searchers have reasonable mastery of the mechanics of searching, this issue of detailed knowledge of the database becomes the most important one and only by study of the database may this knowledge be gained. Luckily, searchers generally require only a few databases and familiarity with them is quickly gained. However, if in any doubt the searcher should consult the online Help Desk, or the database producer.

Perhaps it should again be noted that the Database Summary Sheets (see Section 5.7) are an additional excellent source of help in the first instance. With these, and with the help messages available online, most simple questions may be answered. For example, in Section 16.5.9 the question of EFFCODES in the RTECS File is raised and, from the information shown in Screen 10.1 (particularly the entry HELP EFFCODE), it now is readily apparent how explanation of the codes may be obtained (Screen 10.2). Note in Screen 10.2 how the initial help message also informs how to obtain further help (here on damage codes). Sometimes it is necessary to work through a series of help messages in order to obtain all the information required.

Screen 10.2[a] Specific help (the RTECS File): an explanation of code J15[b]

=> **HELP EFFCODE**
  RTECS has three position (three character) Toxic Effects Codes. The first position is a letter code designating Organ, Tissue, or Functional System. The second and third position is a two digit code designating Damage.

  The following Toxic Effects Codes are used in the RTECS file:
  Organ, Tissue, or Functional System Codes
    A   Brain and Coverings
. . . .
    H   Vascular
    J   Lung, Thorax, or Respiration
    K   Gastrointestinal
. . . .
For lists of Damage Codes associated with each Organ, Tissue, or Functional System Code, enter HELP followed by the Organ, Tissue, or Functional System letter code at an arrow prompt (=>). For example, to see the list of Damage Codes associated with Cardiac, enter HELP G at an arrow prompt (=>).

=> **HELP J**
  The following Toxic Effects Codes are used in the RTECS file:
  J LUNGS, THORAX, OR RESPIRATION
  Damage Codes
. . . .
    13   Fibrosis, interstitial
    14   Fibrosing alveolitis
    15   Acute pulmonary edema
    16   Chronic pulmonary edema
    17   Pleural effusion
. . . .

---

[a]Copyright by the National Institute for Occupational Health and Safety and Reprinted with Permission
[b]See Figure 16.17

The other level at which help messages are available is following an input error by the user. For example, entries may be made which are unacceptable to the system in which case the system will notify the user accordingly. Generally the mistake is a simple one (for example, parentheses may not have been matched) and quickly remedied, but if the searcher is unsure of the problem then HELP may be entered and immediate assistance is obtained.

Important note:
- **HELP messages are there to assist you. Particularly when you are in unfamiliar territory, make sure you take advantage of the messages. There should be nothing that you do not understand, and the way to understand is to ask questions. The better you understand, then the more critical you will be with your inputs and the better the outcomes you will obtain!**

10.1.2 The FILE and INDEX commands

Up until this stage, it has been assumed that the searcher is familiar with the files which are needed, but this sometimes is not the case. Accordingly, sometimes it is necessary to start at a much more general level and this is done with the INDEX command on STN. (A booklet on the use of STNindex is available: *STNindex User Guide*, CAS8062-1293.) The INDEX command is related to the FILE command, but the two commands have some important different features.

In the FILE command:

- single or multiple files are entered;
- connect hour, display and search fees for the file apply and if multiple files are entered, multiple connect hour fees apply;
- all the system commands may be used;
- the search command looks for the actual search terms in the field(s) specified, and gives an *L-numbered answer set*; and
- the answer set may be displayed or modified by any of the commands used by the system.

In the INDEX command:

- single or multiple files are entered;
- a single, and low, connect hour fee applies irrespective of how many files are entered;
- generally only the SEARCH, EXPAND, and FILE commands may be used, although the command D RANK sorts out the files in order of decreasing number of hits;
- the search command looks only at the postings in the field(s) specified, and gives an *L-numbered query*; which then may be used as a search term after the files are entered with the FILE command;
- all the usual tools and techniques (Boolean and proximity operators, truncation, etc.) may be used with the search command; and
- as the L-number generated is a query, there are no answers to be displayed.

The purpose of the INDEX command is to allow the searcher to determine the number of hits the various searches will retrieve either in a single or multifile environment without incurring file-related connect hour and search costs. Accordingly the INDEX command is used particularly when possible files of interest are being sought, although it also may be used to overcome the limitation of the EXPAND command in a single file (that is, that only individual terms may be expanded and only through searches may the number of hits, for terms that need to be connected, be obtained).

Use of the INDEX command in a single file can be cost effective if the hourly cost of access to the file through this option is substantially less than the hourly cost of access to the full file. The advantage here is that the SEARCH command may be used, and search terms may be linked and potential sizes of answers determined. On the other hand, the EXPAND command may be used to identify numbers of entries for individual terms only. That is, a search within INDEX: => **S PHYSIOLOGY AND BACTERIA** will give the number of records which have both of these terms, whereas use of the EXPAND command on PHYSIOLOGY and on BACTERIA will give the number of records which have the two terms individually.

Table 10.3 Examples of the use of the FILE command

COMMAND ENTRY	USE	EXAMPLE[a]
FIL <NAME>	to enter single file	**FIL EMBASE**
FIL <NAME1 NAME2 ..>	to enter a number of files simultaneously	**FIL EMBASE MEDLINE CA**
FIL <CLUSTER>	to enter all files in a cluster	**FIL SAFETY**
FIL <CLUSTER -NAME1 etc>	to enter all files in a cluster except those identified	**FIL SAFETY -CIN -CSNB**
FIL CASLINK	to enter the files linked by CAS[b]	**FIL CASLINK**

[a]It is not necessary to type the full file name. Any abbreviation which unambiguously identifies a file can be used.
[b]CASLINK is mentioned in Section 15.10.1.

Some options for the FILE command are given in Table 10.3. There are a number of points to note about multifile searching, and it is strongly recommended that the booklet on multifile searching (*Multifile Search Aid*, CAS4021-1092) is obtained. However, a few general notes are:

- while there is some overlap (same original articles are indexed) between some files, often the overlap is less than expected and so it is advisable to perform multifile searches when comprehensive searching of the literature is required;
- multifile searching will retrieve some identical records and the DUPLICATE command (see Section 7.5) is used to obtain unique answers only; and
- allowances must be made in the search for file-specific terminology, for the different search fields, and also for the fact that different files have different field groups (for example, the Basic Index in files may be different).

Options to be entered after the INDEX command are identical to those after the FILE command listed in Table 10.3. For example: => **INDEX ENGINEERING -ENERGY** enters the Engineering Cluster except for the ENERGY File.

Some further comments on the INDEX command are:

- the INDEX command is used only as a guide to determine which files might be best suited to provide the information required (however, unless the searcher is aware of database policies for all the files and chooses search terms accordingly, the results may be very misleading!);

- as the INDEX command operates in a multifile environment the normal precautions relating to multifile searching apply (search terms should either be generic or should allow for file-specific terminology);
- if a search term is not appropriate for a particular file (for example, if the fields searched are not appropriate for all the files entered), an asterisk appears adjacent to the number of hits (the asterisk serves merely as a warning that the search might not have been appropriate but having received the warning, the searcher merely needs to think whether an alternative and specific search may need to be conducted but generally such a search is not required);
- the INDEX command indicates how many records in the various files have the search terms entered;
- often it is easiest to rank the answers in decreasing order of hits (=> **D RANK**) and the rank order which now lists F-numbers for the files may be used as synonyms for the name of the file (for example, to next enter the file(s) in order to perform a search); and
- all files which have hits may be entered with: => **FIL HITS** although it is possible to exclude specific files from this list if required: => **FIL HITS -PROMT** (indeed, depending on the intent of the search, generally it is not necessary to search in all the files which have hits, since after all the function of the INDEX command is merely to provide a guide to possible files of importance).

An example of the use of the INDEX command is shown in Screen 10.3. Note that it is important to include the systematic name for animal and plant species since most files index by species names. The popular name, however may be used by the authors in the "free text"

Screen 10.3 Example of use of the INDEX command
(Note that in the display below a tabular format is used. However, the actual online display lists each file on a separate line.)
=> **INDEX BIOSCIENCE**
INDEX 'AIDSLINE, ANABSTR, AQUASCI, BIOBUSINESS, BIOSIS, BIOTECHABS, BIOTECHDS, CABA, CANCERLIT, CAPLUS, CEABA, CEN, CIN, CJACS, CJELSEVIER, CONFSCI, DDFB, DDFU, DISSABS, DRUGB, DRUGLAUNCH, DRUGNL, DRUGU, EMBASE, FSTA, GENBANK, HEALSAFE, IFIPAT, JICST-EPLUS, ...'
Enter SET DETAIL ON to see search term postings or to view search error messages that display as 0* with SET DETAIL OFF.

=> **S (HERRING GULL# OR LARUS ARGENTATUS)**

7	FILE ANABSTR	379	FILE AQUASCI	9	FILE BIOBUSINESS
1320	FILE BIOSIS	189	FILE CABA	4	FILE CANCERLIT
206	FILE CAPLUS	3	FILE CEN	1	FILE CIN
16	FILE CJACS	29	FILE CONFSCI	4	FILE DDFB
2	FILE DDFU	37	FILE DISSABS	4	FILE DRUGB
2	FILE DRUGU	128	FILE EMBASE	3	FILE FSTA
3	FILE GENBANK	29	FILE HEALSAFE	280	FILE LIFESCI
121	FILE MEDLINE	35	FILE NTIS	81	FILE OCEAN
6	FILE PROMT	505	FILE SCISEARCH	256	FILE TOXLINE
117	FILE TOXLIT	1	FILE USPATFULL		

29 FILES HAVE ONE OR MORE ANSWERS, 41 FILES SEARCHED IN STNINDEX
L1 QUE (HERRING GULL# OR LARUS ARGENTATUS)

entries. Then, having performed the initial search the user needs to consider which file(s) to enter and the choice depends on which additional concepts are required. For example, if breeding, population, and life cycle data are required then the BIOSIS and LIFESCI files might be entered; if environmental or toxicity information is sought, then the AQUASCI, CAplus and TOXLINE files should be considered. Of course, a search on the additional concepts required can be performed within the INDEX, and linked with the L-number query (L1 in Screen 10.3) and this will further help with the identification of the most appropriate file(s). However, the searcher should be very careful about searching too many concepts in a multifile environment, and it generally is better to search just one or two concepts (and those for which search terms are most reliably identified in a multifile environment).

Finally, the procedure then is to enter the relevant files using the FILE command (choosing any of the options shown in Table 10.3 but additionally using F-numbers if these have been obtained from the command D RANK within the INDEX feature), and then to perform detailed searches using the techniques discussed in Chapters 6 and 7.

10.1.3 The SELECT command and SmartSELECT

A key feature of online searching is the ability to select terms from one field in one database and then to link them with terms in other fields in the same database, or with terms in fields in other databases.

On STN this is done with the SELECT command. The whole aim of this command merely is to select terms from (somewhere in) a record and then to use these terms as search terms either elsewhere in the record, in other records in the database, or indeed in other records in other databases. The effect of the command is just to save the searcher a lot of typing and sorting.

The subcommands within the SELECT command are very similar to those within the DISPLAY command (see Section 2.2). That is, it is necessary to identify the answer set, then the answer numbers or range of answers, and finally the field from which items are to be selected. (The defaults are the last answer set, answer number 1, and the default field for the file.) The items selected are then identified by E-numbers and the entry: => **D SEL E1-** will list all the E-numbers and the associated terms, but often not all E-numbers may need to be displayed and, for example, **D SEL E1-E10** will display only the first 10 in the list.

These E-numbers then may be searched in the usual manner, in any file, although it may be necessary to specify a different search field from the one in which the items were selected. For example, if index headings are selected from the CT Field, the selected terms would have the /CT suffix and all searches on these terms would be in the CT Field. If these terms are to be searched in the Basic Index, then it would be necessary to edit the selected terms and to add the /BI suffix, and while the EDIT command may be used for this purpose, in actual practice it is merely necessary to add /BI to the search term. That is, if E1-E10 were items selected from the CT Field, the search in the Basic Index would require the entry: => **S E1-E10/BI**.

The Database Summary Sheet for each file indicates which fields are available for implementation of the SELECT command, and the terms from any of these fields may be chosen. However, once chosen, the E-numbers may be searched in any fields desired.

An enhanced version of the SELECT command is available through the SmartSELECT feature. Items are selected in the usual manner, although the extracted information is now placed in an L-number set. The feature has two main functions: first it allows very easy, one-step cross-file searching, and second the data, which is conveniently presented in tabular format, may easily be analysed.

While to the novice searcher the feature can be a little confusing at first, once it has been mastered it is a particularly valuable tool.

There are three ways of turning SmartSELECT "on":

- => **SET SMART ON**
- => **SET TERM L#**
- => **S L# <FIELD>.**

The first two instances are used when information in a single file needs to be analysed, and, in this application, it is necessary to use the SELECT command at the next command prompt. The last instance is used to simplify the procedure whereby terms from one database are used automatically as search terms in another database, that is, in cross-file searching.

Once selected, the terms may be searched or displayed in the usual manner, although the display will be in tabular format and special display options now are available for statistical analyses (Table 10.4).

Table 10.4   Special display options with the SmartSELECT feature

OPTION	FUNCTION
D ENTIRE	to display all of the terms
D 1-	to display all of the terms
D m-n	to display the terms specified (e.g. 1-5)
D TOP n	to display top n occurrences
D OGT n	to display terms with occurrence counts greater than 'n'
D DGT n	to display terms with document counts greater than 'n'
D %GT n	to display terms with percentage counts greater than 'n'
D PGT n	to display terms with percentage counts greater than 'n'
D ALPHA 1-	to display terms in alphabetical order
D ANS 1-	to display the terms with answer numbers indicated

Statistical analyses are useful to determine key terms selected. For example, if a number of records has been obtained, then with the SmartSELECT feature the most frequently posted index headings may be identified and this can assist with the development of the search profile. So, in Screen 10.4, the most frequently posted headings for a quick search on simvastatin in the CAplus File are readily obtained, and this information may then be used in further searches.

Note that L1 and L2 inform that there are 290 records and that in these records there are a total of 296 controlled terms (index headings). The tabular display indicates that LIPOPROTEINS/CT occurs in 54 of the 290 records, but that at least in some of them this index heading appears a number of times (it occurs in total 113 times in the 290 records).

This table offers another (and simple) way to determine index headings (compare, for example, Section 7.1) and these then may be used as search terms as appropriate (for example if information on receptors is of interest the search term RECEPTORS/CT may be added to the search query). Indeed this can be one of the best ways to determine relevant Index Headings. That is, a quick casual search is performed first, then the Index Headings are tabulated. If a very large answer set is obtained in the initial search, it may take a little time for the system to identify all the Headings but a good idea of the Headings may instead be obtained merely by, for example, selecting the Headings from the first 1000 answers (**SEL 1-1000 CT**).

```
                    Screen 10.4ᵃ  Statistical analyses with the SmartSELECT feature
                                 (example from the CAplus File)
=>  S  SIMVASTATIN  OR  79902-63-9
L1      290            SIMVASTATIN OR 79902-63-9
=> SET SMART ON
SET COMMAND COMPLETED
=> SELECT L1 1- CT
L2       SEL L1 1- CT :   296 TERMS
=> D TOP 10
L2       SEL L1 1- CT :   296 TERMS
TERM #  # OCC # DOC  % DOC   CT
------   -------  ------   ------   --------------------------------------
    1     113     54     18.62  LIPOPROTEINS
    2      79     79     27.24  ANTICHOLESTEREMICS AND HYPOLIPEMICS
    3      26     21      7.24  PHARMACEUTICAL DOSAGE FORMS
    4      22     14      4.83  NEOPLASM INHIBITORS
    5      21     20      6.90  LIPIDS, BIOLOGICAL STUDIES
    6      20     20      6.90  LIVER, METABOLISM
    7      18     17      5.86  GLYCERIDES, BIOLOGICAL STUDIES
    8      13     13      4.48  BLOOD ANALYSIS
    9      13     13      4.48  LIVER, COMPOSITION
   10      13     13      4.48  RECEPTORS
```
ᵃCopyright by the American Chemical Society and Reprinted with Permission

Another option for statistical analyses is given in Screen 10.5 which shows the main companies which have patents relating to simvastatin.

```
               Screen 10.5ᵃ  Finding companies with patents on simvastatin (CAplus File)
=>  S  (SIMVASTATIN  OR  79902-63-9)  AND  P/DT
L1       59 (SIMVASTATIN OR 79902-63-9) AND P/DT
=> SET SMART ON
SET COMMAND COMPLETED
=> SELECT
SmartSELECT INITIATED
ENTER ANSWER SET L# OR (L2):L1
ENTER ANSWER NUMBER OR RANGE (1):1-
ENTER DISPLAY CODE (TI) OR ?:CS
L2       SEL L1 1- CS :   14 TERMS

=> DISPLAY
ENTER (L3), L# OR ?:L2
DISPLAY (TOP 10), ENTIRE OR ?:TOP 5

TERM # # OCC # DOC % DOC     CS
------  -------  ------  ------  ----------------
    1      38     38     64.41  MERCK AND CO., INC., USA
    2       9      9     15.25  SQUIBB, E. R., AND SONS, INC., USA
    3       2      2      3.39  MERCK AND CO., INC. , USA
    4       1      1      1.69  APOTEX, INC., CAN.
    5       1      1      1.69  BLOOD CENTER OF SOUTHEASTERN WISCONSIN, INC.,
```
ᵃCopyright by the American Chemical Society and Reprinted with Permission

The examples in Screens 10.4 and 10.5 illustrate the use of the SmartSELECT feature for statistical analysis in a single file. However, the other application of the feature is for one-step cross-file searching, and this is illustrated a number of times in this text (for example, in Sections 9.4.4, 9.4.5, 16.5.3, and 16.5.7). In the multifile environment, it is important to realize that first a search is conducted in one file, then the second file is entered and the search needs to specify only the previous L-number and the field from which the terms are to be selected (remember the Database Summary Sheets indicate the fields from which terms may be chosen and that the field codes must be enclosed in angle brackets, < >).

10.2 Select CHEM

While CAS Registry Numbers are increasingly being used by electronic database producers as index entries for substances, there are many files which presently do not contain CAS Registry Numbers and so searches for substances in these files must involve name based terms. The difficulty is that there may be many names for the substance of interest and naturally all these should be used in the search. This would be a laborious process, but there is a special option, SELECT CHEM, which allows all the complete registered names from the REGISTRY File record to be selected, and the selected items then may be used to search in the bibliographic file of interest.

For example, part of the REGISTRY File record for dioxin is shown in Screen 10.6 in which it is noted that the LIFESCI File does not appear in the LC Field. Yet this file contains extensive information on the environmental effects of substances, and the question is which search terms are to be used if this file is considered to be the file of choice.

Screen 10.6[a] Record for dioxin in the REGISTRY File

RN   1746-01-6 REGISTRY
CN   Dibenzo[b,e][1,4]dioxin, 2,3,7,8-tetrachloro- (9CI) (CA INDEX NAME)
OTHER CA INDEX NAMES:
CN   Dibenzo-p-dioxin, 2,3,7,8-tetrachloro- (6CI, 7CI, 8CI)
OTHER NAMES:

CN 2,3,7,8-TCDD	CN 2,3,7,8-Tetrachlorodibenzo-1,4-dioxin
CN 2,3,7,8-Tetrachlorodibenzo-p-dioxin	CN 2,3,7,8-Tetrachlorodibenzo[b,e][1,4]dioxin
CN aromatic hydrocarbon receptor (human clone hu14)	
CN **Dioxin**	CN Dioxin (herbicide contaminant)
CN TCDBD	CN TCDD

FS   3D CONCORD
DR   56795-67-6
MF   C12 H4 Cl4 O2
CI   COM
LC STN Files: AIDSLINE, ANABSTR, APILIT, APILIT2, APIPAT, APIPAT2, BEILSTEIN*,
BIOBUSINESS, BIOSIS, CA, CANCERLIT, CAOLD, CAPLUS, CAPREVIEWS, CASREACT, CEN,
CHEMLIST, CBNB, CIN, CJACS, CSCHEM, CSNB, EMBASE, GMELIN*, HSDB*, IFICDB,
IFIPAT, IFIUDB, IPA, MEDLINE, MRCK*, MSDS-OHS, MSDS-PEST, MSDS-SUM, PIRA, PNI,
PROMT, RTECS*, TOXLINE, TOXLIT, USPATFULL, VTB
           (*File contains numerically searchable property data)
   Other Sources: EINECS**
      (**Enter CHEMLIST File for up-to-date regulatory information)
=> **SEL CHEM**
E1 THROUGH E11 ASSIGNED

---
[a]Copyright by the American Chemical Society and Reprinted with Permission

The procedure is to use the SELECT CHEM option whereby the 11 different names in Screen 10.6 will be given E-numbers, and these are searched in the LIFESCI File (Screen 10.7). There are 1664 records which contain at least one of these 11 names and this new answer set can then be searched along with keywords which will limit the answers to those with the additional concept present (here the herring gulls).

Screen 10.7   Searching for substances in the LIFESCI File

```
=> FIL LIFESCI
=> S E1-E11
L2   1664   ("AROMATIC HYDROCARBON RECEPTOR (HUMAN CLONE HU14)"/BI
            OR "DIOXIN (HERBICIDE CONTAMINANT)"/BI OR DIOXIN/BI OR
            TCDBD/BI OR TCDD/BI OR 1746-01-6/BI OR "2,3,7,8-TCDD"/BI OR
            "2,3,7,8-TETRACHLORODIBENZO(B,E)(1,4)DIOXIN"/BI OR "2,3,7,8-TE
            TRACHLORODIBENZO-P-DIOXIN"/BI OR "2,3,7,8
            TETRACHLORODIBENZO -1,4-DIOXIN"/BI OR 56795-67-6/BI)
=> S (HERRING GULL# OR LARUS ARGENTATUS) AND L2
      932     "HERRING"
....
      243     LARUS ARGENTATUS
              ("LARUS"(W)"ARGENTATUS")
L3       9     (HERRING GULL# OR LARUS ARGENTATUS) AND L2
```

[a]Copyright by Cambridge Scientific Abstracts and Reprinted with Permission

---

The alternative procedure would be to use SmartSELECT, in which case, if L1 is the REGISTRY File answer set for dioxin, then, in the LIFESCI File the entry would be: => S **L1 <CHEM>**, whereupon the system will then go back to the REGISTRY File, select out the names and search them in the LIFESCI File. The identical answer set, L2, will be obtained.

However, the question is: Is this really necessary, and might not the search be conducted solely in the LIFESCI File, say with the keyword, dioxin?

As seen in Screen 10.7, 9 answers are retrieved when all the registered names are used, but if dioxin alone is the search term then only 6 answers are retrieved, and one of those "missed" is given in Screen 10.8. This clearly is a record of interest and thus indicates the importance of searching on all names, using the SELECT CHEM feature, in files which do not list CAS Registry Numbers.

Screen 10.8[a]   Part of answer from the LIFESCI File in which the term dioxin does not appear

TI   Etiology of chick edema disease in **herring gulls** in the lower Great Lakes.

AB   Severe reproductive failure among fish-feeding birds on the lower Great Lakes was investigated in the early 1970s. Examination of Lake Ontario and Lake Erie **herring gull** (**Larus argentatus**) chicks at hatching showed signs consistent with chick edema disease and thus with the presence of a chick edema factor. Subsequent microcontaminant analysis of stored eggs revealed the presence of **2,3,7,8-TCDD** at concentrations that could account for the poor reproductive success and the signs of chick edema disease.

UT   **TCDD**; edema; pollution effects; **Larus argentatus**; America, Ontario L.; America, Erie L.; association; diseases; chick edema disease; **TCDD**

[a]Copyright by Cambridge Scientific Abstracts and Reprinted with Permission

However, there is a general note here which relates to the final point made in Section 3.6. In the files which were compared at that time, three listed CAS Registry Numbers and there was a low correlation between the numbers listed. Remember that in many files the CAS Registry Numbers are algorithmically assigned, and in turn this process depends on the chemical names which appear in the actual records. So if the names were not in the "free text" or in the indexed parts of the record, then CAS Registry Numbers will not be assigned. Further, even in the CAS files, which feature CAS Registry Numbers as the primary index entry, there are database policies relating to which substances are indexed (essentially these relate to the role of the substance, and the roles now assigned in CAplus records generally reflect CAS policies on substance indexing) and certainly all of the substances mentioned in the original article will not be indexed.

The key issue is for the searcher to realize the implications of the search terms and procedures being used, and to be alert to alternative procedures when problems may occur.

Important notes:
- **For those files which do not have CAS Registry Numbers as index entries, then all the registered names of the substances should be used in the search; and**
- **this is most readily performed by using the feature SELECT CHEM in the REGISTRY File, in which case all the names in the files are selected and the E-numbers may be used as search terms in subsequent files.**

10.3 Current awareness searching

All online systems have a feature in which searches are conducted automatically each time the file is uploaded, and the answers are delivered after each search has been conducted. On STN, the procedure is to construct the search query in the file concerned, and then to implement the SDI command. Any search query may be used, and an example is shown in Screen 10.9.

Screen 10.9   Automatic current awareness search on STN

```
=> SDI
ENTER QUERY L# FOR SDI REQUEST OR (END):L3
ENTER UPDATE FIELD CODE (UP) OR ?:.
ENTER SDI REQUEST NAME OR (END):HERRING/S
ENTER METHOD OF DELIVERY (OFFLINE), ONLINE, OR EMAIL:.
MAILING ADDRESS =        DAMON RIDLEY
                         UNIV OF SYDNEY
                         SCH OF CHEM F11
                         NSW 2006 AUSTRALIA
CHANGE MAILING ADDRESS? (N)/Y:N
ENTER PRINT FORMAT (BIB) OR ?:BIB
HIGHLIGHT HIT TERMS? (Y)/N:Y
PRINT FILE BACKGROUND INFORMATION? N/(Y):N
PRINT MULTIPLE ANSWERS PER PAGE? N/(Y):Y
ENTER MAXIMUM NUMBER OF HITS TO BE PRINTED PER RUN (100):100
SORT SDI ANSWER SET (N)/Y?:N
SEND SDI WITH NO ANSWERS? (Y)/N:N
ENTER SDI EXPIRATION DATE 'YYYYMMDD' OR (NONE):19951231
QUERY 'L3' HAS BEEN SAVED AS SDI REQUEST 'HERRING/S'
```

When the SDI command is entered, all the subcommand prompts are given, and the defaults can be chosen, or overridden, as required. In some files it is possible to choose the frequency with which SDI searches are conducted, in which case another sub-command prompt appears within the command. Choices usually are either weekly, biweekly, or monthly.

Current awareness searches need to be set up for each search in each file, although a link now has been established between the REGISTRY and CAplus Files in such a way that the searches are performed in the former file and the answers are presented from the latter file; that is, the SDI automatically crosses over the new CAS Registry Numbers retrieved to the CAplus File and bibliographic references are obtained. (As with so many aspects of this text, information on the precise details of this operation is available from the vendor.)

Generally searchers should set up SDI searches for their key areas of research. While there is a cost involved with each search, the cost of missing an article, or not keeping up to date, may be far greater in the long run!

10.4 Citations

For over two decades the Institute for Scientific Information (ISI) has maintained an unique database which is focused on the references in the original article. The SCISEARCH File covers the literature from 1974 to date, and provides access to bibliographic information, cited references, and English-language abstracts from more than 4500 scientific and technical journals in a very broad range of scientific disciplines.

While SCISEARCH has over 30 search fields, including the usual bibliographic fields (title, author, abstracts, author specified keywords and database indexing), and while it has features in some of these fields which are unique, by far the most important field is the cited reference field (RE).

Screen 10.10 shows a typical record (although note that abstracts are available only from 1991 onwards). The unique aspect of the bibliographic section is that authors from which reprints are available are highlighted (other records, where appropriate, also list the various addresses of the different authors). Note that indexing is very brief and relatively general.

Screen 10.10[a] A typical record in the SCISEARCH File

ACCESSION NUMBER:	95:75523 SCISEARCH
THE GENUINE ARTICLE:	QB844
TITLE:	AUTHENTICATION OF A SODIUM PRIMARY PHOSPHIDE - SYNTHESIS AND CRYSTAL-STRUCTURE OF [NA(PH(C6H11))(PMDETA)](2) (PMDETA=N,N,N',N'',N''- PENTAMETHYLDIETHYLENETRIAMINE)
AUTHOR:	KOUTSANTONIS G A; ANDREWS P C; RASTON C L (Reprint)
CORPORATE SOURCE:	GRIFFITH UNIV, FAC SCI & TECHNOL, BRISBANE, QLD 4111, AUSTRALIA (Reprint); GRIFFITH UNIV, FAC SCI & TECHNOL, BRISBANE, QLD 4111, AUSTRALIA
COUNTRY OF AUTHOR:	AUSTRALIA
SOURCE:	JOURNAL OF THE CHEMICAL SOCIETY-CHEMICAL COMMUNICATIONS, (07 JAN 1995) No. 1, pp. 47-48. ISSN: 0022-4936.

Screen 10.10 (continued)

DOCUMENT TYPE:	Article; Journal
FILE SEGMENT:	PHYS
LANGUAGE:	ENGLISH
REFERENCE COUNT:	18

ABSTRACT:

The reaction of the primary phosphine PH2(C6H11) with NaBu(n) in the presence of pmdeta gives the first sodium phosphide containing simple organo substituents [Na{PH(C6H11)}(pmdeta)](2), 1 (pmdeta = N,N,N',N",N"-pentamethyldiethylenetriamine) to be structurally characterized.

CATEGORY:	CHEMISTRY
SUPPL. TERM PLUS:	AMIDE CHEMISTRY; METAL-ALKYL; LITHIUM;
	PENTAMETHYLDIETHYLENETRIAMINE; SOLVATE; ADDUCTS

REFERENCE(S):

Referenced Author	IYear	I VOL	I PG	I Referenced Work
(RAU)	I(RPY)	I(RVL)	I(RPG)	I (RWK)
==============	=====	======	======	==================
	I	I1	I	IORGANOPHOSPHORUS CHE
ANDIANARISON M	I1990	I123	I71	ICHEM BER
ANDREWS P C	I1990	I29	I1440	IANGEW CHEM INT EDIT
ANDREWS P C	I1990	I386	I287	IJ ORGANOMET CHEM
BARR D	I1987	I	I716	IJ CHEM SOC CHEM COMM
BARTLETT R A	I1986	I25	I1243	IINORG CHEM
BARTLETT R A	I1987	I26	I1941	IINORG CHEM
FIELD L D	I1994	I35	I1109	ITETRAHEDRON LETT....

However, the unique aspect of the File, the Reference Field, is immediately apparent. Notice that the first named author only is listed, so while the second referenced paper was actually written by Andrews, Clegg, and Mulvey, only the name Andrews appears.

10.4.1 Finding citations to a particular article

If the first named author of the article of interest is known and articles are required in which the work has been cited, then the easiest approach is to expand on the author name in the RE Field. The terms must be entered in the correct format (surname initials, publication year). If the author is first named on numerous occasions, the expanded list may be narrowed by the addition of the publication year.

Screen 10.11 gives an example of the approach required to find references to an article by Beckwith in the *Australian Journal of Chemistry* in 1965. The appropriate E-numbers (here E5 to E9) may then be searched and the records displayed (one is shown in Screen 10.12 in a condensed format which also shows the HIT term, that is, the part of the record which caused the record to be retrieved). Note that the different journal abbreviations in Screen 10.11 occur because of the different ways they were represented in the original articles and indeed it should always be kept in mind that the data in the RE Field very much depends on the way it was presented in the original document!

Screen 10.11[a] Finding citations to a particular article

```
=> E BECKWITH A L J, 1965/RE    10
E1      1          BECKWITH A L J, 1964, V86, P953, J AM CHEM SOC/RE
E2      1          BECKWITH A L J, 1964, V96, P952, J AM CHEM SOC/RE
E3      0 -->      BECKWITH A L J, 1965/RE
E4      1          BECKWITH A L J, 1965, V18, P1023, AUST J CHEM/RE
E5      2          BECKWITH A L J, 1965, V18, P745, AUSTRAL J CHEM/RE
E6      7          BECKWITH A L J, 1965, V18, P747, AUST J CHEM/RE
E7      9          BECKWITH A L J, 1965, V18, P747, AUST J CHEMISTRY/RE
E8      5          BECKWITH A L J, 1965, V18, P747, AUSTR J CHEM/RE
E9      2          BECKWITH A L J, 1965, V18, P747, AUSTRAL J CHEM/RE
E10     2          BECKWITH A L J, 1966, P3055, AUST J CHEM/RE
```

Screen 10.12[a] Display of citation

The paper by Beckwith in Screen 10.11 was cited 25 times. One of the answers is displayed.

```
=> S  E5-E9
=> D TI AU SO HIT
```

ACCESSION NUMBER:	93:545725 SCISEARCH
THE GENUINE ARTICLE:	LV838
TITLE:	NEW CHIRAL BROMINATING AND CHLORINATING AGENTS
AUTHOR:	DUHAMEL L (Reprint); PLE G; ANGIBAUD P
SOURCE:	SYNTHETIC COMMUNICATIONS, (1993) Vol. 23, No. 17, pp. 2423-2433. ISSN: 0039-7911.
REFERENCE COUNT:	40

ABSTRACT IS AVAILABLE IN THE ALL AND IALL FORMATS

REFERENCE(S):

Referenced Author (RAU)	Year (RPY)	VOL (RVL)	PG (RPG)	Referenced Work (RWK)
BECKWITH A L J	1965	18	747	AUST J CHEM <--

10.4.2   Finding citations to a particular author

To find publications by a particular author requires knowledge of the first named author for every article, and this used to be a very tedious process. However, the SmartSELECT feature makes this very easy and the use of the feature involves two key steps.

1. Locate all records in which the author name appears

This is achieved by performing a search on the author name in the author field of the file of interest (that is: => S <NAME>/AU). While this search can be performed in the SCISEARCH File, other files may have more comprehensive information either because they cover a longer time period, or because they index more extensively in the field in which the author publishes. The point is that if the intention is to find citations to a particular author then the answer set must be as comprehensive as possible, and the SCISEARCH File may not be the best file for this part of the search. Probably the easiest way to determine the best file is to search on the author name in the INDEX command, then a few of the more likely files may be entered and specific searches on the author name may be conducted. However, it should be remembered that a single author may have a number of different postings, and that when the individual file(s) is chosen an expand on author names should be conducted (Section 4.3.2).

2.   Enter the SCISEARCH File and use the SmartSELECT feature to find all citations

The general entry to achieve this is: => **S L1 <CIT>** whereupon the system will look at the author and source fields in L1, and reformat them in such a way for automatic searching in the RE Field in the SCISEARCH File. This is equivalent to telling the computer to "go back to the file in which answer set L1 was obtained and automatically select from these answers all the terms, in the correct format, required to search in the new field in the current file."

To achieve this, it doesn't matter how answer set, L1, was obtained. Instead, all that is required is that the two files are linked by the network in a way which enables author names to be selected in the format required for searching in the RE Field in the SCISEARCH File. Currently on STN the SCISEARCH File in linked with over 25 files, and further links are being developed. To obtain an up-to-date list of files which are linked with this feature, it is necessary to enter: **HELP CITATION** in the SCISEARCH File.

Accordingly, to look for citations for all papers published by say Leo Radom, is easy even though he is rarely the first named author. The author is searched in the CAplus File (Professor Leo Radom researches in theoretical chemistry and it is highly likely that records for his publications would be present in the CAplus File) and then the SmartSELECT feature is used in the SCISEARCH File as shown in Screen 10.13.

Screen 10.13[a]   Using the CIT feature in the SCISEARCH File

```
=> FIL  CAPLUS
=> S RADOM LEO/AU OR RADOM L/AU
L1      298         RADOM LEO/AU OR RADOM L/AU
=> FIL  SCISEARCH
=> S L1  <CIT>
SmartSELECT  INITIATED ....
L3      6826        L2
=> S L3 NOT RADOM?/AU
        841         RADOM?/AU
L4      6607        L3 NOT RADOM?/AU
```

[a]Copyright by the American Chemical Society and the Institute for Scientific Information and Reprinted with Permission

---

Sometimes it is desirable to exclude "self-citations", and the answers may easily be narrowed as shown. That is, the 298 papers in the CAplus File are cited 6826 times in the SCISEARCH File and of these 6607 were not cited within papers by the same author.

It is worth taking a brief look at what actually happened during the SmartSELECT process, and Screen 10.14 shows the first 8 terms (of the 298) which were selected from the CAplus File records in the format necessary for searches in the SCISEARCH File. Notice that "V" and "P" were placed in front of the volume and page numbers, and, in particular, note that the journal abbreviation was left unspecified (? = zero or any number of characters), something that automatically allowed for one of the problems seen in Screen 10.11.

```
                    Screen 10.14ᵃ  Selected items from a citation search

=> D L2 1-8
L2      SEL L1 1- CIT :   298 TERMS

TERM #     # OCC     # DOC     % DOC        CIT
------ ------- ------ ------ --------------------------------------------------
1          1         1         0.34         ADENEY P D, 1980, V102, P4069,?
2          1         1         0.34         AGRANAT I, 1991, P80,?
3          1         1         0.34         ARONEY M J, 1968, P507,?
4          1         1         0.34         ARONEY M J, 1976, V29, P581,?
5          1         1         0.34         BAKER J, 1985, P1625,?
6          1         1         0.34         BAKER J, 1986, V7, P349,?
7          1         1         0.34         BALLARD M J, 1979, V32, P1401,?
8          1         1         0.34         BAUMANN B C, 1980, V102, P7927,?
```
[a]Copyright by the Institute for Scientific Information and Reprinted with Permission

10.5 Searching for numeric properties

There are a large number of files which have numeric information. Some of these files are discussed in Chapter 16, but there are other files which specialize in numeric data and the major files are given in Table 10.5. Extensive information on searching for numeric property data is available from a special booklet, *Online with Numeric Files User Guide* (CGA1). There are many issues involved with numeric searching (for example, units, ranges and tolerances) and it is essential that this booklet be consulted before numeric searches are undertaken. Some other aspects of searching in numeric fields are given in Sections 4.3.4 and 16.5.1c.

There are two formats for searches based on numeric properties:

Format 1   S <NUMERIC TERM> / FIELD CODE
                     (example: S 1994/PY)
Format 2   S <FIELD CODE> <NUMERIC OPERATOR> <VALUE>
                     (example: S PY=1994)

and the choice depends on which is the easier option for the question at hand (for example, see Table 4.2).

The easiest way to determine which files might have the numeric property information of interest on STN is to enter the NUMERIGUIDE File, which is a data directory and property file that indicates the numeric properties available in each numeric file on the system. For example, if information on the critical temperature of a material is required, the NUMERIGUIDE File first is checked to determine which files might be relevant (Screen 10.15).

Table 10.5 Some files which have numeric property information

FILE	TYPE OF INFORMATION
AAASD	mechanical and physical property information for commercially available alloys
ALFRAC	aluminium fracture toughness data for 32 aluminium alloys
ASMDATA	property information for engineering materials
BEILSTEIN	all chemical and physical properties for organic substances
COPPERDATA	mechanical and physical property information for copper alloys
CYRSTMET	structural crystallographic information on metals and intermetallic compounds
DETHERM	property data on inorganic and organic substances
DIPPR	property data for commercially important chemical substances
GMELIN	property data for inorganic and organometallic substances
HODOC	property data for common organic substances
HSDB	property data for hazardous substances
IPS	property data for commercial plastics
JANAF	thermochemical data for inorganic substances or substances containing <3 carbons
MDF	property information on nearly all ferrous and nonferrous alloys
METALCREEP	data on creep and rupture stress of Al and Mg alloys and steels
MRCK	property data on important chemicals and drugs
NEWCRYST	crystal structure data of inorganic and organic compounds
NISTCERAM	thermal and mechanical property data for ceramics
NISTTHERMO	thermochemical data for important inorganic and organic substances
PDLCOM	chemical and environmental compatibility of plastics
PLASPEC	property data on plastics
RETCS	factual toxicity data
TRCTHERMO	thermodynamic property data

Screen 10.15[a] Finding which files have property information

=> **FIL NUMERIGUIDE**

This File contains information on all of the numeric properties available in each numeric file on STN, including: appropriate terminology for each property, property definition, files where the property may be searched, and default units for the property in each file.

=> **E CRITICAL TEMPERATURE/PH 5**

E#	FREQUENCY	AT	TERM
--	---------	-------------	---
E1	1	8	CRITICAL SOLUTION TEMPERATURE/PH
E2	1	0	CRITICAL STRESS INTENSITY FACTOR/PH
E3	1	15 -->	CRITICAL TEMPERATURE/PH
E4	1	17	CRITICAL VOLUME/PH
E5	1	0	CRITICAL WAVELENGTH/PH

=> **S E3**

L1   1 "CRITICAL TEMPERATURE"/PH

=> **D**

AN 5013 NUMERIGUIDE

PPN critical temperature

FQ --

FQ	FQ Type S=search D=display	Default Search Unit(*)	File
CRT	S,D	C	BEILSTEIN, GMELIN
CRT	S,D	K	DIPPR, TRCTHERMO
CRT			CHEMSAFE, DETHERM

(*) Original file units. For more information use the HELP UNITS message in the specific file. NTE CHEMSAFE and DETHERM - CRT searchable only in /PROP field.

[a]Copyright by the American Chemical Society and Reprinted with Permission

The expansion on a property name is performed in the Property Hierarchy Field (PH), and, from the display given, it is immediately apparent that the File features a thesaurus (for example, through entries FREQUENCY and AT!). If the original term entered is not posted, then other possible terms are expanded and soon the requisite entry is found. In this case "Critical Temperature" is listed and there are 15 associated terms, which could be investigated by the usual explosion of a thesaurus (see Section 7.1.3).

After the property is searched, the answer is displayed and the search and display field code, search units, and files are listed. Special comments are given, for example in this case the CHEMSAFE and DETHERM Files list critical temperature as a property, and if information concerning critical temperature in these files is required the search term AND CRT/PROP should be added to the search query. The procedure then is to enter the file(s) of interest and to search the property, or specific property values, as needed.

10.6 Costs and saving money

Online searching does cost money, but, as mentioned in the Preface, because of the way online searching has developed in a number of institutions the end-user often has an unrealistic view of the costs compared with those of the print materials. Further, it is the value of the information which is of greatest importance.

Finding information is very much an immediate problem for the scientist. Whether working in the laboratory, in the office, or in the field there will come a need to find out about what others have done. To search almost instantaneously in the world's scientific literature, and to come up with that vital answer has to be the most valuable result possible. The host organization might have a very large print collection, but unless the key information may be found there quickly, then what immediate value is that large print collection for the particular problem at hand?

However, don't go destroying the library! The print materials are the first link in the chain and without them there would be no literature to search, particularly up until recently when no electronic versions of full text journals were available. The print collection in the library, and the online networks, are complementary; they both are very valuable and together make an excellent resource for the scientist.

The costs of online searching involve the purchase and maintenance of the hardware, the cost of the telecommunication connections, and of the interaction with the database. By far the biggest ongoing cost is the last, so it is vital to know how the costs operate and how to minimise them.

Unfortunately, the database costs change, and vendors are constantly negotiating with the database producers on pricing policies. (Some database producers prefer the traditional subscription based pricing since they may estimate their likely budget and plan accordingly. However, there are problems for the vendor, particularly if users start down-loading large sections of the material.) So, as with so many other issues in online searching, this text can only outline the principles and make suggestions on how to operate in general situations.

The first rule is to know the costs involved, and to know exactly what they mean! Vendors publish price lists annually, but they are subject to change and the latest information always is available online. For example, once the file has been entered the HELP COST option lists the costs and Screen 10.16 shows an example (for the CJACS File).

Screen 10.16[a] Finding costs online (CJACS File)

=> **HELP COST**
STN International Fees and Prices Effective January 1, 1995.
CJACS file   U.S. Dollars

Connect Hour Fee (per hour)   29.00

Display Fees (per answer)		Print Fees (per answer)	
BIB	0.50	BIB	0.65
TX	1.00	ALL	3.75
AB	0.50	AB	0.65
Other fields (each)	0.25	TX	1.50
ALL	2.60	Other fields (each) . . .	0.40
KWIC, HIT	0.30	KWIC, HIT	0.45
OCC	FREE	OCC	FREE
PAGE.ALL	15.00	PAGE.ALL	17.00
PAGE.FIRST	3.00	PAGE.FIRST	4.00
PAGE.CONT.	12.00	PAGE.CONT.	13.00

Print Fax Surcharge
(additional per document)   3.00

Download Fees (per answer)
   PAGE.ALL 15.00
   PAGE.FIRST 3.00
   PAGE.CONT. 12.00

SDI Search Fee. 5.00
SDI FREQUENCY:BIWEEKLY

---

[a]Copyright by the American Chemical Society and Reprinted with Permission

The first points to note are the connect hour fees, whether there are search term fees, and the display costs.

10.6.1 Connect hour fees

Clearly the higher the connect hour fees, the more important it is to have the searches well planned beforehand, but some prior planning of searches always is advisable in any case!

The STN network has led the industry in the policy of low connect hour fees along with the (somewhat compensating) introduction of search term fees, since it felt that the time alone in which the searcher was connected should not be such a dominating cost factor. However, it does offer through a few files (currently through the HCA, HCAplus, HCAPreviews, HCHEMLIST, and HCIN Files) the option of either a file which has low connect hour fees and search term pricing, or a file which has higher connect hour fees and no search term pricing. The choice of files here depends on the types of searches to be performed. Simple arithmetic indicates the number of search terms per hour which would need to be performed to make one option cheaper over the other. However, it should be noted that once an option has been chosen, it may be changed at any time simply by entering the alternative file. Nevertheless, searchers should not become too preoccupied with costs since it might distract from the attention needed to perform the most efficient searches.

10.6.2   Search term fees

Files which have search term fees have lower connect hour fees, and with lower connect hour fees the searcher need not feel so pressed to complete the session. While this is a considerable advantage, the main disadvantage of search term fees is that at times a number of search terms must be used to allow for synonymous terms, some of which may be necessary because of the nature of the database.

It is important to understand what is meant by a search term, and to plan to minimise them accordingly. A search term is an individual word in the search query, or an individual E-number. For example, if a search: => S E1-E10 (see Screen 4.1) is conducted, 10 E-numbers are searched and 10 search term fees are charged. However, a search: => S **ANTICHOLEST?** contains only one word in the search query, and only one search term fee is charged even though many individual words in fact are searched. Accordingly there are considerable cost savings in the use of truncation symbols as a number of different terms are searched but only a single search term fee is incurred.

Particularly when search term fees are applied, it is important to check postings with the EXPAND command before searches are conducted. This enables the user to assess the most appropriate search terms, or to identify preferred levels of truncation, without incurring search fees.

Note that L-number answer sets are not counted as search terms. So there is no cost difference for the different ways in which the searches are conducted in Section 6.8. Search term fees apply, however to L-number queries, for example structure queries in structure-searchable files, or L-numbers when used as queries in file crossover situations (into files with search term pricing).

Structure search queries in structure-searchable files may incur fees at two levels: search fees and search terms. For example, there is a search fee for a full structure search in the REGISTRY File, and an additional search term fee (for each L-number structure query in the search statement). That is, if two structure queries L1 and L2 are searched: => **S SSS FUL L1 or L2** there is one search fee and two search term fees. Essentially all single structure search problems may be constructed with a single search query, and if the user is unable to achieve this the STN Service Center should be consulted. It must be noted that SAMPLE structure searches are free and every effort should be made, through SAMPLE searches, to ensure the best search query has been constructed before a full search is conducted, and all these options are discussed in Chapters 14 and 15.

It should be noted that when search term fees apply, CAS Registry Numbers count as search terms, except when L-number crossovers from the REGISTRY File are used. For this reason alone it is highly recommended that answer sets for substances be obtained first in the REGISTRY File, but other reasons include the important use of the LC Field entries for assisting with the determination of the appropriate files in which to find information on the substances, and the fact that when answer sets from the REGISTRY File are involved then the current CAS Registry Number and all deleted CAS Registry Numbers are crossed over.

> **Important ways to minimise search term fees are:**
> • **check on postings first with the EXPAND command;**
> • **use truncation where possible; and**
> • **use CAS Registry Numbers from REGISTRY File answer sets.**

There is a search fee for current awareness searches, but this procedure is a very cost efficient way to keep up to date. The costs associated with regular entry into the file(s), both with respect to database costs and the costs associated with the time taken by the searcher, are much greater than the cost of the current awareness search.

It should also be noted that some files have a small charge associated with select fees, and that there is a single cost associated with the SmartSELECT feature. However, in this latter case, even though many hundreds of terms might subsequently be searched, no search term fees apply.

10.6.3 *Display costs*

Display costs vary considerably with the display formats. While there is a tendency to use cheap display formats (for example, those which do not include abstract or index entries) and then to retrieve the original document, there may be false economies in this approach. It is possible that a more complete display will better identify whether the article is really needed, or indeed a more complete display may give all the information required. The greatest costs in most organizations are those relating to salaries and it may be a very expensive exercise in personnel time in tracing the original documents!

As mentioned throughout this text, extensive use should be made, particularly during the preparation of the search query, of the free D SCAN or the inexpensive D TRIAL formats. Even when the final answer sets have been obtained, sometimes these displays still are used during the process in which unwanted answers are removed.

10.6.4 *Learning files*

Attention is drawn to the learning files on STN which currently include: LBEILSTEIN, LBIBLIO, LCA, LCASREACT, LCJO, LDRUG, LEMBASE, LMARPAT, LMEDLINE, LREGISTRY, and LWPI. The only charges associated with these files are telecommunications and connect hour fees, and the latter are considerably cheaper than the connect hour fees for the full versions of the files. All of the features of the full files may be implemented in these learning files which are subsets of the full files.

Of course, the most cost-effective use of all databases can come only through knowledge of their content, and knowledge of the search mechanics. The better the searcher understands the databases and the tools and techniques to search them, the better and more cost efficient will be the search results!

Summary

- Systems have a number of *commands* and all vendors provide comprehensive manuals which detail command options and applications.
- On STN the HELP command may be used to learn about many aspects of the databases, and on file-specific implementations. Such information also is available particularly through the Database Summary Sheets and Database Catalogues.
- There are many applications of the FILE and the INDEX commands, and the latter is used almost exclusively to identify potential files of interest. When used with the names of clusters, a number of files in a discipline area may be searched at very low cost, and then the individual files of interest may be entered.
- The SELECT command and the SmartSELECT feature are particularly valuable for extracting parts of records, and to use the extracted items as search terms in other fields or files. The SmartSELECT feature additionally allows information to be tabulated.

- In bibliographic databases, a particularly useful way to identify Index Headings is to perform an initial casual search and then to use the SmartSELECT feature to first extract, and then to tabulate the Headings. Tabulation may be presented in a number of ways and the usual forms involve tabulation by frequency of documents, or in alphabetical order.
- Complete names of substances may be selected from REGISTRY File records with the SELECT CHEM option. The selected names may then be searched easily in those databases which do not have CAS Registry Numbers.
- Current awareness searches should always be set up for the primary areas of interest. This is achieved on STN using the SDI command.
- The SCISEARCH File is particularly valuable for locating citations to articles. A limitation is that only first named authors are listed in the RE Field, but the SmartSELECT feature may be used to extract out search terms from other bibliographic databases.
- Numeric searches may be performed using one of two formats. A number of numeric operators are available and the operators are used to connect values with fields.
- The NUMERIGUIDE File is used to identify which databases have the numeric values of interest.
- There are many ways in which online costs may be minimised, but the first rules are to know what the costs are for the databases being searched, and to know what the various costs really mean!

Part 2

Focus on Substances

11

Chemical Substances:
Structure and Indexing

In this chapter we learn:

- *The most general approach to finding information on substances involves first finding the record for the substance in the REGISTRY File!*
- *Some basic chemical concepts relating to substances and their structures.*
- *How various classes of substances are indexed in the REGISTRY File.*
- *Some important points relating to multicomponent substances.*
- *The different approaches to searching for substances.*

11.1 The variety of substances

One of the most challenging tasks in online searching is to find the correct search terms for chemical substances!

Chemical substances have almost infinite variety. Not only can the 92 different naturally occurring atoms connect to each other in numerous ways to form single substances, but also these substances can combine to form complex and bigger substances like polymers, or salts, or mixtures, and each of these constitutes a new substance with its own special properties.

On average, about 10,000 new chemical substances are reported each week in the world's scientific literature, so chemical substance databases increase by around one half a million entries per year. This rate has been relatively constant since the early 1960s when the world's first and largest electronic chemical substance database, the CAS Registry Database, was commenced. The file now contains around 14 million substances.

Each chemical substance has an unique name and this constitutes one form of communication between chemists. There are, however, two main problems with names.

First, names can be very hard to determine, and to describe a substance fully and systematically using text terms (names) can be a very difficult process. A single name may take several lines of text. Although there are rules for naming substances these rules are a study in themselves and understood completely by relatively few.

So why aren't substances given simple names? Actually many are, but the problem here is that simple names do not convey any structural information, so the reader needs to know what the actual substance is in order to understand the science being reported. As these names do not describe the structures, this leads to the second main problem, that is, that a single substance is often described by more than one name. There are many reasons for this and one is that naming systems change in time. What appeared a reasonable name at the time of discovery might not be the most appropriate name years later when the science has developed further.

Each chemical substance has an unique identity and this is mainly described by its chemical structure, which is a picture of the way in which the atoms are connected together in the substance. Most substances have clearly defined structures and often it is easiest for chemists to communicate using structure diagrams.

However, not all substances have a clearly defined structure or known composition, although their source may be well defined. For example, while olive oil and tea-tree oil are actually very complex mixtures of numerous individual substances and have not been fully characterized, their source is well known. Such cases are registered as "substances" in the database, even though they are not single substances in the strict chemical sense.

If the arrangement of the atoms (the structure) is known then the numbers of atoms in the substance is necessarily known, so all substances which have a known structure also have a definite molecular formula. However, a molecular formula is not an unique identifier of a substance since many different substances have the same molecular formula.

In summary, substances are identified by their names, structures, and molecular formulas and nearly all seaches for substances are based on these identifiers.

11.2 Finding information on substances

Almost invariably, it is not the substance alone which is required but instead *information* on the substance, and to find this it is usually necessary to search first for the substance in a substance based file. Nearly all such files also have text or property information which can then be displayed as required.

Some substance based files on STN are listed in Table 11.1 together with a summary of the type of information on the substances they contain.

Substances can be found in a number of ways. Usually searches are based on names, formulas, or structures but sometimes substances with certain properties (for example, specific boiling points) are required, and properties may be used as search terms to find these substances. A summary of the search fields which may be used to identify substances is given in Table 11.2. Even though, as seen in Table 11.2, the CAS REGISTRY File does not contain information on substances, as a general rule it is where the searcher goes first if anything related to chemical substances is sought. There are three main reasons for this.

Table 11.1 Major substance based files on STN and the types of information they contain[a]

FILE	NUMBER OF SUBSTANCES	TYPE OF INFORMATION
BEILSTEIN	6.6 million	chemical and physical property information for organic substances
CHEMCATS	350,000	commercially available substances and their suppliers
CHEMLIST	170,000	EPA TSCA substances[b] and other regulatory information
CSCHEM	130,000	commercial chemicals and their suppliers
DRUGU	28,000	Registry segment contains information on drugs
GMELIN	700,000	chemical and physical property information for inorganic and organometallic substances
HODOC	26,000	chemical and physical data for the most common organic substances (CRC Handbook Data)
HSDB	4,500	toxicology and environmental effects of chemicals
MARPAT[c]		Markush structures (representing several million prophetic substances)
MRCK	10,000	drug descriptions
MSDS-CCOHS	96,000	Materials Safety Data Sheets
PHAR	17,000	information on pharmaceutical products
REGISTRY	14 million	CAS Registry Numbers; citations to files which have information on the substance
RTECS	120,000	factual toxicity data
SPECINFO	100,000	IR, ^{13}C NMR, and mass spectra

[a]Excludes files which have numeric property information only (See Section 10.5), or which are based on chemical reactions (see Chapter 17)
[b]EPA= Environmental Protection Agency; TSCA = Toxic Substances and Chemicals Act
[c]The MARPAT File actually is a bibliographic file but it contains unique chemical substances (Markush structures)

Table 11.2 Substance search fields

FILE	NAME AND NAME SEGMENTS	MF AND MF SEGMENTS	STRUCTURE	PROPERTY INFORM-ATION	CAS REGISTRY NUMBERS
BEILSTEIN	YES	YES	YES	YES	YES
CHEMLIST	YES	NO	NO	YES	YES
CSCHEM	YES	NO	NO	YES	YES
GMELIN	YES	YES	YES	YES	YES
HODOC	YES	YES	NO	YES	YES
HSDB	YES	YES	NO	YES	YES
MARPAT	NO	NO	YES	NO	YES
MSDS	YES	YES	NO	YES	YES
REGISTRY	YES	YES	YES	NO[a]	YES
RTECS	YES	YES	NO	YES	YES
SPECINFO	YES	YES	NO	YES	YES

(Note: Entry YES means that the fields are present and searchable, but not all substances in the file may have information in the fields)
[a]However, the REGISTRY File contains a Locator Field (LC) that flags which files have information on the substance

1. The REGISTRY File is the largest and most comprehensive database of substances. It contains records for all substances reported since 1957 and thus covers the vast majority of substances of current interest.

2. The REGISTRY File contains entries in the name based fields for all substances, including all registered synonyms. It is thus the most comprehensive source of names of substances.

3. The REGISTRY File is *the authoritative source* of CAS Registry Numbers, which are the most widely used identifiers of chemical substances not only in other substance based files (see Table 11.2) and in many bibliographic and numeric databases, but also by government regulatory authorities. As CAS Registry Numbers are readily found in the REGISTRY File, and as they are unique identifiers for each substance, they are often preferred search terms for substances.

A record in the REGISTRY File (see, for example, Screen 7.7) contains in the Locator Field a list of files in which the CAS Registry Number for the substance of interest is present, so effectively it is an index for substances which contain CAS Registry Numbers in other files.

> **Accordingly, the general strategy recommended for searching for information on substances is to:**
> *   **find the substance in the REGISTRY File;**
> *   **check the Locator Field (LC) to see the list of files in which the CAS Registry Number is reported;**
> *   **enter those files which have the type of information required; and**
> *   **search for the substance record by CAS Registry Number and display the information.**

While this strategy works in the overwhelming number of cases, there are four main instances where alternative steps may need to be taken.

1. *When specific substances of interest are not found in the REGISTRY File.*
    In these cases it is necessary to check the BEILSTEIN and the GMELIN Files because the substances may have been reported only prior to 1957, or may be some of the few substances reported since then that are not indexed in the REGISTRY File.
2. *When "prophetic" (Markush) structures from patents are of interest.*
    In these cases it is necessary to check either the MARPAT File which contains Markush structures since 1988, or the structure search files produced by Derwent.
3. *When files which contain information of interest do not list CAS Registry Numbers.*
    In these cases it is necessary to search on substance names in the relevant file(s) (see Section 10.2).
4. *When a generic class of substance is of interest.*
    For example many classes of substances are given general index headings like lipoproteins (Screen 7.6) and in this case text based search terms may need to be used.

In the event, the additional actions which need to be taken can mostly be addressed through links with the REGISTRY File. For example, to check in the BEILSTEIN, GMELIN and MARPAT Files probably requires a structure search query which may have been built already in the REGISTRY File. (The same structure search queries can be used in all the files, although there are some very minor differences in the registration of the bonding in some substances, for example in azides and acid salts.) Additionally, all registered names for the substance are listed in the REGISTRY File, so if a name search is required, the names in the REGISTRY File can be selected and used as search terms in the alternative file (Section 10.2).

When the CAS REGISTRY File was commenced, many policy decisions relating to how all these great variety of substances were to be entered were taken, and the main ones are discussed in this chapter.

However, before describing the policies concerning input of substances in the REGISTRY File, it is necessary to point out an even more far-reaching policy which was taken namely that substances be indexed in bibliographic files as CAS Registry Numbers. Accordingly information on substances in bibliographic files produced by the Chemical Abstracts Service should be searched using CAS Registry Numbers. This numbering system has become increasingly used not only in bibliographic databases built by other organizations, but also by government agencies around the world as the latter develop regulations for the use, manufacture, disposal, and sale of chemical substances.

An unique CAS Registry Number is given to each substance in the REGISTRY File and is a series of numbers with hyphens before the third last, and again before the last, number. Algorithms determine the last number so that there is an internal referencing feature which helps detect incorrect numbers.[*] It is to be noted that CAS Registry Numbers do not have any chemical significance; they are assigned to substances simply in chronological order of registration.

Before proceeding, a comment is needed here for those searchers who do not have specialist training in chemistry. For if chemists themselves have difficulties understanding and representing the complexities of substances, then how much greater are the problems faced by searchers to whom the concepts are unfamiliar?

Accordingly, this chapter describes both the chemical concept involved and the indexing policies. Hopefully even the searcher with little background in chemistry can thereby understand the indexing policies while at the same time learn about the related concepts. (While online searchers don't have to understand what is being searched, it certainly helps!) On the other hand, while chemists may pass over the descriptions of the chemical concepts, they should take particular note how the various classes of substances are indexed. Even though substances are precise entities, there are numerous issues relating to their indexing and unless these are understood then searches will not give the results required or expected.

11.3 A brief description of some basic chemical concepts

The concept of chemical structure is tied to one of the basic concepts of chemistry, that is, that substances are made from combinations of a few building materials. There really is no mystery involving chemical substances - just complexity!

Just a few small bits keep combining together, in a great variety of ways, to produce the vast numbers of substances. The smallest bits are called electrons, protons, and neutrons and together these make up the atoms. In turn, atoms join together to make molecules (which also are called substances). Everything in this world is made from chemical substances!

---

[*]The algorithm is published in the *Registry Handbook* available from CAS.

11.3.1   Atoms, elements and the Periodic Table

There are 92 different elements[*] which occur naturally and some of the more familiar elements and their symbols are:

hydrogen	H	carbon	C	nitrogen	N	oxygen	O
chlorine	Cl	sodium	Na	potassium	K	calcium	Ca
phosphorus	P	iron	Fe	lead	Pb	tin	Sn
gold	Au	silver	Ag	uranium	U		

Symbols are merely a short-hand way of writing the elements. There are 92 elements but only 26 different letters in the alphabet so many elements have two-letter symbols and these are often derived from the Latin name for the element.

All elements consist of the same smaller particles called electrons, protons and neutrons and it is just that the different elements have different numbers of these same small particles. Indeed an atom is like a solar system with a big central sun and smaller planets revolving around the sun. The "planets" in atoms are the electrons and they are negatively charged. In the "sun" (called the nucleus) in atoms there are two types of particles namely protons which are positively charged, and neutrons which have no charge.

Each different atom has a different number of electrons (which, for a single atom, always equals the number of protons in the nucleus). Hydrogen (the smallest atom) has one electron while uranium (the largest naturally occurring atom) has 92 electrons. The other 90 atoms all fit in between, one following the other. It transpires that while all the atoms ultimately have different properties, many behave similarly. For example, sodium (atomic number 11) has similar properties to potassium (atomic number 19) and to rubidium (atomic number 37). Chemists group atoms with similar properties together in a table, called the Periodic Table (see Appendix 2) and similarities occur in the rows across the Table and in the vertical columns. The Periodic Table is simply an arrangement of the atoms in such a way that those with like behavior are grouped together.

11.3.2   Chemical substances

When elements combine (react) together they form new substances. Some of the more familiar substances are:

SUBSTANCE	ELEMENTS FORMING THE SUBSTANCE
water	hydrogen and oxygen
glucose	carbon, hydrogen and oxygen
table salt	sodium and chlorine
penicillin	carbon, hydrogen, nitrogen, oxygen and sulfur

A single chemical substance[#] contains a fixed number of atoms, held together in an unique and constant way. For example, water contains two hydrogen atoms and one oxygen atom. The symbol (called the molecular formula) for water thus is H_2O. The molecular formula for glucose is $C_6H_{12}O_6$, since it is found to contain six carbons, twelve hydrogens, and six oxygen atoms. The atoms are said to be held together in molecules by bonds.

---

[*]The terms elements or atoms essentially are synonyms. Certainly the online searcher does not need to differentiate between them.

[#]The terms chemical substance, molecule and compound also essentially are synonyms.

11.3.3 How atoms are connected in molecules: the two main types of bonds

The bonds between atoms in molecules can be of two basic kinds: covalent and ionic. In what is called a covalent bond there are two electrons which are shared between the atoms. In an ionic bond one atom is positively charged and one atom is negatively charged and the attractive forces between the charges hold the atoms together in the bond. Atoms which have charges are said to be ionic, and the combinations of ions are called salts.

Some atoms like potassium and sodium readily form positively charged ions; other atoms like chlorine and bromine readily form negatively charged ions. The common salt used in foods is sodium chloride (molecular formula $NaCl$) - a combination of positively charged sodium and negatively charged chloride ions.

Other atoms like carbon, hydrogen, nitrogen and oxygen preferably form covalent bonds with other atoms. Indeed carbon is a particularly unusual atom in that it forms molecules in which almost any number of carbon atoms may be linked together, and in a great variety of rings and chains. Carbon also forms strong covalent bonds with most other atoms, particularly hydrogen, nitrogen, sulfur and oxygen. Because of these special properties, the vast majority of substances contain carbon.

For the purposes of searching for substances in computer files it is very important to know from the outset that the registrations of substances with ionic bonds are subject to a number of rules which may, or may not, correspond exactly with the normal chemical representation. In short, most, but not all, ionic substances are treated as multicomponent substances and the individual components may be a little different from those the chemist would anticipate (see Section 11.4.10).

11.3.4 Valence Bond structures

There actually are a few different ways in which chemists visualize substances. The most common way involves linking atoms together by lines (which represent the bonds) and this representation is known as the Valence Bond structure. It turns out that a single atom cannot have an endless number of atoms attached to it through bonds, and indeed that individual atoms have a very precise number of bonds. There can be some variations for a single atom, but mostly each atom has its "favoured" number of bonded attachments. The number of bonds relates to what is known as its "valency"[*] and the most common valencies of some of the more common atoms are given in Figure 11.1. All that needs to be understood is that, for example, carbon virtually always has a valency of four, that is four bonds.

Valency = 1
hydrogen   fluorine   chlorine   bromine   iodine
Valency = 2
oxygen   sulfur
Valency = 3
boron   nitrogen   phosphorus
Valency = 4
carbon   silicon

Figure 11.1 The usual valencies of some common atoms

---

[*]There are numerous terms used in describing substances and the non-expert chemist, who performs searches on substances, need not be concerned with the details of most of them. For example, all the searcher needs to know about valency is that it relates to the number of bonds on an atom.

The chemist uses a number of conventions in drawing the valence bond structures of substances including:

- the carbon framework is shown by lines, with carbon atoms either assumed or drawn at each bend or end;
- sometimes it is important to give some three-dimensional representation in which case heavy lines and dotted lines are used to indicate connections above and below a plane or ring respectively;
- double bonds and triple bonds (that is, bonds in which there are 4 and 6 electrons respectively shared between the atoms) are represented by two and three lines respectively;
- non-carbon and non-hydrogen atoms are always represented in the structure by their chemical symbols (N, O, S etc.); and
- generally hydrogen atoms are not drawn, it being assumed that hydrogens occupy all remaining (non-specified) positions in the molecule to complete the normal valency requirements.

For example, the valence bond structure, as the chemist most commonly draws it, of one of the original penicillin molecules is shown in Figure 11.2 together with a structure which indicates where all the atoms and bonds are. Even with such a simple substance it can be seen why a short-hand convention for carbons and hydrogens is used!

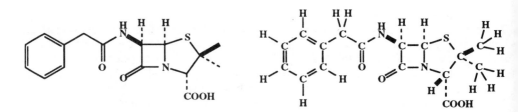

Figure 11.2   Valence bond structures for penicillin G

11.3.5   Areas of chemistry
Traditionally chemistry has been broken up into three general areas, although today the areas overlap extensively. The special branch of chemistry which studies the chemistry of carbon-containing substances is called organic chemistry. Study of the chemistry of non-carbon-containing substances is called inorganic chemistry, while study of the properties of substances is called physical chemistry.

However, chemical substances are studied in most areas of science. For example, biochemistry is the study of the substances which commonly occur in biology, while pharmacology is the study of the effect of chemicals (particularly medicinal substances) on living systems.

Of the major substance based files the REGISTRY File covers all areas of chemistry, while the BEILSTEIN and GMELIN Files cover organic and inorganic substances respectively.

11.3.6 Functional groups

It turns out that bonds between two carbon atoms, and bonds between a carbon and a hydrogen atom, are quite strong. That is, these bonds are not easily broken and this means carbon/carbon and carbon/hydrogen bonds undergo relatively few chemical reactions. Indeed chemical reactions in organic substances most commonly occur at bonds connecting the other atoms present. These other atoms can be present in certain arrangements called groups. As chemical reactions occur with these groups they are called functional groups, that is, they function - they react.

For example, acetic acid (vinegar) is formed from the oxidation of alcohol (present in wines). The spoiling of wines involves the chemical conversion of alcohol to acetic acid (Scheme 1).

Scheme 1

The part of the alcohol which functions (reacts) in this conversion is called the alcohol functional group, while the new group formed in acetic acid is called the acid group (also called the carboxylic acid group). Note that in this reaction nothing happens to the CH_3 group or the bond connecting it with the second carbon atom and accordingly this group is not considered part of the functional group. The concept of functional groups is important not only in chemical reactions, but also in the naming of chemical substances (see Chapter 12).

11.4 Indexing of substances in the REGISTRY File

There are a number of different classes of substances defined in the REGISTRY File, and they differ mostly by how the atoms are bonded together.

11.4.1 Single substances

The most common class is that of the single substances, and a typical record for a single substance is shown in Screen 11.1. It should be noted from the outset that a typical record in the REGISTRY File has seven basic sections:

-   the CAS Registry Number;
-   nomenclature fields (CN);
-   molecular formula field (MF);
-   fields which classify the substance (Class Identifier, CI, and File Segment, FS);
-   a field which indicates files which have information on the substance (Locator Field, LC);
-   the structure of the substance; and
-   the number of records in other CAS files in which the substance is reported.

Screen 11.1[a]   Record for a single substance

RN 53-06-5 REGISTRY
CN Pregn-4-ene-3,11,20-trione, 17,21-dihydroxy- (7CI, 9CI) (CA INDEX NAME)
OTHER CA INDEX NAMES:
CN Cortisone (8CI)
OTHER NAMES:
CN 11-Dehydro-17-hydroxycorticosterone
CN 17-Hydroxy-11-dehydrocorticosterone
CN 17.alpha.-Hydroxy-11-dehydrocorticosterone

CN	Adrenalex	CN	Compound E
CN	Cortisate	CN	Cortivite
CN	Cortogen	CN	Cortone
CN	KE	CN	Kendall's compound E
CN	Reichstein's substance Fa	CN	Wintersteiner's compound F

FS STEREOSEARCH
MF C21 H28 O5
CI COM
LC STN Files: ANABSTR, BEILSTEIN*, BIOBUSINESS, BIOSIS, CA, CABA, CANCERLIT,
   CAOLD, CAPLUS, CASREACT, CEN, CHEMCATS, CHEMLIST, CBNB, CIN, CJACS,
   CSCHEM, CSNB, DDFU, DRUGU, EMBASE, HODOC*, IFICDB, IFIPAT, IFIUDB, IPA,
   MEDLINE, MRCK*, MSDS-OHS, MSDS-SUM, NAPRALERT, PNI, PROMT, RTECS*,
   TOXLINE, TOXLIT, USAN, USPATFULL, VETU
     (*File contains numerically searchable property data)
  Other Sources: EINECS**, WHO
    (**Enter CHEMLIST File for up-to-date regulatory information) DES 4:.PREGN
Absolute stereochemistry.

1	REFERENCES IN FILE CAPREVIEWS
3001	REFERENCES IN FILE CA (1967 TO DATE)
44	REFERENCES TO NON-SPECIFIC DERIVATIVES IN FILE CA
3003	REFERENCES IN FILE CAPLUS (1967 TO DATE)
2	REFERENCES IN FILE CAOLD (PRIOR TO 1967)

[a]Copyright by the American Chemical Society and Reprinted with Permission

There are other parts of the record, for example those which include ring structure data and which include up to the 10 most recent CAplus File references, but these are needed in special cases only and are not shown here.

Notes (Screen 11.1):

- the CA systematic name is given in the first CN Field, together with the Collective Index (CI) in which this systematic name is used (a Collective Index covers 10 volumes of *Chemical Abstracts* and the "9CI" covers Volumes 76 to 85, years 1972 to 1976);

- other registered names appear in separate CN Field repetitions;
- the molecular formula, $C_{21}H_{28}O_5$, is given in the Molecular Formula (MF) Field;
- not surprisingly, information on cortisone, which is a very important substance occurring naturally in animals, is recorded in many files (indicated in the LC Field);
- cortisone has 6 stereocentres (see Section 11.4.12b) and each of these must be described: in the structure drawing the bold and dotted lines indicate the stereochemistry in the structure, while the letters R and S are name based descriptors (in this case the descriptors appear only in the structure diagram, although they commonly occur also in the CN Fields);
- the final section in the record indicates the number of records in the CAS databases in which the CAS Registry Number appears; and
- non-specific derivatives are generic substances which relate to the substance identified by the Registry Number (for example, "cholesterol" in blood refers to a generic group of substances, related to cholesterol, CAS Registry Number 57-88-5).

11.4.2 Alloys

Some *elements* can combine together to form a new material which has properties different from either of the constituent elements. For example, when the metallic elements tin and copper are heated together and the mixture is allowed to cool, a new material, the familiar material called brass, is formed. Different *ratios* of tin and copper can combine and slightly different types of brass are formed. Further, it is found that adding other elements can also change the property of the brass formed. Such mixtures of elements are called alloys, and in alloys the atoms are not bonded together (by covalent or ionic bonds) in the way atoms are bonded together in molecules, but are connected together in a manner similar to that in which the atoms are connected, for example, in a copper wire. (The valence bond theory does not easily explain this form of bonding and another theory, the molecular orbital theory, is used but knowledge of this theory is not needed for the purposes of searching for substances in the REGISTRY File.)

In the REGISTRY File the constituent elements in alloys are arranged in order of decreasing percentage composition in the Index Name (see Screen 11.2).

Screen 11.2[a] Record for an alloy

```
RN       12646-06-9 REGISTRY
CN       Copper alloy, base, Cu 62,Zn 28,Sn 6,Si 4 (9CI)  (CA INDEX NAME)
OTHER NAMES:
CN       Brass LOK-62-06-04
CN       Copper 62, silicon 4, tin 6, zinc 28
MF       Cu  . Si  . Sn . Zn
CI       AYS
```

Component	Component Percent	Component Registry Number
Cu	62	7440-50-8
Zn	28	7440-66-6
Sn	6	7440-31-5
Si	4	7440-21-3
	1	REFERENCES IN FILE CA (1967 TO DATE)
	1	REFERENCES IN FILE CAPLUS (1967 TO DATE)

Notes (Screen 11.2):

- the amounts of the different elements are in name based fields, and in the table (these amounts are searchable in the field MAC, where it is possible to search for alloys with various compositions);
- the elements are arranged in alphabetical order in the Molecular Formula Field;
- in this Field a dot (period) separates the components, and whenever this occurs the substances are called multicomponent substances (see Section 11.6); and
- AYS, the abbreviation for alloy, appears in the Class Identifier Field.

11.4.3 Coordination compounds

In the early stages of the development of chemistry it was thought that organic substances and inorganic substances were unrelated in chemical terms. This was understandable since the two sets of substances behaved very differently. For example, organic substances (like petrol) did not dissolve in water, but inorganic substances (like salt) did. Additionally, most of the metals discovered (copper, calcium, iron, tin, etc.) did not form substances which contained carbon. So the two different branches of chemistry developed independently.

However, by the start of the 20th century it was realized that metals did form substances which contained carbon, and indeed many of the substances found in biological systems contained metals surrounded by carbon-containing substances (organic molecules). For example, haemoglobin found in blood contains a large number of carbon and hydrogen atoms (and lesser numbers of oxygens and nitrogens) arranged around the atom iron (Fe). Compounds which contain metals attached to organic molecules are called coordination compounds.

The representation of the structures of some coordination compounds requires modifications to the normal valence bond definitions. Generally the electrons involved in bonding the organic groups to the metal are provided by the organic groups, and in the language of the discipline there are two types of donors, σ-donors and π-donors, these being distinguished in broad terms in that the electrons in the former case come from atoms, while in the latter case they come from electrons in double bonds.

In the REGISTRY File there are a number of policies relating to the representation of coordination compounds. An example of a σ-donor complex is shown in Screen 11.3, while that of a π-donor complex is shown in Screen 11.4.

Screen 11.3[a] Record for a σ-donor complex

RN   104167-41-1   REGISTRY
CN   Nickel, dichlorotetrakis(1-naphthalenylthiourea-S)-, (OC-6-12)-
         (9CI) (CA INDEX NAME)
OTHER CA INDEX NAMES:
CN   Nickel, dichlorotetrakis[1-(1-naphthyl)-2-thiourea]- (7CI)
CN   Thiourea, 1-naphthalenyl-, nickel complex
OTHER NAMES:
CN   trans-Dichlorotetrakis(1-naphthyl-2-thiourea)nickel
MF   C44 H40 Cl2 N8 Ni S4
CI   CCS
SR   CA
LC   STN Files: CA, CAOLD, CAPLUS, GMELIN*
                     (*File contains numerically searchable property data)
DES   7:OC-6-12

Screen 11.3 (continued)

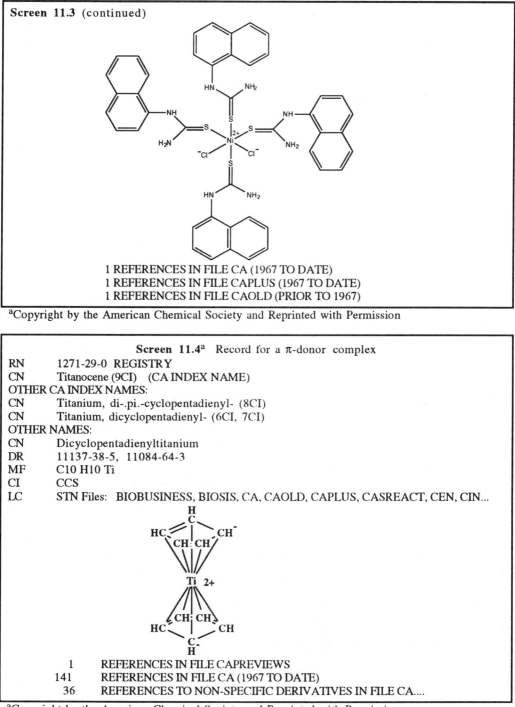

1 REFERENCES IN FILE CA (1967 TO DATE)
1 REFERENCES IN FILE CAPLUS (1967 TO DATE)
1 REFERENCES IN FILE CAOLD (PRIOR TO 1967)

Screen 11.4[a] Record for a π-donor complex

RN	1271-29-0 REGISTRY
CN	Titanocene (9CI) (CA INDEX NAME)

OTHER CA INDEX NAMES:

CN	Titanium, di-.pi.-cyclopentadienyl- (8CI)
CN	Titanium, dicyclopentadienyl- (6CI, 7CI)

OTHER NAMES:

CN	Dicyclopentadienyltitanium
DR	11137-38-5, 11084-64-3
MF	C10 H10 Ti
CI	CCS
LC	STN Files: BIOBUSINESS, BIOSIS, CA, CAOLD, CAPLUS, CASREACT, CEN, CIN...

1 REFERENCES IN FILE CAPREVIEWS
141 REFERENCES IN FILE CA (1967 TO DATE)
36 REFERENCES TO NON-SPECIFIC DERIVATIVES IN FILE CA....

Notes (Screens 11.3 and 11.4):

*   the charges on the atoms involved with bonding to the metal are the same as in the "free state", that is, they relate to the chemical substances which are used to prepare the registered substance (the thiourea attachment has no charge on the sulfur, the chloro attachments have a single negative charge and the nickel has a charge of +2);[*]
*   CCS, the abbreviation for coordination compounds, appears in the Class Identifier Field; and
*   the complex (Screen 11.4) is represented as the individual constituent molecules (it is prepared from titanium 2+ ions and the cyclopentadienyl ion $C_5H_5^-$) except that an additional "single bond" is placed between each of the atoms participating in the π-complex.

11.4.4 Incompletely defined substances

The determination of a structure of a new substance used to be a very difficult task. For example, cholesterol was discovered in 1813 and soon after it was shown to have 27 carbon, 46 hydrogen and 1 oxygen atoms. However, it took over 130 years for its complete structure (that is, the ways in which all the atoms are connected) to be determined.

Today, it would take only a couple of hours to determine the structure of cholesterol, using a variety of instrumental techniques including infrared spectroscopy (IR), ultraviolet spectroscopy (UV), mass spectrometry (MS), nuclear magnetic resonance spectroscopy (NMR) and X-ray crystallography. However, there is a great variety of such techniques for determining structures, and information on the use of these techniques is commonly sought in searches in bibliographic files.

Nevertheless there are substances for which the complete structure is unknown or undefined at least at the time of the report in the literature. For example, if a chemist reports a study on "bromophenol" then unless there is definite evidence elsewhere in the article, on which of the three substances which might be called "bromophenol" is actually being studied, the indexer can only report this work as being on a substance "bromophenol with undefined structure". So a new entry must be placed in the database.

In the REGISTRY File, incompletely defined substances are those which have a known molecular formula, but for which the complete valence bond structure is unknown because the precise attachment of all substituents is not known, because the positions of double bonds are not known, or because the reaction gave a substance of known formula but unknown structure.

An example of the registration of an incompletely defined substance is shown in Screen 11.5. Note that the problem here is that in the original document the substance was reported as a "chlorobenzoyl" substituted benzopyranone but the position of substitution of the chlorine in the benzoyl group was not specified (benzene rings, which are symmetrical and have 6 carbon atoms, can have two substituents in three orientations: on adjacent atoms, on atoms one removed, or on atoms across the ring; the substituents on the benzene ring in this example are the Cl and the C=O, the latter then being attached additionally to the benzopyranone). So the structure diagram is represented as fragments, with the attachments to the single 6-membered ring indicated with the symbols D1.

---

[*]The substance is made from mixing nickel 2+ ions, chloride 1- ions, and thiourea (which is a neutral substance).

Screen 11.5[a] Record for an incompletely defined substance

RN   141230-29-7 REGISTRY
CN   4H-1-Benzopyran-4-one, 6-chloro-3-(chlorobenzoyl)-2-(4-nitrophenyl)-
       (9CI) (CA INDEX NAME)
MF   C22 H11 Cl2 N O5
CI   IDS
SR   CA
LC   STN Files: CA, CAPLUS
DES   8:ID

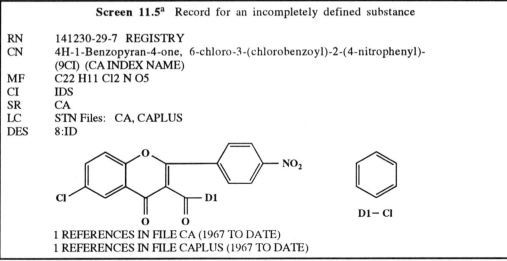

1 REFERENCES IN FILE CA (1967 TO DATE)
1 REFERENCES IN FILE CAPLUS (1967 TO DATE)

---

[a]Copyright by the American Chemical Society and Reprinted with Permission

11.4.5 Minerals

Minerals occur naturally in the Earth's crust and have a definite chemical composition, and usually, a characteristic crystalline form. Some minerals, like sapphire (Screen 11.6), are made from a single chemical substance (Al_2O_3, alumina) while others, like wodginite (Screen 11.6), are made from a mixture of substances (usually oxides of metals). In both of the cases below the atoms which make up the mineral are known, but how they are all assembled in the beautifully crystalline forms of the mineral are not known. (Actually the term "structure" has a variety of meanings to scientists ranging from the way in which the atoms are connected in bonds to the way the atoms are oriented in three-dimensional space, for example packed together in crystals or the actual ways chains curl around. However, the term structure is used in the REGISTRY File only in relation to valence bond representations.)

Screen 11.6[a] Records for minerals

Single chemical substance
RN   1317-82-4 REGISTRY
CN   Sapphire (Al2O3) (9CI) (CA INDEX NAME)
OTHER CA INDEX NAMES:
CN   Sapphire (8CI)
OTHER NAMES:
CN   Leucosapphire
MF   Al2 O3
CI   MNS, COM, MAN
LC   STN Files: BIOBUSINESS, BIOSIS, CA, CAPLUS, CAPREVIEWS, CHEMINFORMRX...
          20   REFERENCES IN FILE CAPREVIEWS
        5183   REFERENCES IN FILE CA (1967 TO DATE)
           1   REFERENCES TO NON-SPECIFIC DERIVATIVES IN FILE CA
        5203   REFERENCES IN FILE CAPLUS (1967 TO DATE)

Screen 11.6 (continued)
Complex oxides
RN   12178-62-0 REGISTRY
CN   Wodginite (Mn(Ta0.5-1Nb0-0.5)2(Sn0.5-1Ta0-0.4)O8) (9CI) (CA INDEX NAME)
OTHER CA INDEX NAMES:
CN   Wodginite (8CI)
MF   Mn . Nb. O . Sn . Ta
AF   Mn Nb0-1 O8 Sn0.5-1 Ta1-2.4
CI   MNS, TIS
LC   STN Files: BIOBUSINESS, CA, CAOLD, CAPLUS
DES 8:IN,MN,WODGINITE

Component		Ratio		Component Registry Number
O		8		17778-80-2
Sn		0.5 - 1		7440-31-5
Ta		1 - 2.4		7440-25-7
Nb		0 - 1		7440-03-1
Mn		1		7439-96-5

          48   REFERENCES IN FILE CA (1967 TO DATE)
          48   REFERENCES IN FILE CAPLUS (1967 TO DATE)
           1   REFERENCES IN FILE CAOLD (PRIOR TO 1967)

[a]Copyright by the American Chemical Society and Reprinted with Permission

     Note that when minerals have more than one component the ratio of the components (rather than the percentage) is presented. Also, MNS, the abbreviation for mineral, appears in the Class Identifier Field. The other abbreviations seen in the Field are COM (indicates substance is also a component in a multicomponent substance), MAN (indicates substance cannot be processed by the CAS Registry System to receive a structure connection table), and TIS (indicates a tabular inorganic substance which does not receive a structure connection table either because its structure is unknown, or it does not exist as a discrete molecule, or it has a three-dimensional lattice, or it has a fractional composition or range of composition).

11.4.6 Mixtures
There are many instances in which two or more chemically discrete components have been deliberately mixed together for a specific use. Commonly these are available commercially under a separate name (for the mixture).
     An example is the mixture known as augmentin (Screen 11.7). It has two components, one is a penicillin antibiotic and the other is a substance (called potassium clavulanate) which inactivates the defense mechanisms some bacteria have developed to overcome the penicillin class of antibiotics. This mixture is a prescribed pharmaceutical in which the presence of both components is important so it has a separate registration. (Indeed pharmaceuticals used today are often mixtures of substances).

Screen 11.7[a] Record for a mixture

RN   74469-00-4 REGISTRY
CN   4-Oxa-1-azabicyclo[3.2.0]heptane-2-carboxylic acid, 3-(2-hydroxyethylidene)-7-
      oxo-, monopotassium salt, [2R-(2.alpha.,3Z,5.alpha.)]-, mixt. with [2S
      [2.alpha.,5.alpha.,6.beta.(S*)]]-6-[[amino(4hydroxyphenyl)acetyl]amino]-3,3-
      dimethyl-7-oxo-4-thia-1azabicyclo[3.2.0]heptane-2-carboxylic acid (9CI) (CA
      INDEX NAME)
OTHER CA INDEX NAMES:
CN   4-Thia-1-azabicyclo[3.2.0]heptane-2-carboxylic acid,
      6-[[amino(4-hydroxyphenyl)acetyl]amino]-3,3-dimethyl-7-oxo-,
      [2S-[2.alpha.,5.alpha.,6.beta.(S*)]]-, mixt. contg. (9CI)
OTHER NAMES:
CN   Augmentin   CN   Augmentin (antibiotic)
CN   BRL 25000   CN   BRL 25000A   CN   BRL 25000G
FS   STEREOSEARCH
DR   74428-36-7
MF   C16 H19 N3 O5 S . C8 H9 N O5 . K
CI   MXS
LC   STN Files: AIDSLINE, BIOBUSINESS, BIOSIS, CA, CANCERLIT, CAPLUS, CBNB,
      CIN, EMBASE, MEDLINE, PHAR, PNI, PROMT, RTECS*, TOXLINE, TOXLIT
            (*File contains numerically searchable property data)

DES 8:MX
      CM 1   CRN 61177-45-5 (58001-44-8)   CMF C8 H9 N O5 . K   CDES *
Absolute stereochemistry.
Double bond geometry as shown.

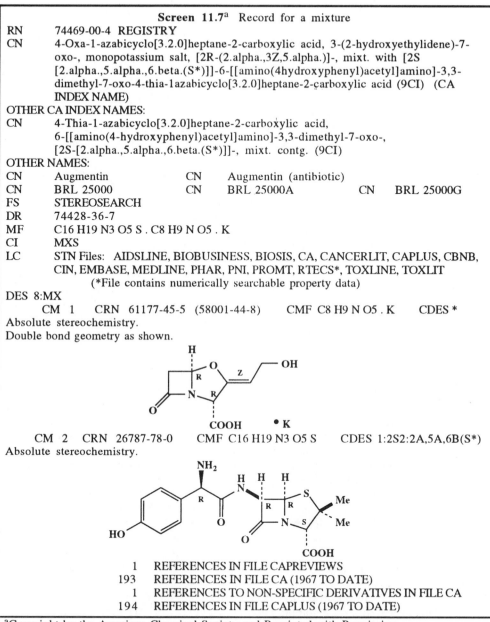

      CM 2   CRN 26787-78-0   CMF C16 H19 N3 O5 S   CDES 1:2S2:2A,5A,6B(S*)
Absolute stereochemistry.

            1   REFERENCES IN FILE CAPREVIEWS
          193   REFERENCES IN FILE CA (1967 TO DATE)
            1   REFERENCES TO NON-SPECIFIC DERIVATIVES IN FILE CA
          194   REFERENCES IN FILE CAPLUS (1967 TO DATE)

[a]Copyright by the American Chemical Society and Reprinted with Permission

Notes (Screen 11.7):

- the substance, augmentin, is registered as a mixture containing two components (that is, it is registered as a multicomponent substance) which are separately identified in the index name, molecular formula and structure fields;
- the first CA Index Name field contains full names for the two components, but the subsequent CA Index Name field contains an index name for the second component only (with qualification: mixt. contg.);
- the trivial names of the components (potassium clavulanate and amoxil) do not appear in the record (and this has real implications for searching for multicomponent substances, see Section 12.8.2);
- the structures of the two components appear separately as CM1 and CM2 (components 1 and 2), and another field, the Component Registry Number (CRN) Field which lists the CAS Registry Number of the components appears; and
- the first component is a salt for which separate indexing issues apply (see Section 11.4.10), although even here it should be further noted that the CRN entry contains the CAS Registry Number for the salt (61177-45-5) and for the free acid (58001-44-8).

11.4.7 Polymers

Polymers are chemical substances, which can either occur naturally (like rubber) or which are synthetic (like polythene and nylon), and which are made by linking together smaller molecules (called monomers) a large number of times. Synthetic polymers are very valuable commercial materials since the different polymers have different properties suitable for a great variety of applications.

There are many ways in which polymers are made and these can often determine how the polymers are registered. For example, *homopolymers*, which are made from a single monomer linked together many hundreds of times (polyvinyl acetate, PVA, is a polymer from the monomer called vinyl acetate), are registered as the individual component monomer. *Copolymers* are made by mixing together a number of monomers (many adhesives are made prior to use by mixing together a number of monomer components) and are registered as multicomponent substances. *Post-treated polymers*, which are polymers which have been further modified chemically particularly at pendant or end groups (polyvinyl alcohol is formed by the complete hydrolysis of polyvinyl acetate), may, or may not, be registered as new substances mainly depending on whether a systematic index name or an unique structure can be determined. *Polymer blends*, which are made by mixing together polymers (but in a way which does not form new covalent bonding) are not assigned their own CAS Registry Numbers and need to be searched with text terms in the CAplus File. Note that the cases described here are just some of the ways in which polymers form, and full descriptions of the registration of polymers are given in a variety of manuals and guides available from CAS.

In the REGISTRY File specific polymers are indexed as their monomer components and examples of the registration of a homopolymer and a copolymer are given in Screens 11.8 and 11.9.

Screen 11.8[a] Record for a homopolymer

RN	9003-53-6 REGISTRY
CN	Benzene, ethenyl-, homopolymer (9CI) (CA INDEX NAME)

OTHER NAMES:

CN	143E

...

CN	Polystyrene

ADDITIONAL NAMES NOT AVAILABLE IN THIS FORMAT - Use FCN, FIDE...

DR	144637-93-4, 117079-77-3, 120037-99-2, 98444-30-5, 86090-91-7, ...
MF	(C8 H8)x
CI	PMS, COM
PCT	Polystyrene
LC	STN Files: ANABSTR, APILIT, APILIT2, APIPAT, APIPAT2, ...

CM 1   CRN 100-42-5   CMF C8 H8

$H_2C = CH - Ph$

199	REFERENCES IN FILE CAPREVIEWS
58470	REFERENCES IN FILE CA (1967 TO DATE)
5022	REFERENCES TO NON-SPECIFIC DERIVATIVES IN FILE CA
58619	REFERENCES IN FILE CAPLUS (1967 TO DATE)

[a]Copyright by the American Chemical Society and Reprinted with Permission

---

Notes (Screen 11.8):

- there are many hundred names for polystyrene and only three of those in the actual record are shown in this screen;
- formerly used CAS Registry Numbers are in the DR (Deleted Registry Number) Field and each of these will probably be mentioned in the CAplus File. However, when an answer set from the REGISTRY File is crossed over to the CAplus File, the current Registry Number and all of the deleted Registry Numbers are crossed over (that is, searched);
- PMS, the abbreviation for polymers, appears in the Class Identifier Field; and
- additional indexing appears in the Polymer Class Term Field (PCT) and relates to the general class of polymer (polystyrene, polyurethane, polyester etc.).

Screen 11.9[a] Example of a copolymer

RN	27321-76-2 REGISTRY
CN	1,3-Benzenedicarboximidic acid, dihydrazide, polymer with 1,3-benzenedicarbonyl dichloride (9CI) (CA INDEX NAME)

OTHER CA INDEX NAMES:

CN	1,3-Benzenedicarbonyl dichloride, polymer with 1,3-benzenedicarboximidic acid dihydrazide (9CI)
CN	Isophthalamide, dihydrazone, polymer with isophthaloyl chloride (8CI)
CN	Isophthalimidic acid, dihydrazide, polymer with isophthaloyl chloride (8CI)
CN	Isophthaloyl chloride, polymer with isophthalimidic acid dihydrazide (8CI)

OTHER NAMES:

CN	Isophthalbisamidrazone-isophthaloyl chloride polymer

Screen 11.9 (continued)
MF   (C8 H12 N6 . C8 H4 Cl2 O2)x
CI   PMS
PCT   Polyother, Polyother only
LC   STN Files: CA, CAPLUS

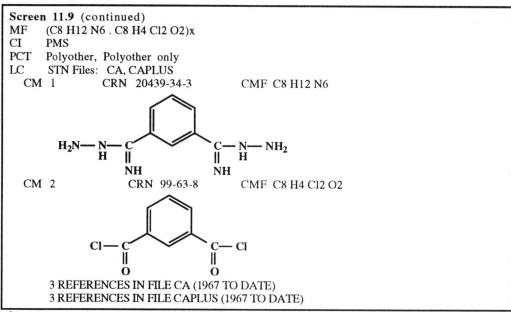

CM 1   CRN 20439-34-3   CMF C8 H12 N6

CM 2   CRN 99-63-8   CMF C8 H4 Cl2 O2

3 REFERENCES IN FILE CA (1967 TO DATE)
3 REFERENCES IN FILE CAPLUS (1967 TO DATE)

[a]Copyright by the American Chemical Society and Reprinted with Permission

Note that in many ways the registration is similar to that of a mixture and all but the last of the notes following Screen 11.7 apply.

11.4.8 Proteins

A very important group of naturally occurring "polymers" are the proteins, which are made from the monomer units called amino acids (so called because they have the amine, NH_2, and acid, COOH, functional groups). There are just over 20 naturally occurring amino acids which nature links together in special ways to form the substances which play a vital part in living systems.

The sequence in which these amino acids are linked is crucial to the property of the protein formed, so an essential part of understanding proteins is the knowledge of the sequence of the amino acids.

The term protein commonly refers to the complete substance, but smaller sequences of amino acids (formed either from breaking down proteins or by synthesis from individual amino acids) are well characterized. These are often termed peptides.

In the REGISTRY File proteins (and peptides) are registered as sequences of amino acids, and an example is shown in Screen 11.10.

Notes (Screen 11.10):

- this display is in the SQIDE (sequence identification) format;
- the SQL Field describes the sequence length (that is the number of amino acids present);
- single letter codes are given for the amino acids, each ten amino acids being listed as a set for easier interpretation ; and
- protein sequence is the class identifier and it appears in the File Segment Field (FS).

```
┌─────────────────────────────────────────────────────────────────────────────┐
│                    Screen 11.10ᵃ  Record for a protein                        │
│                                                                               │
│  RN      162775-31-7 REGISTRY                                                 │
│  CN      338-630-Kinase (phosphorylating), protein (tyrosine) (human gene Syk reduced)  (9CI) │
│          (CA INDEX NAME)                                                       │
│  FS      PROTEIN SEQUENCE                                                      │
│  SQL     292                                                                  │
│  SEQ   1    DTEVYESPYA  DPEEIRPKEV  YLDRKLLTLE  DKELGSGNFG  TVKKGYYQMK         │
│       51    KVVKTVAVKI  LKNEANDPAL  KDELLAEANV  MQQLDNPYIV  RMIGICEAES         │
│      101    WMLVMEMAEL  GPLNKYLQQN  RHVKDKNIIE  LVHQVSMGMK  YLEESNFVHR         │
│      151    DLAARNVLLV  TQHYAKISDF  GLSKALRADE  NYYKAQTHGK  WPVKWYAPEC         │
│      201    INYYKFSSKS  DVWSFGVLMW  EAFSYGQKPY  RGMKGSEVTA  MLEKGERMGC         │
│      251    PAGCPREMYD  LMNLCWTYDV  ENRPGFAAVE  LRLRNYYYDV  VN                 │
│  MF      Unspecified                                                          │
│  CI      MAN                                                                  │
│  SR      CA                                                                   │
└─────────────────────────────────────────────────────────────────────────────┘
```

ᵃCopyright by the American Chemical Society and Reprinted with Permission

While Screen 11.10 gives one example, it must be pointed out that the indexing of proteins is subject to a number of special definitions. For example, there need to be ways to describe proteins which are chemically modified, and proteins which are "cross-linked", and special manuals, available from CAS, describe the full indexing.

11.4.9 Nucleic acids

Another important class of naturally occurring "polymers" is the nucleic acids. DNA, deoxyribonucleic acid, contains the genetic code or fingerprint of life and every individual has its own DNA code. DNA is a polymer which has a backbone comprising phosphate and a sugar called deoxyribose, and attached to every sugar is one of four molecules called a nucleic acid base. These four bases are given the symbols A (adenine), C (cytosine), G (guanine) and T (thymine). Another nucleic acid uracil (U) replaces thymine in the closely related ribonucleic acid (RNA) which, broadly speaking, is the substance which "reads" the DNA code and communicates the message to parts of cells which then conduct the chemical reactions.

The DNA code is effectively that precise sequence of nucleic acid bases attached to the backbone, and, as with proteins, the sequence is the crucially important piece of information. In the REGISTRY File nucleic acids are registered as sequences of the nucleic acid bases and an example is shown in Screen 11.11.

Notes (Screen 11.11):

- this display is in the SQIDE (sequence identification) format;
- the SQL Field describes the sequence length (that is, the number of nucleic acid bases present);
- single letter codes are given for the nucleic acid bases, each ten bases being listed as a set for easier interpretation;
- nucleic acid sequence is the class identifier and it appears in the File Segment Field (FS); and
- the Nucleic Acid Type Field (NA) indicates the numbers of each of the four different nucleic acid bases present.

Screen 11.11[a]   Record for a nucleic acid

RN	162775-37-3 REGISTRY
CN	Deoxyribonucleic acid (human lung cell line T3M-3OLu ferritin heavy chain messenger RNA-complementary) (9CI) (CA INDEX NAME)
FS	NUCLEIC ACID SEQUENCE
SQL	549
NA	161 a 137 c 134 g 117 t
NTE	doublestranded

SEQ					
1	atgacgaccg	cgtccacctc	gcaggtgcgc	cagaactacc	accaggactc
51	agaggccgcc	atcaaccgcc	agatcaacct	ggagctctac	gcctcctacg
101	tttacctgtc	catgtcttac	tactttgacc	gcgatgatgt	ggctttgaag
151	aactttgcca	aatactttct	tcaccaatct	catgaggaga	gggaacatgc
201	tgagaaactg	atgaagctgc	agaaccaacg	aggtggccga	atcttccttc
251	aggatatcaa	gaaaccagac	tgtgatgact	gggagagcgg	gctgaatgca
301	atggagtgtg	cattacattt	ggaaaaaaat	gtgaatcagt	cactactgga
351	actgcacaaa	ctggccactg	acaaaaatga	cccccatttg	tgtgacttca
401	ttgagacaca	ttacctgaat	gagcaggtga	aagccatcaa	agaattgggt
451	gaccacgtga	ccaacttgcg	caagatggga	gcgcccgaat	ctggcttggc
501	ggaatatctc	tttgacaagc	acaccctggg	agacagtgat	aatgaaagc

MF	Unspecified
CI	MAN

Again it must be pointed out that with complex substances of this type there are many subtle variations possible, and each of these needs to be addressed when the substance is indexed. It is beyond the scope of this text to describe all the variations, but it is entirely within the function of this text to point out once again that, in order to obtain comprehensive and precise search results, it is necessary to understand the indexing for the class of substances being sought.

11.4.10 Salts

In the broadest definition, any substance bonded by attractions between ions is called a salt, although a slightly more restrictive definition is that a salt is formed between an acid and a base. For example, if acetic acid is treated with a base (sodium hydroxide) a new substance called sodium acetate is formed (Scheme 2). Sodium acetate contains mainly covalent bonds, but additionally there is an ionic bond between the oxygen and sodium atoms.

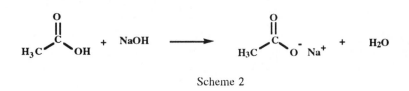

Scheme 2

There are a number of policies relating to the registration of salts but a few broad groups are most commonly encountered.

11.4.10a Salts which do not contain carbon

Simple salts from acids not containing Periodic Table Group VI atoms (oxygen, sulfur, etc.) are registered in the way normally drawn by the chemist. For example, sodium chloride and calcium bromide are represented as $NaCl$ and $CaBr_2$ respectively.

However, salts from acids containing Periodic Table Group VI atoms and bases containing Periodic Table Group I and II atoms (sodium, potassium, calcium, barium, etc.) are registered as the free acid combined with the base which is given the metal symbol. Screen 11.12 shows the record for calcium phosphate, and, in particular, the molecular formula field and the structure diagram should be noted. For example, while chemists write the formula for the substance as $Ca_3(PO_4)_2$, the substance is registered as if the hydrogens were still attached to the phosphate group, that is, as phosphoric acid, H_3PO_4. As the actual salt has three Ca atoms to two phosphate groups the substance is considered as $Ca_3(H_3PO_4)_2$ and the molecular formula, which has the first component in the alphabet as a single atom then becomes Ca.2/3 H3O4P.[*]

Actually, there are two substances called "calcium phosphate" in the File and only one is shown here. The problem lies with the chemical description of the substances in the original literature, since the ratio of calcium and phosphate can vary. If there is not something specific in the article to identify the particular form, the indexer will register the substance as one in which the ratio is not specified. (For example, the Molecular Formula Field entry for the second substance is: MF Ca . x H3 O4 P.) There are currently over 2000 entries for this second substance so a search for information on calcium phosphate should probably include its Registry Number (10103-46-5) as well!

The problem for the searcher is to know when situations like this arise; the solution is to be alert to such situations and to use "chemical intuition", although mostly in cases like this the substance would be retrieved through a name based search (Chapter 12) and this would indicate that more than one substance of this name existed.

Screen 11.12[a] Record for an inorganic salt

RN	7758-87-4 REGISTRY
CN	Phosphoric acid, calcium salt (2:3) (8CI, 9CI) (CA INDEX NAME)

OTHER NAMES:

CN	.alpha.-Tricalcium phosphate	CN	.beta.-Tricalcium phosphate
CN	Bonarka	CN	Calcium orthophosphate
CN	Calcium orthophosphate (Ca3(PO4)2)	CN	Calcium phosphate
CN	Calcium phosphate (3:2)	CN	Calcium phosphate (Ca3(PO4)2)
CN	Calcium tertiary phosphate	CN	Phosphoric acid calcium(2+) salt (2:3)
CN	Posture	CN	Posture (calcium supplement)
CN	Synthograft	CN	Synthos
CN	TCP	CN	TCP 10
CN	Tertiary calcium phosphate	CN	Tribasic calcium phosphate
CN	Tricalcium diphosphate	CN	Tricalcium orthophosphate
CN	Tricalcium phosphate	CN	Tricalcium phosphate (Ca3(PO4)2)
DR	123211-19-8, 1344-15-6		
MF	Ca . 2/3 H3 O4 P		
CI	COM		

---

[*]For reasons which relate to the valencies of the atoms involved, calcium ions have charge 2+, and phosphate ions have charge 3- so in order to obtain a neutral species (in which the charges are balanced) there needs to be three calcium ions to two phosphate groups.

Screen 11.12 (continued)
LC   STN Files: ANABSTR, BIOBUSINESS, BIOSIS, CA, CABA, CAPLUS, CANCERLIT,
         CAOLD, CAPREVIEWS, CASREACT, CEN, CHEMLIST, CBNB, CIN, CJACS, CSCHEM,
         DETHERM*, DDFU, DRUGU, EMBASE, GMELIN*, HSDB*, IFICDB, IFIPAT, IFIUDB,
         MEDLINE, MRCK*, MSDS-OHS, MSDS-SUM, PDLCOM*, PIRA, PHAR, PNI, PROMT,
         TOXLINE, TOXLIT, USPATFULL, VETU, VTB
                    (*File contains numerically searchable property data)
         Other Sources: DSL**, EINECS**, TSCA**
                    (**Enter CHEMLIST File for up-to-date regulatory information)
CRN   (7664-38-2)

$$HO-\overset{\overset{\textstyle O}{\|}}{\underset{\underset{\textstyle OH}{|}}{P}}-OH \qquad \bullet\ 3/2\ Ca$$

         18   REFERENCES IN FILE CAPREVIEWS
       3556   REFERENCES IN FILE CA (1967 TO DATE)
         79   REFERENCES TO NON-SPECIFIC DERIVATIVES IN FILE CA
       3566   REFERENCES IN FILE CAPLUS (1967 TO DATE)
          1   REFERENCES IN FILE CAOLD (PRIOR TO 1967)

11.4.10b Salts from organic acids and Periodic Table Group I/II bases
The registration is similar to the registration described above and Screen 11.13 shows the
record for sodium acetate. In particular, there are two points to note. First, the molecular
formula is C2H4O.Na whereas the actual (chemical) formula for the substance is C_2H_3ONa,
and second, in both Screens 11.12 and 11.13 the entry in the CRN Field is in parentheses
which indicates the actual CAS Registry Number in the field is for the neutral substance.

Screen 11.13[a] Record for an organic salt involving Periodic Table Groups I and II bases
RN   127-09-3 REGISTRY
CN   Acetic acid, sodium salt (7CI, 8CI, 9CI) (CA INDEX NAME)
OTHER CA INDEX NAMES:
CN   Sodium acetate (6CI)
OTHER NAMES:
CN   Anhydrous sodium acetate
MF   C2 H4 O2   . Na
CI   COM
LC   STN Files: ANABSTR, APILIT, APILIT2, APIPAT, APIPAT2, BEILSTEIN*,
         BIOBUSINESS, BIOSIS, CA, CABA, CAOLD, CAPREVIEWS, CASREACT, CEN, ...
CRN   (64-19-7)

$$HO-\overset{\overset{\textstyle O}{\|}}{C}-CH_3 \qquad \bullet\ Na$$

         23   REFERENCES IN FILE CAPREVIEWS
       6703   REFERENCES IN FILE CA (1967 TO DATE)
         54   REFERENCES TO NON-SPECIFIC DERIVATIVES IN FILE CA
       6721   REFERENCES IN FILE CAPLUS (1967 TO DATE)
          5   REFERENCES IN FILE CAOLD (PRIOR TO 1967)

11.4.10c Salts with nitrogen-containing bases
Apart from those involving Periodic Table Group I/II atoms the most common bases are those involving nitrogen atoms, and the salts are represented as the free base and the free acid (which includes the hydrogen donated by the acid). For example, the record for nicotine hydroiodide is shown in Screen 11.14.

Screen 11.14[a] Record for a salt from a nitrogen-containing base

RN   6019-03-0 REGISTRY
CN   Pyridine, 3-(1-methyl-2-pyrrolidinyl)-, monohydriodide, (S)- (9CI)
        (CA INDEX NAME)
OTHER CA INDEX NAMES:
CN   Nicotine, monohydriodide (8CI)
OTHER NAMES:
CN   Nicotine hydriodide
CN   Nicotine hydroiodide
FS   STEREOSEARCH
MF   C10 H14 N2 . H I
LC   STN Files: BEILSTEIN*, CA, CAPLUS
                (*File contains numerically searchable property data) DES 1:S
CRN   (54-11-5)
Absolute stereochemistry.

1 REFERENCES IN FILE CA (1967 TO DATE)
1 REFERENCES IN FILE CAPLUS (1967 TO DATE)

Salts from nitrogen-containing bases involving other acids (for example, sulfuric acid and phosphoric acid) are registered similarly.

11.4.10d Salts from organic acids and organic bases
These salts are registered as the free acid and the free base, but the subtle difference is that now both the acid and the base are registered as individual components. For example, there are two Component Registry Numbers in the record shown in Screen 11.15, while in Screen 11.14 only the Component Registry Number for the base is given, and is in parentheses. (That is, the Registry Number for HI is not shown and a similar situation occurs in Screen 11.13 where the Component Registry Number for the base (Na) is not shown. These substances are not considered to be multicomponent substances in the sense that separate CAS Registry Numbers are not given.)

Screen 11.15[a] Record for a salt involving organic acids and bases

RN	24057-28-1 REGISTRY
CN	Benzenesulfonic acid, 4-methyl-, compd. with pyridine (1:1) (9CI)
	(CA INDEX NAME)

OTHER CA INDEX NAMES:

CN	Pyridine, 4-methylbenzenesulfonate
CN	Pyridine, p-toluenesulfonate (7CI, 8CI)

OTHER NAMES:

CN	PPTS
CN	Pyridinium 4-toluenesulfonate
CN	Pyridinium p-toluenesulfonate
CN	Pyridinium p-tosylate
CN	Pyridinium tosylate
MF	C7 H8 O3 S . C5 H5 N
LC	STN Files: BEILSTEIN*, CA, CAOLD, CAPLUS, CASREACT, CHEMLIST, CJACS, CSCHEM, GMELIN*, IFICDB, IFIPAT, IFIUDB, MSDS-OHS, MSDS-SUM, SPECINFO, TOXLIT, ...

CM 1   CRN 110-86-1   CMF C5 H5 N

CM 2   CRN 104-15-4   CMF C7 H8 O3 S

1	REFERENCES IN FILE CAPREVIEWS
118	REFERENCES IN FILE CA (1967 TO DATE)
1	REFERENCES TO NON-SPECIFIC DERIVATIVES IN FILE CA
120	REFERENCES IN FILE CAPLUS (1967 TO DATE)
1	REFERENCES IN FILE CAOLD (PRIOR TO 1967)

[a]Copyright by the American Chemical Society and Reprinted with Permission

11.4.11 Isotopes

As mentioned in Section 11.3.1, atoms can be broken down into smaller pieces called electrons, protons and neutrons. Protons and neutrons weigh about the same, and they are very, very much heavier than electrons. So the weight of an atom (called its atomic weight) essentially is the sum of the weights of all the protons and neutrons.

While each atom always has its same number of electrons (and protons in the nucleus), the number of neutrons can vary a little. The various forms of atoms which have different numbers of neutrons are called isotopes. All isotopes have essentially the same chemical properties; it is just that since they have different numbers of neutrons they weigh a little different and this can affect how they behave under certain conditions. For example, one isotope of uranium has 92 protons (and of course 92 electrons) and 146 neutrons. It has an atomic weight of 238 (92+146)[*] and is not radioactive. Another isotope of uranium, which necessarily has 92 protons and 92 electrons since these numbers are what distinguish uranium from all the other atoms, has 143 neutrons (atomic weight = 92 + 143 = 235) and this form is highly radioactive. It is the isotope used in one type of nuclear weapon.

However, the online searcher is more likely to encounter the isotopes of the smaller atoms. The normal form of hydrogen has one electron and one proton (atomic weight = 1). A stable isotope of hydrogen is called deuterium (symbol D). It has one electron, one proton and one neutron, and hence an atomic weight of 2. About one deuterium atom occurs naturally to every 10,000 hydrogen atoms. A third isotope of hydrogen is radioactive and is called tritium (symbol T). It occurs only in minute amounts but because it is radioactive it can easily be detected, so is often used in chemistry (and medicine) to study what happens to hydrogen atoms in molecules in living systems. It has atomic weight = 3 (one electron, one proton, two neutrons).

Only the isotopes of hydrogen have different chemical symbols (H, D, T). Isotopes of all other atoms have the same chemical symbol but they are differentiated by putting the weight of the isotope as a superscript before the symbol. However, most elements have mainly one isotope and when this isotope is present, its weight is not given with the symbol. So the symbol C is used for the common form of carbon (it actually has atomic weight = 12, that is, 6 electrons, 6 protons, and 6 neutrons), whereas its isotope of weight 13 (6 electrons, 6 protons, and 7 neutrons) is written as ^{13}C.

Isotopes have many important uses, so many substances in the REGISTRY File have isotopic forms of atoms present. Sometimes it is known exactly where the isotope is while at other times it is not. Each different isotopic substance is registered with its own unique CAS Registry Number.

In the REGISTRY File isotopes of hydrogen are indicated by the symbols D and T, while isotopes of other atoms have the atomic weight as a superscript before the symbol for the atom. These representations appear in the structure diagram and in the name based entries. Screen 11.16 shows examples of a substance containing deuterium and of another containing ^{13}C.

---

[*] Atomic weights are conveniently recorded simply as the sums of the numbers of protons and neutrons. However, the actual weights are very small since protons and neutrons each weigh around 10^{-22} grams!

Screen 11.16[a]   Records for isotopic substances

Deuterium isotope
RN   105089-96-1 REGISTRY
CN   Pyridine, 3-(1-methyl-2-pyrrolidinyl-5-d)-, (2S-cis)- (9CI) (CA
          INDEX NAME)
FS   STEREOSEARCH
MF   C10 H13 D N2
CI   COM
SR   CA
LC   STN Files: CA, CAPLUS, CJACS, TOXLIT
DES *
Absolute stereochemistry.

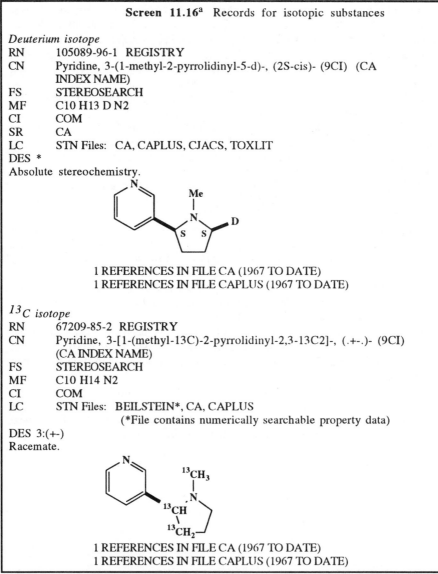

1 REFERENCES IN FILE CA (1967 TO DATE)
1 REFERENCES IN FILE CAPLUS (1967 TO DATE)

^{13}C *isotope*
RN   67209-85-2 REGISTRY
CN   Pyridine, 3-[1-(methyl-13C)-2-pyrrolidinyl-2,3-13C2]-, (.+-.)- (9CI)
          (CA INDEX NAME)
FS   STEREOSEARCH
MF   C10 H14 N2
CI   COM
LC   STN Files: BEILSTEIN*, CA, CAPLUS
                       (*File contains numerically searchable property data)
DES 3:(+-)
Racemate.

1 REFERENCES IN FILE CA (1967 TO DATE)
1 REFERENCES IN FILE CAPLUS (1967 TO DATE)

[a]Copyright by the American Chemical Society and Reprinted with Permission

11.4.12 Isomers

Isomers are different substances with the same molecular formula. There are many different types of isomers, but the two basic types about which searchers should know are *constitutional isomers* and *stereoisomers*. Sometimes many hundreds of substances with a single molecular formula are reported so searches based on molecular formula terms very commonly give large numbers of answers.

11.4.12a Constitutional isomers
In this type of isomer the atoms are connected in different ways. For example, alcohol and dimethyl ether both have molecular formula C_2H_6O but the atoms are connected together differently (Figure 11.3). For larger molecules, there may be several hundreds of ways in which the same numbers and types of atoms can be connected.

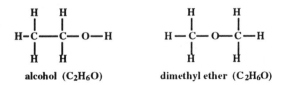

alcohol (C_2H_6O)   dimethyl ether (C_2H_6O)

Figure 11.3   Example of constitutional isomers

11.4.12b Stereoisomers
Stereoisomers have the same molecular formula and the same atoms are connected to each other. However, they differ in the way the atoms are connected in space. Some stereoisomers differ in that they are on opposite sides of a reference plane; others differ in that they are mirror images of each other (yet they cannot be superimposed); still others differ in that while at some parts the arrangements in space are identical, at other parts they are arranged differently in space. Chemists call each of these types of stereoisomers geometrical isomers, enantiomers, and diastereomers respectively.

Examples of each of these types are given in Figure 11.4. All of these substances have important applications in living systems: the geometrical isomers shown are maleic acid and fumaric acid; the enantiomers are the two mirror forms of the important amino acid alanine, and the diastereomers are two forms of glucose.

The ways in which the atoms are arranged in space happen to be critical with respect to how they react and this applies particularly in living systems. For example enantiomers, that is, those substances which are mirror images of each other but which are not superimposable, react, or don't react, with other substances just like a pair of hands (indeed hands are enantiomers!) in a handshake. It is easy to shake another person's right hand with your right hand, but with your same right hand you just cannot shake their left hand. And so it is in nature: if right-handed molecules can react with right-handed molecules they will not react in the same way with left-handed molecules. The various stereoisomers, and their mixed forms, are studied very extensively partly because stereoisomers are so important in living systems.

There is another issue with enantiomers and it relates to whether they are by themselves or mixed. Sometimes (particularly in nature) only the right-handed form is prepared; at other times only the left-handed form is present. The left- and right-handed forms are quite different and are indexed as separate substances. At still other times a mixture of equal amounts of the left- and right-handed forms is prepared. This is called a *racemic mixture* and commonly the searcher will find the symbol (+-) in front of the name of racemic mixtures. At other times the chemist either doesn't know, or doesn't specify, the stereoisomer being investigated and in these cases the substance is indexed as one with *undefined stereochemistry*.

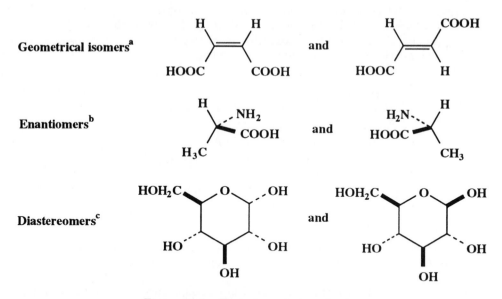

Figure 11.4   Examples of stereoisomers

While there are many aspects of stereisomers the examples illustrate three general situations:

[a]Geometrical isomers arise because of the geometry around a double bond (the two substances shown here cannot easily be converted into each other because a double bond cannot "twist" and also because the atoms are in a single plane)

[b]When a single carbon atom has *four different attached atoms/groups* then left- and right-handed forms (enantiomers) may occur (the central atom concerned is said to be "chiral" or "stereogenic")

[c]Diastereomers commonly have a number of stereogenic atoms but a different handedness will occur at least at one of the centres (the structures here have 5 stereogenic carbon atoms and the arrangements in space are identical except for the carbon at the top right)

There are a number of ways in which the various stereoisomers are named. The letters R, S, E, and Z,[*] and the Greek letters α and β are commonly used to indicate stereochemical arrangements in molecules. Meanwhile structure diagrams often indicate stereochemistry by drawing heavy, or dotted, or wedged bonds.

An example of the registration of an enantiomer is shown in Screen 11.17, and of the racemic form in Screen 11.18. In particular the stereochemical descriptors should be noted in the name fields, that is, the (S), L, and (+) descriptors and the (R,S), DL, dl, and (.+-.) descriptors which are different ways in which chemists describe the enantiomer and the racemate respectively.

---

[*]And D and L which are used mainly for the amino acids and carbohydrates. It is not necessary for non-chemists to understand all these descriptors, but it is important that searchers realize that they relate to the stereochemistry of the substances.

Screen 11.17[a] Example of an enantiomer

RN	56-41-7 REGISTRY
CN	L-Alanine (9CI) (CA INDEX NAME)

OTHER CA INDEX NAMES:

CN	Alanine, L- (7CI, 8CI)

OTHER NAMES:

CN	(S)-(+)-Alanine	CN	(S)-2-Aminopropanoic acid
CN	(S)-Alanine	CN	.alpha.-Alanine
CN	.alpha.-Aminopropionic acid	CN	Alanine
CN	L-(+)-Alanine	CN	L-.alpha.-Alanine
CN	L-.alpha.-Aminopropionic acid	CN	L-2-Aminopropanoic acid
CN	L-2-Aminopropionic acid	CN	Propanoic acid, 2-amino-, (S)-
AR	6898-94-8	DR	115967-49-2
MF	C3 H7 N O2		
CI	COM		
LC	STN Files: ANABSTR, BEILSTEIN*, BIOBUSINESS, BIOSIS, CA, CABA,....		
DES	5:L		

$$\underset{\underset{H}{|}}{\overset{\overset{NH_2}{|}}{Me—C—COOH}}$$

22	REFERENCES IN FILE CAPREVIEWS
22242	REFERENCES IN FILE CA (1967 TO DATE)
792	REFERENCES TO NON-SPECIFIC DERIVATIVES IN FILE CA
22290	REFERENCES IN FILE CAPLUS (1967 TO DATE)
2	REFERENCES IN FILE CAOLD (PRIOR TO 1967)

Screen 11.18[a] Example of a racemic form

RN	302-72-7 REGISTRY
CN	DL-Alanine (9CI) (CA INDEX NAME)

OTHER CA INDEX NAMES:

CN	Alanine, DL- (8CI)

OTHER NAMES:

CN	(.+-.)-2-Aminopropionic acid	CN	(.+-.)-Alanine
CN	(R,S)-Alanine	CN	DL-.alpha.-Alanine
CN	DL-.alpha.-Aminopropionic acid	CN	dl-2-Aminopropanoic acid
CN	dl-Alanine		
FS	STEREOSEARCH		
MF	C3 H7 N O2		
CI	COM		
LC	STN Files: BEILSTEIN*, BIOBUSINESS, BIOSIS, CA, CAPREVIEWS,....		

DES 5:DL
Racemate.

$$\underset{\underset{H}{|}}{\overset{\overset{NH_2}{|}}{Me—C—COOH}}$$

2	REFERENCES IN FILE CAPREVIEWS
1671	REFERENCES IN FILE CA (1967 TO DATE)
90	REFERENCES TO NON-SPECIFIC DERIVATIVES IN FILE CA
1671	REFERENCES IN FILE CAPLUS (1967 TO DATE)

Meanwhile, cortisone (Screen 11.1), augmentin (Screen 11.7), nicotine hydroiodide (Screen 11.14) and the isotopic substances (Screen 11.16) all have stereochemical features and the ways these are presented in the name and structure fields should be noted.

11.5 Class Identifiers and File Segments

Substances are grouped in one of 12 classes and each class is indexed in a special field - the CI (Class Identifier) Field. The class identifiers, their descriptions, and the number of substances in the class are given in Table 11.3.

Table 11.3   Class identifiers in the REGISTRY File

CLASS IDENTIFIER	DESCRIPTION	NO. SUBSTANCES (APPROX)
AYS	ALLOY	480,000
CCS	COORDINATION COMPOUND	960,000
CTS	CONCEPT	23,000
GRS	GENERIC REGISTRATION	13,000
IDS	INCOMPLETELY DEFINED SUBSTANCE	190,000
MAN	MANUAL REGISTRATION	800,000
MNS	MINERAL	8,000
MXS	MIXTURE	49,000
PMS	POLYMER	630,000
RIS	RADICAL ION	24,000
RPS	RING PARENT	98,000
TIS	TABULAR INORGANIC	210,000
UVCB	UNKNOWN/VARIABLE	35,000

Examples of some of these classes are given in the various screens already shown in this chapter, and searchers should study the entries carefully. There is no better way to learn about a database than browse through some actual entries!

Additionally, other classes of substances are grouped in the File Segment Field (Screen 11.19), from which it is seen that almost 400,000 records contain nucleic acid sequences and just over 300,000 contain protein sequences, over two million may be searched using stereochemical search terms and just over five million are part of the three-dimensional (Concord) subset of the file, that is, those which are linked with the Alchemy molecular modelling program. (Molecular modelling and the application of the Alchemy program are advanced chemical concepts which need not be considered in this text.)

```
                    Screen 11.19ᵃ  File Segments in the REGISTRY File
=> E A/FS
**** START OF FIELD ****
E2    5178549    3D/FS          E3          0 -->      A/FS
E4     383142    ACID/FS        E5    5178549          CONCORD/FS
E6     383142    NS/FS          E7     383142          NUCLEIC/FS
E8     319513    PROTEIN/FS     E9     319513          PS/FS
E10    702655    SEQUENCE/FS    E11   2049691          STEREOSEARCH/FS
**** END OF FIELD ****
```

ᵃCopyright by the American Chemical Society and Reprinted with Permission

The Class Identifier and File Segment Fields may be searched in ways similar to searches in specific fields in bibliographic databases. For example, the search term **PMS/CI** will limit answers to polymers.

11.6 Multicomponent substances

Many of the substances illustrated above have more than one component and these are termed multicomponent substances. There are a number of general points which should be noted concerning their registration.

It is important to recognize the different representations for a single component substance and a multicomponent substance. Thus a record for a multicomponent substance will list only a few of the names for the individual substances involved will have a "dot disconnected" entry in the molecular formula field; and will have the individual components presented in the structure display (which also gives the CAS Registry Number of the component). Multicomponent substances are commonly encountered in polymers which have greater than one monomer constituent, in salts, mixtures, minerals, and alloys.

11.7 Searching for substances

The whole concept of searching for substances in online files is quite different from that in the hardcopy literature. In the latter, almost invariably only a single substance may be searched at a time; however, in the former, searches may additionally be performed on a group of related substances very conveniently.

So, when a search involves a substance the searcher first has to ask: Is only a single registered substance required? While it might be considered that the answer is almost invariably YES, in fact in the majority of cases the answer should almost invariably be NO - at least in the first instance, since those who still think only in terms of hardcopy searching would not even be aware that the answer in most cases should be NO! For example, suppose information on potassium clavulanate (CAS Registry Number 61177-45-5) is required, then a search on its CAS Registry Number in the CAplus File would NOT retrieve information on augmentin (Screen 11.7) which contains potassium clavulanate as a component (unless the CAS Registry Number for augmentin is also present in the same CAplus File record).

Additionally, the searcher has to ask what is so special about potassium clavulanate? Would not at least some of the information available on sodium clavulanate, or ammonium clavualante or even clavulanic acid be relevant? Then even more general questions would need to be considered like: Are stereoisomeric substances, or substances which have the *part structure* of clavulanic acid of interest?

Once answers to all these questions have been determined, then the searcher needs to consider the best way to search for the substance or group of substances, and the options involve name based, molecular formula or structure search terms.

This last aspect is quite unique to electronic databases and, in turn there are a number of ways to search a structure query. An EXACT search will retrieve substances which have the same structure as that in the query. A FAMILY search will additionally retrieve all multicomponent substances which have the exact structure searched as one of the components. A SUBSTRUCTURE search will additionally retrieve all substances which have the structure query as part of the substance but with additional groups attached.

Either the full file, or a range or a subset of the file, may be searched. An example of the latter option is searching for specific stereoisomers, when first the full file is searched to obtain an answer set which has all the known stereoisomers, and then this subset is searched to retrieve only those answers which have the required stereochemistry.

Combinations of searches may be performed also. A set of structures may be narrowed by name based searches and vice versa. In effect, different, user-chosen subsets of the file are being searched and these subsets may be chosen in any number of interesting ways. For example, a search: => **S CHEMLIST/LC** will produce an answer set which contains only those substances in the CHEMLIST File (generally those which have regulatory information), and this initial answer set may be narrowed by name, formula or structure search terms.

It is important for searchers to have an overall perspective of searching for substances, that is, to be aware of all the possibilities which exist and the types of situations in which they are best used. The two chapters which follow (Chapters 12 and 13) describe searches based on names and formulas, while Chapters 14 and 15 address the various issues relating to structure searching.

Summary

- *Substances* are made from atoms which are connected together by bonds (either covalent or ionic).
- *Substances* are described by name, molecular formula, and structure.
- *Structures* are *graphic representations* of the connections between the atoms and the *valence bond* representation is used. There are a number of conventions in valence bond representations.
- The CAS REGISTRY File is the major database for chemical substances, and *a general technique for searching for information on substances is to find the substance in this File* and then check the LC Field which gives names of other files in which the CAS Registry Number for the substance is listed.
- The REGISTRY File has a number of *Class Identifiers and File Segments* which group the various types of substances (alloys, coordination compounds, incompletely defined substances, minerals, mixtures, polymers, proteins, nucleic acids, salts, isotopes, and isomers).
- There are special issues with the indexing of each class of substance, and the searcher should be aware of these in order to obtain comprehensive and precise search results.
- Many of the substances in these classes are registered as *multicomponent substances*, that is, they are registered as being made from individual components. The CAS Registry Numbers of each of the components are listed in the Component Registry Number Field (CRN).
- It is important at least to consider at the outset whether only a single substance, or a number of related substances, might have the relevant information and then to use the appropriate search procedure.

12

Finding Substances:
Name Based Terms

In this chapter we learn:

- *The principles of systematic nomenclature.*
- *How the various classes of substances are indexed in name based fields.*
- *How to treat the special keyboard symbols in chemical name fields.*
- *The various name based search fields and when to use them.*
- *The importance of searching in the Component Registry Number Field for multicomponent substances.*

12.1 Nomenclature

Each substance has its own individual name, but naming substances can be an extremely complex task and is often the job for a specialist! Indeed most practising chemists have knowledge of the basic rules only, so searching for substances by name can be a difficult process for both the trained chemist as well as for the information specialist.

There are some general types of names in use and they are classed as: systematic names, trade names, and common names.

12.2 Systematic names

12.2.1 IUPAC
In the early 1950s the International Union of Pure and Applied Chemists (IUPAC) established a nomenclature division whose task was to develop a systematic nomenclature for all substances. The IUPAC rules for organic substances are published in the monograph:

Nomenclature of Organic Chemistry, Sections A,B,C,D,E,F, and H (Pergamon Press, Oxford, 1979); the IUPAC rules for inorganic substances are published in the monograph: *Nomenclature for Inorganic Chemistry* (Butterworths, London, 1971), and the International Union of Biochemistry has published its rules: *Biochemical Nomenclature and Related Documents* (Biochemical Society, London, 1978).

However, modifications are made from time to time, it being understood that it never is easy to foresee how chemistry will develop and that better ways of naming substances may only be realized after the area has progressed.

12.2.2   Chemical Abstracts Index Nomenclature

CAS has another systematic nomenclature which is closely allied to the IUPAC nomenclature, and the rules also have been published. (The CA Index Guide contains an appendix, which can also be obtained independently: *Naming and Indexing of Chemical Substances for Chemical Abstracts*) The two systems are not identical, partly because CA Index names must be produced as soon as possible after the substance is reported (so the indexers don't have the "advantage of hindsight"), and partly because, for computer-search purposes, it is better to arrange the name a little differently (see below).

12.2.3   Beilstein Nomenclature

The Beilstein Institute has developed another systematic nomenclature plus a chemical naming program (called AUTONOM). Again, it is based on IUPAC nomenclature but there are important differences. However, presently only about one third of the substances in the Beilstein File have systematic names, and name based searching in this File currently is not recommended as a general procedure.

12.2.4   How systematic nomenclature works

In many ways chemical substances may be thought of as a tree with a central stem and attached branches. The key to systematic nomenclature is to identify the main stem, then to name all the branches as parts attached to the stem, and finally to name sub-branches within the branch.

It is necessary to identify where the branches are attached and this is done by use of locants (usually numbers, but sometimes letters - including Greek letters). If things get complicated, then branches (and sub-branches within them) are put in parentheses (using as many sets of parentheses as are needed) immediately following the locant and mostly separated by a hyphen.

Finding the stem can be more difficult than at first expected, but the guiding rule is to find the principal group which could be a functional group or ring system.

Nomenclature systems have assigned the various functional groups (see Section 11.3.6) in order of priority for nomenclature purposes. A carboxylic acid group has priority over an alcohol functional group, so if a molecule has both an acid and an alcohol functional group, the name of the alcohol part becomes a branch (of the stem which is based on the carboxylic acid). However, unless the searcher wishes to specialize in name based searching it is not necessary to know all the details of nomenclature, for example of priority rules for functional groups. However, it is valuable to know in general how names are constructed since this will allow easier interpretation of the name based fields.

The CA Index name actually places the stem first, then the branches follow. This is very useful at times since the main name (the stem) often describes a special set of related substances, and a simple search on this stem can retrieve all these substances. The special field in which such searches are performed is the Heading Parent Field (HP).

12.3 Trade names and common names

Many substances are most commonly referred to by their trade names, that is, by the names under which they are sold. Different manufacturers generally have different product names so a single substance may be marketed under a number of synonyms.

Other substances, particularly those in common use, are referred to by simple names. They are a bit like nicknames! For example, PVC, acetone, acetylene, morphine, aspirin, and cholesterol are the names given to some very familiar compounds.

Searchers do not need to understand the difference between trade names or common names. It is sufficient to know that very simple names have been given to the commonly used substances, and that these substances are most easily searched in the REGISTRY File by use of these trade or common names.

12.4 Indexing in name based fields

12.4.1 Single substance

A typical example of an entry in a name based field for a single substance which has considerable commercial application is given in Screen 12.1. This substance is one of the major penicillin antibiotics in current use, and the record is typical of common commercial substances. However, substances used mainly in research laboratories have few synonyms.

Screen 12.1[a] Nomenclature fields for a penicillin antibiotic

CN   4-Thia-1-azabicyclo[3.2.0]heptane-2-carboxylic acid,
         6-[[amino(4-hydroxyphenyl)acetyl]amino]-3,3-dimethyl-7-oxo-,
         [2S-[2.alpha.,5.alpha.,6.beta.(S*)]]- (9CI) (CA INDEX NAME)

OTHER CA INDEX NAMES:

CN   4-Thia-1-azabicyclo[3.2.0]heptane-2-carboxylic acid,
         6-[2-amino-2-(p-hydroxyphenyl)acetamido]-3,3-dimethyl-7-oxo-, D- (8CI)

OTHER NAMES:

CN   6-[D-(-)-2-Amino-2-(p-hydroxyphenyl)acetamido]-3,3-dimethyl-7-
         oxo-4-thia-1-azabicyclo[3.2.0]heptane-2-carboxylic acid

CN[b]   6-[D-(-)-p-Hydroxy-.alpha.-aminobenzyl]penicillin

CN[b]   6-[D-.alpha.-Amino-.alpha.-(4-hydroxyphenyl)acetamido]penicillanic acid

CN[b]	Amoclen	CN[c]	Amolin	CN[c]	Amopen
CN[b]	Amopenixin	CN[c]	Amoxi	CN[c]	Amoxi-Mast
CN[b]	Amoxicillin	CN[c]	Amoxil	CN[c]	Amoxipen....

CN[b]   D-(-)-.alpha.-Amino-p-hydroxybenzyl penicillin

CN[b]   D-(.alpha.-Amino-p-hydroxybenzyl)penicillin

CN[b]   D-2-Amino-2-(4-hydroxyphenyl)acetamidopenicillanic acid

CN[c]	D-Amoxicillin	CN[c]	Delacillin	CN[c]	Efpenix
CN[c]	Histocillin	CN[c]	Ibiamox	CN[c]	Imacillin
CN[c]	Metafarma capsules	CN[c]	Metifarma capsules	CN[b]	p-Hydroxyampicillin
CN[c]	Piramox	CN[c]	Sawacillin	CN[c]	Sumox

---

[a]Copyright by the American Chemical Society and Reprinted with Permission
[b]A common name for the substance
[c]A trade name for the substance

Notes (Screen 12.1):

- the current index name is listed first followed by index names used in earlier Collective Indexes;
- index names have the heading parent listed first, then the branches (in alphabetical order);
- the heading parent (principal name stem) for this substance remained unchanged in the Collective Indexes and is:
  4-Thia-1-azabicyclo[3.2.0]heptane-2-carboxylic acid;
- other names are listed in alphabetical order;
- a maximum of 50 names is listed in the default display format, but other names may be seen in the FCN (full chemical names) format;
- common and trade names are indicated;
- Greek letters are spelt between periods (for example, .alpha., and .beta.);
- symbols D and S are stereochemical descriptors; and
- for the purpose of application of the proximity operator (L), each CN is a separate index entry.

Note also that this substance is the second component (CRN 26787-78-0) in the record shown in Screen 11.7. Only the name from the 9th Collective Index for the substance in Screen 12.1 corresponds with one of the names listed in Screen 11.7, and the question then is: "How is amoxil, and all substances containing amoxil in a registered mixture, retrieved if only a very complex index name is in common?" Clearly name based searches are not the answer, and this issue is addressed below and again in Section 12.8.2.

12.4.2 Multicomponent substances

Examples of entries are shown in Chapter 11 (Screens 11.2, 11.6, 11.7, 11.9, and 11.15), and a further example, given in Screen 12.2, is the record for a mixture of morphine, phenacetin, caffeine and aspirin. All of these records should be studied carefully, and, in particular it should be noted that, while in the first CN Field (which contains the current CA Index Name) the Index Names for all components in a mixture are given (although only the first is in inverted format), subsequent CN fields contain only one systematic name. It should be further noted that no name based terms are listed for the individual components in the Component Registry Number Field (CRN).

So while there are many synonyms for aspirin, caffeine, morphine and phenacetin in their individual records, only their CA Index Names, and one or two of their synonyms, appear in records in which they are present as components. On the other hand, the CAS Registry Number for the component substances appear, so in a way *substances are indexed in multicomponent substances as CAS Registry Numbers* in the same manner as they are indexed as CAS Registry Numbers in the CAplus File. For this reason, CAS Registry Numbers should be used as search terms in the CRN Field (and common or trade names should not be used) to retrieve answers relating to queries concerning individual components in multicomponent substances! The question as to why searchers should perhaps seek multicomponent substances which contain specific individual components is discussed in Section 12.8.2.

A similar situation arises with the indexing of polymers where systematic names are given in the CA Index Name Field, but then subsequent fields contain systematic names for only one of the components and the words "polymer with" precede a name term for some of the other components (Screen 11.9).

Screen 12.2[a]   Name fields for a mixture
(structure diagrams are omitted in this display)

RN   37262-70-7 REGISTRY
CN   Morphinan-6-ol, 7,8-didehydro-4,5-epoxy-3-methoxy-17-methyl-, (5.alpha.,6.alpha.)-
,   mixt. with 2-(acetyloxy)benzoic acid, 3,7-dihydro-1,3,7-trimethyl-1H-purine-2,6-dione
       and N-(4-ethoxyphenyl)acetamide (9CI) (CA INDEX NAME)
OTHER CA INDEX NAMES:
CN   1H-Purine-2,6-dione, 3,7-dihydro-1,3,7-trimethyl-, mixt. contg. (9CI)
CN   Acetamide, N-(4-ethoxyphenyl)-, mixt. contg. (9CI)
CN   Benzoic acid, 2-(acetyloxy)-, mixt. contg. (9CI)
OTHER NAMES:
CN   Phenacetin mixt. with acetylsalicylic acid and caffeine and codeine
FS   STEREOSEARCH
MF   C18 H21 N O3 . C10 H13 N O2 . C9 H8 O4 . C8 H10 N4 O2
CI   MXS
LC   STN Files: CA, TOXLIT
DES 8:MX

CM	1[b]	CRN 76-57-3	CMF C18 H21 N O3
CM	2[b]	CRN 62-44-2	CMF C10 H13 N O2
CM	3[b]	CRN 58-08-2	CMF C8 H10 N4 O2
CM	4[b]	CRN 50-78-2	CMF C9 H8 O4

---

[a]Copyright by the American Chemical Society and Reprinted with Permission
[b]The components are morphine, phenacetin, codeine, and aspirin respectively

Alloys, coordination compounds, minerals, mixtures, proteins, nucleic acids, salts, isotopes, and stereoisomers all have their own naming conventions and examples of these are given in Chapter 11. Finally, Table 12.1 summarizes some other features of index names for some common groups of substances, and searchers should be aware of these, since at times name based searches can assist greatly in obtaining answer sets for groups of substances.

Table 12.1 Examples of names of some other classes of substances

CLASS	NOTES and EXAMPLES
ACRONYMS	All common acrynonyms are entered. Examples: DDT, DMF, HMPA, THF etc.
DYES	Color Index substances are entered both as the C.I. code and C.I. name. For example, the napthalene dye, CAS Registry Number 84-84-4, has entries: C.I. 37205 C.I. Azoic Diazo Component 23
ENZYME	Enzyme Commission numbers (E.C. - numbers) are entered in a single CN Field. For example, the enzyme chymotrypsin has entry: E.C. 3.4.24.12
ISOTOPES	With the exception of the isotopes of hydrogen, the atomic mass precedes the symbol for the element. Example: 14C
RADICAL	The term radical[a] is used in the Index Name and, if the radical has an associated charge this is indicated subsequently in parentheses. The radical anion obtained by adding an electron to anthraquinone is named : Anthraquinone, radical ion (1-)

---

[a]A radical is a substance which has an unpaired electron.

12.5 Special symbols in CN fields

For two reasons, some of the symbols in CN fields need special consideration when being entered into search terms. First, some symbols (like the Greek letters) are not readily available on computer keyboards, and, second, some names contain characters or words (like parentheses) which are reserved by the system.

The list of such situations, and the action needed to be taken, is given in Table 12.2.

Table 12.2 How to treat special symbols in name based fields

ENTRY	EXAMPLE	ACTION
UPPER/LOWER CASE		either can be used (Benzene, BENZENE)
SUPERSCRIPTS	^{13}C	normal type (13C)
SUBSCRIPTS	d_2	normal type (d2)
ITALICS	*italics*	normal type
HYPHENS	-	normal type
COMMAS	,	normal type
PERIODS	.	normal type
PRIMES	'	mask with quotations (")
PARENTHESES	( )	mask with quotations
BRACKETS	[ ]	replace with parentheses and mask
GREEK LETTERS	α	spell and place spelling inside periods
RESERVED WORDS	OR AND	mask with quotations
RESERVED SYMBOLS	+ -	place inside periods (.+-.)

Examples

CHEMICAL NAME	SEARCH ENTRY[a]
tricyclo[6.2.0.0^{2,10}]decane	"tricyclo(6.2.0.02,10)decane"
α,β,β-trichlorostyrene	.alpha.,.beta.,.beta.-trichlorostyrene
D and C Orange No. 17	"d and c orange no. 17"
2-piperidinone-3,3-d_2	2-piperidinone-3,3-d2

[a]The exact search term depends on the search field (See Section 12.6)

12.6 Name based search fields

Segmentation for entries in the Chemical Name Segment and Basic Index Fields in the REGISTRY dictionary database differs with the different systems. Thus even though the same tapes are provided, the different systems have slightly different fields and capabilities for searching name segments.

The various fields in which name based terms may be searched in the REGISTRY File on STN are summarized in Table 12.3.

On STN the segmentation occurs in four stages.

1. All hyphens and parentheses/brackets are removed.
2. All other punctuation (commas and periods) are removed.
3. The remaining segments are further broken into all chemically distinct name units (common segments are published in the Manual: *Name Segments in the REGISTRY File*).
4. All possible, chemically significant, recombinations of units formed in Step 3 are made.

Table 12.3 Name based search fields on STN

FIELD	FIELD CODE	CONTENTS
CHEMICAL NAME	CN	complete name as bound phrase
CHEMICAL NAME SEGMENTS	CNS	name segments obtained by removing all hyphens and enclosures (parentheses and brackets)
BASIC INDEX	(BI)[a]	entries in CNS plus segments after: • removing all punctuation (including commas and periods); • breaking remaining entries into all chemically distinct name units; and • making all possible recombinations of chemically distinct name units without crossing CNS boundaries
HEADING PARENT	HP	stem of CA Index Name
	INS.HP[b]	index name segment in the Heading Parent
	INS.NHP[b]	index name segment not in Heading Parent
	ONS	name segment not in Heading Parent

[a]Field code need not be included in the search query
[b]Some search fields have subfields which follow the field (separated by a period)

The segments obtained in Step 1 are placed in the Chemical Name Segment Field (CNS) while the segments obtained in all the Steps listed are placed in the Basic Index. For example, just the fifth CN Field entry for the substance in Screen 12.1 will have CN, CNS and BI entries as indicated in Figure 12.1.

Entry in CN Field
6-[D-.alpha.-Amino-.alpha.-(4-hydroxyphenyl)acetamido]penicillanic acid
Entries in CNS Field

6	D	.alpha.	amino	4
hydroxyphenyl		acetamido	penicillanic	acid

Additional **entries in the BI Field**

hydroxy	oxy	phen	phenyl	yl
acet	amido	pen	penicill	anic

Figure 12.1 CN, CNS and BI entries

It is apparent that even for a single substance like that in Screen 12.1 there are large numbers of CNS and BI segments indexed!

Finally, while a "chemically distinct name unit" relates to all prefixes and suffixes, and name parts, there are further complications when some of these actually are an integral part of a name stem. This occurs in four situations (Table 12.4).

Table 12.4 Name segments which deviate from system generated patterns

SEGMENT WITH	EXAMPLE
Multiplicative prefixes	TRITRIACONT
DE or DES prefixes	DEOXY, DESACETYL
Ring system names	DIOXAPHOSPHOLE
Rings with ISO prefix	ISOTHIAZOLE

Thus the prefix "tri" refers to three and is a chemically distinct name unit. Meanwhile the group "tritriacont" refers to thirty-three, and to segment the latter into "tri, tri, acont" would completely alter the meaning of the original group, so in this and in all of the cases in Table 12.4 segmentation does *not* occur. For example, isothiazole is not broken down further which means that a search: **S THIAZOLE**, will not retrieve ISOTHIAZOLE. Indeed, to retrieve thiazoles and isothiazoles it is necessary to use left- and right-hand truncation in the CNS Field: => **S ?THIAZOLE?/CNS** (see below).

12.7 Search tools in name based fields

12.7.1 Proximity operators and truncation

Proximity operators and truncation tools may be used in the normal manner, and it is to be noted that each separate CN Field constitutes a single information unit, so the (L) operator is used to restrict search terms to a single CN Field. It is not advisable to overspecify proximity since segments may appear in inverted order, or at very least in an order the searcher might not necessarily anticipate, so often it is better to link segments with the (L) operator in a single CN Field rather than the (A) or (W) operators. While the AND operator may be used, it will retrieve terms that appear anywhere in the record, that is, in different CN Fields, and this may not be desirable in most cases.

12.7.2 Restricting searches to special name fields

On the other hand, it is possible to restrict searches either to the CA Index Name, or to CN entries other than the Index Name entry. This is done through the INS.HP, INS.NHP, and ONS Fields. This is particularly useful to those searchers who are very familiar with nomenclature systems, and is also useful when selecting individual answers from a large answer set (see Section 13.4.3). Thus, for example, the searches:

=>   S   **AZABICYCLO/INS.HP**
=>   S   **HYDROXYPHENYL/INS.NHP**
=>   S   **PENICILLIN/ONS**

could be used to retrieve the record shown in Screen 12.1.

12.7.3 Left-hand truncation in CNS Field

Left-hand truncation may be used in the REGISTRY File only in the CNS Field and this can be helpful in some instances. However, as discussed in relation to the restriction of answers in bibliographic searches in Section 7.3, the effect of using more restrictive terms should always be carefully considered and sometimes this can be achieved only by trying a variety of searches and analysing the outcomes.

For example, some search terms and the size of answer sets are shown below, and it is necessary to determine why the results are so different.

	Search Term	Number of Answers
1.	**?THIAZOLE?/CNS**	77,000
2.	**THIAZOLE?**	64,000
3.	**THIAZOLE**	64,000
4.	**?THIAZOLE/CNS**	45,000
5.	**THIAZOLE?/CNS**	41,000
6.	**THIAZOLE/CNS**	20,000

Note that searches 2. and 3. are in the Basic Index and give identical answer sets since THIAZOLE is a chemically distinct name unit. However, as mentioned in Section 12.6, ISOTHIAZOLE is considered as a single unit and so isothiazoles will not be retrieved in search 2. (but will be retrieved in search 1.). Meanwhile THIAZOLECARBOXYLIC acids are a name segment in many substances and will be retrieved in searches 2. and 5. above, but not in search 6.

It cannot be overemphasized that in a database of many millions of substances there can be many subtle variations, and the full implications of search terms should be considered. Indeed it can be a hazardous exercise to retrieve classes of substances using name based search terms unless simple names are available. However, as discussed in Chapter 15, a structure is an exact entity and searches for classes of substances based on structure components are usually more precise and more comprehensive.

12.8 Search strategies in name based fields

As with all substance based searches, it is necessary to keep in mind whether information on a single substance, or on a group of substances, is required. The searcher should always consider from the outset whether a single substance, the substance and its salts or isotopic forms, or the substance as a component in a mixture or even in a polymer should be retrieved. For example, the biological activity of a substance might be known only for its salts and isotopic forms so only through searching for these might the most relevant information be found.

The overall strategy for any name based search is:

1. **EXPAND to check the presence of the name or name segment in the required field(s);**
2. **SEARCH on the E-number(s); and**
3. **DISPLAY the answer(s).**

The appropriate search terms should first be checked otherwise, in those files which have search term pricing, needless expense may be incurred. Then, once the term has been identified, it is much easier to enter the E-number than a lengthy string of characters.

12.8.1 Single substance
If only a single substance is required, and if a common or trade name is known, then the easiest way to find the record is:

1. **EXPAND on the name** *in the CN Field;*[*]
2. **SEARCH the E-number; and**
3. **DISPLAY the answer.**

The files listed in the LC Field are checked, and information on the substance is then sought from the appropriate file(s).

Fortunately this procedure works for a majority of questions commonly asked. It does not work when simple names are not available and this applies mainly to the specialized

---

[*]Remember that searches in the CN Field must exactly match the actual entry, that is, searches are conducted as bound phrases.

substances used in research laboratories. When the latter applies, while search terms may be connected with proximity operators in the CNS, BI, or HP Fields, it may be more cost effective either to explore a search based initially on the molecular formula (see Section 13.4.3) or to proceed straight to an EXACT structure search (see Sections 14.9 and 15.8.1).

However, even when a single substance, with what might be thought to be a simple name, is required the searcher still needs to be aware that potential problems may arise if the substance may exist in stereoisomeric forms, or if it may form salts. For example, if the search requirement is for information on the substance known as fexofenadine, the first step is to expand on the full name (**E FEXOFENADINE/CN**) and from the display it is noted that there are no entries under the name "fexofenadine" but that "fexofenadine hydrochloride" is posted. When this name is searched and displayed it is noted that the CAS Registry Number, 153439-40-8, relates to the hydrochloride for the substance in which the stereochemistry is undefined.

The structure of the parent base and a summary of the entries for the various stereoisomeric forms and salts are shown in Figure 12.2. All the substances are listed under their index names (the general name is shown in the figure while the specific names also contain the stereochemical descriptors and salts). *All* the trivial and trade names listed in the database, and the number of postings in the CAplus File, are shown under the different CAS Registry Numbers in Figure 12.2, and, with knowledge of this information, the searcher should consider how any (or which) of these substances might be retrieved through name based terms. It should also be considered as to which of the 9 different registered substances are of interest!

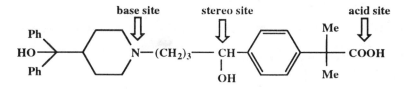

General index name is:
Benzeneacetic acid, 4-[1-hydroxy-4-[4-(hydroxydiphenylmethyl)-1-piperidinyl]butyl]-
.alpha.,.alpha.-dimethyl-

	Parent base	**Hydrochloride**
Stereo undefined	83799-24-0	153439-40-8
	carboxyterfenadine	fexofenadine hydrochloride
	MDL 16455	MDL 16455A
	terfenadine acid metabolite	
	(16 references)	(2 references)
Racemic substance	159389-12-5	138452-21-8
	(1 reference)	(1 reference)
(R) enantiomer	139965-10-9	138515-57-8
	(5 references)	(1 reference)
(S) enantiomer	139965-11-0	138515-56-7
	(5 references)	(1 reference)
Tritium isotope	166759-34-8	
	(1 reference)	

Figure 12.2 Fexofenadine and related susbtances in the REGISTRY File

The point here is that, even in apparently straightforward cases, there are indexing issues of which the searcher needs to be aware. (All of the substances listed in Figure 12.2 are retrieved very readily through a FAMILY search, see Section 15.8.)

12.8.2 Multicomponent substances

If a single multicomponent substance is required (for example, a mixture, a salt, or a polymer) a name based search is generally feasible only with simple salts. (The problems in more complicated cases already have been mentioned in Sections 12.4.1 and 12.4.2.) Again an expansion on the main component name in the CN Field will indicate the E-numbers for such salts (for example, Screen 12.3 indicates the procedure for finding the ammonium salt of benzoic acid and the sodium salt of clavulanic acid). Simple salts like these are generally listed in both formats: ammonium benzoate and benzoic acid, ammonium salt; sodium clavulanate and clavulanic acid, sodium salt, although it should be noted that "clavulanic acid sodium salt" but not "clavulanic acid potassium salt" is posted. Hence the importance of expanding first (and clearly other expansions would need to be done to find the potassium salt by a name based search).

Screen 12.3[a] Expanding in CN to find a simple salt

```
=> E AMMONIUM BENZOATE/CN   5
E1      1          AMMONIUM BENZHYDROXAMATE/CN
E2      1          AMMONIUM BENZIDINE-2,2'-DISULFONATE-PYROMELLITIC
                   ANHYDRIDE POLYMER/CN
E3      1-->       AMMONIUM BENZOATE/CN
E4      1          AMMONIUM BENZOATE-FORMALDEHYDE-1,1-
                   DIMETHYLHYDRAZINIUM OXALATE MIXTURE/CN
E5      1          AMMONIUM BENZYL MALEATE/CN


=> E CLAVULANIC ACID/CN   13
...
E3      1-->       CLAVULANIC ACID/CN
E4      1          CLAVULANIC ACID 1-AMINOADAMANTANE/CN
E5      1          CLAVULANIC ACID 2-AMINO-2,4,4-TRIMETHYLPENTANE SALT/CN
...
E9      1          CLAVULANIC ACID NONYL ESTER/CN
E10     1          CLAVULANIC ACID PHENYL ESTER/CN
E11     1          CLAVULANIC ACID PHTHALIDYL ESTER/CN
E12     1          CLAVULANIC ACID PIPERIDINE SALT/CN
E13     1          CLAVULANIC ACID SODIUM SALT/CN
```

[a]Copyright by the American Chemical Society and Reprinted with Permission

---

For other than simple salts it is recommended that searches be conducted in the Component Registry Number Field (CRN) since, as pointed out in Section 12.4.1, relatively few name terms appear in the name fields for multicomponent substances. Provided that the CAS Registry Numbers can easily be found for the components by individual searches (for example, in the CN Field), this technique is recommended for all multicomponent substances including salts, mixtures and polymers.

Important note:
- **Multicomponent substances are best retrieved by searches in the Component Registry Number Field**

For example, Screen 12.4 shows how to retrieve pyridinium salicylate, while Screen 12.5 shows how to find mixtures containing caffeine, aspirin and morphine. (The CAS Registry Numbers for caffeine, aspirin and morphine may be found through searches in the CN Field, and are 58-08-2, 50-78-2 and 76-57-3 respectively. If required, the number of components in a mixture may be specified and the search term, **NC=4**, will retrieve all mixtures with 4 components. One of the answers would be that given in Screen 12.2.)

Chemists should review the actual entries in the CN Fields in Screen 12.4 and it would be realized that searches based on name terms would not have been easy to formulate. Meanwhile it is noted that there were 13 registered mixtures (Screen 12.5) which had these three substances as components.

```
                  Screen 12.4ᵃ   Finding salts from organic acids and bases
=> S PYRIDINE/CN;D RNᵇ
L1          1 PYRIDINE/CN
RN          110-86-1 REGISTRY
=> S SALICYLIC ACID/CN; D RNᵇ
L2          1 SALICYLIC ACID/CN
RN          69-72-7 REGISTRY
=> S 110-86-1/CRN AND 69-72-7/CRN AND NC=2ᶜ
          5044    110-86-1/CRN
          1638    69-72-7/CRN
     1987937      NC=2
L3          1 110-86-1/CRN AND 69-72-7/CRN AND NC=2
=> D
RN          15039-34-6 REGISTRY
CN          Benzoic acid, 2-hydroxy-, compd. with pyridine (1:1) (9CI)  (CA
            INDEX NAME)
OTHER CA INDEX NAMES:
CN          Pyridine, 2-hydroxybenzoate
CN          Pyridine, salicylate
CN          Salicylic acid, compd. with pyridine (7CI)
CN          Salicylic acid, compd. with pyridine (1:1) (8CI)
MF          C7 H6 O3 . C5 H5 N
LC          STN Files:  BEILSTEIN*, CA, CAOLD
                        (*File contains numerically searchable property data)
            CM 1ᵈ              CRN 110-86-1        CMF C5 H5 N

            CM 2ᵈ              CRN 69-72-7         CMF C7 H6 O3
```

[a]Copyright by the American Chemical Society and Reprinted with Permission
[b]Note that commands can be "stacked" by separation with semi-colons, but of course the searcher needs to be sure that the first command will give the answer expected!
[c]This specifies the number of components (NC) to be present in multicomponent substances.
[d]The structures for pyridine and salicyclic acid appear here as usual, but are not shown in this screen.

Screen 12.5[a] Finding mixtures using the CRN Field

=> S   **58-08-2/CRN AND 50-78-2/CRN AND 76-57-3/CRN**
          539   58-08-2/CRN
          437   50-78-2/CRN
          198   76-57-3/CRN
L1   13   58-08-2/CRN AND 50-78-2/CRN AND 76-57-3/CRN

---

[a]Copyright by the American Chemical Society and Reprinted with Permission

It should be remembered that a search based on Component Registry Numbers retrieves all substances in which that original CAS Registry Number appears, but that this excludes all isotoptic substances and stereoisomers (which can be retrieved most readily through structure searches). Nevertheless such a search will retrieve all CAS Registry Numbers for mixtures containing the original substance of interest and then information on the original substance and registered mixtures can be obtained by crossing over the answer set to the CAplus File or to any other file which allows CAS Registry Numbers as search terms.

For example, a search on the Component Registry Number for amoxil (CAS Registry Number 26787-78-0, Screen 12.1) retrieves 77 registered substances. These substances are reported in 562 records in the CAplus File, and, of these, 339 records do not contain the CAS Registry Number for amoxil. So failure to search for these mixtures may mean that important information on amoxil is not obtained.[*]

Finally searches for single substances in the CNS, BI and HP Fields are often done in conjunction with searches in the Molecular Formula Field (Section 13.4.3). If a group of substances is required then the possibility of searches in these fields should always be kept in mind - provided that the general limitation of name based searching (that is, the complexity of nomenclature itself) is recognized.

12.9 When name based searches must be done

There are some substances which do not have structures, or molecular formulas, in which cases name based searches must be performed. For example, an expansion on **TEA TREE OIL/CN** indicates that such an entry is present in the REGISTRY File, and the record is shown in Screen 12.6.

Note that the MF is unspecified and the structure diagram is not available, since tea tree oil, a known "substance" from a definite source, actually is a complex mixture of substances. It should also be noted that the CA Index Name is OILS, TEA-TREE and this will be the index entry under which the "substance" will appear in CAS files.

---

[*]That is, when the search was done for CAS Registry Number 26787-78-0 in the CAplus File, 2108 records were retrieved. Meanwhile 562 records reported information on the 77 registered mixtures, and of these 339 were unique (did not contain 26787-78-0).

Screen 12.6[a] Finding substances which do not have structure or molecular formulas
RN   68647-73-4 REGISTRY *
*   Use of this CAS Registry Number alone as a search term in other STN files may result in incomplete search results. For additional information, enter HELP RN* at an online arrow prompt (=>).
CN   Oils, tea-tree (CA INDEX NAME)
OTHER NAMES:
CN   Oil of Melaleuca alternifolia (cheel)
CN   Tea tree oil
DEF   Extractives and their physically modified derivatives. Melaleuca alternifolia, Myrtaceae.
MF   Unspecified
CI   MAN, CTS
LC   STN Files: CHEMLIST, CIN, CSCHEM, IPA, MEDLINE, RTECS*, TOXLINE....

The record in the REGISTRY File intentionally does not indicate the number of records in the CAplus File in which the CAS Registry Number appears because indeed use of this Registry Number as a search term is unreliable. Instead name based searches in the CAplus File should be performed and an example is given in Screen 12.7.

Screen 12.7[a] Search in the CAplus File for tea tree oil
=> S ((TEA(W)TREE)(L)OIL#) OR (MELALEUCA(L)EXT?)
       10356   TEA
       19628   TREE
      313583   OIL#
          31   (TEA(W)TREE)(L)OIL#
         124   MELALEUCA
     1222174   EXT?
          19   MELALEUCA(L)EXT?
L1   48   ((TEA(W)TREE)(L)OIL#) OR (MELALEUCA(L)EXT?)
=> D 10 HIT
TI   A disinfecting composition containing **tea tree oil** biocidally active terpenes
AB   A disinfecting compn. comprises stable aq. solns. of a blend of biocidally active terpenes of **tea tree oil**, .gtoreq.1 biocidally active surfactants, .gtoreq.1 proton donor type biocides, and a salt of mono-, di or trihydroxy aliph. or arom. acids. The **tea tree oil** contains terpinen-4-ol and 1,8-cineole. The compn. may act as a carrier for secondary compns. for ...
ST   disinfecting compn biocide **tea tree oil**; terpene Melaleuca oil disinfectant compn; terpinenol surfactant disinfectant compn
IT   Bactericides, Disinfectants, and Antiseptics
     Fungicides and Fungistats
        (biocidally active terpenes of **tea tree oil** and surfactants and proton donor type biocides and hydroxy acids in)
IT   Terpenes and Terpenoids, biological studies
     RL: BIOL (Biological study)
        (biocidally active, of **tea tree oil**, in disinfecting compn.)
IT   562-74-3, Terpinen-4-ol
     RL: USES (Uses)
        (biocidally active, of **tea tree oil**, in disinfecting compn.)
IT   470-82-6, 1,8-Cineole
     RL: USES (Uses)
        (of **tea tree oil**, in disinfecting compn.)

Summary

- Every substance has a name, but systematic nomenclature may be difficult to determine.
- Many substances, particularly those in common use, have relatively *simple trade or common names*.
- Name fields contain the CA Index Name, and then other names which may be former systematic names, or trade or common names.
- All registered names for single substances are entered, and *individual names of substances are entered in each CN Field* in the REGISTRY File.
- For *multicomponent substances* the CA Index Names for the individual components are listed in separate fields and each of these fields will have either a name for one of the other components, or a descriptor (example: mixt. or polymer) indicating that the registered substance has further components. However, all the names for the various components are not given and so name based searches for multicomponent substances are reliable only with simple substances (for example, simple salts or organic acids and bases).
- Many *names contain special symbols* for which there are a number of policy decisions concerning the actual entry in the File.
- Searches based on names may be conducted in the CN Field, CNS Field, Basic Index, or in a few fields based on index names.
- Searches in the CN Field must match exactly the entries in the field (that is, the field is searched as a *bound phrase*), although truncation symbols may be used.
- Searches in the CNS Field may additionally be conducted with *left-hand truncation*.
- *Proximity operators* may be used in the CNS Field and in the Basic Index, and it is recommended that proximity is not overspecified (for example, it is preferable to use the (L) operator).
- It always is advisable to *expand first* on likely terms to verify their presence in the database.
- In most instances searches for multicomponent substances should be performed by searching for the *CAS Registry Numbers* in the CRN Field.

13

Finding Substances: Formula Based Terms

In this chapter we learn:
- *Atoms in molecular formulas are arranged in a special order (Hill order).*
- *There are rules for the arrangement of components within multicomponent substances.*
- *Searches can be performed in the Molecular Formula Field, in the Basic Index, or in a number of fields derived from molecular formulas.*
- *A general strategy to find a single substance record is to combine molecular formula searches with searches based on name segments.*
- *Searches based on molecular formulas can always be used to narrow answer sets obtained by alternative searches.*

13.1 The representation of molecular formulas

A substance with a known composition has a specific molecular formula which is a count of the various atoms that combine together to form the substance. Formulas are generally represented in the format: $A_xB_yC_z$ where A, B, and C are different atoms and x, y, and z are the numbers of each of these atoms in the substance respectively. A molecular formula can always be worked out from a structure diagram, the only point to remember is that in some structure drawing conventions the carbon and hydrogen atoms are not specifically shown (see Section 11.3.4).

For all single substances molecular formulas are arranged in a standardized order, called the Hill System, for which there are two simple rules:

1. if the substance does not contain carbon then the atoms are arranged in alphabetical order; and
2. if the substance contains carbon, the carbon is placed first, hydrogen (if present) second, and then all other atoms in alphabetical order.

Some examples of molecular formulas for single component substances are shown in Figure 13.1, and it is important to note the arrangement of the elements (for example, sulfuric acid is H2O4S in the Hill order rather than H2SO4 as normally described by chemists).

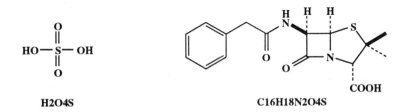

H2O4S   C16H18N2O4S

Figure 13.1   Some examples of molecular formulas

For multicomponent substances the atoms in each single component are again arranged in the Hill system order, and the individual components are arranged according to some additional rules (Figure 13.2).

COMPONENTS CONTAINING	ORDER OF ARRANGEMENT OF COMPONENTS
No carbon	Alphabetical using the first atom of each component
Carbon and non-carbon	Carbon-containing component first
All carbon-containing	Component with highest number of carbons first then in order of decreasing number of carbons
Same number carbons	Component with highest number of hydrogens first
Same number carbons and hydrogens	Alphabetical using the remaining atoms

Figure 13.2   Arrangement of components in multicomponent substances

13.2 Indexing in the Molecular Formula Field

There are a number of points which always need to be kept in mind with the registrations of the different classes of substances. The screens in Chapter 11 show the formulas for the classes but for convenience the entries in the Molecular Formula Field are repeated in Table 13.1 along with comments on the indexing.

Table 13.1 Examples of molecular formula entries for various classes of substances

CLASS and ENTRY	NOTES
Alloys	
MF Cu . Si . Sn . Zn	elements are arranged in alphabetical order; AF (Alternative Formula) Field (when present) additionally gives percentages of elements[a]
Coordination compounds	
MF C44 H40 Cl2 N8 Ni S4	indexing rules for single substances or salts apply
Incompletely defined substance	
MF C22 H11 Cl2 N O5	IDS entries have specific formulas, but not specific structures!
Mineral	
MF Mn . Nb. O . Sn . Ta	elements are arranged in alphabetical order; AF (Alternative Formula) Field (when present) additionally gives percentages of elements[a]
AF Mn Nb0-1 O8 Sn0.5-1 Ta1-2.4	
Mixtures	
MF C16 H19 N3 O5 S . C8 H9 N O5 . K	indexing rules for multicomponent substances apply
Polymers	
MF (C8 H12 N6 . C8 H4 Cl2 O2)x	indexing rules for multicomponent substances apply, with entries in parentheses followed by "x"
Proteins and *Nucleic Acids*	formulas not specified.
MF unspecified	However, sequences of amino acids and nucleic acid bases can be searched; otherwise proteins and nucleic acids are found through name based terms[b]
Salts	
MF Ca . 2/3 H3 O4 P	rules for multicomponent substances
MF C2 H4 O2 . Na	apply; hydrogen atoms from acid
MF C10 H14 N2 . H I	components remain as with the free
MF C7 H8 O3 S . C5 H5 N	acid
Isotopic substances	
MF C10 H13 D N2	symbols for D and T are used; isotopes
MF C10 H14 N2	of other atoms are not specifically identified in the MF Field
Substances of undefined composition	
MF Unspecified	no molecular formula available!

[a]AF Field entries may be searched but apply only in special situations (see the manual: *REGISTRY File: Dictionary Searching*)
[b]See the Database Summary Sheet: *REGISTRY (Biosequence Searching)*

13.3 Molecular formula search fields

There are three main classes of search fields based on molecular formulas.

13.3.1 Molecular Formula Field

Molecular formulas are entered as bound phrases in the Molecular Formula Field so the rules stated in Section 13.1 must be applied exactly if the desired substance is to be retrieved.

In the Molecular Formula Field spaces may be optionally inserted between the different atoms, that is a formula $C_6H_{12}O$ may be searched either as: => S C6H12O/MF or => S C6 H12 O/MF. This helps overcome ambiguities when two single-letter symbols together make the symbol for a different atom. For example, indium (In) contains the single letters I (iodine) and N (nitrogen) so the search => S I N O/MF will produce a different answer set from the search => S INO/MF since the latter will also retrieve, *inter alia*, indium oxide. The issue of spaces in the Molecular Formula Field is critical and there are special considerations which apply to multicomponent substances (Table 13.2).

Table 13.2 Spaces in molecular formula search fields[a]

TYPE OF FORMULA	INPUT	NOTES
Single substance	C6 H12 O/MF	Spaces between elements
Multicomponent substance	C7 H8 O3 S . C5 H5 N/MF	Spaces before and after periods
Multicomponent (with ratios)	C5 H6 O5 . 2 C3 H4 N2/MF	Spaces before and after coefficient
Multicomponent (fractional ratios)	"Ca . 2/3 H3 O4 P"/MF	Spaces before and after fraction; slash must be masked
Polymers	"(C8 H12 N6 . C8 H4 CL2 O2)X"	No spaces before or after parentheses; mask parentheses

[a]Note that once a space is used, then spaces must be used consistently throughout. However, the absence of *all* spaces is also acceptable.

13.3.2 Basic Index

The various component molecular formulas are searched in the Basic Index as bound phrases and in this field no spaces are allowed between atoms in the formula. This is necessary since text terms are also searched in the Basic Index and if spaces were allowed in formula based searches the system would not differentiate between say A for Argon and the letter A as a text term. Note that the total formula for multicomponent substances is not posted in the Basic Index.

13.3.3 Fields based on molecular formulas

Additionally there are a number of fields which are *based* on the molecular formula and some are summarized in Table 13.3. Each of these fields refers to a formula fragment, that is, the molecular formula of a single substance or of a component of a multicomponent substance.

Table 13.3 Some fields based on molecular formulas

FIELD	USE
ATC (Atom Count)	to indicate total number of atoms
ELC (Element Count)	to indicate number of each type of atom present[a]
ELF (Element Formula)	to indicate elements present in each component[b]
ELS (Element Symbol)	to indicate the presence (or absence) of an element
PG (Periodic Table Group)	a group code is assigned for each element corresponding to the vertical columns or horizontal rows of the Periodic Table
FW (Formula Weight)	to indicate formula weight in each component
NC (Number Components)	to indicate the number of components in a multicomponent substance

[a]In a multicomponent substance the element count is generated for each component
[b]Without numeric coefficients and with spaces between each element

For example, augmentin, which has molecular formula C16 H19 N3 O5 S . C8 H9 N O5 . K (Screen 11.7) has postings in the following fields (note that the second line of entries does not list a field since these are the entries in the Basic Index):

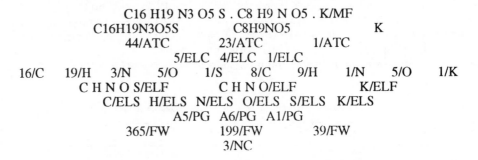

C16 H19 N3 O5 S . C8 H9 N O5 . K/MF

C16H19N3O5S   C8H9NO5   K

44/ATC   23/ATC   1/ATC

5/ELC 4/ELC 1/ELC

16/C   19/H   3/N   5/O   1/S   8/C   9/H   1/N   5/O   1/K

C H N O S/ELF   C H N O/ELF   K/ELF

C/ELS H/ELS N/ELS O/ELS S/ELS K/ELS

A5/PG A6/PG A1/PG

365/FW   199/FW   39/FW

3/NC

13.4 Search strategies in molecular formula fields

13.4.1 Proximity operators

Proximity operators are not allowed in searches in the Molecular Formula Field since entries here are bound phrases, but the (L) operator may be used to link bound phrases in the Basic Index. That is, the search: => S C8H9NO5 (L) K would retrieve, *inter alia*, the record for augmentin. The AND operator can be used but additionally it will link entries in the MF Field with those in the AF Field (when present), and such links are rarely necessary.

Table 13.4 Examples of use of proximity operators in molecular formula based fields[a]

FIELD	OPERATOR	APPLICATION
ATC	AND	includes links between MF and AF Fields
	(L)	restricts links to same field (MF or AF)
	(L)	links ATC with other formula derived fields
		(Example: S 44/ATC (L) K/ELS)
ELC	(L)	links element counts in different components
		(Example: S 5/ELC (L) 4/ELC)
	(P)	links ELC with other formula derived fields in a single component
		(Example: S 5/ELC (P) 44/ATC)
ELF	AND	includes links between MF and AF Fields
	(L)	restricts links to same field (MF or AF)
		(Example: S C H N O/ELF (L) K/ELF)
ELS	(L), (P)	links element symbols within a single component
or		(Examples: S C/ELS (L) O/ELS
(elements)		S 16/C (L) 19/H)
	(W), (A)	links element symbols within a single component
		(W) = adjacent, (A) = adjacent (any order)
PG	(L)	restricts links to same field (MF or AF)
		(Example: S A6/PG (L) A1/PG)
	(P)	links PG with other formula derived fields in a single component
		(Example: S A6/PG (P) C=16)
FW	(L)	restricts links to same field (MF or AF)
		(Example: S 365/FW (L) 199/FW)
NC	(L)	links NC with other formula derived fields
		(Example: S C8H9NO5 (L) 3/NC)

[a]The search examples chosen would all retrieve, *inter alia*, the record for augmentin

In fields based on molecular formulas (Table 13.3) the overall rule is that the MF and AF Fields are each single information units, although in the ELS and specific element fields each component in a multicomponent substance is a single information unit. Actually there are a number of aspects of the application of the proximity operators in these fields on STN and they are summarized in Table 13.4.

The subtle differences in the applications of the operators in the different fields relate to whether searches "make sense" within a single component level. For example, the ELF Field refers to the whole component and it makes no sense to combine the whole element formula with one or more elements within the component formula. That is, the (P) operator has no meaning.

On the other hand, the individual elements within a single component formula have independent postings and it is sensible to link them within the single component (using the ELS or element symbol fields).

13.4.2 Numeric search fields

Many search fields based on molecular formulas are numeric search fields in which case the two formats mentioned in Section 4.3.4 may be used. For example, the options shown in Table 4.2 apply, and it is possible to enter either 16/C or C=16 as a search term to find components with 16 carbons. Additionally other numeric operators may be used and 16-18/C or C>30 would retrieve answers which had components with 16,17,18 or 31 and larger numbers of carbons respectively.

Important note:
- **Numeric searches can be performed in one of two ways:**
=> S <NUMERIC VALUE>/FIELD CODE
                              or
=> S FIELD CODE <NUMERIC OPERATOR> <NUMERIC VALUE>

13.4.3 Single substance

If only a single substance of known molecular formula is required, and if an expansion on entries in the CN Field is not successful, then a general strategy on STN is to:

1. EXPAND on the molecular formula in the MF Field;
2. SEARCH on the E-number;
3 DISPLAY SCAN to check at minimum cost what additional search terms might narrow the answer set;
4. SEARCH answer set with added search terms; and
5. DISPLAY answer.

This procedure is particularly useful either when there are only relatively few isomers with the molecular formula of interest or if there are many isomeric substances, then when a few additional search terms, which can quickly narrow the size of the answer set, can be added. For example, while the systematic name for the thione (1) might be difficult to derive, its molecular formula ($C_{10}H_8O_2S$) is readily obtained. However, an expansion on this formula indicates that there are 207 such isomeric substances.

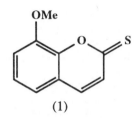

(1)

Nevertheless the THIONE and METHOXY groups are likely chemical name segments and the initial answer set is quickly narrowed to such a level that all answers may be scanned and the substance of interest identified (Screen 13.1).

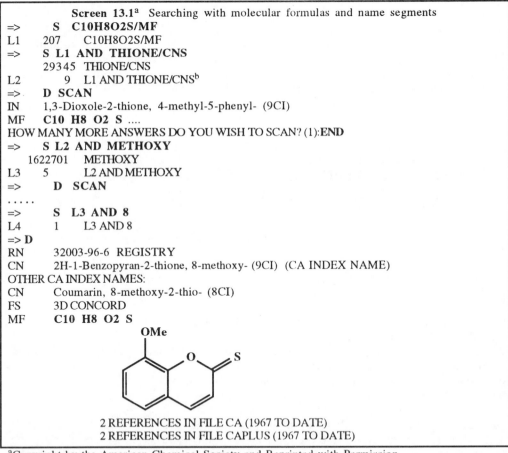

Screen 13.1[a] Searching with molecular formulas and name segments
=>   **S   C10H8O2S/MF**
L1   207   C10H8O2S/MF
=>   **S L1 AND THIONE/CNS**
       29345   THIONE/CNS
L2   9   L1 AND THIONE/CNS[b]
=>.   **D SCAN**
IN   1,3-Dioxole-2-thione, 4-methyl-5-phenyl- (9CI)
MF   **C10 H8 O2 S** ....
HOW MANY MORE ANSWERS DO YOU WISH TO SCAN? (1):**END**
=>   **S L2 AND METHOXY**
   1622701   METHOXY
L3   5   L2 AND METHOXY
=>   **D SCAN**
. . . . .
=>   **S L3 AND 8**
L4   1   L3 AND 8
=> D
RN   32003-96-6 REGISTRY
CN   2H-1-Benzopyran-2-thione, 8-methoxy- (9CI) (CA INDEX NAME)
OTHER CA INDEX NAMES:
CN   Coumarin, 8-methoxy-2-thio- (8CI)
FS   3D CONCORD
MF   **C10 H8 O2 S**

2 REFERENCES IN FILE CA (1967 TO DATE)
2 REFERENCES IN FILE CAPLUS (1967 TO DATE)

[a]Copyright by the American Chemical Society and Reprinted with Permission
[b]Note that since only 9 answers are retrieved all could be scanned at this stage and the required substance identified. It would be found that the terms METHOXY and 8 are needed to select out the single answer. However, as shown here, the process is executed in a number of steps, it being immediately realized on scanning L2 that the term METHOXY may be safely used to narrow answers further.

13.4.4 Single multicomponent substance

If a single multicomponent substance is required then, taking note of the order in which the component formulas are entered, an expansion in the MF Field will quickly indicate whether this procedure is likely to be successful. For example, Screen 13.2 indicates how a molecular formula based search might also have been used to find pyridinium salicylate (see Screen 12.4).

Screen 13.2[a] Finding a salt through a molecular formula search: pyridinium salicylate

=>	E C7H6O3.C5H5N/MF 5	
E1	1	C7H6O3.C5H4N4O.NA/MF
E2	1	C7H6O3.C5H4O2/MF
E3	1 -->	C7H6O3.C5H5N/MF
E4	4	C7H6O3.C5H5N3O.NA/MF
E5	3	C7H6O3.C5H5N5/MF
=>	S E3	

Note that this expand merely informs that there is an entry C7H6O3.C5H5N/MF and only a search (on E3), followed by a display of the answer, would verify that this formula did indeed correspond with pyridinium salicylate.

13.4.5 Multicomponent substances containing specific components

The difficulty with nomenclature identified in the search for substances containing aspirin, caffeine and morphine (see Section 12.4.2) can be overcome if instead a search based on the molecular formulas is used, but now the problem with molecular formula based searches (that is, isomeric substances) arises. However, the 'ambiguity' relating to molecular formula searches (the issue of isomers) may be used to advantage. Thus, if it were of no concern as to which isomer was used, searches in the Basic Index can yield useful (and unique) answer sets. For example, if polymers containing any of the monomers

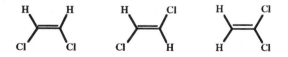

were required then a search using C2H2Cl2 (in Basic Index) could be used, and in order to restrict the answer set to polymers it would be necessary merely to add the search term PMS/CI.

13.4.6 Isotopic substances

For substances which contain deuterium or tritium, two separate formulas are posted in the Molecular Formula Field and in the Basic Index. One formula contains the symbol for deuterium or tritium, and the second formula replaces these isotopes with hydrogen. Accordingly the substance shown in Screen 11.16 is posted both as C10 H13 D N2 and C10 H14 N2.

If the isotope D or T is included in the formula only that isotopic form is retrieved, while to exclude these isotopic forms it is necessary to add the search terms NOT D/ELS or NOT T/ELS to the search statement. Abnormal isotopes of the other elements are not shown in the Molecular Formula Field, but are reflected in the Index Name (see Section 11.4.11 and Screen 11.16). Accordingly the search term to retrieve substances with ^{235}U would be: => **S 235U/CNS**.

13.4.7 Other applications of searches based on molecular formulas
The various search fields based on molecular formulas (Table 13.3) are useful for obtaining groups of substances particularly when used in combination, or with other search terms. Table 13.5 shows some examples in which, progressively, more restricted answer sets are retrieved.

Table 13.5 Examples of search options in molecular formula based fields

SEARCH TERM	RETRIEVES
C/ELS AND H/ELS AND X/ELS	substances containing carbon, hydrogen, halogens and any other atoms
C/ELS AND H/ELS AND X/ELS AND 3/ELC	substances containing only carbon, hydrogen, and (one of the) halogens
12/C AND H/ELS AND X/ELS AND 3/ELC AND BIPHENYL	halogenated biphenyls
12/C AND H/ELS AND Cl/ELS AND 3/ELC AND BIPHENYL	chlorinated biphenyls

Meanwhile searches based on molecular formulas may always be performed on any subset of the REGISTRY File that has been obtained through any other search procedure. Thus, an answer set may have been obtained through a structure search and, if, for example, the structure searched included the variable atom for metals, M (see Section 15.3.1b), a number of substances may have been retrieved with different metals present. Those substances which had ruthenium, or had metals in the second row of transition elements, present could be selected with the search terms **RU/ELS** and **T2/PG** respectively.

Alternatively, suppose that the mass spectrum of an unknown substance indicated that it had formula weight 340, and that the NMR spectrum indicated the presence of 8 CH3 groups, and 10 CH2 groups. All those substances of formula weight 340 may be retrieved (=> **S FW=340**) and a structure search, identifying the structure components, may be conducted on the initial answer set (as a SUBSET search, see Section 15.5.3b). As with all online searching, quite ingenious searches may be used to retrieve relevant answers to the most intricate problems.

It is important to be aware of all the various chemical name and molecular formula based searches which may be used, since only then may the best search option be chosen to solve the problem at hand. Naturally, structure based search terms may be used also and these will be discussed in the following two chapters.

Summary

- Substances of known composition have entries in the Molecular Formula Field.
- Molecular formulas are entered in the *Hill system order* and the rules are extended to multicomponent substances so that components are entered in order of decreasing number of carbons, then hydrogens, then atoms in alphabetical order.
- A major difficulty with molecular formula based searches is that many isomers of the formula often exist, but the answer sets may be narrowed with other search terms (usually those based on name fragments).
- Complete formulas are searched as *bound phrases* in the Molecular Formula Field.
- Molecular formulas for *individual components* are searched as bound phrases in the *Basic Index*.
- There are a number of numeric search fields based on counts of atoms in molecular formulas.

14

How Structure Searching Works

In this chapter we learn the theory behind the searching for substances by structure on STN!

That is, with the CAS structure search system, screen numbers define structure fragments and when a structure is built the system automatically generates all the screen numbers relating to the query.

When the query is searched, the system first matches the screen numbers with screen numbers for substances on the file, and those substances which pass the screen test are then matched atom-by-atom with the search query.

Structure searching is not hard. It just is different! Further, different database producers have different search engines and the ways the searches are performed are different. What the searcher really wants is to be able to draw the structure in the usual manner and then to let the system interpret the structure in the way appropriate for the file to be searched.

The communications software, STN Express, does exactly that! That is, before the structure is drawn, the software asks for the format in which the structure is to be interpreted and the options on STN are: STANDARD (that used by the CAS databases), SPECINFO (that used in the SPECINFO File which contains ^{13}C nmr and IR spectra), and WPI (that used by the Derwent files). Additionally, an option exists for structure searching directly on Questel.

In most structure searches all the screens necessary to execute the search are generated automatically and so it is not essential that the searcher knows how the structure search operates. However, even when working with the STN Express software, an understanding of how the system operates will help the searcher in the application of some of the search options available.

14.1 Connection tables

Structures are encoded in the CAS Registry system as connection tables that detail which atoms are connected to which other atoms and by what type of bonds. Atoms are connected either in rings or in chains and while in the normal representation of structures it is obvious which atoms and bonds are in rings, this needs to be specifically described in connection tables.

For example, the chemist's picture of nicotine and the corresponding computer "drawing" is shown in Figure 14.1 in which the node numbers on the structure diagram correspond with the node numbers in the structure connection table. Accordingly the computer drawing describes the nitrogen (number 3) in the five-membered ring as connected by a ring single exact bond (RSE) to a carbon it numbers 5, a similar connection to another carbon it numbers 2, and a chain single exact bond (CSE) to a carbon it numbers 1.

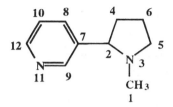

```
***************CONNECTIONS***************
```

NOD SYM	NOD/BON/SIT/STE	NOD/BON/SIT/STE	NOD/BON/SIT/STE
1 C	3 CSE		
2 C	7 CSE	4 RSE	3 RSE
3 N	5 RSE	2 RSE	1 CSE
4 C	6 RSE	2 RSE	
5 C	6 RSE	3 RSE	
6 C	4 RSE	5 RSE	
7 C	9 RN	8 RN	2 CSE
8 C	10 RN	7 RN	
9 C	11 RN	7 RN	
10 C	12 RN	8 RN	
11 N	12 RN	9 RN	
12 C	11 RN	10 RN	

Figure 14.1   Structure connection table for nicotine

Every specific structure has its own complete connection table and the bonds are characterized by symbols: R = ring, C = chain, SE = single exact, and N = normalized (see Sections 14.4 to 14.6). Stereoisomers and isotopically labeled substances have the same structure connection table, and the different substances can be distinguished only by additional search terms (for example, by name based terms or a structure stereosearch, although some Graph Modifier screens (see below) may be associated with the record for the substance on the File).

The atoms are numbered in the connection table in a way determined by the system and do not relate to the normal numbering conventions used in chemical nomenclature, while the

SIT and STE headings shown in Figure 14.1 are relevant to chemical reaction site and stereochemical searches (for general discussion see Sections 17.4.3 and 15.9 respectively).

In order for a structure to be retrieved through a structure search query, the computer must match up the chemist's drawing with the computer drawing, and while it would be possible for the computer to determine the full connectivities in the search query and match them with the full connectivities of structures on the file, in practice this would be a very demanding process in CPU time. Further, since a chemist often wishes to identify all related structures of a given type then this specific connectivity matching process would soon become very inefficient with databases containing large numbers of structures.

Accordingly, the system executes structure searching in a two-stage process. First the database is screened for potential answers, and then the atom-by-atom matching is conducted.

14.2 What is the nature of the screening process?

In setting up the first chemical structure database (the CAS Registry Database), the Chemical Abstracts Service defined just over 2000 different screens, and these same screens are now used in the chemical structure databases available on STN (except the SPECINFO File). This is important since essentially the same search query may be searched in any one of the databases. Actually, there are a few very minor differences in the ways in which structures are encoded in the REGISTRY File and in the BEILSTEIN File, and in almost all cases these differences are of no concern to the searcher. They occur only in some cases where ions are involved in resonance structures, for example in salts of acids, and occur in some functional groups like the azide group. While the screens used for structures in the Questel database are somewhat different, however, as already noted, the STN Express software has an option under which Questel structures can be saved automatically in the necessary format.

Screens relate to features of parts of structures, and the list of the different types of screens is given in Table 14.1. (The full list of the actual screens is given in the *Screen Dictionary* available from CAS.)

Table 14.1 Types of screens

	TYPE OF SCREEN	CONTENTS
AA	AUGMENTED ATOM	non-hydrogen attachments and bonds
AS	ATOM SEQUENCE	linear atom sequences of 4 to 6 atoms and bonds
BS	BOND SEQUENCE	linear bond sequences of 3-5 bonds
CS	CONNECTIVITY SEQUENCE	exact number of non-hydrogen connections in a linear sequence
RC	RING COUNT	minimum number of rings
TR	TYPE OF RING	atom types (isolated/embedded) in 3-7 rings
AC	ATOM COUNT	minimum number of non-hydrogen atoms
DC	DEGREE CONNECTIVITY	minimum number of atoms having at least a specified number of non-hydrogen attachments
EC	ELEMENT COMPOSITION	minimum number of atoms of each element (except H, D, T)
GM	GRAPH MODIFIER	various screen types including substance Class Identifiers

14.3 Augmented Atom screens

For example, there are around 400 screens in the Screen Dictionary which are called Augmented Atom screens. These describe which atoms are augmented (connected) to the central atom in question, and the nature of the bond which makes the connection.

A few Augmented Atom screens are shown in Table 14.2. That is, screen number 1344 is an AA (Augmented Atom) screen relating to a carbon atom which is connected to an arsenic atom (As), and to a carbon atom (C). The hyphen and asterisk refer to the *type of bond* (chain and ring respectively), and the frequency of occurrence of this screen number 1344 in substances in the database is 2.63%.

Table 14.2 Augmented Atom screens[a]

SCREEN NUMBER	FRAGMENT DEFINITION			FREQ %
1344 AA	C	-As	*C	2.63
1345 AA	C	-1As	*1C	0.28
1346 AA	C	-1As	*4C	2.41
1190 AA	C	-1As	-3C	0.17

[a]This screen type describes attachments to the central atom

More specific screens relating to the same connections of atoms are 1345, 1346, and 1190, the only differences now being that numbers precede the As atom and the second C atom, and these numbers refer to the *value of the bond*.

The full list of bond types and bond values, together with some of the common combinations, is shown in Table 14.3.

Table 14.3 Bond types and bond values

BOND TYPES		BOND VALUES	
*	ring	1	single exact
-	chain	2	double exact
(blank)	ring/chain	3	triple
		4	normalized
EXAMPLES			
*	any ring bond	-	any chain bond
*1	single exact ring bond	-1	single exact chain bond
*2	double exact ring bond	-2	double exact chain bond
*3	triple ring bond	-3	triple chain bond
*4	normalized ring bond	-4	normalized chain bond
(blank)	any bond		

So screen number 1346 (Table 14.2) is for "a central carbon atom attached by a single exact chain bond to an arsenic atom and by a normalized ring bond to a carbon atom".

14.4 Bond values

Connections between atoms in computer generated connection tables follow the valence bond definitions for bonds. Recall from Chapter 11 that the valence theory of bonding says each bond is made of two electrons, and, because of various limitations on the number of electrons which can be around an atom, this means atoms may have only a specific number of bonds. The maximum number of bonds an atom can have is equal to (what is called) its valency. Carbon has a valency of 4 and that means it has a maximum of 4 bonds.

However, the chemist will immediately recognize that the terminology in Table 14.3 is a little different from that traditionally used in the chemical literature, and Table 14.4 shows how the terminologies compare. Thus, what a chemist traditionally calls a single bond is defined as a single exact bond in the connection table.

An unspecified bond means one of any value, and screens with unspecified bonds are automatically selected when the structure query does not define the nature of the bond. For example, if compounds containing either the C-O or the C=O bond in a certain position are required then the bond between the atoms should be left unspecified in the structure query.

Table 14.4 Correlation between bond descriptions

CHEMICAL DEFINITION	SYSTEM DEFINITION
SINGLE BOND	SINGLE EXACT (SE)
DOUBLE BOND	DOUBLE EXACT (DE)
TRIPLE BOND	TRIPLE (T)
UNSPECIFIED BOND	
AROMATIC BOND	No single correlation but
DONOR or σ- BOND	instead the system handles these
π- BOND	bonds in various ways

However, in chemical substances, there are two situations when a single valence bond structure does not truly represent the properties of the substance and to overcome this problem chemists use two concepts to supplement the valence bond theory. These concepts are resonance and tautomerism.

While, in general, a bond with a system-defined normalized value correlates with either resonance or tautomerism, the correlation is not perfect and there are very important exceptions to this general statement.

14.5 Normalized bonds

System-defined normalized bonds occur in two situations.

14.5.1 Alternating single and double bonds in a ring with an even number of atoms
When alternating single and double bonds occur in a ring with an even number of atoms then all bonds in the ring are described as normalized. Some examples of substances with normalized bonds are shown in Figure 14.2.

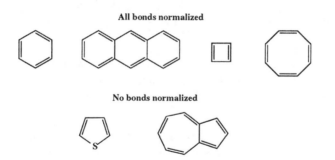

Figure 14.2   Examples of normalized bonds

However, this definition does not directly correlate with resonance (or aromaticity) since other substances shown in Figure 14.2 do not have normalized bonds defined by the system (even though the chemist will recognize they have significant resonance structures). Also, chemists will recognize that cyclobutadiene and cyclooctatetraene (the structures on the top right in Figure 14.2) are definitely not aromatic compounds. It is important to realize that normalized bonds occur only when the rings have even numbers of atoms.

14.5.2   Tautomers
The system also defines normalized bonds between atoms in the situations covered in Figure 14.3. The two very important factors to note are first, that either X or Z must have a hydrogen (or deuterium or tritium) atom attachment or a charge (charged ions of this type do occur in the REGISTRY File, for example in "inner salts" like $(CH_3)_2S^+CH_2COO^-$ (compare Section 11.4.10)); and second that neither X nor Z may be carbon.

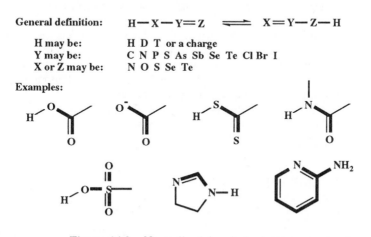

Figure 14.3   Normalized bonds in tautomers

The first point means, for example, that the bonds in carboxylic acids, and primary and secondary amides, are normalized whereas the bonds in esters and tertiary amides are exact (Figure 14.4).

The second point means that ketones and enols are represented by exact bonds! (Chemists will recognize that this is the situation in which tautomerism is very commonly considered.) However, the vast majority of carbonyl compounds are present as the keto form only and it would have been very confusing if normalized bonding was system-defined for the carbonyl group. If there is the possibility that a particular carbonyl compound (for example, a β-ketoester) might have been reported as the enol form, then structures (with exact bonds) for both the keto and the enol forms should be built and searched (using the OR operator between the structure query L-numbers in the search statement).

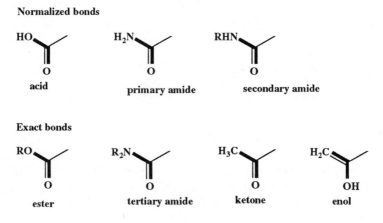

Normalized bonds

acid   primary amide   secondary amide

Exact bonds

ester   tertiary amide   ketone   enol

Figure 14.4   Examples of normalized and exact bonds

Searchers must be very aware of these differences between "chemical" and "system" definitions of bond values, even if they build their structures using the STN Express software. The first point to realize is that normalized bonding in rings occurs only when there are an even number of ring atoms, and the second is that the "tautomer equation" must involve a hydrogen atom (or deuterium or tritium or charge).

Possible structures for the screens shown in Table 14.2 can now be imagined, and some examples are shown in Figure 14.5.

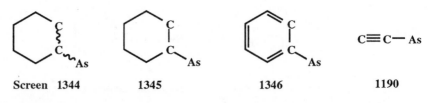

Screen 1344   1345   1346   1190

Figure 14.5   Structures corresponding with screen numbers in Table 14.2

14.6 Other cases in which the valence bond theory does not directly apply

While normalized bonding covers the general areas of resonance and of tautomerism, there are two other chemical bond types which need special attention.

14.6.1 π-bonds

There are many cases, particularly when metals are involved, in which bonds are formed by electrons which are shared between more than two atoms. Such bonds are generally called π-bonds. The system treats such multi-atom bonds as if there was a single bond between each of the atoms involved (see also Section 11.4.3).

For example, the classical case of π-bonding occurs in the substance ferrocene and Figure 14.6 shows the structures in the ways represented by chemists and by the system.

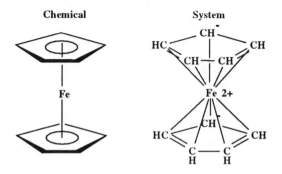

Figure 14.6 Representation for ferrocene

14.6.2 Donor bonds

Generally, in a covalent bond between two atoms each of the atoms contributes one electron. However, there are cases where the two electrons are provided by one atom only (this often occurs as the second bond between the atoms, the atoms having already been formally connected through another bond in which each atom has contributed one electron in the usual manner) and these are called donor bonds. Chemists represent the structures of such molecules either by a single bond between the atoms with each atom (necessarily from a chemical viewpoint) bearing a charge (one positive and one negative), or by a double bond between the two atoms (and no charges on either atom).

Unfortunately chemists themselves are often inconsistent in the way they draw the structures. For example, chemists commonly draw the sulfone and the sulfoxide functional group using the different representations (Figure 14.7) even though the same principle is involved, that is, that in the second bond between the sulfur and the oxygen, the sulfur provides both the electrons in each case.

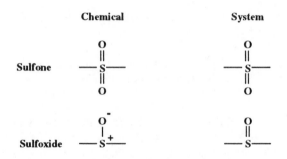

Figure 14.7   Representations for donor bonds

However, computers cannot allow such inconsistencies and must have one representation or the other. Accordingly the rule is that connection tables treat such donor bonds as double bonds and no charges are associated with the individual atoms. (The main cases which vary considerably from the chemical representation are with the amine oxides and nitro compounds, which on the system are represented as $R_3N=O$ and (1) respectively.)

(1)

14.7 Other structure based screens

14.7.1 Atom Sequence

Other screens relate to sequences of between 4 and 6 atoms, and an example of an Atom Sequence screen is shown in Table 14.5. Screen numbers often describe similar fragments and screen number 474 applies to six atom sequences in which either oxygen or sulfur atoms are at the end of 4 carbons, with all bonds except the central bond being in chains. Screen number 475 differs in that only chain bonds are involved.

Table 14.5   Atom Sequence screen[a]

SCREEN NUMBER	FRAGMENT DEFINITION		FREQ %
474	AS	O - C - C * C - C - O	1.28
		O - C - C * C - C - S	
		S - C - C * C - C - S	
475	AS	O - C - C - C - C - O	2.88
		O - C - C - C - C - S	
		S - C - C - C - C - S	

[a]This screen type describes linear sequences of 4, 5, or 6 atoms and their bonding

14.7.2 Type of Ring

Examples of Type of Ring screens are shown in Table 14.6. In this class of screens, ring atoms are differentiated only by whether the atoms are present in a single ring or whether they are common to more than one ring. The former are given the symbol D, while the latter are given the symbol T. If the fragment definition contains only three such symbols then the screen refers only to three-membered rings.

Table 14.6 Type of Ring screens[a]

SCREEN NUMBER		FRAGMENT DEFINITION	FREQ %
1848 TR		DDD	1.71
1849 TR	2	DDD	0.17
1850 TR		DDT	0.26
1851 TR		DTT	2.18
1851 TR		TTT	2.18

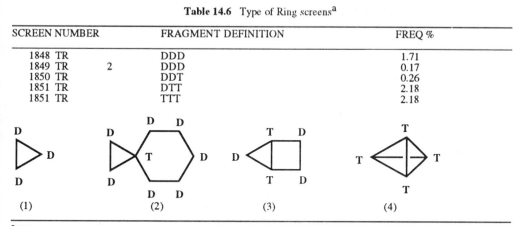

(1) (2) (3) (4)

[a]This screen type characterizes ring atoms depending on whether they are in isolated (D) or fused (T) ring systems

Also shown in Table 14.6 are some examples. For example, structure (1) would be indexed with screen number 1848 while structure (2) would be indexed with screen number 1850 (and also with screen number 1873 which has fragment DDDDDT), although it should be noted that these Type of Ring screens are not automatically selected by the system unless the rings are isolated (see Section 15.2.2b).

14.7.3 Bond Sequence
Another type of screen is the Bond Sequences screen and some examples are shown in Table 14.7. These screens are generated when, for example, the bonding sequence is defined in the structure query, but various options are allowed for some of the atom nodes.

Table 14.7 Bond Sequence screens

SCREEN NUMBER	FRAGMENT DEFINITION		FREQ%
795	BS	A * A - A * A	15.81
803	BS	A * A - A * A * A - A	10.42
804	BS	A * A - A* A - A	9.55
805	BS	A * A - A * A - A * A	1.25
734	BS	A *1A * 1A *1A *1A	40.52

Accordingly, screen number 734 defines the situation in which five atoms (A = any atom other than hydrogen) are connected by single bonds in a ring, while the other screens have atoms linked (by unspecified bonds) in rings and chains.

14.8 Screens which are number-based and Graph Modifier screens

There are other classes of screens which are number-based and these are ATOM COUNT (minimum number of non-hydrogen atoms present), RING COUNT (minimum number of rings), and ELEMENT COMPOSITION (minimum number of atoms of each element). Finally, Graph Modifier screens refer to a variety of special features possible in structures, and some of the more commonly used screens are shown in Table 14.8.

Table 14.8 Some Graph Modifier screens

SCREEN NUMBER	DESCRIPTION
2039	abnormal mass - all isotopic specifications
2040	abnormal valence
2127	2 or more components
2077	3 or more components
2078	4 or more components
2050	alloy
2049	coordination compound
2052	manual registration
2052	mineral
2051	mixture
2043	polymer

In most structure searches all the screens necessary to execute the search are generated automatically and there is no need to add additional screens. Nevertheless, it is important to know how structures are input into the system, and how the search operates, since then the importance of various options within structure building are understood. However, there are cases where screens need to be added and this may be done through one of the drop down menus in the STN Express software, or manually. For manual inclusion of screens it is necessary to identify the screen number from the Screen Dictionary, although these screens may be applied through STN Express under the **View Query Refinement** option within **QueryDef** in the structure building program. (Further details are given in Section 15.5.3a.)

14.9 The search process: types and scopes of searches

Once the structure has been built it is then searched. There are four types of searches which may be conducted and they are called EXACT, FAMILY, CLOSED SUBSTRUCTURE and SUBSTRUCTURE. There are three scopes of searches which may be conducted and they are called SAMPLE, RANGE, and FULL. These are discussed in Chapter 15.

All structure searches are executed in two steps: first, a screening process, and then an atom-by-atom iterative matching process. For example, the system might be able to generate 20 specific screen numbers from the *structure query*. If an EXACT structure search is requested, the system will search for all substances which have *only those same 20 screen numbers* and thus will identify them as potential answers. Having completed this screening, the system does an atom-by-atom match of each potential answer against the actual search query and only those which exactly fit are placed in the final answer set.

On the other hand, if a SUBSTRUCTURE search is requested, the system will search for all substances which have those same 20 screen numbers but will allow to pass in this screen step any substances which have any additional screens.

There are two main reasons for the execution of the iterative stage. First, most screen numbers have more than one fragment definition and the fragment in the query, which caused selection of that screen number, might have been different from the related fragment in the potential answer. For example, the query might have had the atom sequence O-C-C-C-C-O whereas the potential answer might have had the atom sequence O-C-C-C-C-S. Both of these fragments are defined by screen number 475 (Table 14.5).

Second, the different fragments which caused selection of the different screens might have been connected differently in the query and in the potential answer. This is illustrated in Figure 14.8. Both of these structures contain two fragments defined by two screens numbered 475, but their connections are very different!

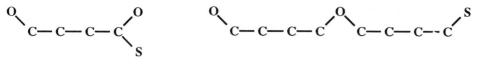

Figure 14.8   Identifying the correct connectivity between the atom fragments

14.10 Files in which structures may be searched and displayed

Currently there are a number of files in which structures may be searched or displayed on STN, and the list is given in Table 14.9. Those files which support "standard STN" queries use the structure connection tables discussed in this chapter. While the remaining files in which structure searches are available have different search processes, the queries may easily be generated in the correct format through the STN Express software. (For details see the *STN Express User Guide*. Remember that structure queries for the Questel system may also be built through STN Express.)

Table 14.9 Structure files

FILE	STRUCTURE SEARCH	STRUCTURE DISPLAY
BEILSTEIN	Standard STN	Yes
CASREACT	Standard STN	Yes
CHEMINFORMRX	Standard STN	Yes
CHEMREACT	Standard STN	Yes
CSCHEM	Not available	Yes
DRUGU	Standard STN	Yes
DRUGUPDATES	Not available	Yes
GMELIN	Standard STN	Yes
HSDB	Not available	Yes
MARPAT	Standard STN	Yes
MARPATPREV	Standard STN	Yes
MRCK	Not available	Yes
PHAR	Not available	Yes
REGISTRY	Standard STN	Yes
RTECS	Not available	Yes
SPECINFO	Special calculation packages	Yes
USAN	Not available	Yes
WPI	Derwent fragmentation codes	Yes

Summary

- Structures are entered in the system on STN as *connection tables based on valence bond theory*.
- Bond descriptions generally correlate with normal definitions (single exact bond in the system = single bond in valence bond definition), although "exceptions" arise with definitions of normalized and unspecified bonds, and in the manner in which π- and donor-bonds are treated.
- It is necessary for the system to identify bonds (and atoms) which are in rings and which are in chains.
- *Screens* define fragments or features of structures.
- The search involves a screening process and then an atom-by-atom match of potential answers against the original query.

15

Searching by Structure

In this chapter we learn first of the steps involved in performing structure searches.

In particular, we learn:

- *Issues in defining the structure query.*
- *Structure building defaults both at the system level and within STN Express.*
- *Options for allowing variables in the structure query.*
- *How to perform sample searches and analyse results.*
- *Options to modify initial structure queries.*
- *How to find information on the substances we retrieve in the final search.*

We do not learn here about structure building details which are fully explained in manuals provided by STN. Instead we concentrate more on the special issues related to building structures for search queries.

Having learnt the principles we then work through an actual example, showing the different types of searches and indicating where the problems arise and how they may be overcome.

There are two main reasons why a structure search is undertaken. First, it may not have been possible to find the substance quickly by a name or formula based search. Names may be difficult to determine, and formulas are not unique. Sometimes relatively simple substances may be very difficult to find through either of these methods, and by the time a number of search terms have been used it would have been quicker and more economical to find the substance through a structure search. After all, a structure is an unique and precise description of a substance and provided the search query is built correctly then a structure search will provide a comprehensive and precise answer set.

Second, it simply may not be possible to define the question in any way other than through a structure diagram. This applies particularly to substructure searching.

The steps involved in a structure search are shown in Figure 15.1 and are discussed in turn in this chapter.

1.   DEFINE THE QUERY
2.   BUILD THE STRUCTURE QUERY
3.   ENTER THE FILE
4.   UPLOAD THE QUERY
5.   PERFORM A SAMPLE SEARCH
6.   SCAN SOME OF THE ANSWERS
7.   REVISE THE STRUCTURE QUERY (if needed)
8.   PERFORM A FULL SEARCH
9.   FIND INFORMATION ON THE SUBSTANCE(S)

Figure 15.1   Steps involved in a structure search

Important notes:
*   **The actual process of searching for structures is quite easy - that is, once you have built the structure you use the SEARCH command and then you DISPLAY the chemical substances retrieved.**
*   **However, some structure files are very large, and structures have many subtle variations, so the difficult aspect is to know how to build the right initial structure and then, if necessary, to know the tools needed to modify it to give the substances you really want.**

15.1 Define the query

As mentioned in Section 11.7, a whole new way of thinking about searching for substances in electronic databases needs to be developed. In particular, it is possible, and through using very simple techniques, to search for either a single substance or a group of substances. The group of substances can be related by name, formula, or structure and of these the last option offers the greatest precision.

So, the first consideration about searching for a substance is to decide whether only the single substance, the substance and its isotopic or stereoisomeric forms, the substance as a component in a multicomponent substance, or substances which have a specific part structure best provide the answers.

Structure searches are most commonly performed in one of three types. An EXACT search gives all substances whose structure connection tables are exactly the same as the structure connection table for the search query; a FAMILY search will *additionally* retrieve all multicomponent substances which have one of the components with the same structure connection table as that of the search query; and a SUBSTRUCTURE search will additionally retrieve all substances which have the structure connection table of the query embedded within the full structure connection table of the actual substance. Note that an EXACT and a FAMILY search may give different results from a search on the CAS Registry Number and on a search on this number in the CRN Field respectively, because the latter searches will not retrieve isotopic substances and stereoisomers.

When contemplating a structure search it is also important to consider the scope of the database and the variability possible in the search query. Databases of the size of the BEILSTEIN and REGISTRY Files contain quite extraordinary varieties of structures, and often there are many hundreds of structures of any given type. So sometimes very specific structures need to be searched in order to obtain the quite specific information required.

On the other hand, the particular substance of interest may not be in either of the files, in which case it is necessary to search for related substances or even for synthetic precursors. That is, very general structures need to be searched. For example, if the target substance is a methyl ester of the type (1) in which the ring system is of quite unusual structure, it may either not have been reported or, if reported, there may be only one method of preparation which may not be practical for the current purposes. In such cases it may be desirable to search not only for other esters but also for the acid and even for its precursors.

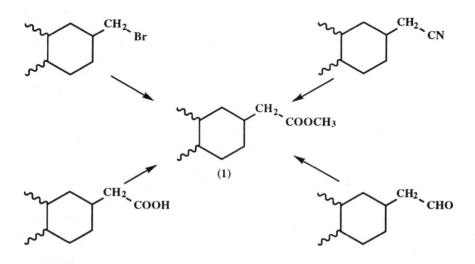

Essentially any variation may be built into the structure query. There may be different sizes and types of rings, or chains. Bonds may be exact or left unspecified and either single atoms, or groups of atoms, may be allowed. Further, the searcher need not necessarily specify where the groups are attached: attachments may be left completely open (groups may be attached anywhere), or the attachments may be optional but only in specified locations.

Important notes:
- **There is no parallel to structure searching in the hardcopy literature and the chemist really has to learn a new way of thinking about searching for substances!**
- **Searches may be very specific or very broad, and may even involve synthetic precursors, isotopic substances, and stereoisomers to name a few.**
- **There is no structure-related problem which cannot be solved through a structure search!**

15.2 Build the structure

A structure search query may be built either with keyboard commands or through a structure drawing program like STN Express. Prior to the introduction of STN Express, structures had to be built by the former method, but both options for structure building are now available and the structure drawing program in STN Express is the method of choice to most since it eliminates the need to remember what can be quite complicated keyboard instructions. In either case, similar steps are involved. That is, the atom skeleton is built first and the default definition for the nodes (atom positions) is that they are carbon. This node default is then overridden by specifying the non-carbon nodes, and finally the bonds are specified.

Detailed descriptions of structure building methods are available in a number of manuals (for keyboard commands see the manual: *Building and Searching Structures on STN*; for structure drawing with STN Express see the manual: *STN Express User Guide* which is provided with the software). Attention also is drawn to the STN Workshop: *Structure Searching with STN Express*. In this workshop not only are the various structure building mechanics explained, but also actual online practice is provided and this can be a very effective way of learning to search by structure.

15.2.1 *Traps for the unwary - particularly experienced chemists!*
Structures may also be built with other structure drawing software and these structures may be imported into STN Express. As STN Express has automatic "uploading" (see Section 15.8) the unwary chemist thinks that all that is involved with structure searching is to draw the structure say in CHEMDRAW, import the structure into STN Express, then upload and search. This is true - but only when an EXACT or FAMILY search is required, although EXACT and FAMILY searches also allow variations in bonds (but not variations in atoms), and special modifications may need to be made to imported structures to allow for such possibilities.

However, with a SUBSTRUCTURE search there are many system defaults and search options which need to be addressed, and if they are not then the import/upload and search procedure just outlined will give either a very large number of false hits or will not give optimal answers since full structure search possibilities will not have been exploited.

15.2.2 *Structure building defaults: system level*

15.2.2a *Chain default*
When atoms are drawn in a chain, all the atoms and bonds are automatically assigned chain values. Accordingly all screens generated will have chain values only (for discussion of chain values in screens see Section 14.3). Often it is necessary to override this default, and this may be done either for the bonds or for the atoms.

For example, if substances (1) and (2) are representative of the structures required in a substructure search then the basic common skeleton is structure (3).

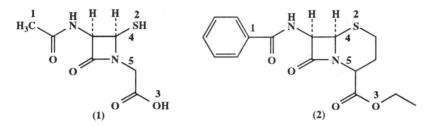

(1)   (2)

However, if structure (3) is built without changing the defaults, and searched, then structure (1) will be retrieved but structure (2) will not because in structure (2) the node marked 1, and the bonds marked 4 and 5, are in a ring whereas in structure (3) they are chain atoms and bonds only since the defaults have not been changed.

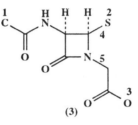

(3)

It is possible to override the default either for an atom or a bond and the procedure using the STN Express software is to use the highlighter tool to tag either the atom or the bond, and then choose options as required with **Bond Characteristics** or **Node Characteristics** under **QueryDef**. (All modifications also may be made using keyboard commands (see the manual: *Building and Searching Structures on STN*).)

When making these changes, it is to be noted that when the bond characteristics are changed the characteristics of the attached nodes are changed automatically, while when the node characteristics are changed, no changes are made to the characteristics of the attached bonds(s) and this is essential since very often it is just the node default which needs to be overridden. Further, node (or bond) specification R (ring) may also be used in cases where the searcher needs an attached atom (or bond) to be in a ring but wants to specify that atom only, leaving all the other atoms which will make up the ring unspecified.

15.2.2b   Ring default
When atoms are drawn in a ring, all the atoms can either be in a single ring only or common to two or more rings. That is, the rings default to "isolated or embedded" since no Type of Ring screens are generated, and all ring atoms can be either D or T (see Section 14.7.2).

There are some very important and subtle implications! For example, consider the structures (4) to (8) (Figure 15.2) all of which have the substructure corresponding to structure (4). However, if substructure (4) is built without overriding any system defaults and then searched, all structures except structure (5) would be retrieved. There are two reasons for this. First, the bond between rings A and B in structure (4) would have been defined by the system as a chain bond (in structure (5) the bond is in a ring), and second, the default for atoms in rings is that they are isolated or embedded so further ring fusions on each of the rings A and B is allowed.

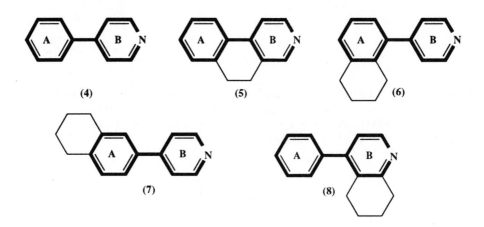

(4)   (5)   (6)

(7)   (8)

Figure 15.2 Possible variations on a given substructure

Thus if, additionally, structures of the type (5) were required then it would be necessary to define the bond between the rings in the structure query as ring or chain.

On the other hand, suppose more specific structures are required, in which case there are three broad possibilities:

1. fusion between the rings;
2. fusion only on ring A or only on ring B; and
3. fusion more specifically in a single ring, for example orientation shown either in (6) or in (7).

Case 1. The bond characteristic between the rings is changed to ring only, and this is done on STN Express by highlighting the bond and changing the **Bond Characteristics** under **QueryDef**. It might be wondered whether such a course of action is ever required - but it is! For example, if a ring of any type between the rings specified in structure (4), including of any size or with any number of heteroatoms, is acceptable then the best way to build the query would be to build structure (4) and specify the bond between the rings as a ring bond only.

Case 2. Any single ring system (it may contain either a single ring or already contain fused rings) may be isolated. (With STN Express, the procedure is to use the highlighter tool to tag any one atom in the ring and then choose options as required with **Ring Isolation** under **QueryDef.** If there are a few separate rings which need to be isolated, then holding down the "Shift Key" while tagging atoms enables the different rings to be tagged at the one time.)

Case 3. The connectivities at the atoms of interest are specified.[*] The number of connected atoms may be any required and the connectivity specified may be EXACT, MINIMUM or MAXIMUM and either RING, CHAIN or RING/CHAIN. Note that connectivities refer to numbers of attached atoms (irrespective of whether a single, double, or triple bond is required), so a connectivity specification of M3 R indicates a minimum three atoms all attached by ring bonds to the atom highlighted (and it does not matter whether single or double bonds are involved).

Accordingly to allow answers of the type (6) and not (7) it would be necessary to specify that two of the atoms in Ring A in structure query (4) have exactly three ring attachments and that the others have exactly two ring attachments. The effect is to specify the Type of Ring code T and D to the various atoms (see Section 14.7.2).

15.2.3   Special cases: system definitions and STN Express defaults

There is another general situation which is commonly encountered and of which the searcher should be particularly aware. It highlights the need to consider very carefully how both the system definitions and STN Express defaults operate.

Consider the three structures (9), (10), and (11) which contain the common substructure (12). If answers of the type indicated in (9), (10), and (11) are required then the searcher has to think carefully about the way they are actually described in the database.

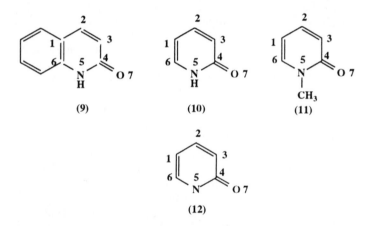

(9)   (10)   (11)

(12)

In particular, every bond in structures (9) and (10) will be normalized! Because there is a hydrogen atom on the nitrogen in the amide, this means the group satisfies the "tautomer" equation (see Section 14.5.2) which effectively allows for the alternative structure (13). Chemists will be well familiar with this problem, the question being whether pyridones are actually 2-hydroxypyridines! However, this is an example of a general issue relating to tautomers and it is because of this general issue that the special system definition for tautomers is needed.

---

[*]With STN Express, the procedure is to use the highlighter tool to tag the atom, and then choose options as required with **Non-H Attachments** under **QueryDef**. This procedure also is followed to allow substitution at certain positions only (Closed Substructure Search, for example, see Figure 15.4). The alternative to Closed Substructure Search is to add hydrogens to the structure query to block substitution (Section 15.5.2a).

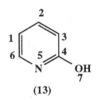

(13)

In this structure (13) there are alternating single and double bonds in an even-membered ring, so another of the definitions of normalized bonding is satisfied. Accordingly all bonds in the actual substances (9) and (10) on the file are normalized.

However, there is no hydrogen on the nitrogen in structure (11) and the tautomer definition (Figure 14.2) does not apply, so bonds 4-5 and 4-7 will be exact. No longer does the entire ring have alternating single and double bonds, so the other ring bonds will also be exact.

Using keyboard commands, the way to build a single structure which then allows all answers of the type (9), (10), and (11) to be retrieved is to use the bond values S and D. Value S (single) allows either SINGLE EXACT or NORMALIZED, while D (double) allows DOUBLE EXACT or NORMALIZED.

However, the structure building program in STN Express has "chemical intelligence". That is, it automatically recognizes situations in which EXACT or NORMALIZED bonds may occur and defaults to EXACT/NORMALIZED when both are possible. So when structure (12) (without any attachment specified on the nitrogen) is built on STN Express, the program will describe all bonds as EXACT/NORMALIZED. It does not need to further define them as single or double, since it already "sees" that single or double bonds have been drawn in the structure.

Actually another problem arises here since STN Express applies the most generic situation possible. So if structure (14) is built and the ring is not isolated, STN Express allows for answers of the type (15) since the part structure (14) is present in the left-hand ring in (15).* Because bond 3-4 in (15) is normalized by virtue of its presence in the right-hand ring, STN Express needs to define bond 3-4 in (14) as EXACT/NORMALIZED to allow for the most generic situation. As all the other bonds in structure (14) could also be part of larger rings in which the bonds are normalized, then STN Express automatically assigns all bonds in (14) as EXACT/NORMALIZED. This being the case, then structure (16) represents a potential answer, and the problem here is that the chemist does not expect benzene (16) to be retrieved in a substructure search of what was intended to be cyclohexane (14)!

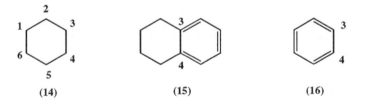

(14)   (15)   (16)

---

*This is a database policy matter! It was considered better to be as generic as possible in the default situation and then to allow the searcher to make input when more specific situations were required.

However, if the ring in query (14) is isolated, then STN Express "knows" that answers like (15) are not required and it can happily define all bonds in the query as EXACT and only substituted cyclohexanes will be retrieved.

The defaults used by STN Express may always be checked through **Query Verification** under **QueryDef** and if anything is not to satisfaction then it should be changed. Indeed the searcher should always strive to set up the most precise search query, not only because it is through critical analysis of the query that all potentialities are covered (a critical review of the structure query will make the searcher more alert to the outcomes of the query, and to potential answers in the file, and will help in building better queries in the future) but also because the search conducted by the host computer will be more efficient in computer terms (CPU time).

Quite commonly the bond values may need to be made more specific. The procedure is to check all bonds which have been specified exact/normalized and then to consider carefully, using chemical knowledge and knowing the types of structures required, which bonds need to be made more specific (that is, changed either to exact or to normalized).

> **Important notes:**
> - **when chains are built, all atoms and all bonds default to chain values;**
> - **when rings are built, all rings default to isolated or embedded; and**
> - **bond values in STN Express default to the more generic definition (that is, to exact/normalized).**
>
> **It is always necessary to consider the implications of these defaults and to change them when needed. Options are checked in STN Express through the** Query Verification **option under** QueryDef **in the structure building menu.**

15.3 System options

Experienced chemists should also be aware of the variations which may be built into a search query. All of these options may be implemented either through keyboard commands or through the menus in the structure building program within STN Express, and while those who are very experienced with the commands may still prefer to use them it is much easier if the new searcher learns the options through STN Express. The menus within STN Express are easily followed, and help messages are available. Essentially there are so many options and it now is not necessary for the practising chemist to learn the keyboard commands for them all.

It is intended here merely to alert searchers to the possibilities, and for the implementation of the options, the searcher should consult the full manuals.

*15.3.1   Options within the **DRAW** menu of STN Express[*]*
The options within the **DRAW** menu are summarized in Table 15.1, and may be illustrated through the structure query (17).

---

[*]Keyboard commands can also be used to achieve all the outcomes described in this section. See the manual: *Building and Searching Structures on STN.*

Table 15.1   Options within the DRAW menu of STN Express

OPTION	NOTES
Shortcut symbols	50 system-defined shortcut symbols for the common groups of atoms found in substances
Variable	8 system-defined variables for generic atoms and groups
G-groups	used to define user-variations in nodes
Variable point of attachment	used when groups must be present only at certain points in the structures
Repeating groups	nodes or groups of nodes may be repeated a user-specified range of times

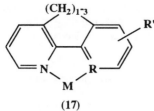

R = N P As
R' = X COOH or its esters or amides
M = any metal

(17)

15.3.1a Shortcut symbols

There are 50 system-defined shortcut symbols which include methyl (CH_3), methylene (CH_2), and methine (CH) groups, simple alkyl groups (ethyl, isopropyl, etc.), and common functional groups (nitro, acid, acetyl, etc.). When the shortcut symbols are used no substitution on the group is allowed, so the phenyl shortcut (Ph) and the ethyl shortcut (Et) are used for the C_6H_5 and C_2H_5 groups only. Shortcut symbols are particularly useful when only the precise group is required in the search and they include the correct bond specifications for groups like the acid group (COOH) and the nitro group (NO_2), which have issues of normalized and donor bonding respectively.

Accordingly in the structure query (17), the CH_2 and COOH shortcuts may be used (at the ring node and in the definition of R' respectively).

15.3.1b Variable

The 8 main system-defined variable symbols are listed in Table 15.2 together with the further qualifications for the generic groups. That is, it is possible to define a node as an alkyl group and to further require that the group be either linear or branched, saturated or unsaturated, or have carbon count greater than or equal to 7 carbons, or less than seven carbons. The only limitation on the use of the alkyl group is that it must be attached to a node which is *not a chain carbon node*, so while it is acceptable to attach an alkyl chain to a ring, or to a heteroatom, the option Ak-C(O)- is not allowed since the alkyl group is attached to a chain carbon (the carbon in the C=O).

Accordingly, the M and X variables may be used in the structure query (17).

Table 15.2 System-defined variables

SYMBOL	DEFINITION	GENERIC GROUP CATEGORIES
A	all atoms except hydrogen	
M	all metals	
Q	all atoms except carbon and hydrogen	
X	all halogens	
AK	alkyl group	linear, branched, saturated, unsaturated, C<7, C>=7
CY	cyclic group	monocyclic, polycyclic
CB	cyclic group containing carbon only	saturated, unsaturated, C<7, C>=7, monocyclic, polycyclic
HY	cyclic group with at least one non-carbon atom	saturated, unsaturated, C<7, C>=7, monocyclic, polycyclic, one heteroatom, more than one heteroatom

15.3.1c G-groups

Shortcut symbols and variables are *system-defined* but it is possible for the *user to define any options* required through the use of a "G-group". The procedure here is to define the group and then to insert it into the structure query, that is, to specify the group at the node required. Any number of G-groups from 1 to 20 can be used, and the system numbers each group defined successively.

Two G-groups need to be used to set up the structure query (17). The procedure is straightforward for the first group since it contains the (system-recognized) atoms N, P, and As. However, while X and COOH in group R' are system-defined options, the ester and amide options are not system-defined and need to be user-defined. This is achieved by drawing the structure fragments:

and then including the carbons which are part of the C=O within the definition of the G-group together with the X and COOH. (Note that the usual way to allow for esters and acids is to build the group O=C-O and to define the bonds as exact/normalized (Figure 14.4), and this strategy may have been used as an alternative. However, if say acids and *alkyl* esters only were required then it would be necessary to build the acid, and the ester fragments as shown here, and to specify the terminal carbon node as an alkyl group or leave the node specification as chain.)

15.3.1d Variable point of attachment

Sometimes the attachment of a group at a number of select positions is required and this is achieved through the variable point of attachment (VPA) option. To achieve this, through STN Express, the substituent(s) to be attached and the possible positions of attachment are highlighted, and the **VPA** option under the **DRAW** menu is chosen.

In this way the substituent R' in query (17) may be specifically attached to the atoms in the right-hand ring, and then answers will include at least one of the definitions of R' in at least one of the indicated positions.

15.3.1e Repeating groups
Any node or defined set of nodes (for example, $O\text{-}CH_2\text{-}CH_2\text{-}$) may be repeated a variable number of times through the repeating group option ([ ] **m-n**) under the **DRAW** menu.

Using all of the options just presented, the structure query (17) may be built with STN Express and the final structure would appear as in Figure 15.3. The specific definitions of the G-groups may be checked under **Query Verification** in which case it will be found that G_2 includes X, COOH, and the nodes marked @^{1} and @^{2}.

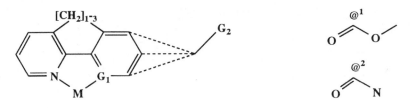

Figure 15.3   Structure built with STN Express

*15.3.2   Options within the **QueryDef** menu of STN Express*
There are many structure building options within the **QueryDef** menu of the structure building program of STN Express. The options are listed in Table 15.3 together with some notes on when they are used. In order to fully understand how they are implemented the searcher is referred to the *STN Express User Guide*.

Table 15.3   Options within the QueryDef menu of STN Express

OPTION	USE
Ring Isolation	to isolate a ring system (see Section 15.2.2b)
Bond Characteristics	to define bonds as RING/CHAIN or EXACT/NORMALIZED (see Section 15.2.2a)
Stereochemistry	to define stereochemical requirements for enantiomers, diastereomers and geometric isomers (see Section 15.9)
Node Characteristics	to define nodes as RING/CHAIN (see Section 15.2.2a)
Hydrogen Attachments	to specify the number of hydrogens on a node (see Section 15.5.2a)
Non-Hydrogen Attachments	to specify connectivities (see Section 15.2.2b)
Other Attributes	to specify charges, valencies, or isotopes
Generic Definition	to specify options for generic groups (see Section 15.3.1b)
Markush Attributes	to specify options for searches in the MARPAT File (searching generic structures) (see Section 15.10.1)
Element Count	to limit counts of elements in generic groups
Delocalized Charge	to specify a charge is delocalized over a group of atoms
Free Sites	to define connections in WPI and Questel structures only
View Query Refinement	to see list of refinement filters (see Section 15.5.3a)
Query Verification	to check the specifications of the structure built

15.4 Perform a SAMPLE search and evaluate answers

It now is necessary to create an L-number for the structure query. If the structure has been built within the STRUCTURE command with keyboard instructions the L-number is generated automatically as soon as the STRUCTURE command is terminated. If the structure has been built within the **Prepare Structure Query** menu of STN Express, the structure needs to be saved, and this is done following usual procedures for saving files. The searcher then logs into the network, enters the structure file and uploads the structure. All of these actions may be done within menus in STN Express. Once uploaded the system assigns an L-number to the structure query.

A structure may be built in, or uploaded into, any file which allows structure searching, and most commonly either the BEILSTEIN or REGISTRY File is used. The same L-numbered query may be searched, and the same search procedure is involved.

The subcommands within the search command in a structure file, and the various options are summarized in Figure 15.4.

=> **SEARCH**
ENTER LOGIC EXPRESSION, QUERY NAME, OR (END):
ENTER TYPE OF SEARCH (SSS), CSS, FAMILY, OR EXACT:
ENTER SCOPE OF SEARCH (SAMPLE), FULL, RANGE, OR SUBSET:

OPTION	USE
(LOGIC EXPRESSION	to search with name- or formula- based terms)[a]
QUERY NAME	to search an L-numbered structure query

Type

SSS (substructure search)	to search for substances which have the substructure defined in the query (the default)
CSS (closed structure search)	to search for substances which have the substructure defined in the query but with substituents only where additional connectivities have been added
FAMILY	to search for substances which exactly match the query (no other non-hydrogen atoms allowed), but allowing answers in which such a component is in a multicomponent substance
EXACT	to search for substances which exactly match the query (no other non-hydrogen atoms allowed) in single component substances only

Scope

SAMPLE	to search a system-defined subset of the file
FULL	to search the full file
RANGE	to search a user-defined range of Registry Numbers of the file
SUBSET	to search the query within a user-defined subset of the file

Figure 15.4   Subcommands within the SEARCH command in the BEILSTEIN and REGISTRY Files

[a]Remember that terms other than structures may be searched in the File and this prompt covers these possibilities!

A SAMPLE search should always be undertaken first. A SAMPLE search is free and:

• searches a subset of the total file (5% in the case of the REGISTRY File; 10% in the case of the BEILSTEIN File) and may be performed in any of the search types (EXACT, FAMILY, CSS, SSS);

- searches a subset which the system identifies as being the most appropriate subset for the search query (the system evaluates the screens in the query and then selects a representative subset of the file based on those screens);
- searches only that specific subset (hence for a given query the same subset will be searched, and the same answers will be retrieved, if multiple SAMPLE searches are conducted);
- projects how many answers there might be in a FULL file search and whether a FULL file search will run to completion (that is, whether it might exceed the system limits: see Screen 15.1); and
- gives an answer set which then can be evaluated (free or inexpensive display formats are available).

The system limits for a SAMPLE search are 50 answers or 1000 iterations, but this always is sufficient to evaluate answer sets.

The next step is to evaluate the answers using the inexpensive DISPLAY SCAN format. As with searching in bibliographic files, the searcher should critically review answers. It is very important when scanning through answers that the searcher asks:

- Is this a good answer, and why? or
- Why is this not a good answer?

Precise answers to these questions will help greatly in determining ways in which the query may be revised.

15.5 Revise query and perform new SAMPLE search; evaluate answers

Even if all the answers in the SAMPLE search are of the type required, it still is worth evaluating what has been done. The problem is that, while all the answers retrieved may be good, the searcher still has to question what the search query might be *missing*!

If, however, some of the answers are undesired, then the search query should be carefully revised in such a way to exclude only the unwanted answers. It is worth keeping in mind that usually structures are being sought in order to find some information about them (in alternate files) and that if only a few of the answers are unwanted, then it might be more appropriate to exclude them from the final answer set manually. This applies particularly to those situations where unwanted answers might be difficult to exclude in the structure search. For example, sometimes the odd answer may be removed only by very complicated modifications of the search query and in these cases either great care should be taken with the modifications, or else it may be easier to remove the answers manually after the full search is done.

The only time when a SAMPLE search may not give an indication of the appropriateness of the query is if no answers are obtained. In such cases the course of action is to check the query very carefully to ensure there are no mistakes. Sometimes to have no answers is the preferred result, since the search may simply have been done to check on the uniqueness of the substances which may have been, or are to be, made in the laboratory. However, at other times it may be that the search is too narrowly defined and that a slightly more general search, particularly for analogous substances or for possible synthetic precursors, may be worth attempting.

15.5.1 Ways to narrow answer sets
There are numerous ways in which a potential answer set may be narrowed, although they fall into two main groups. Either it is necessary to be more specific in the structure query, or to restrict the search to a subset of the file. The approach depends upon the searcher's requirements and on the types of answers being retrieved in the SAMPLE search. However, as with searching in the bibliographic files, the aim should always be to obtain the most relevant answers and any restrictions should be made in a planned and understood way!

15.5.2 Being more specific in the structure query
There are many ways in which the query may be made more specific.

15.5.2a Block substitution by adding hydrogens
Hydrogen atoms may be added either by using shortcut symbols, by drawing in hydrogen nodes, or by using hydrogen counts.[*] In each of these ways it is possible to define a minimum, a maximum, or an exact number of hydrogens. For example, to block substitution in benzene rings the shortcut CH may be used. Thus if structure (18) is searched, substitution is allowed in all positions in the ring, while if structure (19) is searched, substitution is allowed only on the position adjacent to the metal.

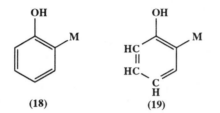

(18)   (19)

Although adding hydrogens to ring atoms sometimes effectively blocks ring fusion (because of valency considerations) the system will not add Type of Ring screens automatically. Consistent with the good practice of trying to define search queries as precisely as possible (even if only to optimize CPU time), the ring should be isolated in these cases whereupon the Type of Ring screens will be added automatically.

Indeed, it should be noted that none of the screens used by the system have specific hydrogen atoms, so hydrogens always are checked in the iterative process. It follows that adding hydrogens to search queries will not affect the number of substances which pass the screen test and this has implications if system limits are being exceeded (projections of too many substances passing the screen test) since adding hydrogens to the search query will not reduce the number of substances which need to undergo the iteration process, even though the number of answers will be reduced.

15.5.2b Isolate rings
Sometimes it is sufficient to search for substances with the ring systems exactly as specified and not to allow further rings to be attached. Isolation of the ring(s) can substantially reduce the number of answers retrieved (see Section 15.2.2b).

---

[*]With STN Express, shortcut symbols are chosen from the **DRAW** menu, hydrogen nodes are added by drawing in bonds and specifying hydrogens at the required nodes, and hydrogen counts are entered through **Hydrogen Attachments** under **QueryDef.**

15.5.2c Define bonds and atoms more exactly
When searchers first realize the power of structure searching and with the options of finding many related substances easily, the search queries may be overgeneralized. That is, too much variation is put into the queries, either by having large numbers of G-groups or undefined bonds. The problem that arises here is that databases of several millions of substances might have many thousands of substances fitting into broad categories. In these cases the query may need defining more precisely through the bond or atom specifications. Indeed, one of the most common sources of errors relates to the bond specifications, and often the first thing to do is to check the bond values (for example, see Section 15.2.3).

15.5.2d Search a larger structure
In bibliographic files, answer sets are narrowed by adding more search terms. In the same way, adding more atoms to the structure query effectively adds more "terms", and the size of the answer set may be reduced to better fit requirements.

For example, the nature of the extra ring substituent (next to the metal) in structure (19) may be specified and either a G-group, or a system-defined variable (for example, the generic atom symbol, A), or an additional sequence of atoms may be added. However, when additional chains are added in this way it must be remembered that the default is that the nodes and bonds are chain only, so the need to change the node or bond characteristics should be considered (see Section 15.2.2a).

15.5.3   Restricting the search to a subset of the file
A structure search may be performed in any user-defined subset of the file, and this is commonly done in one of two general ways. Of course, structure queries are directing the search in a user-defined way, but the point being made here is that more general ways, which do not involve specific structure features, may be used to define the part of the file to be searched.

15.5.3a Adding screens manually
When a structure is built and searched, the system automatically uses all the possible screen numbers, but there are ways in which additional screens may be added by the searcher. For example, the query may be refined so that it contains any of the screens not automatically generated and such screens typically are those listed in Section 14.8.

Using STN Express, this is done at the stage in which the structure is saved. Thus when **Save** is chosen under the **File** menu, a prompt appears for the name of the file and after this is entered a dialog box appears which includes the entry **Refine Query**. When this box is checked a very extensive list of **Refinement Filters** appears and just a few examples are shown in Figure 15.5.

1 or more C-CH3	2 or more C-CH3
1 or more rings	1 or more O
Presence of an isotope	Presence of a charge
Presence of one or more deuterium isotopes	Presence of a tautomer
Substance with 2 or more components	Substance with 3 or more components
Presence of an element with abnormal valency	Presence of a delocalized charge

Figure 15.5   Examples of STN Express Refinement Filters

Each item may be highlighted and another dialog box enables the searcher to include the filter in the search through either the AND or NOT operators. For example, to attach AND to the refinement "Substance with 2 or more components" and NOT to the refinement "Substance with 3 or more components" will mean that only substances with exactly two components will be retrieved. The effect of this process is to add the screen number 2127 (2 or more components) and to exclude the screen number 2077 (3 or more components). Screens may also be added manually through the SCREEN command (see the manual: *Guide to Commands*).

15.5.3b Subset searches

The other way in which the user may define a specific part of the file is to first obtain a subset of the file and then perform the search in this subset. It is important to realize that the subset may be obtained through any type of search acceptable in the file. As long as an L-number answer set in the file is obtained first, this may be used as the subset within which the structure search is conducted.

For example, in the REGISTRY File, the searches:

```
=>      S   CSCHEM/LC
=>      S   PMS/CI
=>      S   C/ELS  AND  H/ELS  AND  2/ELC
```

would give all substances which had records in the CSCHEM File (commercially available substances), which were polymers, or which contained only carbon and hydrogen respectively, and these answer sets may then be searched for specific structures.

Options for subset searches in the BEILSTEIN File are even greater since the File contains well over 100 search fields (see Section 16.5.1). For example, if only substances with reported dipole moments are required then a search: => S DM/FA will give a subset which includes only those substances for which dipole moments have been reported, and then, as this is quite a small subset of the file, very general structure search queries may be searched in this subset without exceeding system limits. For example, if dipole moments of alkyl halides are required then the structure query may be as simple as: C-X (making sure the C is RING/CHAIN if cyclic halides are additionally required!). Such a simple search query in a search of the full file would greatly exceed system limits.

The format for a subset search, where L1 is the subset of the file and L2 is the structure query is: => S L2 SUB=L1 and the type or scope of the structure search may be chosen in the usual way.

15.5.4 Exceeding system limits

The search techniques above are needed simply because the number of answers exceeds the *limits set by the searcher*. However, on rarer occasions the search needs to be narrowed because *system limits* have been exceeded.

Screen 15.1 shows a typical example of a SAMPLE search which detects a potential problem. It is of little concern that the system limits for the SAMPLE search are exceeded since an answer set of 50 answers is more than sufficient to assess whether the initial query is producing the best answers.

Screen 15.1[a] System limits in SAMPLE SEARCH

```
=> S L1
SAMPLE SEARCH INITIATED 22:07:40
SAMPLE SCREEN SEARCH COMPLETED -  4826 TO ITERATE
 20.7% PROCESSED   1000 ITERATIONS                     50 ANSWERS
INCOMPLETE SEARCH (SYSTEM LIMIT EXCEEDED)
SEARCH TIME: 00.00.08

FULL FILE PROJECTIONS:             ONLINE **INCOMPLETE**
                                   BATCH  **COMPLETE**
PROJECTED ITERATIONS:              92367 TO   100673
PROJECTED ANSWERS:                  4331 TO    6285

L2      50 SEA SSS SAM L1
```

[a]Copyright by the American Chemical Society and Reprinted with Permission

However, the problems are that a full search will not run to completion online, and that searches on this query project around 5000 answers.

The search may be narrowed in any of the ways described above, but if no refinement can be used that would not remove wanted answers, a BATCH search may be requested. A BATCH search query is saved on the system as a file:

=> **BATCH   <L-NUMBER>   <QUERYNAME>/B**

and is searched by the system when there is less demand on CPU time (usually overnight). The system then saves the result as: <QUERYNAME>/A and this file can be activated at the next logon. Any name of 8 or less letters and not starting with a number may be used for the queryname (for example => **BATCH L1 STEROID/B**), and an actual example is discussed in Section 15.9.

15.6 Perform a FULL file search

When happy with the results of the SAMPLE search, and if projections are that system limits will not be exceeded in the full search, the next step is to proceed with a search of the appropriate scope. The commands are given in Table 15.4 for some of the various SUBSTRUCTURE searches. To obtain searches of similar scope for CLOSED SUBSTRUCTURE, FAMILY, and EXACT searches it is merely necessary to add CSS, FAM or EXA to the search statement. It does not matter in which order the instructions are given and: => **S L1 FAM FUL**, or **S FUL FAM L1** both are acceptable.

Table 15.4 Entries to initiate substructure search

SEARCH TERM	USE
S L1 FUL	to perform a substructure search of the full file
S L1 RAN=XXX-XX-X,	to perform a substructure search from CAS RN XXX-XX-X onwards
S L1 RAN=,XXX-XX-X	to perform a substructure search from CAS RN XXX-XX-X forwards (that is, earlier)
S L1 RAN=XXX-XX-X,XXXX-XX-X	to perform a substructure search for substances added between CAS RNs XXX-XX-X and XXXX-XX-X
S L1 FUL SUBSET=L2	to perform a full search of query L1 within the subset L2

15.7 Display answers; find information on the substances

At this stage the searcher may wish to display all the answers, in which case the default display format is usually acceptable. The format varies with the different files but generally it gives the File Registry Number, and the name, molecular formula and structure of the substance. However, any of the fields may be displayed and sometimes it is sufficient to display only the Registry Number (RN) and structure fields (STR).

Otherwise, if the search has been performed in the REGISTRY File the searcher may wish to search for information on the substances in any one of the files which contain CAS Registry Numbers. In particular the CAOLD and CAplus Files may contain the information required. If the REGISTRY File answer set obtained is L2, then the bibliographic files may be entered in turn and the search: => S L2 will retrieve all records in which the CAS Registry Numbers in the answer set L2 appear. What this so-called "file crossover" is doing is taking all the CAS Registry Numbers from the answer set and automatically using these Registry Numbers as search terms in the new file. If the crossover to the CAplus File is performed then the CAS Registry Numbers are searched irrespective of whether in the CAplus File they appear with either of the suffixes P (preparation) or D (derivative). This new answer set may be combined with the usual bibliographic search terms.

If individual substances in the REGISTRY File answer set appear in many CAplus File records then the number of records in the new answer set will be very much larger than the number of substances in answer set L2. However, sometimes many of the related substances in L2 are reported in a single publication and now the CAplus File answer set will contain many fewer records than there are substances. Other reasons why the CAplus File answer set may contain a fewer number of records are because some of the REGISTRY File substances have been manually registered (for example, by organizations to comply with government regulations - yet the organizations have not published the scientific reports), or because although the substances may appear in the REGISTRY File they may have been very recently reported and the articles may not yet have been fully indexed.

Important notes:
- **an answer set in the REGISTRY File may be crossed over to any file which allows CAS Registry Number search terms;**

- the process simply takes the CAS Registry Numbers from the answer set and uses them as search terms in the new file; and
- any other search terms allowable in the new file may be added to the search query in order to obtain specific information on the substance(s) crossed over.

15.8 Examples of searches

The applications of the principles of structure searching can be almost of infinite variety! Each problem needs its own specific solution, but at least the above discussion gives the searcher an idea of the necessary tools. However, some structure searches can be quite complicated and, as always, inexperienced searchers are encouraged to check with the STN Help Desks prior to the execution of full searches.

The difficulties need to be addressed as they are encountered, and some representative examples are now worked through using the part structure (20) as an example.

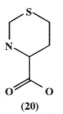

(20)

It is instructive at this stage to consider a few initial questions.

Q1 How many records might there be for this exact substance (that is, for the substance with the structure above, MF $C_5H_9NO_2S$, in which hydrogens are placed in all of the available positions)?

Q2 Would name based, molecular formula then name segment, or EXACT structure searches be the best way to find these record(s), and what terms might be used?

Q3 Would multicomponent substances having the exact substance also be of interest?

Q4 How many substances might be retrieved if a full substructure search was conducted?

Of course, only the most experienced searcher/chemist would guess near the correct numbers of answers retrieved through an EXACT, a FAMILY, or a SUBSTRUCTURE search - 4, 10, and 1516 respectively! Even knowing this, the question is which of these substances really are of interest, and only the intending searcher can answer this.

15.8.1 The EXACT search
Screen 15.2 shows the EXACT search, and there are a number of points to note. First, the structure was built using the structure drawing program in STN Express, was saved as THIAZINE (although any name may have been used), and was uploaded. Once uploaded, it is useful to display the query as a cross check (**D QUE L1**).

Screen 15.2[a] EXACT structure search of query (20)

=>	Uploading "THIAZINE" in the current file
L1	STRUCTURE UPLOADED
=>	**D QUE L1**
L1	STR

=>	**S L1 EXA**
L2	0 SEA EXA SAM L1
=>	**S L1 EXA FUL**
L3	4 SEA EXA FUL L1
=>	**D 1-4 CN**
CN	2H-1,3-Thiazine-4-carboxylic acid, tetrahydro-, (S)- (9CI) (CA INDEX NAME)
CN	2H-1,3-Thiazine-4-carboxylic acid, tetrahydro-, (R)- (9CI) (CA INDEX NAME)
CN	2H-1,3-Thiazine-4-carboxylic acid, tetrahydro-, (.+-.)- (9CI) (CA INDEX NAME)
CN	2H-1,3-Thiazine-4-carboxylic acid, tetrahydro- (6CI, 7CI, 9CI) (CA INDEX NAME)

[a]Copyright by the American Chemical Society and Reprinted with Permission

---

Second, in an EXACT search no other non-hydrogen atoms may be present, so an EXACT search of structure (20) would effectively mean that the 9 hydrogens would be added at the positions which were left open (see Section 11.3.4).

Third, a SAMPLE search was conducted first (the entry: => **S L1 EXA** accepts the default search type which is SAMPLE). However, in this case the SAMPLE search gave no answers. This is not unusual for an EXACT search since a SAMPLE search searches only 5% of the File. When zero answers are retrieved in the SAMPLE search, it could be because there were no hits in the SAMPLE conducted, or else the structure query may be wrong. A searcher would be confident that the former applied here since it is a very simple structure to draw and since zero answers are commonly retrieved in a SAM EXA search. However, in most other cases where a SAMPLE search does not produce an answer, the searcher seriously has to question whether there are errors in the search query.

Fourth, accordingly the full search was conducted and four answers were retrieved (all of these related to the fact that stereoisomers existed). That is, the carbon atom in the ring next to the COO group has four different substituents and so can exist in left- and right-handed forms (enantiomers) (see Figure 11.4).

Finally, the names only of the 4 answers are indicated in Screen 15.2. The first two answers are the enantiomers, the third is the racemate, and the last is the one in which the stereochemistry is not specified.

Clearly all of these answers may have been retrieved by name based or molecular formula with name segment searches, but there are very few names listed for these substances and the searcher would have to be careful that the right nomenclature was used!

Indeed it is worth considering here the answer to Question 2 (Section 15.8), particularly now that the answer is known! Thus if an expansion on possible names in the CN field was undertaken, it would have to be known that the names started with "2H-1,3-thiazine .....". Alternatively if the search involved: => **S THIAZINE/CNS (L) CARBOXYLIC/CNS (L) TETRAHYDRO/CNS** many answers would be retrieved and considerable effort may have to be expended to narrow the answer set.[*] Meanwhile an expansion on the molecular formula C5H9NO2S/MF indicates there are 148 isomers, and another 49 which have this formula as one formula in a multicomponent substance. The value of proceeding to an EXACT structure search may thus been seen!

15.8.2 The FAMILY search

A full FAMILY search (which involved the procedure first: => **S L1 FAM**, then => **S L1 FAM FUL**) gave 10 answers, and the name and formula fields for the additional 6 answers are given in Screen 15.3. (Naturally the 4 answers retrieved in the EXACT search were retrieved from the FAMILY search also.)

Screen 15.3[a]   Unique answers from FAMILY search

RN	147666-00-0 REGISTRY
CN	2H-1,3-Thiazine-4-carboxylic acid, tetrahydro-, (S)-,
	[S-(R*,R*)]-2,3-dihydroxybutanedioate (1:1) (9CI) (CA INDEX NAME)
MF	C5 H9 N O2 S . C4 H6 O6
RN	147665-99-4 REGISTRY
CN	2H-1,3-Thiazine-4-carboxylic acid, tetrahydro-, (R)-,
	[R-(R*,R*)]-2,3-dihydroxybutanedioate (1:1) (9CI) (CA INDEX NAME)
MF	C5 H9 N O2 S . C4 H6 O6
RN	143174-34-9 REGISTRY
CN	2H-1,3-Thiazine-4-carboxylic acid, tetrahydro-, monohydrate (9CI)
	(CA INDEX NAME)
MF	C5 H9 N O2 S . H2 O
RN	89417-43-6 REGISTRY
CN	2H-1,3-Thiazine-4-carboxylic acid, tetrahydro-, hydrochloride (7CI)
	(CA INDEX NAME)
MF	C5 H9 N O2 S . Cl H
RN	67639-40-1 REGISTRY
CN	2H-1,3-Thiazine-4-carboxylic acid, tetrahydro-, hydrochloride,
	(.+-.)- (9CI) (CA INDEX NAME)
MF	C5 H9 N O2 S . Cl H
RN	61414-26-4 REGISTRY
CN	2H-1,3-Thiazine-4-carboxylic acid, tetrahydro-, monohydrate, (.+-.)-
	(9CI) (CA INDEX NAME)
MF	C5 H9 N O2 S . H2 O

[a]Copyright by the American Chemical Society and Reprinted with Permission

---

[*]This search actually gave 244 answers.

The additional answers are the salts of the parent substance with tartaric acid (a standard chemical procedure to isolate enantiomers from racemic mixtures involves crystallizing salts and here the tartaric acid salts were obviously used), and the hydrochlorides and hydrates of the racemic form and the form in which the stereochemistry is not specified.

> **Important note!**
> **If a scientist came to you and asked for information on the thiazinecarboxylic acid (20), you would have to alert the scientist to the possibility of stereochemical complications and to salt (and hydrate) formation. You would then have to choose the appropriate search terms .... and they probably would NOT involve name based terms!**

15.8.3 The SUBSTRUCTURE search

Since the default within the SEARCH command in the REGISTRY File is that a SAMPLE, SUBSTRUCTURE search is conducted it is sufficient to enter the search term: => **S L1** and the result of the search is shown in Screen 15.4. The large number of projected answers is because the thiazinecarboxylic acid group is part of many of the cephalosporin group of antibiotics and this immediately becomes apparent when the answers are scanned!

Screen 15.4[a] SAMPLE SUBSTRUCTURE search on query (20)

```
=> S L1
SAMPLE SEARCH INITIATED 21:41:51
SAMPLE SCREEN SEARCH COMPLETED -              198 TO ITERATE
100.0% PROCESSED        198 ITERATIONS            50 ANSWERS
INCOMPLETE SEARCH (SYSTEM LIMIT EXCEEDED)
SEARCH TIME: 00.00.05
FULL FILE PROJECTIONS:             ONLINE  **COMPLETE**
                                   BATCH   **COMPLETE**
PROJECTED ITERATIONS:              3116 TO   4804
PROJECTED ANSWERS:                 1147 TO   2253
L2      50 SEA SSS SAM L1
=> D SCAN

IN      5-Thia-1-azabicyclo[4.2.0]octane-3-acetic acid, 2-hydroxy-2-[[(4-nitrophenyl)
        methoxy]carbonyl]-8-oxo-7-[(phenylacetyl)amino]-, 1,1-dimethylethyl ester, 5,5-
        dioxide, [2R-(2.alpha.,3.alpha.,6.alpha.,7.beta.)]- (9CI)
MF      C28 H31 N3 O11 S
Absolute stereochemistry.
```

Screen 15.4 (continued)

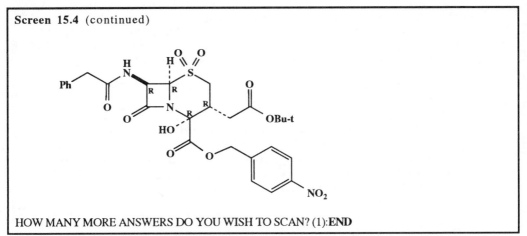

HOW MANY MORE ANSWERS DO YOU WISH TO SCAN? (1):**END**

This is a typical outcome of a search in such a large file. Suddenly the searcher is confronted with a very large number of potential answers (note that the projected number of answers is between 1147 and 2253) and the search query would now probably need to be revised to give only those types of substances required.

For example, in Section 15.5.2 four different ways of being more specific in the structure query are outlined and illustrations of applications of three of these follow. (The fourth option, Section 15.5.2c, involves defining bonds or atoms more exactly. However, in the original query, EXACT bonds had already been specified in the ring, that is, the STN Express default, Section 15.2.3, already had been addressed.)

Application of 15.5.2a: block substitution by adding hydrogens
For example, the structure query (20) may be modified in a way which prevented substitution in part of the ring and a query (21) may be built. That is, the structure "THIAZINE" was opened in the structure building menu of STN Express and was modified by nominating CH2 groups at the nodes indicated. The **Save As** option under the **File** menu was then chosen and the new structure was named as "THIAZ CH2".

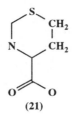

(21)

A SAMPLE, SUBSTRUCTURE search on this query gave 5 answers and the key parts of the search and display are given in Screen 15.5. If this modification was acceptable, then a full search would be performed and in this case the full search gave 87 records.

Screen 15.5[a] Blocking substitution with hydrogen atoms
=> Uploading "THIAZ CH2" in the current file
L1   STRUCTURE UPLOADED
=> S L1
SAMPLE SEARCH INITIATED 21:49:26
SAMPLE SCREEN SEARCH COMPLETED -   198 TO ITERATE
100.0% PROCESSED   198 ITERATIONS   5 ANSWERS
SEARCH TIME: 00.00.03
FULL FILE PROJECTIONS: ONLINE **COMPLETE**
                                     BATCH **COMPLETE**
PROJECTED ITERATIONS: 3116 TO   4804
PROJECTED ANSWERS: 5 TO   234
L2   5 SEA SSS SAM L1
=> D SCAN

IN   5-Thia-1-azabicyclo[4.2.0]octane-2-carboxylic acid, 7-chloro-8-oxo-,
         methyl ester (9CI)
MF   C8 H10 Cl N O3 S

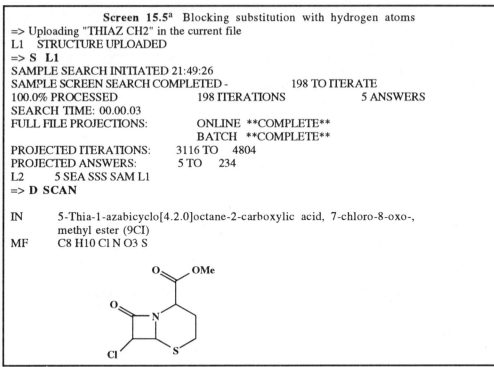

Application of 15.5.2b: isolate rings
Alternatively, the ring may be isolated (see Section 15.2.2b) and the outcome is given in
Screen 15.6.

Screen 15.6[a] Isolation of the ring
=> Uploading "THIAZ ISOL" in the current file
L1   STRUCTURE UPLOADED
=> S L1
....
PROJECTED ITERATIONS: 3116 TO   4804
PROJECTED ANSWERS: 5 TO   234
L2   5 SEA SSS SAM L1
=> D SCAN

IN   2H-1,3-Thiazine-4-carboxylic acid, tetrahydro-2-[[[4-(2-
         propenyloxy)phenyl]thio]methyl]-, ethyl ester (9CI)
MF   C17 H23 N O3 S2

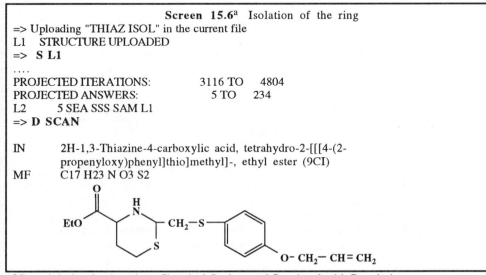

A full search of this query (which had been saved as "THIAZ ISOL") gave 90 answers.

Application of 15.5.2d - Search a larger structure
Third, a larger structure may be built. The SAMPLE search on the further modified structure query (22) did not retrieve any answers (since now a very specific structure was searched in only 5% of the database), but a full search afforded 5 answers of which one is shown in Screen 15.7.

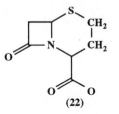

(22)

Screen 15.7[a] Sample answer from full search of query (22)

RN   101470-16-0 REGISTRY
CN   5-Thia-1-azabicyclo[4.2.0]octane-2-carboxylic acid, 7-[(5-amino-5-carboxy-1-
          oxopentyl)amino]-8-oxo-, [2R-[2.alpha.,6.alpha.,7.beta.(R*)]]- (9CI) (CA INDEX
          NAME)
OTHER NAMES:
CN   Antibiotic 13285A1
FS   STEREOSEARCH
MF   C13 H19 N3 O6 S
SR   CA
LC   STN Files: CA, CAPLUS
DES   1:2R2:2A,6A,7B(R*)

Absolute stereochemistry.

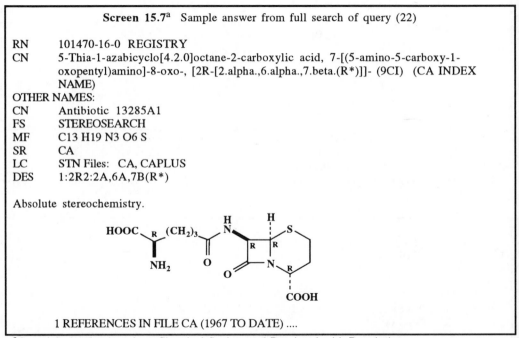

1 REFERENCES IN FILE CA (1967 TO DATE) ....

These three applications illustrate just three of the ways in which the problem identified in the initial SAMPLE search (Screen 15.4) may be addressed. Other options may include retrieval only of the acids (in which case it would be necessary to attach the shortcut COOH to the thiazine ring), or may include elimination of oxidised forms at the sulfur (in which case the valence at the sulfur would be set at exactly two using **Other Attributes** within the **QueryDef** menu). Alternatively specific stereoisomers may be searched!

15.9 Stereosearch

The BEILSTEIN File has about 1.8 million substances with stereo centres and almost 0.4 million with geometric double bonds. The REGISTRY File has over 3 million stereo substances. Most of these can be searched by structure.

A search which does not define stereochemistry, a so-called "flat search", retrieves all substances including stereoisomers, racemates, and those substances with stereochemistry undefined. Even though the searcher may be interested in specific stereo substances, at times everything about related isomers may be useful. For example, a study on asymmetric synthesis may need knowledge of all possible stereoisomers.

A stereosearch gives only those stereoisomers specified in the query, although it is acceptable to define only one stereocentre and leave other stereocentres open.

While individual search queries require different approaches, the recommended approach is to perform the flat search first and then SCAN some of the answers. If the number of answers is large, and if there really are a lot of structures of marginal interest, then a stereosearch should be undertaken.

The steps involved in a stereosearch are:

1. build two structures - the structure with the stereochemical requirements and the flat structure;
2. perform the flat search; and
3. perform the stereosearch as a SUBSET search of the flat search answer set.

The easiest way to build the stereostructure is with STN Express, using the options under **Bond** (in the **DRAW** menu) to indicate bonds above and below the plane, and using **Stereochemistry** from the **QueryDef** menu to specify the nature of the stereochemistry required. (For full details see the *STN Express User Guide*.) While there are no problems indicating stereochemistry associated with rings, care must be taken to represent stereochemistry in chains in an unambiguous way. (Searchers unfamiliar with stereo drawings should consult a specialist chemist. The problem with drawing stereoisomers is that a three-dimensional object is being represented in two dimensions and to do this there are a number of specific conventions. The Masamune representation is probably the best for drawing stereoisomers in chains; that is, the chain is drawn in a zig-zag way with wedged bonds to illustrate stereo arrangements.) Once the stereostructure has been saved, it may be "flattened" (stereochemical features removed) with an option under the **Stereochemistry** menu and this "flattened" structure is saved also.

Stereosearch can be extremely powerful and give very valuable answer sets. As an example of a stereosearch, and of a search which brings together a number of the features of structure searching, consider a search for all 5β-steroids which have 3β,7β oxygen substituents (that is, structures of the type (23)).

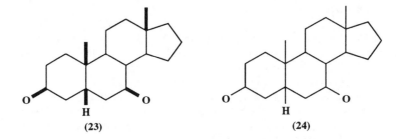

(23)   (24)

A flat (24) and a stereo structure (23) are built and the flat structure query is uploaded, giving an online structure query L1. However, a SAMPLE search of L1 quickly shows that system limits would be exceeded (this sample search is the one actually presented in Screen 15.1). The SAMPLE screening passed 4826 substances for iteration and only the system limit (for a SAMPLE search) of 1000 iterations was checked. All the answers SCANned were acceptable. Still, there are too many iterations projected to complete a full search online, and this needs to be considered.

The reason why so many substances passed the screening process was because the query contained mainly carbon atoms connected in rings. Only a few screens would have been generated and these screens would have occurred in a large number of substances. After all, carbon-carbon ring bonds and carbon-oxygen chain bonds are very common in organic substances!

The options listed, and numbered in Section 15.5.2, to narrow answer sets were considered in turn.

First, blocking substitution by adding hydrogens was not acceptable since all steroids of the type (23) were required. In any case, adding hydrogens would not have affected the screening process as no screens contain hydrogens and so no additional screens would have been assigned to the query.

Second, isolation of the rings certainly would have helped with the screening process since specific Type of Ring screens would have been generated automatically, but larger ring systems which contained the steroid skeleton were acceptable.

Third, the bonds already were defined precisely, that is, all bonds had been specified EXACT in order to exclude any aromatic rings (see Section 15.2.3). And finally, to search a larger structure (insertion of more atoms) would also have ruled out possible answers required.

Other options contemplated also were not useful. For example, a subset of the file might have been made by extracting only those substances which could be searched for stereochemistry,[*] but as there are over three million of these and as a system limit is that no more than 2 million answers may be held for the session this approach would be of no value in this case.

While the SAMPLE search for the flat structure query projects a full file answer set of between 4331 and 6285 answers, clearly only a few of these would have the required stereochemical features, and so this large flat answer set was of little concern at this stage. It should always be kept in mind also that a large answer set in the REGISTRY File may be

---

[*]All substances searchable by stereochemistry are listed in the STEREOSEARCH File Segment. However, a search: **S STEREOSEARCH/FS** would give an answer set which would exceed system limits.

transferred to the CAplus File or other files which allow CAS Registry Number search terms, and then any number of text-based search terms may be used to narrow answers.

So it was decided to continue with the BATCH search, and the answer set was obtained at the next logon (Screen 15.8).

Screen 15.8ª Obtaining a BATCH search

=> **BATCH**
ENTER QUERY L# FOR BATCH REQUEST OR (END):**L1**
ENTER BATCH REQUEST NAME OR (END):**STEROID/B**
ENTER TYPE OF SEARCH (SSS), CSS, FAMILY, OR EXACT:.
ENTER SCOPE OF SEARCH (FULL) OR RANGE:.
QUERY 'L1' HAS BEEN SAVED AS BATCH REQUEST 'STEROID/B'

Next session
=> **ACT STEROID/A**
L1   STR
L2   5595 SEA FILE=REGISTRY SSS FUL L1
=> Uploading "steroid stereo" in the current file
L3   STRUCTURE UPLOADED
=> **S L3 SUB=L2 FULL**
FULL SUBSET SEARCH INITIATED 21:52:28
FULL SUBSET SCREEN SEARCH COMPLETED - 5595 TO ITERATE
100.0% PROCESSED   5595 ITERATIONS   99 ANSWERS
SEARCH TIME: 00.00.14
L4   99 SEA SUB=L2 SSS FUL L3
=> **D SCAN**
L4 99 ANSWERS REGISTRY COPYRIGHT 1995 ACS
IN   Cholan-24-oic acid, 3,7,12-trihydroxy-, 2-(4-bromophenyl)-2-oxoethyl
      ester, (3.beta.,5.beta.,7.beta.,12.alpha.)- (9CI)
MF   C32 H45 Br O6

Absolute stereochemistry.

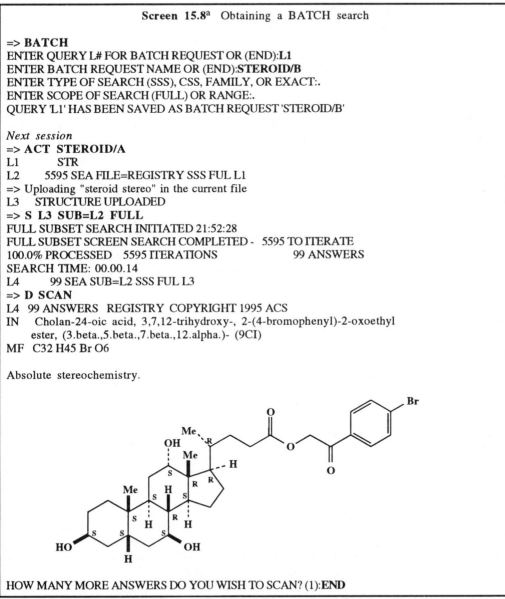

HOW MANY MORE ANSWERS DO YOU WISH TO SCAN? (1):**END**

As with nearly all the screen displays in this text, there are a number of points to note. First, a BATCH search was initiated and the structure query was saved as STEROID/B. The system acknowledged the request: QUERY 'L1' HAS BEEN SAVED AS BATCH REQUEST 'STEROID/B'.

Second, at the next session, the ACTIVATE command is used to obtain the answer set. Note that once the BATCH request has been executed the system returns the answer set under the name of the BATCH request with suffix /A. (For details on the operation of the BATCH and ACTIVATE commands see the manual: *Guide to Commands*.)

Third, the full search of the flat structure query (24) gave 5595 answers (L2), and finally, the stereostructure query (23) was uploaded, then searched as a subset of L2, and 99 answers were retrieved (one of them is displayed).

This example shows a number of the features of structure searching, and shows that very careful thought is needed to obtain answers of the type required. Even the novice searcher may need to have quite a broad perspective of online search possibilities, and a broad knowledge of the potential substances in the database in order to obtain the best answer set! Partly for this reason, all online vendors have "Help Desks" that offer search advice, and help should be sought whenever needed. Even the most experienced searcher will come across difficult problems, and, further, the Help Desk operator may not immediately know the best solution. However, vendors also have file specialists who will help tackle even the most complex problem!

15.10   Other structure-searchable files

Presently there are a number of structure-searchable files on STN (Table 15.5).

Table 15.5 Structure-searchable files on STN

FILE	CONTENT
BEILSTEIN	over 6,000,000 organic substances from 1779
CASREACT	over 1,000,000 reactions since from 1985
CHEMINFORMRX	180,000 reactions covered in *Chemischer Informationsdienst*
CHEMREACT	370,000 records (1978-1988) from former Soviet/East German database
DRUGU	Derwent Drug File records
GMELIN	700,000 inorganic and organometallic substances from 1817
MARPAT	Markush structures from 1988
MARPATPREV	Markush structures (most recent)
REGISTRY	over 14,000,000 substances since 1957
SPECINFO	^{13}C NMR and IR spectra for 100,000 substances

As mentioned in Chapter 11, while the CAS produced files (CASREACT, MARPAT, MARPATpreviews, and REGISTRY) are based on the same search system, there are differences with the other files. However, the differences are very minor except for the SPECINFO and Derwent Files, but in these cases the STN Express software has special features to convert structure queries into the correct formats.

15.10.1 The MARPAT Files

Quite often only generic structures are reported in the literature, and this applies particularly to the patent literature since patents often cover both specific and related structures. The patent assignee wants patent protection on all substances of a general type, even though perhaps only a few of them have actually been prepared at the time the patent application was made. These generic substances are often referred to as Markush substances, and are "prophetic" substances in the sense that the substances and their properties are predicted.

Up until the beginning of 1988, CAS indexed only those substances which had been characterized. However, since 1988 generic structures reported in patents have been included in the MARPAT File. Records in the MARPAT File contain the Markush structures found in the claims and often the disclosure of the patent, the bibliographic information, in-depth substance and subject indexing including CAS Registry Numbers, and an abstract. The structures in the MARPAT File are structure-searchable.

Markush structure queries are built in the same way as queries for specific structures, the only difference being that the **Markush Attributes** within **QueryDef** in the structure building program of STN Express may need to be changed. Thus the default setting for chain nodes is that structure matches operate either at the class or the atom level, and it is only if more specific requirements are needed that the default needs to be changed. For example, to retrieve structures which have generic options at some of the atoms but specific options at others, it is necessary to change the match level for the latter group of atoms.

Searches are conducted in the same way as in the REGISTRY File, and, as an example, Screen 15.9 shows the search for the structure query (21) in the MARPAT File.

It was unfortunate that no answers were retrieved in the SAMPLE search since this did not allow the query to be checked. Nevertheless the full search was undertaken and 32 answers were retrieved in the MARPAT File. That is, 32 different patent records were retrieved (since the MARPAT File is a bibliographic file the number of answers refers to the number of bibliographic records and not to the number of structures).

Screen 15.9[a] Search for Markush structures in the MARPAT File
```
=> FIL MARPAT
=> S L1
SAMPLE SEARCH INITIATED 22:13:02
SAMPLE SCREEN SEARCH COMPLETED -    52 TO ITERATE
100.0% PROCESSED        52 ITERATIONS              0 ANSWERS
SEARCH TIME: 00.00.11
FULL FILE PROJECTIONS:          ONLINE **COMPLETE**
                                BATCH  **COMPLETE**
PROJECTED ITERATIONS:              609 TO    1471
PROJECTED ANSWERS:                   0 TO     0
L2      0 SEA SSS SAM L1
=> S L1 FUL
L3      32 SEA SSS FUL L1
```

[a]Copyright by the American Chemical Society and Reprinted with Permission

---

Part of one of these is shown in Screen 15.10 while part of the Markush structures in the record is shown in Screen 15.11. Those familiar with Markush structure representations will be able to follow this latter screen (which contains just a small part of the very extensive Markush structure representations in this record). For those who are not familiar with this form of reporting, suffice it to say that it shows the different variations on a basic structure claimed within the patent.

Screen 15.10[a] Answer from the MARPAT File

```
=> D IBIB
```

ACCESSION NUMBER:	122:106520 MARPAT
TITLE:	Preparation of novel amino acid derivative
INVENTOR(S):	Ishizuka, Masaaki; Kawazu, Masaji; Katsumi, Toshiaki; Fuse, Yoshihide; Maeda, Kenji;Takeuchi, Tomio
PATENT ASSIGNEE(S):	Zaidan Hojin Biseibutsu Kagaku Kenkyu Kai, Japan; Kanegafuchi Kagaku Kogyo Kabushiki Kaisha
SOURCE:	PCT Int. Appl., 56 pp. CODEN: PIXXD2

```
                                    NUMBER                 DATE
                                    --------------         ------
```

PATENT INFORMATION:	WO9408947 A1	940428
DESIGNATED STATES:	W: CA, JP, US	
	RW: BE, CH, DE, FR, GB, IT, NL, SE	
APPLICATION INFORMATION:	93WO-JP01482	931015
PRIORITY APPLN. INFO.:	92JP-0301559	921015
DOCUMENT TYPE:	Patent	
LANGUAGE:	Japanese	

[a]Copyright by the American Chemical Society and Reprinted with Permission

---

Screen 15.11[a] Representation of Markush structures

MSTR 1A

G1—G8—G31

G1   = alkylcarbonyl<(1-8)> (SO (1-4) G2) / alkylcarbonyl<(1-8)> (SO G7)
G2   = OH / 4 / 9 / SH / alkylthio<(1-3)> / CO2H / alkoxycarbonyl<(1-3)> / Ph / Ph

O—G3   G5
N
9
        G6

G3   = alkyl<(1-3)> / CHO / COMe / COCH2Me / Ph / 6

G4—Ph

G4   = (1-3) CH2
G5   = H / alkyl<(1-3)> / CHO / COMe / COCH2Me
G6   = H / alkyl<(1-3)>
G7   = OH / NH2
G8   = 16-1 104-3 / 117-1 120-3

G9 —G11 —CH2—C(O)   N—————CH2—C(O)
16   104   117   118   120
                                    G35

[a]Copyright by the American Chemical Society and Reprinted with Permission

While searches in the REGISTRY and MARPAT Files may be done separately, a special feature, CASLINK, is available on STN. This feature links the REGISTRY and MARPAT Files with the CAplus File, and part of this feature is that through a single search entry, a structure is searched first in the REGISTRY and MARPAT Files and then the answers are automatically crossed over to the CAplus File so that bibliographic records are obtained directly from a structure search!

Important notes:
- **You should search in the MARPAT Files if you require "prophetic" substances (reported in the patent literature since 1988).**
- **The same structure search query may be used in the MARPAT Files, although in rare cases it might be necessary to specify that matches be specific at certain chain nodes.**

15.10.2 *Structure search in the BEILSTEIN File*
While the BEILSTEIN File is discussed in more detail in Chapter 16, it is to be noted here that standard STN structure search queries may be searched in the File, and the search on structure (21) is illustrated in Screen 15.12.

Screen 15.12[a] Structure search in the BEILSTEIN File

```
=> S L1
L2      4 SEA SSS SAM L1
=> D MF STR
Molecular Formula (MF):   C13 H19 N3 O6 S
```

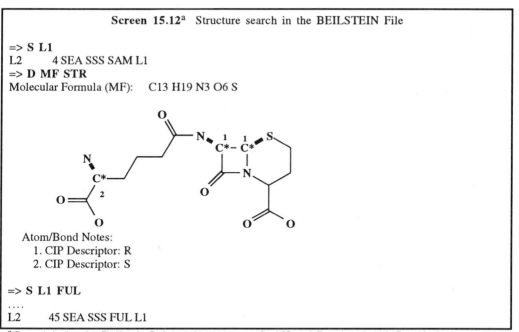

```
Atom/Bond Notes:
  1. CIP Descriptor: R
  2. CIP Descriptor: S

=> S L1 FUL
. . . .
L2     45 SEA SSS FUL L1
```

[a]Copyright by the Beilstein Informationssysteme GmbH and Reprinted with Permission

In this case 45 answers were found (compared to the 87 answers which were found in the full search in the REGISTRY File) and the unique substances in the File may be found through a search: => **S L2 NOT RN/FA**. This will remove from the answer set those records which have CAS Registry Numbers. When this was done there were 14 substances which were not reported in the REGISTRY File, although this is an unusually high proportion and is not typical!

Summary

- *Structure searching* involves a number of steps from building the structure to performing a full structure search, and it is important to understand fully what is involved in each step.
- Structures search queries may be quite specific, or very general, and may include all types of variations in rings, chains, bonds, and types of atoms.
- There are a number of system and STN Express defaults which need to be addressed when the structure is being built.
- Structure variations may most easily be incorporated into structures using the **DRAW** and **QueryDef** menus in the structure building program in STN Express.
- Structure searches may be of various types and *EXACT, FAMILY and SUBSTRUCTURE* searches are most commonly used.
- A *SAMPLE structure search should always be conducted first* to check on the types of answers being retrieved.
- There are a number of tools which may be used to refine structure queries so that precise and comprehensive answer sets are obtained.
- Specific stereoisomers may be retrieved through searching with *stereostructure queries*.
- Markush structures (reported in patents since 1988) may be searched in the MARPAT Files.
- In almost all cases the same structure queries may be searched in the BEILSTEIN and REGISTRY Files, and duplicate records may easily be eliminated.

16

Substance Files
with Property Information

*In this chapter we survey those files which have chemical substances as accession points.
We learn:*

- *There may be a large number of fields containing property information and that the
  Database Summary Sheet is an excellent initial guide.*
- *The general procedure to find property information involves searching on the CAS
  Registry Number, displaying the list of fields available, and then displaying the fields of
  interest.*

We also highlight the particular features of some of the different files.

16.1 Substance-based files

A substance-based file is one in which the accession number relates to a chemical substance.
The REGISTRY File contains the largest number of substances, covers all areas of
chemistry and is the major database for chemical substances. However, it does not contain
information on substances. (Actually, up to the most recent 10 references from the CAplus
File may be displayed, but the information in these references is not searchable in the
REGISTRY File and in practice there is little need ever to display bibliographic information
in the File.)

Instead, the REGISTRY File contains the Locator Field (LC) which lists the files which
contain the CAS Registry Number for the substance, and in this way the link between
substance and property information is achieved.

However, there are many substance-based files which do contain property information
and some of these are listed in Table 11.1. The organization of these files is similar. First,
there are a number of fields which identify the substance, and then there are the fields which
give the property information.

16.2 Types of property information

Property information may be either text or numeric, and some files have information in well over 100 fields, nearly all of which may be searched as well as displayed. Clearly with such a variety of information available it is not possible in this text to cover all fields. However, there are a number of general areas.

The biggest area is physical property information which on STN has been grouped into 11 main classes:

Electrical and Magnetic Data	Electrochemical Behavior
General Data	Mechanical Properties
Multi-Component System Data	Optical Data
Spectral Data	Structure and Energy Parameters
State of Aggregation	Thermodynamic Data
Transport Data	

Within each of these classes there are a number of individual fields. For example, some of the fields within the general class **State of Aggregation** are:

Boiling Point	Critical Density	Critical Pressure
Critical Temperature	Critical Volume	Crystal Lattice Parameter
Crystal Transition Point	Crystal Property Description	Crystal Space Group
Crystal System	Decomposition Point	Liquid Transition Point
Melting Point	Sublimation Point	Triple Point
Vapor Pressure		

Nearly all these fields are numeric and are searchable, and the techniques for searching numeric information are summarized in Section 10.5.

Chemical property fields generally contain information on preparations and reactions, although some files additionally have information on related areas like on the isolation of substances from natural sources. Meanwhile, a number of other fields contain data on the toxicity and pharmacology of substances, including the mechanism of action, absorption, distribution and excretion of drugs, biological half-life, human and non-human toxicity, maximum drug dose, minimum fatal dose and therapeutic use.

The handling and use of many substances are subject to Government regulations, and different fields contain information on regulations including occupational health, fire storage and flammability, storage, threshold limit value, bioconcentration and biodegradation, and environmental fate and exposure. Finally, other fields give information on the commercial availability of substances.

The point is that essentially all known information on substances may be retrieved, and the question for the searcher is to know which files to enter, and when. While detailed knowledge of the individual databases is required to fully answer the question, there are some general principles which can be applied.

Important notes:
- very extensive data and information on properties are available;
- this chapter discusses basic techniques for accessing the information;
- but detailed questions may be answered only if the searcher has intimate knowledge of the databases and of the special search techniques.

16.3 Database Summary Sheets

With so many different databases and so many fields, the resource materials provided by the database producer and the vendor are invaluable, and the initial reference material again is the Database Summary Sheet (see Section 5.7).

Before attempting a search, the user should at least be familiar with the search and display field codes, and the display formats. Remember that Database Summary Sheets provide basic information on the construction of the database and on the search mechanics, but more detailed information is found in the Database Descriptions and Index Guides.

16.4 Field Availability

While a single database may have many fields, the majority of substance records may contain information in only a few of these fields simply because the properties for the substance relating to the specific fields have not been reported (or indexed). Accordingly, to assist with search and display in these databases, most of the files have an option that lists the fields in which information for each substance is available. The entry to obtain the display of the fields available for the record is: => **D FA** that is, display the Field Availability. In most files the display of fields available is free but the notable exception is the BEILSTEIN File for which costs are based only on displays (no search term or connect hour fees), and display costs vary with volume of usage per month.

A typical example of a record in a substance-based file is given in Screen 16.1, which shows the substance identifying information for simvastatin from the BEILSTEIN File.

Screen 16.1[a] Substance identifying information in the BEILSTEIN File

Beilstein Reg. No. (BRN):	4768037 Beilstein
Molecular Formula (MF):	C25 H38 O5
Synonym (SY):	simvastatin
Autonom Name (AUN):	2,2-dimethyl-butyric acid 8-<2-(4-hydroxy-6-oxo-tetrahydro-pyran-2-yl)- ethyl>-3,7-dimethyl-1,2,3,7,8,8a-hexahydro-naphthalen-1-yl ester
Beilstein Reference (SO):	6-18
General Comments (NTE):	Stereo compound
CAS Reg. No. (RN):	79902-63-9; 123049-81-0
Formula Weight (FW):	418.57
Lawson Number (LN):	19072; 1185

Screen 16.1 (continued)
Ring System Data:
Number of Rings (CNR):	3
Ring Systems (CNRS):	2
Diff. Ring Systems (CNDRS):	2
Ring Heteros (CNRH):	1
Acyclic Heteros (CNAH):	4

Beilstein Ring Index (BRIX)	Ring System Formula (RF)	BRIX Count
10.2.6-0.0-2.13	C10	1
6.1.0-1.2-0.0	C5O	1

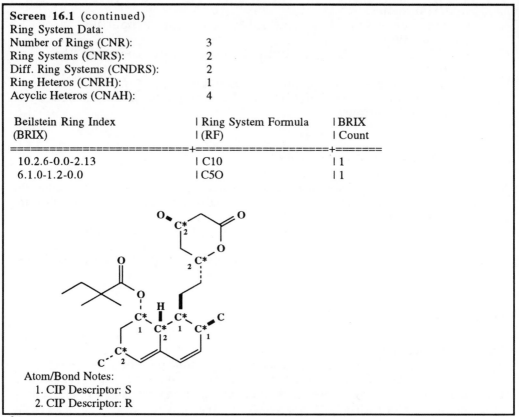

Atom/Bond Notes:
  1. CIP Descriptor: S
  2. CIP Descriptor: R

Note that the information in this part of the record is similar to that in the REGISTRY File since after all, as discussed in Section 11.1, the three key factors which identify a substance are its name, molecular formula and structure. However, there are differences!

Once the record has been obtained the next step is to display the list of fields available: => **D FA** (Screen 16.2).

Note that the Field Code, full name of the field, and the number of repetitions in the field are listed, that the first 9 fields are the substance-identifying fields (which are seen in Screen 16.1), that in this case there are 10 additional fields which contain property information on the substance, and that the information contained in these fields may be displayed by entering the DISPLAY command followed by the field code.

While Screens 16.1 and 16.2 illustrate the procedure in the BEILSTEIN File, the procedure in other substance-based files is very similar. Since the information is so readily displayed, the key factor in finding information in these substance-based files becomes finding the record for the substance, and searches in name and molecular formula-based fields, and in some instances searches by structure, may be used (for example, see Table 11.2).

```
                    Screen 16.2ᵃ  Display of list of fields available (BEILSTEIN File)

=>  D  FA
                |                                        | (OCC)
        ========+========================================+==========

   MF           | Molecular Formula                      |    1
   SY           | Synonym                                |    1
   AUN          | Autonom Name                           |    1
   FW           | Formula Weight                         |    1
   SO           | Beilstein Citation                     |    1
   LN           | Lawson Number                          |    2
   RN           | CAS Registry Number                    |    2
   NTE          | Notes                                  |    1
   SF           | Stereo Family                          |    1
   PRE          | Preparation                            |    2
   CTCPL        | Coupling Phenomena                     |    2
   MP           | Melting Point                          |    1
   NMRA         | NMR Absorption                         |    5
   IRM          | Infrared Maximum                       |    1
   EAM          | Electronic Absorption Maximum          |    1
   SLB          | Solubility                             |    1
   CTLLSM       | Liquid/Liquid Systems                  |    2
   REA          | Chemical Reaction                      |    1
   BF           | Biological Function                    |    4
```

ᵃCopyright by the Beilstein Informationssysteme GmbH and Reprinted with Permission

However, all of the substance-based files have CAS Registry Numbers which may be used as search terms, and this is by far the preferred method for finding the substances. If the CAS Registry Number for the substance of interest is known then the best procedure is to find the substance in the REGISTRY File and cross over the answer to the file of interest.

There are two main reasons for this. First, name fields in many of the substance-based files do not contain the extensive list of synonyms (present in the REGISTRY File) which is so vital for finding substances through common/trade names, and second, many of the files are not searchable by structure and, as seen in Chapter 15, a structure search provides the best option for finding substances for which name and formula based searches do not readily give precise answers.

Problems occur sometimes with CAS Registry Number searches in the BEILSTEIN and GMELIN Files where isotopic and stereo substances are involved (see Sections 16.5.1a and 16.5.4), and in some other files where a number of different records may appear for a single substance. However, a search on the CAS Registry Number will retrieve all the records and it then is necessary to sort through the records manually. This problem also occurs in the GMELIN File when different physical states of the substance are indexed separately and in the CSCHEM File when suppliers list different names for the substances.

General strategy for finding information on a substance in substance-based files:

1. **Find the CAS Registry Number in the REGISTRY File;**
2. **Browse the LC Field;**
3. **Enter File which contains the type of information required;**
4. **Search for substance by CAS Registry Number;[a]**
5. **Display Field Availability; and**
6. **Display field(s) of interest.**

[a] Note that the L-number answer set from the REGISTRY File or the actual CAS Registry Number in the RN Field may be used as the search term

The only modification to this general strategy which may be required occurs when a number of substances are in the REGISTRY File answer set. In order to cross over only those substances which have information in the file of interest, the REGISTRY File answer set is narrowed with the search term **AND <FILE>/LC** (for example: => **S L1 AND HSDB/LC**). This new answer set is then searched in the substance-based file. However, this modification is not needed if information on a single substance is required in which case it is a simple matter merely to check for the file name in the LC Field.

Accordingly, if information on aspirin is required, the record is retrieved in the REGISTRY File (the easiest search option is: => **S ASPIRIN/CN**) and the Locator Field is displayed (Screen 16.3).

Screen 16.3[a] Entries in the Locator Field (REGISTRY File) for aspirin

=> **S ASPIRIN/CN; D LC**

....

LC STN Files: AIDSLINE, ANABSTR, BEILSTEIN*, BIOBUSINESS, BIOSIS, CA,
     CABA, CANCERLIT, CAOLD, CAPREVIEWS, CASREACT, CEN, CHEMINFORMRX,
     CHEMLIST, CBNB, CIN, CJACS, CSCHEM, CSNB, DETHERM*, DDFU, DIPPR*,
     DRUGU, EMBASE, GMELIN*, HODOC*, HSDB*, IFICDB, IFIPAT, IFIUDB,
     IPA, MEDLINE, MRCK*, MSDS-OHS, MSDS-SUM, NAPRALERT, PDLCOM*, PIRA,
     PHAR, PNI, PROMT, RTECS*, SPECINFO, TOXLINE, TOXLIT, USAN,
     USPATFULL, VETU, VTB....

---

[a]Copyright by the American Chemical Society and Reprinted with Permission

In this case the names of all of the substance-based files listed in Table 11.1 appear, and now those files are entered that cover the specific type of property information required. Since all the files allow CAS Registry Numbers as search terms, the answer set (L1) obtained in the REGISTRY File may be searched in each file in turn using the entry: => **S L1**.

As some of the substance-based files have related print materials, and since the general strategy outlined above resembles the process for searching in the print versions, it is reasonable to question why the electronic versions should be searched. First, the print versions might not be readily available to the scientist or else may be relatively expensive. This latter aspect applies particularly to the Beilstein and Gmelin Handbooks, but the issue is a much more general one (for example, see Section 1.4).

Second, the ability to be able to proceed very easily from one database to another is very useful. In the online networks all the information is available in the one location and the databases are linked, so specialist pieces of information may readily be retrieved.

Finally, through electronic networks, searches may be conducted that are just not possible through print materials. For example a part-structure search query can be created and searched in the REGISTRY File then information on the answers may be retrieved in any of the substance-based files. Alternatively, if a single property is of interest then it is very easy to search for substances which have this property. In these respects, note that print materials do not allow searches by structure to be performed, and, as the print materials also are organised by substance, if a single property is of interest then it would have to be searched manually in all the substance records!

16.5 Specific files: contents and notes

It is outside the scope of this text to discuss details of all of the various substance-based files so searchers should consult the major source material available from the database producer. So only a general overview, and some general notes about searching the files, are given here. Of the files listed in Table 11.1, the BEILSTEIN File is by far the largest, and some aspects of this file are considered first. Then the other files will be considered in turn, and the records for aspirin in these files compared when applicable. (Actually, the record for aspirin in the BEILSTEIN File is very detailed and will not be compared here. It contains information in 70 different fields and many of these have substantial field repetitions. For example, there were 303 occurrences in the Biological Function Field!)

16.5.1 BEILSTEIN File
The File contains nearly all of the information in the Beilstein Handbook up to 1960 and from 1980 onwards. All the substances in the Handbook period 1960-1979 are included in the File together with some of their basic physical properties (melting point, boiling point, density and optical rotation). However, references only are given for other information reported in this period. (The Beilstein Institute, which was founded late in the 19th century, commenced recording the Handbook Data in electronic form in the early 1980s. As sections are completed they are made available through the online networks, so the BEILSTEIN File is updated periodically.)

General classifications are given to the types of information in these different periods and they are: Handbook Data (up to 1960); Unchecked Data (1960-1979); and Primary Literature (1980 onwards).

However, searchers need not be too concerned about the differences particularly if searches are restricted to the general strategy outlined above. All that needs to be known is that for the different time periods the information is entered a little differently; sometimes the actual data and literature references are presented, while at other times only the literature references are given.

An example of the content of a record in the BEILSTEIN File has been given already (Screens 16.1 and 16.2) and some of the fields (identified in the display of Field Availability) are shown for simvastatin in Screen 16.4. (The entry to display this information is: **D MP PRE NMRA.**)

Screen 16.4[a] Display of individual fields in the BEILSTEIN File; melting point, preparation and NMR absorption fields for simvastatin[b]

Melting Point:
Value |Ref.
(MP) (Cel) |
=============+====
139.50 |1
Reference(s):
    1. Askin, D.; Verhoeven, T. R.; Liu, T. M.-H.; Shinkai, I., J.Org.Chem., 56 <1991> 16, 4929-4932, LA: EN, CODEN: JOCEAH

Preparation:
PRE
    Start: BRN=4836426 C25H39O6(1-)*NH4(1+)
    Time: 6 hour(s)
    Yield: 94.20 %
    Solv: toluene
    Temp: 100.0 Cel
    Reference(s):
        1. Askin, D.; Verhoeven, T. R.; Liu, T. M.-H.; Shinkai, I., J.Org.Chem., 56 <1991> ...
PRE
    Start: BRN=5364343 C31H52O5Si
    Reag: acetic acid, Bu4NF*3H2O
    Time: 18 hour(s)
    Solv: tetrahydrofuran
    Reference(s):
        1. Hoffman, W. F.; Alberts, A. W.; Anderson, P. S.; Chen, J. S.; Smith, R. L.; Willard, A. K., J.Med.Chem., 29 <1986> 5, 849-852, LA: EN, CODEN: JMCMAR

NMR Absorption:
NMRA
    Nucl: 1H   Solv: CDCl3
    Reference(s):
        1. Uchiyama, Naotaka; Kagami, Yayoi; Saitoh, Yuko; Ohtawa, Masakatsu, Chem.Pharm.Bull., 39 <1991> 1, 236-238, LA: EN, CODEN: CPBTAL
NMRA
    Nucl: 1H   Solv: CDCl3
    Reference(s):
        1. Askin, D.; Verhoeven, T. R.; Liu, T. M.-H.; Shinkai, I., J.Org.Chem., 56 <1991> ...
NMRA
    Nucl: 13C   Solv: CDCl3
    Reference(s):
        1. Askin, D.; Verhoeven, T. R.; Liu, T. M.-H.; Shinkai, I., J.Org.Chem., 56 <1991> ...
NMRA
    Nucl: 1H   Solv: CD2Cl2
    Reference(s):
        1. Smith, George B.; DiMichele, Lisa; Colwell, Lawrence F.; Dezeny, George C.; Douglas, Alan W.; et al., Tetrahedron, 49 <1993> 21, 4447-4462, LA: EN, CODEN: TETRAB
NMRA
    Nucl: 13C   Solv: CD2Cl2
    Reference(s):
        1. Smith, George B.; DiMichele, Lisa; Colwell, Lawrence F.; Dezeny, George C.; Douglas, Alan W.; et al., Tetrahedron, 49 <1993> 21, 4447-4462, LA: EN, CODEN: TETRAB

[a]Copyright by the Beilstein Informationssysteme GmbH and Reprinted with Permission
[b]The substance identifying fields, and lists of fields available are given in Screens 16.1 and 16.2.

In the majority of cases, all the information required by the searcher is presented in the fields. For example, Screen 16.4 gives the reference to the ^{1}H and ^{13}C NMR spectra (in deuterochloroform and deuterated methylene chloride). Additionally the references for the preparation are listed, and while the actual starting material is not named, nevertheless the Beilstein Registry Number is given and it may be searched in the File.

While property information for simvastatin appears in only 10 fields there are over 150 search and display fields in the File. Couple these large number of possible fields with the almost 7 million substances in the File and it is clear that the BEILSTEIN File contains a wealth of information. For example, it is estimated that the File currently contains information on over 3 million spectra and on over 8 million chemical reactions and preparations!

Thus shown in Table 16.1 are the numbers of records which have information in the 20 fields listed. (These fields were chosen simply to give an idea of the volume of information available in the File, and they are representative only.) In some cases the actual property values, while in other cases some key data and references, are given. An example of the former is seen in the Melting Point Field (Screen 16.4) which lists the actual melting point, while an example of the latter is shown in the NMRA Field which gives the nucleus being studied plus the literature reference.

Table 16.1 Number of substance records in selected fields (BEILSTEIN File)

FIELD	NO. ENTRIES	FIELD	NO. ENTRIES
Reaction	576,000	Preparation	5,261,000
Density	203,000	Dipole moment	24,000
Boiling point	647,000	UV maximum	412,000
Vaporization enthalpy	3,300	IR maximum	1,069,000
Natural product	88,000	Mass spectra	490,000
Optical rotation	500,000	NMR spectra	1,570,000
Half-wave potential	19,500	Raman spectra	11,800
Surface tension	5,500	Toxicity	33,500
Solubility data	35,600	Fluorescence maximum	11,100
Mutarotation	3,000	Calorific data	9,300

The BEILSTEIN File covers organic substances only, and, together with the REGISTRY File, the two files cover all the organic chemical literature from the late 18th century to the present day. While the BEILSTEIN File contains almost 7 million, and the REGISTRY File a little over 12 million organic substances there is not complete overlap and indeed about one quarter of the substances in the BEILSTEIN File are not in the REGISTRY File. While many of these substances which are not common to both files are only in the pre-1957 literature (and often relate to derivatives of substances used for characterization purposes or to substances which at the time were not fully identified) there are substances, reported post-1957, which are indexed in only one file, so for comprehensive results searches should be done in both files.

When this is done, duplicate answers (substances) may need to be identified or excluded. The search term in the BEILSTEIN File which identifies REGISTRY File records is **RN/FA**, and the corresponding search term in the REGISTRY File is **BEILSTEIN/LC**. So to find unique records in the BEILSTEIN File the search term is: **S L1 NOT RN/FA** (where L1 is the BEILSTEIN File answer set). However, if the substance is found in the first file, then, depending on the type of information required, it may not be necessary to search in the second file.

16.5.1a Finding substances in the BEILSTEIN File

The Registry Number systems in the BEILSTEIN and REGISTRY Files were set up independently, and the accession numbers are Beilstein Registry Numbers (BRN) and CAS Registry Numbers respectively. Late in the 1980s the structure connection tables for substances in the two files were matched. This enabled CAS Registry Numbers to be entered in the BEILSTEIN File and the BEILSTEIN Locator Field to be flagged in the REGISTRY File.

Since the structure connection tables were matched and since these do not contain information on isotopes or stereochemical information, a single Beilstein Registered Substance may list a number of CAS Registry Numbers in the RN Field (and vice versa). That is, the structure connection table for L-alanine in the BEILSTEIN File will match the structure connection table in the REGISTRY File for the D- and L- forms of alanine, the racemic mixture, the substance with stereochemistry undefined, and all the isotopic forms.

Further matches between the files on name based terms could not be carried out easily, partly because there are significant differences in the nomenclature in the files, and partly because only about one third of the substances in the BEILSTEIN File have entries in the Chemical Name or Synonym Fields. Accordingly, the searcher usually needs to sort through the records manually.

The numbers of entries in the main substance identifying fields in the two files, and also in the GMELIN File (see Section 16.5.4), are listed in Table 16.2 and from this it is evident that *comprehensive searches* on name based fields in the BEILSTEIN and GMELIN Files are not possible.

Table 16.2   Numbers of entries in the main IDE fields[a]

FIELD	NUMBER OF SUBSTANCES		
	BEILSTEIN	GMELIN	REGISTRY
Total Substances	6,700,000	1,000,000	13,500,000
CAS Registry Numbers	4,400,000	182,000	13,500,000
Chemical Name	2,100,000[b]	380,000	14,300,000
Molecular Formula	6,700,000	1,000,000	14,300,000
Structures	6,700,000	1,000,000	13,000,000

[a]The numbers given are approximate and merely give an indication of the entries. only
[b]There also are 2,400,000 substances which have names in the synonym field, but many of these also have entries in the Chemical Name Field

Indeed effective comprehensive searches are possible only through structure searches. Accordingly, to find a substance in the BEILSTEIN File, it is recommended that either the CAS Registry Number is searched in the RN field and, if there is more than one hit, the answers are displayed and the required substance is identified manually, or if there is no CAS Registry Number then possible terms be expanded in the CN, SY, or MF Fields and unless the substance can be identified readily then it is recommended that an EXACT structure search be undertaken.

Nevertheless, as soon as the substance is found, the list of fields available is displayed followed by a display of the fields of interest. While this general procedure always may be used, on occasions, depending on the type of question involved, it may be more economical to perform an additional search (see Section 16.5.1c(2)). This is because of the current pricing in the File under which searches are free but note that display costs vary, for example with monthly frequency of usage.

Groups of substances may be obtained in the same way as in the REGISTRY File. Since all substances in the File have molecular formulas and structures, searches based on formulas (or molecular formula derived fields like those in Section 13.3.3) or on structures yield comprehensive results.

16.5.1b Chemical information

Unlike with the CASREACT File (see Section 17.3), preparations and reactions are treated separately in the BEILSTEIN File, and within the PRE and REA Fields there are a number of subfields (Figure 16.1).

OVERALL CHEMICAL REACTION

[A]	+	[B]		=====>		[E]		+		[F]

[C] (solvent)
[D] (catalyst;
    inorg. reagent)

For a PREPARATION of [E]

Substance	....	will appear in subfield entry[a]
[A] , [B]		PRE.SM
[C] , [D]		PRE.RGT
[E]		(Entries are within PRE for this substance record)
[F]		PRE.BPRO

For a REACTION of [A]

Substance	....	will appear in subfield entry[a]
[A]		(Entries are within REA for this substance record)
[B]		REA.RP
[C] , [D]		REA.RP or REA.RGT
[E] , [F]		REA.PRO

Figure 16.1 Indexing of preparations and reactions in the BEILSTEIN File
[a]The major subfield is indicated. However, the distinction between a reagent and a starting material, or a reaction partner and a reagent, can be a fine one and all options should be searched if comprehensive results are required

Again the general procedure to find chemical information is to find the registered substance and display the PRE and REA field entries as required. A reaction will appear in the PRE or in the REA field depending upon whether, in the view of the indexer, the primary focus of the reaction in the original article was on a preparative procedure or on a reaction. Since almost 90% of records have entries in the PRE Field and less than 20% have entries in the REA Field the chemical reaction of interest is often better found by searching or displaying in the PRE Field.

There are two main instances where the general procedure (Section 16.4) may be inappropriate for finding preparations. This occurs first when there are a very large number of entries in the PRE Field for a single substance (note that the number of occurrences is displayed in the FA list), and second when the preparations of many related substances are required.

In the former case it still is best to display all the entries in the field and to sort through them manually, while in the latter case, if preparations from a given set of starting materials are required then this should be attempted only after consultation with the vendor's Help Desk. Such searches are indeed possible but generally should be attempted only by those very familiar with the File. For example, entries in the PRE.SM Field can include names (most of which are not systematic), Beilstein Registry Numbers, or molecular formulas, and special techniques are needed to identify the appropriate search terms. Fortunately, with no search term or connect hour pricing, all of these issues can be sorted out at no cost, and when such searches are done, they can provide excellent information on chemical reactions for a time period covering well over a century!

16.5.1c Physical property information
There are three common types of searches which may be performed and which relate to physical property information.

1. Find a property for a single substance
The general strategy here is exactly the same as the general strategy outlined earlier. That is, the substance record is found, and then the list of fields available (FA), followed by the specific fields of interest, are displayed. For example, to find the melting point of simvastatin, the record is found, the Fields Available listed (Screen 16.2) and the Melting Point Field is displayed (Screen 16.4). Indeed this procedure is so easy that arguably it affords the most cost effective method for finding property information on a single substance.

The only additional point to note here relates to the current pricing structure in the File under which searches are free and displays only are charged. Since the display of fields available now incurs a charge, it may be more cost effective to approach the question of finding a property for a substance by first finding the record for the substance and then searching to determine whether the field of interest is present. That is, if a melting point is required and the substance record is L1, then the search: => **S L1 AND MP/FA**, will immediately inform as to whether the information required is present. If so, the final answer set is displayed in the usual manner.

2. Find a property for a group of substances
The first step is to find the group of substances, for example by a structure or perhaps molecular formula based search. However, any subset of the File may be chosen. For example, a search: => **S INP/FA** will give all those substances which are isolated from natural sources and then other properties of this group of substances (for example, ultraviolet absorption maxima) may be found. Such a search might be valuable, for example, to those interested in identifying natural substances which might be useful for sunscreens.

If there are a large number of substances, it is hardly feasible to display the lists of fields available for each, and there certainly is no point in displaying the property field for all the substances since many may not have information in the field of interest. However, only those substances (in the initial answer set, say L1) which have information in the field required may be obtained through a search:

> => **S L1 AND <REQUIRED FIELD CODE> / FA**
> (example: **S L1 AND EAM/FA**)[*]

---

[*]EAM is the field code for ultraviolet absorption maximum.

Answers may now be displayed, and, since in the BEILSTEIN File the default display format is that with the HIT terms, it is sufficient to enter: => **D 1-** . However, lesser information may be displayed and a useful (and perhaps more cost-effective) option is to display just the STR and the field of interest, for example: => **D 1- STR EAM.**

For example, in Section 15.10.2 the structure search in the BEILSTEIN File gave 45 answers and if the property required related to nmr spectral information, then the answer set is searched with the NMRA (NMR absorption) and NMRS (NMR spectrum) Fields (Screen 16.5).

Screen 16.5[a]   Finding NMR data for a group of substances (BEILSTEIN File)

```
=> S L2 AND NMR#/FA
     1603355       NMR#/FA
L4        7       L2 AND NMR#/FA
=> D BRN STR HIT
Beilstein Reg. No. (BRN):          6880293   Beilstein
```

Atom/Bond Notes:
   1. CIP Descriptor: R
   2. CIP Descriptor: S

NMR Absorption:
NMRA
   Nucl: 1H
   Reference(s):
   1. Baldwin, Jack E.; Abraham, Edward P.; Adlington, Robert M.; Chakravarti, Bulbul; Derome, Andrew E.; et al., J.Chem.Soc.Chem.Commun., <1983> 22, 1317-1319, LA: EN, CODEN: JCCCAT

[a]Copyright by the Beilstein Informationssysteme GmbH and Reprinted with Permission

---

3. Find substances which have a property of interest

There are a number of steps involved and each needs special attention. They may be illustrated with the sample question: "Find substances which have a sublimation point of between 120 and 140 °C at pressures lower than 10^{-4} Torr."

First it is necessary to check for the property by looking up the Database Summary Sheet or the Database Description. (The point is that there are many fields and it is necessary to check exactly the field in which the property of interest will be present.) The entry for sublimation point is shown in Figure 16.2 and from this essentially all the relevant information may be obtained. For example, it is noted that sublimation point temperatures are in °C and that the pressure at which the measurement is performed is in Torr. (Clearly the proper units have to be used otherwise completely the wrong results will be obtained!) If the units in which the question is asked are different from the (default) units in the File then the latter may be changed with the command: => **SET UNIT <FIELD CODE=UNIT>** (for example, => **SET UNIT BP=K** sets the units to degrees Kelvin) or otherwise the value required may be recalculated by the searcher so that the default units apply.

FIELDS	UNITS	SEARCH CODE	SEARCH EXAMPLES	DISPLAY CODES
Sublimation Point	Cel	/SP	**S 340-360/SP**	SP
Keyword	(none)	/SP.KW	**S 340/SP(NOTP)OPEN/SP.KW**	SP
Pressure	Torr	/SP.P	**S 340/SP(P)0.04/SP.P**	SP
Range	Cel	/SP.RAN	**S350/SP.P(P)SP.RAN<=20**	SP

Figure 16.2 Sublimation Point in the BEILSTEIN File; entry from the Database Summary Sheet

When a property has a dependent parameter (for example, boiling point and sublimation point depend on pressure), it is necessary to link the terms with the (P) operator. Thus for a single substance the sublimation point may have been recorded at a number of pressures and it is only through linking the search terms with the (P) operator that the correct temperatures and pressures are connected.

It now is necessary to apply the correct numeric operators (see Figure 4.8) with the search fields, and this is shown in Screen 16.6 together with part of one of the 14 answers retrieved.

Screen 16.6[a] Finding substances with specific sublimation points

```
=> S  120<=SP<=140  (P)  SP.P<0.0001
       1430          120 CEL <=SP<=140 CEL
         92          SP.P<0.0001 TORR
L1     14            120 CEL <=SP<=140 CEL (P) SP.P<0.0001 TORR
=> D  CN SP
```

Chemical Name (CN):   1-<.beta.-hydroxy-phenethyl>-4-phenyl-piperidine-4-carboxylic acid
                               ethyl ester 1-<.beta.-Hydroxy-phenaethyl>-4-phenyl-piperidin-4-
                               carbonsaeure-aethylester

Sublimation Point:

Value	Press.	Ref.	Note
(SP)	(.P)		
(Cel)	(Torr)		
===============+==============+======+=======			
125.00	1.0E-05	1	1

Reference(s):
    1. Perrine; Eddy, J.Org.Chem., 21 <1956> 125, CODEN: JOCEAH
Notes(s):
1. Handbook Data

---

[a]Copyright by the Beilstein Informationssysteme GmbH and Reprinted with Permission

This example shows the principle involved in finding substances with specific property values. A database of the size and complexity of the BEILSTEIN File offers a very wide range of such search possibilities!

Important notes (BEILSTEIN File):
- almost 7 million organic substances;
- literature covered from early 19th century to present day;
- records best found through structure searches or searches on CAS Registry Numbers;
- while you may use DISPLAY FA to list fields present for the substance and then display required fields, remember that currently connect hour and search fees do not apply and this can affect strategies for finding information in the File.

Used in this way the BEILSTEIN File is an extremely valuable source of chemical and physical property information, and the information can be found very easily and cost effectively.

While specialized searches can be conducted, and can solve the most complicated questions to give unique answers, they should be conducted only by those very experienced in the File, or only after consultation with the online vendor or database producer.

16.5.2 CHEMLIST File

The CHEMLIST File currently covers information on chemical substances listed in national inventories including the Environmental Protection Agency Toxic Substances Control Act, the European Inventory of Existing Commercial Chemical Substances, the Canadian Domestic Substances List, and the Korean Existing Chemicals List. Similar listings from other countries, for example Japan and Australia, will be added in the future, so that the CHEMLIST File will become the major source of regulated chemicals listings. It should also be noted that the CHEMLIST File is not the only file which contains information relating to Government regulations. STN has a cluster of files (GOVREGS) in this area, in which STN also publishes a number of documents and manuals, and a CD-ROM product. For full information on searching for regulatory and compliance information, these additional resource materials should be consulted.

The CHEMLIST File also contains some state "right-to-know" lists and other US regulatory information such as the Superfund Amendments and Reauthorization Act, OSHA Regulations, US State Regulations, CERCLA and the Marine Pollutants List. One of the most significant benefits of the CHEMLIST File is that it merges all regulatory lists together under the individual substances.

The record for aspirin is given in Screen 16.7 and a number of the features of the File immediately become apparent.

That is:

- the FS Field (File Segment) lists countries (and Acts) in which regulatory information has been listed;
- the CBI Field (Confidentiality Status) gives status of the original document;
- the RLN Field (Regulatory List Number) gives registration numbers for the various original listings;
- the INV Field (Inventory Status) refers to the latest regulatory document; and
- the FA Field (Field Availability) lists the fields for which information on the substance is available.

```
                    Screen 16.7ᵃ  Entry for aspirin in the CHEMLIST File
AN      18 CHEMLIST
RN      50-78-2
CN      Benzoic acid, 2-(acetyloxy)- (TSCA, DSL)
        Acide O-acetylsalicylique (French) (DSL, EINECS)
        O-acetylsalicylic acid (EINECS)....ᵇ
FS      CANADA: DSL; EEC: EINECS; KOREA: ECL; USA: STATE, TSCA
CBI     Public
RLN     EINECS No.: 200-064-1
        ECL Serial No.: 3-1917
INV     On TSCA Inventory
           January 1995 Inventory Tape.
        On DSL
           Supplement to Canada Gazette, Part I, January 26, 1991.
        On EINECS
           Annex to Official Journal of the European Communities, 15 June 1990.
        On ECL
           Korean Existing Chemicals List, 1992 Ed.
FA      RN; RLN; INV; 4A; PROP65; SNJ; SPA
```

[a]Copyright by the American Chemical Society and Reprinted with Permission
[b]All the synonyms for aspirin in the REGISTRY File also appear in the CHEMLIST File

In this File the list of fields available appears in the default display format (that is, following entry of the DISPLAY command: => **D**, meaning that it is not necessary to separately ask for a display of field availability) and any of the fields listed may be displayed in detail in the usual manner. Thus Screen 16.8 shows the display of two of the fields. Many of the fields have numeric codes, for example field code 4A refers to a Test Rule under TSCA Section 4A. While the different codes might seem overwhelming at first it should be remembered that HELP options always are available (see Section 10.1.1) and that field codes may be checked in the Database Summary Sheet in the usual way.

```
                    Screen 16.8ᵃ  Display of fields in the CHEMLIST File
=>      D PROP65   4A
==== U.S. State Regulations ====
PROP65  California Proposition 65 Carcinogens and Reproductive Toxins
        Office of Environmental Health Hazard Assessment, California EPA
        January 1994 Status Report.
        Listed Name(s): Aspirin
        Special Health Hazard Code(s): Chemicals known to the state to cause reproductive
        toxicity (Developmental toxicity) Special Health Hazard Code(s): Chemicals known to
        the state to cause reproductive toxicity (Female reproductive toxicity).
==== U.S. EPA Regulations - TSCA ====
4A      Test Rule - TSCA Section 4a
        U.S. EPA/OPTS Public Files 40-81421237.
        title: FINAL REPORT TO BATTELLE COLUMBUS LABORATORIES & EPA-OTS,
        SUBCONTRACT NO. T-6419 (7197)-033, 100179 - 093081. DEVELOPMENT OF
        TEST FOR DETERMINING ANAEROBIC BIODEGRADATION POTENTIAL
        ..completion date: 081481 ..submitted by: U S EPA ..microfiche
        number: OTS0518842 ENVIRONMENTAL FATE** ..Biodegradaton Mixture
```

[a]Copyright by the American Chemical Society and Reprinted with Permission

However, the CHEMLIST File may be searched independently. Indeed, apart from the fact that it is a substance-based file and contains a Chemical Name Field (CN) which may be searched similarly to the corresponding field in the REGISTRY File using the full name or name segments, in all other respects the text fields may be searched using text terms in the same manner as searches may be done in the non-bibliographic text fields in bibliographic files, noting, however, that substance-based files do not contain Title, Author, Corporate Source and Source Fields which are inappropriate to substance-based files.

Important notes (CHEMLIST File):
- **The feature of the File is that it contains references to the original documents produced by major international regulatory authorities concerning regulations or acts relating to the substance;**
- **the information from a large number of sources is located in the one place, that is, within a single substance record; and**
- **while individual fields may be searched and displayed, the general usage of the file is to find the substance record and to display the fields of interest.**

16.5.3   CSCHEM File

There are numerous companies worldwide which supply chemical substances, and the CSCHEM File contains names of those companies from which the individual chemicals can be purchased.

The preferred search term is the CAS Registry Number since the same substance may appear in the file in different records under different names because in general the substances are indexed separately under the names used by the chemical supplier.

Only the abbreviations for the companies are listed in the CSCHEM File (although the D ALL format also spells out company names), and these abbreviations are then searched in the companion file, the CSCORP File, which gives contact information for the supplier.

For example, a search on the CAS Registry Number (50-78-2) gives two records, and the main entry is shown in Screen 16.9. (The other entry is under the Chemical Name aspirin, but as usual a search on the CAS Registry Number overcomes this difficulty with nomenclature.)

Screen 16.9[a]   Record for aspirin in the CSCHEM File

```
AN        1945  CSCHEM
RN        50-78-2
CN        ACETYLSALICYLIC ACID
COC[b]    ABOUS, ACO, AFC, ALHUS, ANECA, ARFPK, ASI (HP), AUBDE, BAYDE, BECZA,
          CAC, CHGDE, CHM, CIHPL, CREUS, CSIUS, DICZA, DOLCH, EMI, FABES, FIS, ....
```

---

[a]Copyright by the Directories Publishing Company, Inc and Reprinted with Permission
[b]COC is the Company Code Field and gives the acronym used for the company

In the CSCORP File addresses of the parent company, and of their international agencies are given, and it is often necessary to identify only the local supplier. This is most easily achieved by the following procedure which uses the SmartSELECT feature (see Section 10.1.3):

1. locate the record(s) in the CSCHEM File (answer set L1);
2. enter the CSCORP File (=> FIL CSCORP);
3. search: => S L1 1- <CO> (answer set L3);
4. search: => S L4 AND COUNTRY
   (for example: => S L4 AND UNITED STATES); and
5. display answer(s): => D 1- HIT.

In Step 3. the example given above effectively tells the computer: "go back to the file in which the answer set L1 was created and for each answer select all the company names then search for these companies in the CSCORP File". (Note that is is not essential that Step 4. be used, and if it is not then addresses of the company and its agencies around the world will be retrieved.)

Naturally, the accuracy of the files depends upon the companies to notify the database producer when new products become available, or when existing products are discontinued. So at times the information may not be completely up to date, but at least the two files represent an excellent guide to the commercial availability of substances.

> **Important notes (CSCHEM File):**
> * **The feature of the File is that it lists those substances which are commercially available;**
> * **substances are indexed under the names of the substances used by the suppliers, so a search on a single CAS Registry Number may produce more than one record in the File; and**
> * **the CSCORP File contains the full names and addresses of the suppliers of the substances.**

(Note that the recently released CHEMCATS File also contains records for commercially available substances, and additionally the File contains company addresses, prices of chemicals, toxicity, and health and safety data. Like other substance-based files it is best searched through CAS Registry Numbers, and then the relevant fields are displayed. It is now the preferred first option to search for commercially available substances.)

16.5.4   GMELIN File

The GMELIN File contains information on inorganic and organometallic substances,[*] and in some ways is the companion to the BEILSTEIN File which contains information on organic substances.

---

[*]Organometallic substances are those which contain a bond from a *carbon* atom to a metal. They differ from coordination compounds (Section 11.4.3) which contain bonds between the metal and atoms other than carbon.

The GMELIN File is the electronic version of the well-known print series: *GMELIN Handbook of Inorganic and Organometallic Chemistry* which has been the major resource material in the area covering the literature from the late 18th century. Like the BEILSTEIN File, the GMELIN File has been assembled since the early 1980s and the process of conversion of the print to electronic versions is continuing.

Since relatively few substances have entries in the name fields (see Table 16.2), searches based on name terms will not produce comprehensive results. Indeed, the recommended procedure to find substances in the File is through molecular formula or structure search terms, particularly since only about 20% of the substances in the File have CAS Registry Numbers.

While a record for aspirin actually appears in the GMELIN File, this File would not be entered to find information on this substance (which is registered here for the purposes of identifications relating to other records in the File), since the focus of the File is on inorganic and organometallic substances. So Screen 16.10 shows instead one of the records for calcium phosphate. Note that the registration of this substance is quite different from the registration in the REGISTRY File (Screen 11.12). In particular the indexing of salts in the GMELIN File corresponds exactly with the chemist's representation and hydrogen atoms are not attached to the parent acid.

Further, there actually are 13 records in the GMELIN File which have the molecular formula Ca3 O8 P2 and they relate to different crystalline forms or physical states of the substance (that is, to various liquid and solid forms).

On the other hand, the record in Screen 16.10 indicates that 10 different CAS Registry Numbers may apply, and these CAS Registry Numbers are those for the different isotopic forms and the REGISTRY File substances which have different ratios of the calcium and phosphate groups. The need to know the specific database indexing policy again is emphasised and in this case it is noted that details of indexing in the GMELIN File can be obtained from the Gmelin Institute.

Screen 16.10[a]   A record for calcium phosphate in the GMELIN File

GMELIN Reg. No. (GRN):	15665 GMELIN
CAS Reg. No. (RN):	7757-93-9; 7758-23-8; 7758-87-4; 10103-46-5; 13767-12-9; 16460-52-9; 18372-33-3; 19476-29-0; 29819-43-0; 36412-25-6
Molecular Formula (MF):	Ca3 O8 P2
Comp. Mol. Formula (CMF):	Ca3O8P2
Fragm. Mol. Formula (FRAGMF):	6850: Ca(2+):1
	1997: O4P(3-):1
Chemical Name (CN):	tricalcium diphosphate
Formula Weight (FW):	0.310176E3
Lin. Struct. Formula (LSF):	3Ca(2+)*2PO4(3-)=Ca3(PO4)2

    FRAG 1   FRAGGRN 6850
    Ca
    FRAG 2   FRAGGRN 1997
    O4 P

As there are 13 different "calcium phosphates" in the GMELIN File, the searcher would need to scan these and identify the one(s) of particular interest in order to obtain the requisite property information. Once this has been ascertained, the fields available may be listed and the specific information displayed.

Important notes (GMELIN File):
- **The feature of the File is that it contains factual information on almost one million inorganic and organometallic substances;**
- **substances are most reliably retrieved through molecular formula or structure searches;**
- **a single CAS Registry Number may relate to a number of Gmelin Registry Numbers and vice versa; and**
- **fields of interest, identified through a display of the Field Availability, are displayed as with other substance-based files.**

16.5.5 HODOC File

For over half a century CRC Press has published a series of Handbooks containing data in chemistry and physics, and the HODOC File is a numeric file representing the *CRC Handbook of Data on Organic Compounds*. The file features physical data on the most frequently used organic compounds, and is an extensive source of spectral data. Physical data, when available for the substance, is restricted to boiling point, melting point, density, refractive index, optical rotatory power, solubility, and crystal property. Spectral data, when available, covers infrared, Raman, ultraviolet, NMR, and mass spectra.

If property information on a substance is required and if the HODOC File is listed in the Locator Field in the REGISTRY File, then the HODOC File should be checked. The field availability is listed and relevant fields are displayed (Screen 16.11).

```
                    Screen 16.11ᵃ  Part record for aspirin in the HODOC File
RN      50-78-2 HODOC
HN      05855
MF      C9 H8 O4
LSF     2(CH3CO2)-C6H4CO2H
CN      Benzoic acid, 2-(acetyloxy)-
CN      AC 5230...ᵇ
=> D FA
Code       Field Name                    Code       Field Name
-------+----------------------------     -------+----------------------------
RN         CAS Registry Number           CN         Chemical Name
CPD        Crystal Property Description   HN         HODOC Number
IRS        IR Spectrum                   LSF        Linear Structural Formula
MS         Mass Spectrum                 MP         Melting Point
MF         Molecular Formula             MW         Molecular Weight
NMRS       NMR Spectrum                  HNMR       NMR Spectrum, H1
OS         Other Source                  RAS        Raman Spectra
SLB        Solubility                    UVS        UV and Visible Spectrum
```

Screen 16.11 (continued)
=> **D RAS SLB**
 Raman Spectrum
Peak   RAS.PP   cm**-1
===
3090 3070 2940 1740 1620 1600 1480 1430 1290 1250 1220 1190 1150 1040
780 750 700 640 550 420 320 290 170 120 100

Reference: Sadtler Research Laboratories spectral collection (No. 417)

Solubility
  Description | Solvent
    SLB.TX | SLB.SOL
====================+=========================
Slightly soluble |benzene
Soluble |water; ether; chloroform
Very soluble |alcohol

[a]Copyright by CRC PRESS INC and Reprinted with Permission
[b]70 different synonyms appear in the record

The HODOC and the BEILSTEIN Files contain similar property and spectral information, although a major difference is that the former file contains records only for the most commonly encountered organic substances.

Important note (HODOC File):
*   **The feature of the File is that it contains numeric data (particularly melting and boiling points) and spectral information for the most frequently used organic substances.**

16.5.6   HSDB File
The Hazardous Substances Data Bank contains very extensive information on the toxicology and environmental effects of over 4000 substances. A look through the fields for which information on aspirin is available (Screen 16.12) gives a quick idea of the exact type of information which is available under the 10 major headings!

Screen 16.12[a] Fields in which information is available for aspirin in the HSDB File

Code	Field Name		
Substance Identification			
RN	CAS Registry Number	CN	Chemical Name
CR	Cross Reference	HSN	HSDB Number
MF	Molecular Formula	MW	Molecular Weight
NC	Number of Components	PG	Periodic Group
RDAT	Revision Date	RTN	RTECS Number
WLN	Wiswesser Line Notation		

Screen 16.12 (continued)

Manufacturing Information

APP	Application	CO	Corporate Name (of Producer/Manufacturer)
COMP	Composition	CPAT	Consumption Pattern
MMFG	Method of Manufacture	EXPT	U.S. Exports
IMPT	U.S. Imports	USPR	U.S. Production

Physical Properties

CPD	Crystal Property Description	DISK	Dissociation Constant
MP	Melting Point	NTE	Note
LKOW	Octanol-Water Distribution Coefficient		
ODOR	Odor	SLB	Solubility
SPGR	Specific Gravity	SPECT	Spectral Property
VP	Vapor Pressure		

Safety and Handling

FPOT	Fire Potential	IRR	Irritation
OPRM	Other Preventative Measures	STRG	Storage

Toxicity

ACTN	Action Mechanism	ADE	Absorption, Distribution and Excretion
ANTR	Antidote and Emergency Treatment		
BHL	Biological Half-Life	HTOX	Human Toxicity
HTXE	Human Toxicity Excerpt	INTC	Interaction
METB	Metabolism-Metabolite	NTOX	Non-Human Toxicity
NTXE	Non-Human Toxicity Excerpt		

Pharmacology

IDIO	Drug Idiosyncracy	WARN	Drug Warning
MXDD	Maximum Drug Dose	MFD	Minimum Fatal Dose
THER	Therapeutic Use		

Environmental Fate/Exposure Potential

ABIO	Abiotic Degradation	ARTS	Artificial Source
CBIO	Bioconcentration	BIOD	Biodegradation
COEV	Concentration in Environment	CHMN	Concentration in Humans
ENVF	Environmental Fate	ENVS	Environmental Fate/Exposure Summary
PBEX	Probable Exposure	KOC	Soil Adsorption/Mobility
VWS	Volatilization from Water/Soil		

Exposure Standards and Regulations

OSHA	OSHA Standards and Regulations	TLV	Threshold Limit Value

Monitoring and Analysis Method

ALAB	Analytical Laboratory Method	CLAB	Clinical Laboratory Method

Additional References

(none)

[a]Copyright by the National Library of Medicine and Reprinted with Permission

Any of the fields may be displayed in the usual manner and, for example, Screen 16.13 shows part of the record in the THERapeutic Use Field for aspirin.

Screen 16.13[a] Part display of information in THERapeutic Use Field for aspirin (HSBD File)

Pharmacology
Therapeutic Uses (THER):
ANTIPYRETIC THERAPY IS RESERVED FOR CASES IN WHICH FEVER IN ITSELF MAY BE
DELETERIOUS, & FOR PATIENTS WHO EXPERIENCE CONSIDERABLE RELIEF WHEN FEVER IS
LOWERED. ... ANTIPYRETIC DOSE ... FOR ADULT IS 325 MG-1.0 G ORALLY EVERY 3 OR 4 HR
... CHILDREN 10-20 MG/KG EVERY 6 HR, NOT TO EXCEED TOTAL DAILY DOSE OF 3.6 G.
/SALICYLATES/ **PEER REVIEWED** [Gilman, A.G., T.W. Rall, A.S. Nies and P. Taylor (eds.).
Goodman and Gilman's The Pharmacological Basis of Therapeutics. 8th ed. New York, NY.
Pergamon Press, 1990. 652]

ANALGESIA. SALICYLATE IS VALUABLE FOR NONSPECIFIC RELIEF OF CERTAIN TYPES OF
PAIN, FOR EXAMPLE HEADACHE, ARTHRITIS, DYSMENORRHEA, NEURALGIA, & MYALGIA.
... IT IS PRESCRIBED IN SAME DOSES & MANNER AS FOR ANTIPYRESIS. /SALICYLATES/
PEER REVIEWED [Gilman, A.G., T.W. Rall, A.S. Nies and P. Taylor (eds.). Goodman and
Gilman's The Pharmacological Basis of Therapeutics. 8th ed. New York, NY. Pergamon Press,
1990. 652] ....

[a]Copyright by the National Library of Medicine and Reprinted with Permission

It should be noted that, in common with most substance-based files, each field displayed
incurs a display charge but generally only a few fields are required and the general procedure
(find substance => display FA => display fields) offers a very cost effective way of finding
information exactly of the type required.

Important notes (HSDB File):
- **The feature of the File is that it contains *very extensive information* on the toxicology and environmental effects of substances.**
- **So if the HSDB File is listed in the Locator Field in the REGISTRY File, and if information in these general areas is required, then the HSDB File provides an excellent source of such information.**

16.5.7 MRCK File
The MRCK File is the electronic version of the hardcopy *Merck Index* which contains
descriptions of important chemicals, drugs, biologically active substances, and agricultural
and natural products. The File contains a Field Availability Field so specific information on
substances is retrieved using the general procedure already outlined.

While this chapter has focused on the general procedure for finding the various types of
property information, all the unique aspects of online searching may be employed. These
particularly apply to the reverse process, that is, finding substances which have specific
properties of interest. The only limitation here is the resourcefulness of the searcher!

For example, consider the request: "Find substances which have been isolated from
natural sources and which are currently in use as anti-inflammatory agents."

Although the MRCK File contains information on the therapeutic use of important drugs,[*] it does not contain any general heading which would identify substances which have been isolated from natural sources since natural products are not routinely highlighted in the text in the MRCK File. However, such information is available in the BEILSTEIN File but while this file has some information on biological function it does not indicate which substances might be currently in clinical use. Accordingly specific searches need to be performed in each of the files and the records connected in the way required to best respond to the request.

A solution is to match entries under ANTI-INFLAMMATORY in the THER Field in the MRCK File with those substances isolated from natural sources (INP Field) in the BEILSTEIN File. This requires that the CAS Registry Numbers from one search be matched with the CAS Registry Numbers with the second search and this is performed with the SmartSELECT option (Screen 16.14). While in theory the answer set from either file could be matched with the answer set from the second file, the SmartSELECT feature currently allows only 50,000 items to be selected and there are more than 50,000 substances in the BEILSTEIN File which have CAS Registry Numbers and which have been isolated from natural sources. So the search must be conducted in the order shown in Screen 16.14.

Screen 16.14[a] Finding anti-inflammatory substances which have been isolated from natural sources

```
=> FIL MRCK
=> S ANTI INFLAMMATORY/THER
L1      174         ANTI INFLAMMATORY/THER
           ((ANTI(W)INFLAMMATORY)/THER)
=> FIL BEIL
=> S L1 <RN>
SmartSELECT INITIATED
L2      364         L1
=> S L2 AND INP/FA
        87828       INP/FA
L3      14          L2 AND INP/FA
=> D RN INP
CAS Reg. No (RN):           29908-03-0
Isolation from Natural Product:
INP Isolierung aus Hefekulturen nach Zusatz von L-Methionin
       Reference(s):   1. Schlenk et al., Arch.Biochem., 83<1959>28,29, CODEN: ARBIAE ....
=> FIL MRCK
=> S  29908-03-0
L4      1 29908-03-0
```

---

[*]The relevant field in the MRCK File is the THER Field (therapeutic use), in which single words are posted so the hyphenated term, anti-inflammatory, is searched as two words.

Screen 16.14 (continued)

=> D STR THER

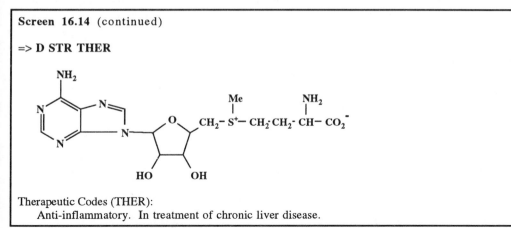

Therapeutic Codes (THER):
   Anti-inflammatory. In treatment of chronic liver disease.

Note that 14 substances fit the requirements (that is, answer set, L3) and all of these may be displayed in either of the files. Parts of the record for one of the substances in the two files is shown.

This example shows the power of online searching in which answers from one file may easily be used as search terms in a second file to solve unique problems!

Important note (MRCK File):
- **The feature of the File is that it contains descriptions (and properties) for important chemicals in current use for medicinal purposes.**

16.5.8 MSDS Files
Material Safety Data Sheets are available online for almost 100,000 substances. While they are organized by substances, they actually are full text files, and contain extensive information on the handling of, and risks associated with, substances. Most of the safety sheets contain very extensive technical information, but in the MSDS-SUM File there are particularly useful records which contain summaries in lay terms. For example, part of the record in this File for aspirin is shown in Screen 16.15.

MSDS information is often required by government, industry, and university authorities before sale or use of the substances is allowed, and indeed they often are supplied at the point of sale. However, if not readily available from other sources it should be kept in mind that they may be retrieved readily on the STN network. In the first instance it is merely necessary to find the substance in the REGISTRY File and to check whether there is a listing in one of the MSDS Files.

Screen 16.15   MSDS-SUM: summary for aspirin
(Note this shows part of the record only)
OHS MSDS Summary Sheet

SUBSTANCE: ACETYLSALICYLIC ACID
CAS#: 50-78-2   FORMULA: C-H3-C-O2-C6-H4-C-O2-H

DESCRIPTION: Odorless, white crystals or white, crystalline powder with a slight bitter taste.

HEALTH AND FIRST AID:
INHALATION:
 SHORT TERM EFFECTS: May cause irritation. Additional effects may include asthma.
 LONG TERM EFFECTS: No information available on significant adverse effects.
SKIN CONTACT:
 SHORT TERM EFFECTS: May cause irritation. May cause effects as reported in short term
ingestion.
 LONG TERM EFFECTS: May cause effects as reported in long term ingestion.
EYE CONTACT:
 SHORT TERM EFFECTS: May cause irritation. Additional effects may include burns.
 LONG TERM EFFECTS: No information available on significant adverse effects.
INGESTION:
 SHORT TERM EFFECTS: May be harmful if swallowed. May cause allergic reactions. May cause
rash, fever, ringing in the ears, nausea, vomiting, difficulty breathing, asthma, dizziness,
hyperactivity, visual disturbances, blood disorders, convulsions, shock and coma. May also cause
reproductive effects.
 LONG TERM EFFECTS: May cause effects as reported in short term exposure. In addition
yellowing of the skin and eyes, diarrhea, bloody vomit, low blood pressure, high blood pressure,
headache, drowsiness, hearing loss, bluish skin color, lung congestion, kidney damage, liver
enlargement and heart failure may occur.....

[a]Copyright by the Occupational Services, Inc and Reprinted with Permission

Important note (MSDS Files):
* **The feature of the Files is that they contain detailed information on toxicity and health effects of substances including:**
  general health hazards;
  reactivity with other materials;
  spill or leak procedures;
  toxicity;
  exposure limits and threshold values; and
  chemical and physical property data.

16.5.9 RTECS File
The Registry of Toxic Effects of Chemical Substances File contains a compendium of
toxicity data and includes information on over 120,000 substances on irritation data,
mutation data, tumorigenic effects, reproduction effects, and toxicology data. The general
fields of information can be appreciated by scanning those available for aspirin (Screen
16.16).

```
                 Screen 16.16ᵃ  Fields available for aspirin in the RTECS File

Code              Field Name
-------------------+-------------------------------------------------
RN                CAS Registry Number
CN                Chemical Name
CI                Class Identifier
ASTA              Federal Agency Status (EPA, NIOSH, NTP, OSHA)
MF                Molecular Formula
MUT               Mutation Data
NREC              NIOSH Recommendations
SREG              Regulations and Standards
REP               Reproductive Effect Data
RTN               RTECS Number
SO                Source
SURV              National Occupational Survey (NOHS, NOES)
TLV               Threshold Limit Value
TOX               Toxicity Data
TREV              Toxicology Review
WLN               Wiswesser Line Notation
```

ᵃCopyright by the National Institute for Occupational Health and Safety and Reprinted with Permission

Fields may be displayed in the usual manner, although if complete references for the source information are required then the suffix FULL must be added to the field code. For example, Screen 16.17 shows part of the entry in the toxicity data field for aspirin.

```
                 Screen 16.17ᵃ  Toxicity data for aspirin in the RTECS File
                         (Note this shows a minor part of the record only)
=> D TOXFULL
TOXICITY DATA (TOX):
```

Effect EFF	Route RTE	Organism ORGN	Dose DOSE	Duration DUR	Source SO
J15;M03	oral	child	TDLo 10 mg/kg	1D-I	CTOXAO 18,247,81
F24;J26	oral	man	TDLo 857 mg/kg		HUTODJ 7,161,88
L01	oral	woman	TDLo 525 mg/kg	5D-I	AIMEAS 80,74,74
	oral	rat	LD50 200 mg/kg		34ZIAG -,67,69
	intraperitoneal	rat	LD50 340 mg/kg		NYKZAU 62,11,66

Screen **16.17** (continued)
....

F05;J25	loral	ldog	lLD50 700		lARZNAD
	l	l	lmg/kg	l	l21,719,71
F29	lintravenous	ldog	lLD50 681		lAIPTAK
	l	l	lmg/kg	l	l149,571,64
F17	loral	lrabbit	lLD50 1010 l		lGTPZAB
	l	l	lmg/kg	l	l24(3),43,8
F05;F07	loral	lguinea pig	lLD50 1075		lJAPMA8
	l	l	lmg/kg	l	l47,479,58

TOXICITY DATA REFERENCES:
CTOXAO Clinical Toxicology (New York, NY) V.1-18, 1968-81. For publisher information, see JTCTDW.
HUTODJ Human Toxicology   (Macmillan Press Ltd., Houndmills, Basingstoke, Hants., RG 21 2XS, UK) V.1-   1981-
AIMEAS Annals of Internal Medicine   (American College of Physicians, 4200 Pine St., Philadelphia, PA 19104) V.1-   1927-
....

[a]Copyright by the National Institute for Occupational Health and Safety and Reprinted with Permission

While most of the information in Screen 16.17 may be understood readily, it is not obvious to what the EFFect codes (left-hand column in the screen) refer. Further, they are not explained in the Database Summary Sheet for the File. While the database print materials explain these codes, it should be pointed out here that there are many online HELP options. This specific case is discussed in Section 10.1.1, but all that needs to be realized here is that online HELP messages are available and that the RTECS has three character Toxic Effects Codes in which the first letter designates a part of the animal and the two digits designate type of damage. Hence J15 relates to J (Lung, Thorax, or Respiration) and 15 (Acute pulmonary edema), while M03 relates to M (Kidney, Ureter, and Bladder) and 03 to changes in tubules including acute renal failure and acute tubular necrosis.

Clearly very extensive information, from a number of different sources, is assembled in the one record so the File provides an excellent single source of factual toxicity data.

Important note (RTECS File):
• **The feature of the File is that it contains text and numeric data on the registered toxic effects of chemical substances. In many instances it gives details of the organism, the dose involved, and the route of administration/exposure.**

It will be noted that the CHEMLIST, HSDB, MSDS and RTECS Files are substance-based files, all of which contain data relating to the toxicity of substances and the question is which of the files should be considered first when information in this general area is required.

Actually this question is further complicated, since there are additionally a number of bibliographic files which also contain information in the area, and these files include, *inter alia*, the BIOSIS, CAplus, CSNB, EMBASE, FSTA and MEDLINE Files.

The answer to the question comes only through the searcher's knowledge of the databases. While the features of the substance-based files considered in this chapter are presented, they give a quick guide only, and, when needed, further information should be obtained from the online vendors. Nevertheless since chemical substances are involved, and since the REGISTRY File lists in the Locator Field those Files which contain CAS Registry Numbers, the first step is to scan this list. Commonly only a few of the files are indicated and they are often sufficiently different for the searcher to be able to determine quickly the files of choice.

16.5.10   SPECINFO File

The SPECINFO File contains infrared, NMR, and mass spectral data for a representative group of organic substances. This type of information may also be present in other substance-based files, particularly the BEILSTEIN, GMELIN and HODOC Files, but the feature of the SPECINFO File is that records may contain the actual spectra, or the spectral assignments, as well as the references.

For example, Screen 16.18 shows the fields available for aspirin in the File, and it is apparent that there are four different sets of ^{13}C NMR spectral information, namely those which refer to different solvent systems, or different methods of measurement. Examples of entries in the CNMR and the CNMRS Fields are shown and they clearly illustrate the different types of information available. The display formats shown in this screen are text based only. In order to display the actual spectra (with communications software like STN Express which supports graphics presentations) the formats NMRS.GSP, IR.GSP, and MSS.GSP must be entered.

Screen 16.18[a]   Spectral information in the SPECINFO File

Fields available for aspirin (and occurrences)

CNMR	l 13C-NMR Data	l 4
CNMRS	l 13C-NMR Spectrum	l 4
IR	l Infrared Data	l 1
IRS	l Infrared Spectrum	l 1
MS	l Mass Data	l 1
MSS	l Mass Spectrum	l 1

Sample entry in the CNMR Field

13C-NMR Data :

 Spectrum Number (.NR) : CNCC-81626-585
Instrument (.INS)   : Bruker HX-90
Solvent (.SOL)   : CDCl3
Standard (.STD)   : TMS
Temperature (.T)   : ambient
Literat. Ref. (.REF) : W.J.ELLIOT,J.FRIED,J.ORG.CHEM.43,2708(1978)....

```
Screen 16.18 (continued)
Sample entry in the CNMRS Field
13C-NMR Spectrum :
------------------

Peak          | Peak            | Multi-          | Equiv.
Assig.        | Position        | plicity         | Lines
              | .PP             | .MUL            | .IN
              | (ppm)           |                 | (no.)
=========+===============+==============+========
   1          |    122.20       |    s            |   1
   2          |    151.30       |    s            |   1
   3          |    122.30       |    d            |   1
   4          |    134.80       |    d            |   1
   5          |    126.10       |    d            |   1
   6          |    132.50       |    d            |   1
   7          |    170.00       |    s            |   1
   8          |    169.70       |    s            |   1
   9          |     21.00       |    q            |   1
```

[a]Copyright by Chemical Concepts GmbH and Reprinted with Permission

The SPECINFO File may also be used to predict ^{13}C NMR chemical shifts, and to match known chemical shifts with possible structures or structure fragments. For example, a part structure may be built in the File and the system will estimate the chemical shift for the various atoms involved.

Important note (SPECINFO File):
- **The feature of the File is that it contains actual spectral data and spectra for a cross section of organic substances.**

16.5.11 Other substance-based files
There are a number of other substance-based files which may be listed in the LC Field in the REGISTRY File, and the user should check with the Databases Catalogues or Summary Sheets to determine whether the specific information of interest may be found in one of these files.

Databases which have particular relevance to the pharmaceutical industry are the Derwent Drug Registry, the PHAR and the USAN databases.

The Drug Registry segment of the Derwent databases contains almost 28,000 substances and is available in the DRUGU File. The DRUGU File is available only to Derwent subscribers and is structure searchable (WPI structures). The companion file, which is available to STN users but which is not structure searchable, is the DDFU File. The database covers all aspects of drug synthesis, development, evaluation, manufacture and use.

The PHAR File contains around 18,000 substances, and, in addition to the usual substance identification fields, research and pharmacological activity codes, contains detailed information on originating companies, licensees, information on the stage of development and availability for commercial licensing. When available, records also contain information on the development history of the product, and key literature and patent references.

The USAN File contains over 8000 records and is the authorative drug dictionary for names of nonproprietary drugs in the health care industry. Names include those registered in the US, UK and Japan, and miscellaneous older names and trade names, and the file additionally is a valuable source of information on the supplier and on the US status of the drug.

While these files may be entered independently, and searched, it should be noted that they are linked with the REGISTRY File and unless the searcher is very familiar with the files, it usually is easier to identify the REGISTRY File record and then to check the LC Field.

The other consideration with all of the substance-based files mentioned in this chapter is the cost. Information costs money and in some instances the costs of accession of the files may be substantial, although since many are electronic versions of print materials there often are substantial discounts for those who additionally subscribe to the hardcopy.

Summary

- *Substance-based files* have chemical substances as the accession points, that is, they are organised by chemical substances.
- *Very extensive numeric and text property information* can be retrieved from substance-based files, especially in the areas of chemical and physical properties, and regulatory and toxicology information.
- Many substance-based files have well over a hundred fields containing information; important aids are the *Database Summary Sheets* which provide a quick reference resource and indicate the mechanics of searching and displaying in the files.
- *A general search technique involves locating the substance in the REGISTRY File, scanning the Locator Field, and entering the file(s) of interest.* The list of fields available for the substance then is displayed and the individual fields finally are displayed.
- Some of the substance-based files have similar types of information (for example, on toxicity properties, or spectral data) and the *searcher needs to be aware of the strengths* of each file in order to assess which may be the best file to enter in the first instance. One way to obtain this experience is to consider the content of some records carefully and the various examples in this chapter, those other examples in the Database Summary Sheets, and the information obtained from the supplementary materials provided by the database producers are useful starting points.
- Information on substances may also be found in bibliographic files where often the property of the substance, but not necessarily the specific numeric data, is reported (for example, many bibliographic databases may contain information on toxicity, government regulations, and environmental aspects and the information is found through keyword searches particularly those relating to index headings).

17

Searching for Chemical Reactions

In this chapter we learn:

- *On STN, chemical reaction databases describe chemical reactions and conditions, and search terms involve Registry Numbers.*
- *Reaction roles, (reactant, reagent, product, etc.) are added as suffixes to the search terms.*
- *When information on groups of substances is involved it is necessary to specify bond sites and to map atoms.*
- *The STN Express software can be used to draw required chemical reactions, and to assign roles and bond sites/atom maps automatically. Saved queries are then uploaded and searched in chemical reaction databases.*

17.1 What does a chemical reaction involve?

A central feature of chemistry is the chemical reaction, that is, the conversion of one substance into another. A chemical conversion does not occur spontaneously, but needs some influence to cause it to happen. In the vast majority of cases this involves another chemical substance although sources of energy like heat or light may be sufficient to overcome the energy barrier required to effect the reaction.

In the language of the science, a starting material or reactant is converted into a product with a reagent (or reactant) under certain conditions. The difference between a reactant and a reagent is often an arbitrary one although, in general, in chemical reaction databases:

- a *reactant* is a substance, usually organic, which participates in a chemical reaction by contributing a major portion to the product; and
- a *reagent* is a substance, often inorganic, which participates in a chemical reaction to help the overall reaction occur but which does not contribute a major portion to the product.

A reaction between a single reactant and a single reagent rarely gives a single product, but instead a mixture of products is formed. While the term by-product is used to describe minor products, the best way of stating amounts of products formed is by their "yield" as a percentage of the maximum yield possible. There is a fundamental rule in chemistry that matter cannot be created or destroyed and a given weight of starting materials will produce a given weight of products.   So the theoretical weight of a product may be calculated and the actual weight obtained in the reaction is expressed as a percentage of the maximum weight possible.

Besides the actual chemicals involved in the conversion, it is important to describe the conditions under which a reaction occurs. Generally reactions are done in a solvent and at a specified temperature, while sometimes another chemical substance, called a catalyst, is added. A catalyst actually remains unchanged in a reaction, and it is there merely to make the reaction proceed much faster; in the absence of a catalyst some reactions simply do not occur. All of these aspects need to be reported to fully describe the chemical reaction.

Whereas in the early stages of development of chemical reactions, the chemist was more concerned with finding out what happens if a group of chemicals was mixed together, today, with the wealth of chemical reaction information at hand, the chemist almost invariably focusses on the outcome - and needs to find out what to do in order to achieve it. That is, a particular substance is required as the target and the question is how might it be achieved using known chemical reactions. This constitutes the main reason why chemical reaction databases are used; if the substance is known then known synthetic procedures are of interest, while if it is not known procedures used for the preparations of analogous substances may help in the determination of the synthetic method to be used.

Another reason for searching reactions is that planned chemical reactions sometimes go wrong. Something unexpected occurs and the chemist then wants to know whether anything similar has been reported before.

A major issue in chemical reaction searching is that the desired target might not be achievable in a single chemical reaction but instead a series of reactions is required from the nearest available known starting material. So a series of steps:

$$A \rightarrow B \rightarrow C \rightarrow D \rightarrow E \rightarrow F \rightarrow G \rightarrow H$$

is needed, each with its own set of reagents and conditions.

Actually such a "linear" sequence is not usually the best way to proceed, and instead a so-called convergent synthesis, which makes bigger pieces separately and puts them together in a few final steps is preferred (Figure 17.1).

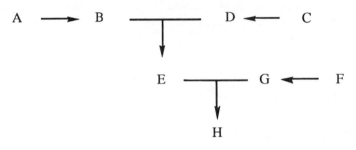

Figure 17.1   A convergent syntheses
Note that in a convergent synthesis bigger pieces are assembled independently and then put
together. That is, a number of steps might be involved in the preparation of B and of D, then these
are combined to give E etc. Such a synthetic process is more efficient than a linear process.

So a chemical reaction database ideally needs to index *multistep* reactions as well as
single step reactions, since the chemist might need to know literature which reports not only
the conversion of A to B, but also A to E and even A to H.

While the number of new chemical substances reported increases by over 1000 per day,
the number of new reactions performed daily is possibly many times that figure.
Computerized chemical reaction databases are invaluable in helping chemists 'keep up' with
the literature. These databases can, however, be quite difficult and expensive to construct,
and, additionally, special techniques are needed to search and display the information.
Unfortunately their cost of preparation means in turn that searching such databases may be
relatively expensive, although once again it is the value of the information which should be
considered. A chemist may struggle with a preparation for say two weeks and the salary and
chemical bill might be a few thousand dollars; however, if the literature had been carefully
searched beforehand, analogous reactions might have been discovered for a fraction of the
cost. Chemical reaction databases provide information which would be very difficult (and
expensive) to obtain in any other way, including by trial and error at the bench!

17.2 Electronic chemical reaction databases

A chemical reaction database is one specifically designed for chemical reactions and enables
the searcher to find specific information on chemical conversions and reaction conditions.
Some of the more important reaction databases available *online* are listed in Table 17.1.
There are a number of "inhouse" reaction databases available, particularly those produced by
MDL. Generally they are much smaller, and have more restrictive search options, than
online databases like CASREACT. However, they can be obtained on a subscription basis
and once so obtained charges for each individual search are not incurred.

There are a number of points to note. First, all these databases allow searches in which
a specific starting material is converted to a product. This distinguishes them from other
chemical databases, like the CAplus File, which index substances but which do not
specifically indicate in the record which substances are involved in specific chemical
reactions.

Table 17.1 Major online databases with chemical reaction information

DATABASE	APPROX. NUMBER OF SINGLE STEP REACTIONS[a]	YEARS COVERED
BEILSTEIN	10,000,000	1779-
CASREACT	1,300,000	1985-
CHEMINFORMRX	250,000	1991-
CHEMREACT	400,000	1975-1988
GMELIN	465,000	1817-

[a]Note that the number of reactions given in the BEILSTEIN and GMELIN Files is very approximate since many reactions may be listed under a single substance record. Further, the coverage of reactions can depend on the time periods involved.

Second, the CASREACT database permits searches based on specific reaction centers to be undertaken. The so-called reaction sites are important if information on conversions involving specific parts of substances is required.

Third, while in theory all these databases may be searched for multistep reactions (for example, by looking at various single step reactions in turn) only the CASREACT File permits true multistep reactions to be searched easily. This has advantages, for example although a single overall conversion may be required it may be irrelevant how many intermediate steps (perhaps involving protecting groups) there are. Unless a single set of reagents and conditions was used (even though they may affect a series of related reactions) a conversion involving sequential reactions leading to a desired goal would not be indexed in single-step reaction databases.

Finally, while the years covered are indicated in Table 17.1, very often only a specific subset of the literature in that time period may be indexed. For example, the CASREACT File covers just over 100 selected serials since 1985 and patents since 1991.

It should be pointed out also that while some chemistry-related files are not specifically designed for searching chemical reactions, they can provide very useful reaction information, not only for broader time periods but also from a wider range of the literature. Thus, the CAplus File appends CAS Registry Numbers with the letter "P" if the original article reports the preparation of the substance (for other "roles" see Section 5.5.2) and, particularly when this information is linked with CAS Registry Numbers for potential starting materials, actual chemical conversions may be retrieved. Naturally it is necessary to employ this procedure to search for chemical reactions on the CAS databases prior to 1985 when the CASREACT File commences.

Indeed, if it is sufficient merely to know how a substance is prepared (irrespective of what starting materials are used), the easiest approach is to search for the CAS Registry Number (or Registry Numbers) in the CAplus File with the P suffix added. Such a search may either be => S **79902-63-9P**, to search for the preparation of substance with Registry Number 79902-63-9 in the CAplus File, or => S **L#/P** to search for the preparation of substance(s) retrieved in the REGISTRY File, or => S **L#/ROLE** where the ROLE is any one of the letter codes given in Table 5.3. Note that is is important to add the slash (/) since this instructs the system software to interpret the command as a request to add P after all the CAS Registry Numbers in the answer set. As the CAplus File is a text file, the search L#P (for example, L1P) would otherwise be interpreted as a search for the string of letters/numbers L1P.

17.3 Indexing in the CASREACT File

A CASREACT File record is shown in Screen 17.1 for the reaction scheme in the original article (Figure 17.2).

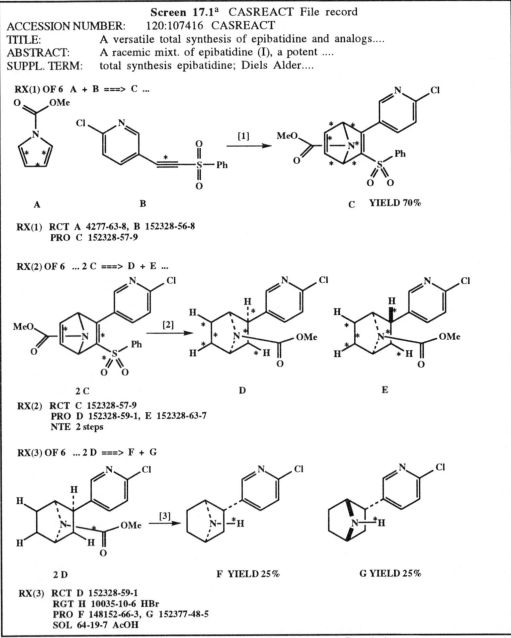

Screen 17.1[a] CASREACT File record
ACCESSION NUMBER: 120:107416 CASREACT
TITLE: A versatile total synthesis of epibatidine and analogs....
ABSTRACT: A racemic mixt. of epibatidine (I), a potent ....
SUPPL. TERM: total synthesis epibatidine; Diels Alder....

RX(1) OF 6 A + B ===> C ...

A   B   C   YIELD 70%

RX(1) RCT A 4277-63-8, B 152328-56-8
       PRO C 152328-57-9

RX(2) OF 6 ...2 C ===> D + E ...

2 C   D   E
RX(2) RCT C 152328-57-9
       PRO D 152328-59-1, E 152328-63-7
       NTE 2 steps

RX(3) OF 6 ...2 D ===> F + G

2 D   F YIELD 25%   G YIELD 25%

RX(3) RCT D 152328-59-1
       RGT H 10035-10-6 HBr
       PRO F 148152-66-3, G 152377-48-5
       SOL 64-19-7 AcOH

[a]Copyright by the American Chemical Society and Reprinted with Permission

Again there are many points to note. First, this is actually a very short record (deliberately chosen). Some original articles may contain a very large number of reactions, real and "imaginary"! Here "imaginary" is used to describe reactions which actually were not performed at the bench but which are indexed in order to allow searches on multistep processes (see below).

Second, the record in Screen 17.1 is displayed in the IALL format (although most of the bibliographic, abstract and index sections have been omitted). For the CASREACT File the IALL format gives the bibliography, abstract, index entries and the SSRX display field (the single-step reactions display which has the map, diagram and summary for all single-step reactions). As usual, there are a number of display options and the Database Summary Sheet contains the full list.

Third, there are three major portions in the CASREACT reaction display. The *REACTION MAP* (example: RX(1) OF 6   A + B ===> C ...) indicates which reaction is displayed and gives the identifying letters for the substances (periods before or after a letter indicate that there are earlier, or later, steps in the sequence respectively). The *REACTION DIAGRAM* indicates the structures for reactants and products with asterisks indicating bonds involved in the reaction. The *REACTION SUMMARY* gives all of the reaction participants using CAS Registry Numbers and role indexes where here roles relate to reactant, reagent, product, solvent, and catalyst etc.

Fourth, the CASREACT File actually is a bibliographic (document based) file to which chemical reaction information has been added. So answer numbers in searches relate to the number of documents and not to the number of reactions. The text entries are exactly the same as the text entries for the same article in the CAplus File, and the same Accession Number is used. While the main use of the CASREACT File is for searching specific reactions, it should always be remembered that bibliographic search terms may be used in exactly the same way as they are in the CAplus File. Such text-based terms may be valuable for narrowing answer sets in the CASREACT File.

Fifth, part of the actual publication from which this record was derived is shown in Figure 17.2. In particular it should be noted that while the original document actually reported 4 reactions, the CASREACT File record refers to 6 reactions, although only 3 reactions are indicated.

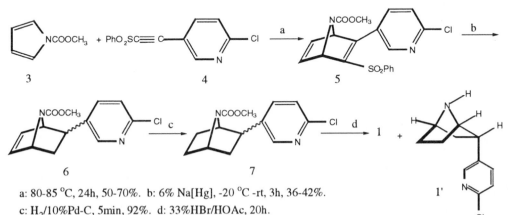

a: 80-85 °C, 24h, 50-70%. b: 6% Na[Hg], -20 °C -rt, 3h, 36-42%.

c: H_2/10%Pd-C, 5min, 92%. d: 33%HBr/HOAc, 20h.

Figure 17.2 Reaction scheme from original article

Reprinted from *Tetrahedron Letters*, 1993, 34, 4477 with Permission from Elsevier Science Ltd., The Boulevard, Langford Lane, Kidlington OX5 1GB, UK

Only after very careful study of the information in Screen 17.1 and Figure 17.2 can an insight into the chemical reaction indexing of the CASREACT File be obtained. Before this is discussed chemists will realize that the scheme in Figure 17.2 involves 4 steps:

Step 1   A Diels Alder reaction to give substance (5);

Step 2   Reduction of a conjugated double bond and sulfone with sodium amalgam to give a mixture of stereoisomers (6):

Step 3   Reduction of an alkene with hydrogen/palladium charcoal to give a mixture of stereoisomers (7); and

Step 4   Hydrolysis of carbamate to give the required amine (1) and its stereoisomer (1'). (Note that this amine (1) is not shown in Figure 17.2, but it is the important substance epibatidine which has the pyridine ring in the *exo* position.)

So it is seen that a number of indexing issues have been applied in the CASREACT File record:

1.   the "chemical" steps 2 and 3 above have been incorporated into a single reaction (RX(2)) in the CASREACT File;

2.   the issue of stereoisomeric products formed in this RX(2) has been dealt with by saying that two molecules of C are involved and that each one gives a different stereoisomer (the map for RX(2) says ...2C ===> D + E ...; and

3.   the CASREACT File record refers to "RX(1) OF 6" since it considers there are 6 reactions (Figure 17.3). It needs to assign these "imaginary" reactions RX(4), RX(5), and RX(6) so that multistep reactions can be searched!

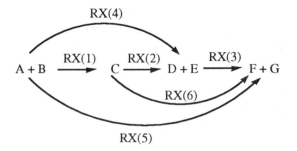

Figure 17.3   How CASREACT handles multistep reactions

Finally, much information is entered in the reaction information in the CASREACT File: there is a reaction map and reaction information (CAS Registry Numbers) for each reaction; letter codes are given to each chemical substance for quick identification purposes; each reaction has separate subfields: RCT (reactant), RGT (reagent), PRO (product), SOL (solvent); NTE (note); CAT (catalyst) (although only some of these appear in Screen 17.1); entries in these sub-fields are CAS Registry Numbers, although simple names or formulas may also be given to help ready identification; and bonds involved in reactions are tagged and this allows specific reaction site information to be searched.

While not shown in the CASREACT File record, each functional group in each substance is noted by the system, so, for example, in RX(3) (Screen 17.1) it would be noted that the reaction involves the conversion of the CARBAMATE functional group to the SECONDARY AMINE functional group. The full list of functional groups indexed in the File is given in Appendix 3, but the list may also be obtained online through **HELP DIRECTORY** followed by **HELP FGA**. (Comments on the HELP command are given in Section 10.1.1.)

In summary, reactions are indexed as shown in Figure 17.4 with each substance entered in a specific field which relates to its role.

Substance conversion (search terms are CAS Registry Numbers)

			reaction conditions		
	A	+	B	----------->	C	% yield
ROLE	RCT		RGT	SOL	PRO	YD
	(or RRT)[a]		(or RRT)[a]	CAT		
				NS[b]		

Functional group conversions (search terms are functional group names)

FG.RCT	FG.RGT	----->	FG.FORM

Figure 17.4   Reaction roles in the CASREACT File

[a]Since the line between a reactant and a reagent may be a narrow one, the terms may need to be searched in both fields at the same time and this is done using the field code RRT.
[b]NS = number of steps

17.4   Searching in the CASREACT File

Chemical reaction searching in the CASREACT File may be performed with *substance-based terms* or with *functional group terms*.

The *first option* uses CAS Registry Numbers as search terms, and the general format of the search is:

> => S   <CAS RN FOR SUBSTANCE A>/<ROLE OF A>   <L>
>   <CAS RN FOR SUBSTANCE B>/<ROLE OF B>

Note that almost invariably the (L) operator is used since this restricts the search terms to the same single-step or multistep reaction. (The AND operator would retrieve answers in which the terms were anywhere in the record and this generally is too broad a search.)

The CAS Registry Number(s) for the substance(s) may be obtained through any of the methods discussed in Chapter 12 (names and name segments), Chapter 13 (molecular formulas) and Chapter 15 (structures), and either the individual CAS Registry Numbers or the L-number answer sets from the REGISTRY File searches may be used.

Structure based queries may also be undertaken using options within the structure building menu in STN Express. After the structures are drawn on the screen the **RXN** icon is chosen, whereupon reaction roles, reaction sites and atom mapping may be specified. The structure query may be saved, and uploaded to a chemical reaction file. It then appears as a single L-number and when this L-number is searched the roles and proximity operator are automatically assigned.

The *second option* uses the names of functional groups as search terms, and the general format of the search is:

=> S   <FUNCTIONAL GROUP A>/FG.RCT (S)
        <FUNCTIONAL GROUP B>/FG.PRO

Note the (S) operator retrieves reactions in which the reactant functional group is converted to the product functional group.

Which of the these options should be used depends on the nature of the query, and it is best to illustrate this through some of the common questions which need to be answered:

1.   conversion of a specific substance A to a specific substance B;
2.   reaction of a specific substance A with a specific reagent C;
3.   conversion of a group of substances A to a group of substances B, or reactions of a group of substances A with a specific (or group of) reagent(s) C;
4.   conversion of one functional group to another; and
5.   reaction involving a specific reagent or a group of related reagents.

17.4.1   Conversion of a specific substance A to a specific substance B
Unlike in the BEILSTEIN File (see Section 16.5.1b), in the CASREACT File there is no distinction between the reaction of A to form B, or the preparation of B from A, since the identical search terms are used:

=>   S <CAS RN FOR A> /RCT (L) <CAS RN FOR B> /PRO

Since the (L) operator restricts answers to the same single-step or multistep reaction, answers will be retrieved as long as the two substances are on the reaction path. So, if the search was: => S <CAS RN FOR A> (L) <CAS RN FOR H> then a multistep synthesis like that in Figure 17.1 would be retrieved.

Accordingly, if the preparation of the aldehyde (2) from cyclohexanone (1) was required, then the CAS Registry Numbers of the two substances would be found in the REGISTRY File, for example using the searches: => S   CYCLOHEXANONE/CN and S CYCLOHEXANECARBOXALDEHYDE/CN, and the search would be conducted in the CASREACT File (Screen 17.2).

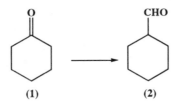

(1)   (2)

Screen 17.2[a] Conversion of specific substance A to specific substance B

=> S   **108-94-1/RCT (L)   2043-61-0/PRO**
   1523 108-94-1/RCT
   60 2043-61-0/PRO
L1   4 108-94-1/RCT (L) 2043-61-0/PRO

=> **D SCAN**

TI Synthesis of spiro[cycloalkane-1,3'-[3H]indoles] from cycloalkanecarboxaldehydes.
   Acid-catalyzed rearrangement to cycloalkano[b]indoles

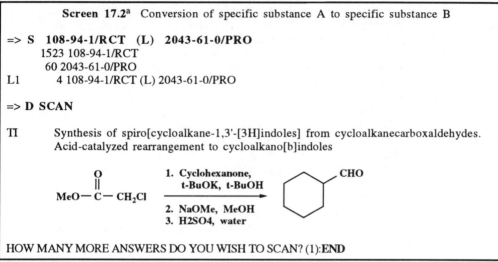

HOW MANY MORE ANSWERS DO YOU WISH TO SCAN? (1):**END**

   The search gives 4 answers, and the easiest option, as usual, is to use the free D SCAN format as an initial verification that the answers are those required (Screen 17.2).
   However, there are many display options in the CASREACT File since not only does the file have the full bibliographic, abstract and index formats, but it also has reaction formats. While the BIB format will give the literature reference and then the original article may be obtained, generally the most useful display for the chemist is the CRDREF format which gives the compact reaction display and the source information (Screen 17.3).
   It must be emphasized, however, that there are a large number of display formats and that the costs vary. Individual searchers will have their own preferences (which will somewhat depend on the costs involved and the availability of the original article), but the display shown in Screen 17.3 is a good compromise in that it gives considerable details of the reaction involved in the normal chemical presentation, and gives the reference.

Screen 17.3[a] Compact reaction display and source information (CASREACT File)

=> **D 3 CRDREF**

L1 ANSWER 3 OF 4 CASREACT COPYRIGHT 1995 ACS
RX(50) OF 92 - 3 STEPS

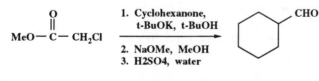

REF: J. Heterocycl. Chem, 22(5), 1207-10; 1985

It is possible to draw the reaction, for example the structures (1) and (2) and to specify the reaction roles (here reactant and product), within the structure drawing menu of STN Express, then to upload and search. However, the uploaded structure will have a single L-number and the only search options, for L-number reaction queries in the CASREACT File, are either a Substructure or Closed Substructure Search. To perform an exact search of the type required may be done with a Closed Substructure Search but this may be a more expensive option than the search shown in Screen 17.2. Essentially, it depends on how easily the CAS Registry Numbers for the individual substances can be found, for example, in the REGISTRY File. If they can be found easily by name based terms then it will be cheaper to find the substances in the REGISTRY File and then search on the CAS Registry Numbers in the CASREACT File. However, if two EXACT searches are required, then the Closed Substructure Search option in the CASREACT File will be cheaper.

> **Important note:**
> **For the conversion of one specific substance into another the steps are either:**
>
> 1. **Find CAS Registry Numbers for the two substances in the REGISTRY File; and**
> 2. **Enter the CASREACT File and search the CAS Registry Numbers, with roles assigned and using the (L) operator.**
>
> **OR**
>
> 1. **Draw the two structures in the structure building menu of STN Express and assign roles using the options under the RXN icon; and**
> 2. **Enter the CASREACT File, upload the query and search the L-number using a Closed Substructure Search.**
>
> **Once the answer set has been obtained, first use the D SCAN format to check results, then perhaps use the CRDREF display format to obtain sufficient information to proceed to check the details of the reaction in the primary literature.**
>
> **The option chosen depends on how easy it might be to find the original CAS Registry Numbers, and is an issue of cost versus convenience (and chemists often find the second option more convenient).**

17.4.2 Reaction of a specific substance A with a specific reagent C
Reactions of this type require the CAS Registry Number search terms similar to those described in Section 17.4.1, the only difference being that the different roles need to be specified:

> **<CAS REGISTRY NUMBER FOR A> /RCT**   (or **RRT**)
> **<CAS REGISTRY NUMBER FOR C> /RGT**   (or **RRT**)

Since reagents apply to specific reactions the (L) operator is used, and the problem becomes one of finding the CAS Registry Numbers and then deciding which role is appropriate. CAS Registry Numbers may be found in the usual way, while if unsure of which role to specify the searcher may always expand the listings first to see how many postings there may be in the RCT or RGT role fields. (For example, => E 108-94-1/RGT 5 will show the number of postings in which cyclohexanone appears as a reagent.) Alternatively the structures may be built through STN Express and the issues relating to the option chosen are the same as those given in Section 17.4.1.

17.4.3 *Conversion of a group of substances A to a group of substances B, or reactions of a group of substances A with a specific (or group of) reagent(s) C*

The search terms required here are:

<CAS REGISTRY NUMBERS FOR A> /RCT	(or RRT)
<CAS REGISTRY NUMBERS FOR B> /PRO	
<CAS REGISTRY NUMBERS FOR C> /RGT	(or RRT)

and the terms are connected by the (L) operators.

The groups of CAS Registry Numbers may be obtained in any way to solve the specific problem but now a new issue arises. For example, if methods for the conversion of cyclohexanones (1) to cyclohexanecarboxaldehydes (2) were required, if substructures (1) and (2) were built and searched in the REGISTRY File, and finally if these answers were searched with the appropriate roles in the CASREACT File, then the reaction shown in Figure 17.5 would be retrieved. That is, the starting material contains a cyclohexanone, and the product contains a cyclohexanecarboxaldehyde, but the required conversion did not take place in this reaction.

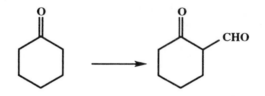

Figure 17.5 Conversion of cyclohexanones to cyclohexanecarboxaldehydes

The solution to the problem is to *specify bond sites* which remain the same or are changed, and also to *map specific atoms* in the reaction. While all this may be done with keyboard commands, by far the easiest way is to build the query through the structure building menu in STN Express. That is, the structures (1) and (2) are drawn on the screen and then the **RXN** icon is selected. A new tool box appears which enables the roles of the substances and the bond sites to be specified, and also for the individual atoms to be mapped.

As with all searching, it is desirable to specify the query as precisely as possible and in chemical reaction searching this frequently involves specifying all three options: roles, bond sites, and mapped atoms.[*]

> **Important note:**
> • **when conversions involving groups of substances are involved it is always necessary to specify bond sites and to map specific atoms, otherwise false hits will be obtained.**

The final query then appears on the screen as shown in Figure 17.6. That is, the tag on the C=O bond indicates the bond is completely changed, the number indicates that the ring atom has been mapped in the starting material and in the product, and the roles are indicated below the structures.

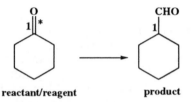

reactant/reagent   product

Figure 17.6   Display of final reaction query on STN Express

When this structure is uploaded in the usual way, the STN Express software recognizes that this is a reaction query and so prompts for confirmation that the search is to be conducted in a chemical reaction file. The CASREACT File is entered, the sample search is conducted, and the results obtained are shown in Screen 17.4.

Notes (Screen 17.4):

• Substructure search is the default search type, and **S L1** uses this default. The only other search type possible is Closed Substructure which assigns hydrogens to all open positions (unless connectivities have been specified).
• The default search scope is SAMPLE, and sample searches should always be performed first.
• System limits are different for the CASREACT File. In a SAMPLE search only 3000 reactions may be verified. System limits are 60,000 verifications for a FULL search online and 120,000 for a BATCH search.

---

[*]Details of the procedure to specify roles, bond sites and atoms are not given here. However it is very easy to do with STN Express and, if needed, the *STN Express User Guide* may be consulted.

Screen 17.4[a] SAMPLE search in the CASREACT File

=> S L1
SAMPLE SEARCH INITIATED 02:23:22
SCREENING COMPLETE - 5781 REACTIONS TO VERIFY FROM 366 DOCUMENTS
      46.8% DONE   2705 VERIFIED   1 DOCS
      51.9% DONE   3000 VERIFIED   4 HIT RXNS   1 DOCS
INCOMPLETE SEARCH (SYSTEM LIMIT EXCEEDED)
SEARCH TIME: 00.00.29
FULL FILE PROJECTIONS: ONLINE **INCOMPLETE**
                              BATCH **INCOMPLETE**
PROJECTED VERIFICATIONS: 111145 TO   120095
PROJECTED ANSWERS: 1 TO   113
L2   1 SEA SSS SAM L1 (4 REACTIONS)

=> D SCAN
L2 1 ANSWERS CASREACT COPYRIGHT 1995 ACS

TI   A short-step synthesis of 14,15-dinoreudesmanolides using intramolecular cyclization of
      an allylsilane

RX (17) OF 352 - 2 STEPS

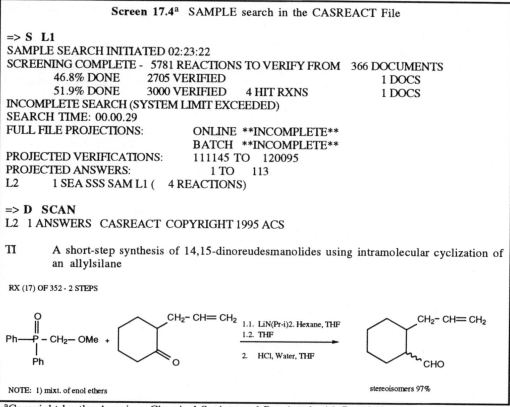

NOTE: 1) mixt. of enol ethers   stereoisomers 97%

[a]Copyright by the American Chemical Society and Reprinted with Permission

- The CASREACT File is a bibliographic file, so the answer L2 refers to a single bibliographic record, which has 4 different HIT reactions. It is quite common for a number of different HIT reactions to appear in a single record, since the same type of reaction often appears for a series of related substances in the original article.
- As usual, the free SCAN display format is used and in this file it gives the title and the first hit reaction in the compact display format. Screen 17.4 shows reaction 17 of 352 (real and "imaginary") reactions in the record!
- This answer was exactly of the type required so the decision had to be taken as to how to modify the search query so that the full search would run within system limits. Any of the options discussed in Section 15.5 could have been used, but in this case, as the projected verifications only just exceeded system limits (and at the upper end of the projection) it was decided to proceed with a BATCH search (for example, see Screen 15.8).

The BATCH search did run to completion and the answer set, L2 showed:

    L2   73 SEA FILE=CASREACT SSS FUL L1 (204 REACTIONS)

At this stage any display format may be used, although some most useful options are either:

- **D SCAN** to check a few answers to confirm they all are of the type required; or
- **D 1- CBIB** to obtain the references so that the original articles may be looked up; or
- **D 1- CRDREF** to obtain all answers in the compact display format with references (Screen 17.5 shows two examples).

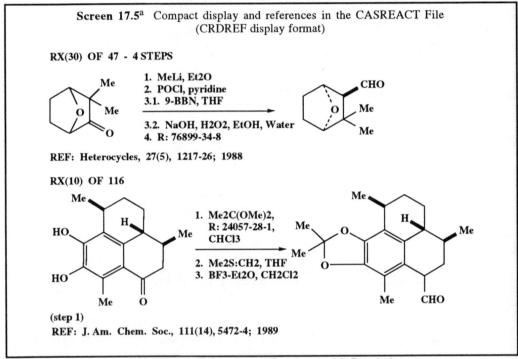

Screen 17.5[a] Compact display and references in the CASREACT File
(CRDREF display format)

RX(30) OF 47 - 4 STEPS

1. MeLi, Et2O
2. POCl, pyridine
3.1. 9-BBN, THF

3.2. NaOH, H2O2, EtOH, Water
4. R: 76899-34-8

REF: Heterocycles, 27(5), 1217-26; 1988

RX(10) OF 116

1. Me2C(OMe)2,
   R: 24057-28-1,
   CHCl3

2. Me2S:CH2, THF
3. BF3-Et2O, CH2Cl2

(step 1)
REF: J. Am. Chem. Soc., 111(14), 5472-4; 1989

While this example focuses on the conversion of a group of substances to a second group of substances, the same principles apply to questions relating to reactions of a group of substances with a specific reagent or group of reagents. Bond sites may need to be specified, but since a specific target substance is not identified the mapping of atoms usually is not relevant.

However, depending upon the actual search, it may be better to approach the question: "What happens when A and C react together" from the perspective of one of the substances being converted into a product. For example, if the question is to determine reactions of cyclopentenyl Grignard reagents (or lithium derivatives) with carbonyl compounds (Scheme 1) then there are a number of issues to address.

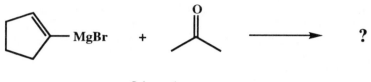

Scheme 1

The first is that searches are based on CAS Registry Numbers, and there will be very few Grignard reagents registered in the file since normally they are prepared *"in situ"* and are not characterized. So this part of the problem is far better approached by building a cyclopentenyl halide as one of the reactants. While the carbonyl substructure may be built, and searched as a second reactant, in practice it would be better in such cases to build the substructure for the product. So this search would in fact be better executed by the search outlined in Scheme 2 (with suitable mapping of the atoms and bonds).

Scheme 2

Again by far the easiest approach is to use the STN Express software and to specify the roles of the substances as required. Even though one or more substructure searches may be conducted, a full substructure search in the CASREACT File is considerably cheaper than a single substructure search in the REGISTRY File.

17.4.4   Conversion of one functional group to another
The functional groups defined in the CASREACT File are listed in Appendix 3 and any of these may be used in the three functional group search fields shown in Table 17.2.

Table 17.2 Functional group search fields

SEARCH FIELD	USE
FG.FORM	to restrict to reactions in which the functional group is formed
FG.RCT	to restrict to reactions in which the functional group reacts
FG.NON	to restrict to reactions in which the functional group is unchanged

While the conversion of one functional group into another is a fundamental aspect of organic chemistry, it is almost as important to be able to effect the process selectively. That is, it is often required to effect a specific conversion while at the same time leaving all other functional groups unchanged.

Not surprisingly in such a large database, many thousands of entries involve the formation or reactions of some of the more common functional groups, so functional group fields are generally searched in combinations. That is the functional group in the reactant and the functional group in the product are linked (with the (S) operator). When an additional requirement is to exclude a reaction involving another functional group, the (L) operator is used.

For example, Screen 17.6 shows a search that requests reactions in which the sulfoxide group is converted to the sulfone group, but the sulfide group remains unreacted.[*]

Screen 17.6[a] Selective oxidation of sulfoxides to sulfones in the presence of sulfides

=> S SULFOXIDE/FG.RCT (S) SULFONE/FG.FORM (L) SULFIDE/FG.NON

     2116   SULFOXIDE/FG.RCT

     2086   SULFONE/FG.FORM

   10424   SULFIDE/FG.NON

L1   12   SULFOXIDE/FG.RCT (S) SULFONE/FG.FORM (L) SULFIDE/FG.NON

=> D SCAN

TI   Atropisomeric sulfur compounds in organic synthesis: generation and reactions of the carbanions of dinaphtho[2,1-d:1',2'-f][1,3]dithiepine and its oxides

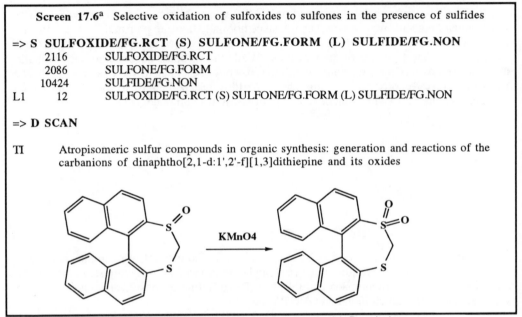

^aCopyright by the American Chemical Society and Reprinted with Permission

---

17.4.5 Reaction involving a specific reagent or a group of related reagents

Sometimes it is necessary to seek reactions involving specific reagents, and this is easily achieved in the CASREACT File since it is necessary merely to specify the role of the reagent (that is, RCT or RGT). For example, if the use of iodobenzene diacetate, $PhI(OAc)_2$, as an oxidizing reagent is of interest then it is necessary to find the CAS Registry Number for the substance. An expansion: => **E 3240-34-4/RGT** will indicate the number of records which will be retrieved, and if there are too many, then specific types of starting materials can be targeted. For example, in this case, it might be useful to build the structure query for p-substituted phenols (for which the oxidant iodobenzene diacetate is particularly useful) and to specify the reaction role (RCT) for this structure in the search.

---

[*]Sulfides may be oxidized to sulfoxides, and sulfoxides may be further oxidized to sulfones. As in many chemical reactions there is need to perform reactions (here oxidation) selectively!

17.5 Other online chemical reaction files

The two other chemical reaction databases available on STN are the CHEMINFORMRX and CHEMREACT Files. Like the CASREACT File, both are document-based and give the bibliographic details before the chemical reaction information. The same reaction search queries may be built in STN Express for all three files, and roles, bond sites and atom maps are specified in the same manner although bond sites involving hydrogen bonds may not be specified in the CHEMREACT File.

Features of the databases are:

CHEMINFORMRX
* Journals covered from 1991 onwards and currently approximately 250,000 reactions (including single-step and multistep) are listed.
* CAS Registry Numbers may be searched for all reaction participants. For example, to retrieve all documents which list iodobenzene diacetate as a reagent requires the search term: **S 3240-34-4/RGT**.
* Separate RCT and RGT roles are listed in a manner similar to the listings in the CASREACT File.

CHEMREACT
* Reactions for the period 1975-1988 selected by the All-Union Institute of Scientific and Technical Information of the Academy of Science of the former USSR.
* Approximately 370,000 reactions (single-step only).
* Search terms are CHEMREACT Registry Numbers.
* Reactants and reagents are not differentiated, and all starting materials are thus searched with the RCT role.

The REGISTRY File contains an entry in the LC Field for substances which are listed in the CASREACT and CHEMINFORMRX Files, but the CHEMREACT File does not contain CAS Registry Numbers so no such connection is available.

CHEMREACT Registry Numbers are found only through structure searches. Accordingly a Closed Substructure Search on the structure query for iodobenzene diacetate searches for reactions involving the substance, and it is necessary to display one answer (the D HIT format commonly is used) to obtain the CHEMREACT Registry Number which in this case is 6994800.

As a comparison between the three chemical reaction files, searches on the query shown in Figure 17.6, and the number of listings for iodobenzene diacetate as a starting material are listed in Table 17.3. For example, it is noted that in both the CASREACT and the CHEMINFORMX Files iodobenzene diacetate is mainly indexed as a reagent, although in each file there is a considerable number of entries in which it is listed as a reactant. This is a common issue in chemical reaction databases and clearly the recommended search field is the RRT Field.

Table 17.3 Comparison of search results in the CASREACT, CHEMINFORMRX, and CHEMREACT Files

	CASREACT		CHEMINFORMRX		CHEMREACT	
	Rxns	Docs	Rxns	Docs	Rxns	Docs
Query Fig 17.6	204	73	2	2	11	11
Iodobenzene diacetate						
S 3240-34-4/RCT		43		25		35[a]
S 3240-34-4/RGT		201		76		n/a
S 3240-34-4/RRT		239		99		n/a

[a]Note that in this File the search is: => **S 6994800/RCT**.

If comprehensive searching is required then clearly all databases need to be searched, and it is to be noted that the time period for the CHEMREACT File (1975-1988) complements that for the CASREACT File (1985 onwards). However, in the first instance generally key reactions are required in which case, provided the chemistry has been reported since 1985, it often is sufficient to search in the CASREACT File.

Summary

- *Chemical reaction databases* specifically index chemical reactions and conditions.
- *The CASREACT File* covers selected literature from 1985 onwards, and is the most comprehensive chemical reaction database for the current literature. Searches for single-step and multistep reactions are possible.
- *General preparations* of substances are most readily obtained by searching for CAS Registry Numbers (with P suffix) in the CAplus File, which covers the literature since 1967: chemical reaction databases are used when preparations from specific starting materials are required.
- *Search terms* in the CASREACT and CHEMINFORMRX Files are CAS Registry Numbers. It is necessary to specify reaction roles, and, when reactions involving groups of substances are of interest, it is further necessary to specify bond sites and to map atoms.
- The STN Express software may be used very conveniently for building the chemical reaction query, and all the necessary parameters for the chemical substances involved can be specified.

Appendices

APPENDIX 1

COMMAND COMPARISON

STN and DIALOG

Command Description	DIALOG	STN
Enter a file	BEGIN <file name>	FILE <file name>
Start a multifile search	BEGIN <file1> <file2>	FILE <file1> <file2>
View inverted index	EXPAND [E]	EXPAND [exp, e]

Search
  in steps
  by field code
	SELECT [s]
	SUPER SELECT [ss]
	S FC=(term)
		SEARCH [s]
		S STEPS [s ste]
		S term/FC

Create offline prints	PRINT [pr]	PRINT [pri]
Remove duplicate answers from the results of a multi-file search	REMOVE DUPLICATES [rd]	DUP REM
View online history	DSETS [ds]	DISPLAY HISTORY [dis his, d his]
View cost	COST	D COST
View answers online	TYPE [t]	DISPLAY [dis, d]
Save information	SAVE	SAVE
Retrieve saved information	RECALL	ACTIVATE
Delete unwanted search statement	RELEASE	DELETE
Automatic current awareness search	SAVE ALERT	SDI
Convert display items to search terms	MAP	SELECT [sel]
Analyze answer sets	RANK	D SELECT [d sel]
Set system parameters (customize search)	SET	SET
Sort answer set	SORT	SORT
End online session ...with temporary hold	LOGOFF LOG HOLD	LOG Y LOG H (60 minutes)

APPENDIX 1

COMMAND COMPARISON

STN and ORBIT

Command Description	ORBIT	STN
Enter a file	FILE <file name>	FILE <file name>
Start a multifile search	FILE <file1> <file2>	FILE <file1> <file2>
View inverted index	NEIGHBOR [nbr]	EXPAND [exp, e]
Indicate a search	No command necessary	SEARCH [s] No command necessary when AUTOSEARCH SET ON
Search in steps	Not available	S STEPS
View answers online	PRINT [prt]	DISPLAY [dis, d]
General format for search/ display in specified field	/<FIELD CODE>	/<FIELD CODE>
Create offline prints	PRINTOFF	PRINT [pri]
Remove duplicate answers from the results of a multi-file search	PRT GROUP EXCL DUPS	DUP REM
View online history	HISTORY	DISPLAY HISTORY [dis his, d his]
Save information	STORE	SAVE
Retrieve saved search	RECALL	ACTIVATE
Delete unwanted search statement	PURGE	DELETE
Convert display items to search terms, statistical analysis	SELECT GET	SELECT [sel] DISPLAY [dis, d] DISPLAY SELECT [d sel]
Set system parameters (customize search)	TERM PROFILE	SET
Sort answer set	SORT PRTOFF SORT	SORT
End online session Save session on logoff	STOP Y STOP H	LOG Y LOG H (60 minutes)

APPENDIX 2

THE PERIODIC TABLE OF ELEMENTS

	A1	A2	B3	B4	B5	B6	B7	B8	B8	B8	B1	B2	A3	A4	A5	A6	A7	A8
1	H																	He
2	Li	Be											B	C	N	O	F	Ne
3	Na	Mg											Al	Si	P	S	Cl	Ar
4	K	Ca	Sc	Ti	V	Cr	Mn	Fe	Co	Ni	Cu	Zn	Ga	Ge	As	Se	Br	Kr
5	Rb	Sr	Y	Zr	Nb	Mo	Tc	Ru	Rh	Pd	Ag	Cd	In	Sn	Sb	Te	I	Xe
6	Cs	Ba	LAN	Hf	Ta	W	Re	Os	Ir	Pt	Au	Hg	Tl	Pb	Bi	Po	At	Rn
7	Fr	Ra	ACT															

T1-> Sc   T2-> Y   T3-> LAN

LNTH	La	Ce	Pr	Nd	Pm	Sm	Eu	Gd	Tb	Dy	Ho	Er	Tm	Yb	Lu
ACTN	Ac	Th	Pa	U	Np	Pu	Am	Cm	Bk	Cf	Es	Fm	Md	No	Lr

Comments:

- The Periodic Table is presented in seven rows and each row represents a different "orbit" in which the electrons may be present (think of Row 1 like the orbit for the planet Mercury, Row 2 for Venus, Row 3 for Earth, Row 4 for Mars, etc.)

- Row 1 has the first two elements (hydrogen and helium)

- Row 2 has the next eight elements numbered 3 to 10 (lithium, beryllium, boron, carbon, nitrogen, oxygen, fluorine and neon)

- The other elements follow in rows, although after barium and radium come the "lanthanides" and "actinides" respectively

- Because of their special, and similar, properties the lanthanides and actinides are grouped separately. In a similar way the "transition metals" come in three different groups which are labeled T1, T2, and T3

- Chemists give group names to the elements in the different columns. Thus the elements in Column A1 (except hydrogen) are called "alkali metals", those in Column A2 are called "alkali earth metals", and those in Column A7 are called "halogens", etc.

- However, the most important point is that the table is set out in such a way that elements with similar properties are grouped together! Sometimes it is valuable to search for the related elements by groups and so the PG (Periodic Group) Field is searchable in the BEILSTEIN and REGISTRY Files. That is, a search: => S T1/PG retrieves all substances which have elements in the first transition series (scandium to copper)

Functional Group Class Terms in the CASREACT File

Class term	Functional Groups Searched
ALCOHOLS	ALLYL ALCOHOL or CYANOHYDRIN or CYCLIC ALCOHOL or ENOL or GLYCOL or HALOHYDRIN or EMIACETAL or HYDROXYLAMINE or PHENOL or PRIMARY ALCOHOL or SECONDARY ALCOHOL or TERTIARY ALCOHOL
ALKENES	ACYCLIC ALKENE or CYCLIC ALKENE
ALKYNES	ALKYNE or ENYNE or PI-ALKYNE
AMINES	AMINE OXIDE or AZIRIDINE or CHLORAMINE or CYANAMIDE or ENAMINE or HYDROXYLAMINE or IMINE or PRIMARY AMINE or SECONDARY AMINE or TERTIARY AMINE
CARBONATE DERIVS	CARBAMATE or CARBONATE or GUANIDINE or HALOFORMATE or THIOUREA or UREA
CARBOXY DERIVS	ACID HALIDE or AMIDE or AMIDINE or ANHYDRIDE or CARBOXYLATE or CARBOXYLIC or HALOFORMATE or IMIDE or LACTAM or LACTONE or PEROXY ACID or PEROXY ESTER or THIOAMIDE or THIOCARBOXY
HALIDES	ACID HALIDE or ALKYL HALIDE or ALLYL HALIDE or ARYL HALIDE or CHLORAMINE or GEM-DIHALIDE or HALOFORMATE or HALOHYDRIN or METAL HALIDE or SULFENYL HALIDE or SULFINYL HALIDE or SULFONYL HALIDE or TRIHALIDE or VIC-DIHALIDE or VINYL HALIDE
HETEROCYCLES	1,2-C3N2 or 1,2-C3NO or 1,2-C3NS or 1,2-C3O2 or 1,2-C3OS or 1,2-C3S2 or 1,2-C4N2 or 1,2-C4NO or 1,2-C4NS or 1,2-C4O2 or 1,2-C4OS or 1,2-C4S2 or 1,3-C3N2 or 1,3-C3NO or 1,3-C3NS or 1,3-C3O2 or 1,3-C3OS or 1,3-C3S2 or 1,3-C4N2 or 1,3-C4NO or 1,3-C4NS or 1,3-C4O2 or 1,3-C4OS or 1,3-C4S2 or 1,4-C4N2 or 1,4-C4NO or 1,4-C4NS or 1,4-C4O2 or 1,4-C4OS or 1,4-C4S2 or 1,4-C5N2 or C2S or C3N or C3O or C3S or C4N or C4O or C4S or C5N or C5O or C5S or C6N or C6O or C6S or AZIRIDINE or CEPHEM or EPOXIDE or PENAM or PURINE
KETONES	ACYCLIC KETONE or CYCLIC KETONE or O-QUINONE or P-QUINONE
ORGANOMETALLICS	ACYLMETAL or METAL ARENE or METAL CARBENE or METAL CARBONYL or METAL CYCLOPENTADIENYL or METAL HALIDE or METAL HYDRIDE or METAL METAL BOND or METAL NITROGEN or METAL NITROSYL or METAL PHOSPHINE or METAL SULFUR or METALLOCARBOCYCLE or MU-CARBONYL or ORGANOMETAL or PI-ALKENE or PI-ALKYNE or PI-ALLYL

APPENDIX 3

Functional Groups in the CASREACT File

1,2-C3N2	ALLYL HALIDE	ISOTHIOCYANATE	QUATERNARY
1,2-C3NO	AMIDE	KETAL	AMMONIUM
1,2-C3NS	AMIDINE	KETENE	S-O GROUP
1,2-C3O2	AMINE OXIDE	KETENIMINE	SE GROUP
1,2-C3OS	AMINES	KETONES	SECONDARY
1,2-C3S2	ANHYDRIDE	LACTAM	ALCOHOL
1,2-C4N2	ARYL HALIDE	LACTONE	SECONDARY AMINE
1,2-C4NO	ARYLSULFONYL	MESYL	SELENIDE
1,2-C4NS	AZIDE	METAL ARENE	SELENOL
1,2-C4O2	AZINE	METAL CARBENE	SILYL
1,2-C4OS	AZIRIDINE	METAL CARBONYL	SILYL ENOL ETHER
1,2-C4S2	AZO	METAL	SULFENYL HALIDE
1,3-C3N2	AZOXY	CYCLOPENTADIENYL	SULFIDE
1,3-C3NO	CARBAMATE	METAL HALIDE	SULFINATE
1,3-C3NS	CARBONATE	METAL HYDRIDE	SULFINYL HALIDE
1,3-C3O2	CARBONATE DERIVS	METAL METAL BOND	SULFONAMIDE
1,3-C3OS	CARBOXY DERIVS	METAL NITROGEN	SULFONE
1,3-C3S2	CARBOXYLATE	METAL NITROSYL	SULFONYL HALIDE
1,3-C4N2	CARBOXYLIC	METAL PHOSPHINE	SULFONYLOXY
1,3-C4NO	CEPHEM	METAL SULFUR	SULFOXIDE
1,3-C4NS	CHLORAMINE	METALLOCARBOCYCLE	SULFUR YLIDE
1,3-C4O2	CYANAMIDE	MU-CARBONYL	TE GROUP
1,3-C4OS	CYANATE	NITRILE	TERTIARY ALCOHOL
1,3-C4S2	CYANOHYDRIN	NITRILE OXIDE	TERTIARY AMINE
1,4-C4N2	CYCLIC ALCOHOL	NITRITE	THIOACETAL
1,4-C4NO	CYCLIC ALKENE	NITRO	THIOAMIDE
1,4-C4NS	CYCLIC KETONE	NITRONE	THIOCARBONYL
1,4-C4O2	CYCLOPROPYL	NITROSAMINE	THIOCARBOXY
1,4-C4OS	DIAZO	NITROSO	THIOCYANATE
1,4-C4S2	DIAZONIUM	NITROXIDE	THIOKETAL
1,4-C5N2	DIENE	NULL	THIOL
C2S	DIIMIDE	O-QUINONE	THIONE
C3N	DISULFIDE	ORGANOMETAL	THIOPHENOL
C3O	ENAMINE	ORGANOMETALLICS	THIOUREA
C3S	ENOL	ORTHO ESTER	TRIAZENE
C4N	ENOL ETHER	OXIME	TRIHALIDE
C4O	ENYNE	OXONIUM	UNSATD ACID
C4S	EPISULFIDE	P-N GROUP	UNSATD ALDEHYDE
C5N	EPOXIDE	P-O GROUP	UNSATD AMIDE
C5O	ETHER	P-QUINONE	UNSATD ESTER
C5S	GEM-DIHALIDE	P-S GROUP	UNSATD KETONE
C6N	GLYCOL	PENAM	UNSATD NITRILE
C6O	GUANIDINE	PEROXIDE	UNSATURATED ACID
C6S	HALIDES	PEROXY ACID	UNSATURATED
ACETAL	HALOFORMATE	PEROXY ESTER	ALDEHYDE
ACETYL	HALOHYDRIN	PHENOL	UNSATURATED
ACID HALIDE	HEMIACETAL	PHOSPHATE	AMIDE
ACYCLIC ALKENE	HETEROCYCLES	PHOSPHITE	UNSATURATED
ACYCLIC KETONE	HYDRAZIDE	PHOSPHONATE	ESTER
ACYLMETAL	HYDRAZINE	PHOSPHONIUM	UNSATURATED
ALCOHOLS	HYDRAZONE	PHOSPHORUS YLIDE	KETONE
ALDEHYDE	HYDROPEROXIDE	PI-ALKENE	UNSATURATED
ALKENES	HYDROXYLAMINE	PI-ALKYNE	NITRILE
ALKYL HALIDE	IMIDE	PI-ALLYL	UREA
ALKYNE	IMINE	PRIMARY ALCOHOL	VIC-DIHALIDE
ALKYNES	IMINO ETHER	PRIMARY AMINE	VINYL HALIDE
ALLENE	ISOCYANATE	PURINE	
ALLYL ALCOHOL	ISONITRILE		

Index

Abstract Field
    general entries 48
    in Basic Index only 49
Abstracts
    writing abstracts 6
Accession Number Field
    search example 49
Alloys
    indexing of 181
    molecular formulas of 222
Amine oxides
    bonds in 238
Amoxil
    REGISTRY File record 207
Anticholesteremics
    Index Headings in CAplus File 75
Antiinflammatories
    naturally occurring 300
Aspirin
    LC entry in REGISTRY File 282
Atom maps
    in reaction searching 319
Atom sequence screens 238
Atoms
    description 176
    valency 177
Augmented atom screens 233
Augmentin
    postings in MF fields 224
    REGISTRY File record for 186
Author Field
    general entries 44
    search example 49
Author names
    appearance in bibliographic databases 30
    example in CAplus File 45

BATCH search
    in CASREACT File 321
    saving 260
    stereosearch example 271
BEILSTEIN File
    chemical information in 287
    description and content 283
    display costs 279
    display of field availability 281
    duplicate records and REGISTRY File 285
    finding substances 286
    number of substances 286

    physical property information 288
    structure and property searches 289
    structure search in 275
    table of records with property information 285
Bibliographic databases
    Basic Index 18
    broadening searches 69
    choosing initial search terms 74
    clusters 26
    comparison with full text databases 108
    comprehensive searches
        issues in 65
    comprehensive searching in 65
    content 7
    fields 18
    figure showing hierarchy 26
    general structure of index entries 51
    hierarchy 26
    individual words 40
    location of index entries 53
    narrowing searches 69
    patent records in 123
    preliminary searches 68
    revision of search profile 69
    search principles 64
    search summary 98
    similarities and differences
        implications to authors 38
        implications to searchers 38
    structure and content 25
    structure of 26
    summary of commands 100
    text as individual entries 17
BIOSIS File
    coverage 4
    sample online record 32
Bond sequence screens 239
Bond values 234
Bonds
    covalent 177
    ionic 177
    normalized, definitions 234
    representation of donor bonds 237
    representation of pi.bonds 237
    tables of types and values 233
Bonds sites
    specifying in reaction searching 319
Boolean operators
    applications 17
    linking concepts 66

spaces in 19
terms in fields 45
Bound phrases
  in author field 44
Business and news databases 115
Business databases
  general search strategy 115

CA Collective Index 180
CA File
  brief description of 29
Calcium phosphate
  GMELIN File record 295
  REGISTRY File record 193
CAOLD File
  brief description of 29
CAplus File
  brief description of 29
  comments on specific fields 30
  crossover to WPI Files 137
  general structure 28
  index examples 58
  indexing of chemical substances 58
  initial search for anticholesteremics 76
  patent legal status information 126
  preparations of substances 59
  roles for substances 59
  sample record 22
  search for asymmetric tandem additions 22
CAPreviews File
  brief description of 29
Carboxylic acids
  bond definitions 236
CAS Registry Numbers
  as index terms 6
  comparison of listings 35
  description 175
  in CAplus File 59
  indexing in bibliographic files 175
  use in searching substance-based files 281
CAS Standard Abbreviations 31
CASLINK 275
CASONLINE
  network 5
CASREACT File
  CRDREF display format 317
  functional group conversions 323
  functional groups in 332
  indexing in 312
  indexing of multistep reactions 314
  REACTION MAP 313

reaction roles 315
SAMPLE search 321
single and multistep reactions in 311
structure search options 318
structure search limits 320
CD-ROMs
  advantages and disadvantages 9
CHEMCATS File 294
CHEMDRAW
  structure import from 246
Chemical Abstracts database
  broad classifications 56
  general indexing 56
  Index Headings 57
  sections in 28
Chemical reaction databases
  content 7
  coverage in 311
  electronic 310
Chemical substance databases
  content 7
Chemical substances
  indexing in CAplus File 58
CHEMINFORMRX File 325
Chemistry
  branches of 178
CHEMLIST File
  general description 291
CHEMREACT File 325
CIN File
  thesaurus in 53
Citation searching 157
  single article 158
  single author 159
Cited references
  SCISEARCH File 35
CJACS File
  bibliographic entries 103
  references and captions 105
  search example 113
  text entries 104
Class identifiers
  table of 202
Clusters
  METALS 52
  of bibliographic databases 26
  table of 27
CN Fields
  special symbols in 210
  table of special symbols 210
CNS Field 211

Command comparison charts
    STN/Dialog 329
    STN/Orbit 330
Command defaults
    automatic selection 16
    for the 5 common commands 16
Commands
    table of 145
Common names 207
Communications
    software
        text and graphics options 12
COMPENDEX File
    coverage 4
Component Registry Numbers
    example 208
Concepts
    choice of in initial searches 67
    conversion to search terms 68
    setting out in natural language form 66
CONFSCI File 106
Connect hour fees 164
Connecting online 12
Connectivities
    defining of 249
Constitutional isomers
    definition of 199
Convergent synthesis 310
Coordination compounds
    indexing of 182
    indexing of π complexes 183
    indexing of σ complexes 182
Copolymers
    indexing of 189
Corporate Source
    appearance in bibliographic databases 30
Corporate Source Field
    general entries 45
    sample abbreviations 45
    search example 49
Cortisone
    REGISTRY File record 180
Costs
    connect hour 164
    displays 166
    effect on end-users 7
    EXPAND command 43
    general comments 163
    online versus hardcopy 7
    search terms 165
    structure search 165

CRN Field
    searches in 215
CSCHEM File
    for commercial substances 293
CSCORP File
    finding company addresses 294
Current awareness searching 156
Cyclohexanecarboxaldehyde
    preparation 316

Database Summary Sheets
    identifying SELECT fields 151
    information contained in 61
    TOXLINE File 61
Databases
    different types 7
    errors 8
Deleted Registry Numbers 189
Dialog
    network 5
    software packages 10
Dialog
    commands 14
    comparison chart 329
Dioxin
    REGISTRY File record 154
Directory databases
    content 7
DISPLAY BROWSE
    in full text databases 111
    searches within 114
    table of options 112
DISPLAY command
    common display formats
        table of 72
    display formats 71
    display of hit terms 46, 71
    general features 15
    SCAN format 68
Display format 15
    IALL 29
Display of answers
    online, offline, email 70
DISPLAY SCAN
    use in CAplus File 90
DISPLAY TRIAL 90
Document Type Field
    general entries 48
    search example 49
DRAW option and STN Express
    table of 252

DRUGU File 306
DUPLICATE command
    use of 96

E-mail
    delivery of answer sets by 71
EDIT command 151
EFFECT codes
    RTECS File 304
Electronic database producers
    table of major 4
Electronic databases
    future possibilities 9
EMBASE File
    coverage 4
    sample online record 33
    search in 83
Enantiomers
    REGISTRY File example of 201
ENERGY File
    CHI and ET Fields 37
    coverage 4
Epibatidine
    preparation 313
    record in CASREACT File 312
EXACT search
    example 262
    screens in 240
EXPAND command
    applications in thesaurus fields 53
    EXPAND back 43
    EXPAND left 43
    for finding author postings 42
    general features 42
    general use of 41

FAMILY search
    example 264
FAX
    delivery of records 71
Fexofenadine
    name based search 214
Field availability
    listing of 279
Field repetitions
    in bibliographic databases 26
FILE command
    default 16
    table of options 149
File crossover
    from REGISTRY File 261

File segments
    list of 202
Free text
    in Abstract Field 48
FSEARCH command 138
Full text databases
    comparison with bibliographic database
    108
    display options 111
    table of 102
    when to search in 105
Full text records
    electronic and hardcopy 102
Functional groups
    conversions in CASREACT File 323
    definitions 179

G-groups
    in structure building 253
GeoRef File
    coverage 4
    searching for origin of life 20
GMELIN File
    general description 294
    number of substances 286
Graph Modifier screens 240
Graphic images 103

Hardcopy
    ownership 5
    searching 6
Heading Parent Field 206
HELP command
    features 145
HELP COST command 163
HELP directory
    RTECS File 146
Hill system
    classification of molecular formulas 22
Hit term highlighting
    display of 21
Hit terms
    within D SCAN 91
HODOC File
    general description 296
HSDB File
    general information 297
Hydrogens
    adding to structure queries 257
Hypercholesterolemia
    Index Heading in EMBASE File 78

thesaurus in EMBASE File 79

E Fields
 number of substances in 286
 Files
 comparison 123
 coverage 4
 PAT File
 examples of claims in 133
 patent legal status information 127
house databases
 advantages and disadvantages 9
completely defined substances
 indexing of 184
DEX command
 Bioscience example 150
 use of and applications within 149
ex Headings
 Chemical Abstracts Database 31, 57
 general application 56
 options for finding headings 74
 smartSELECT feature 152
ex name fields 212
ormation specialists
 roles in online searching 8
S File 4
PADOC File
 coverage 4
 finding legal status information 141
 patent families and legal status information
 136
SPEC File
 CHI and ET Fields 37
 coverage 4
 in STN clusters 26
 sample record 35
ernational Patent Classification
 codes 128
ernet
 access to scientific databases 10
 delivery of answers through e-mail 71
VESTEXT File
 display scan 117
 search example 116
obenzene diacetate
 as oxidant 324
mers
 definition of 198
opes
 definition of 196
 indexing of 198

MF fields and 227
 molecular formulas of 222
IUPAC nomenclature
 print sources 205

JICST-E File
 coverage 4

Language Field
 entries in the BIOSIS File 48
 search example 49
Language Fields
 general entries 48
Learning files 166
Legal status information
 from INPADOC File 141
 in patent databases 125
LIFESCI File
 coverage 4
 searching for substances 155
Lowe G
 original article 27

MAC Field
 for alloys 182
Markush structures
 in MARPAT File 274
MARPAT File
 sample answer 274
 structure search in 273
MATH File
 coverage 4
MEDLINE File
 sample online record 33
 thesaurus 87
 updating of index headings 57
METADEX File
 coverage 4
MF Field
 searches in 222
Minerals
 indexing of 185
Mixtures
 indexing of 186
 molecular formulas of 222
Molecular Formula Field
 indexing 221
Molecular formulas
 Basic Index searches 223
 CNS searches and 226
 for substance classes 222

Hill system 221
numeric search fields 225
search fields 222
search strategies 225
table of search fields based on 223
MRCK File
general description 299
MSDS Files
general description 301
Multicomponent substances
general indexing 203
general search strategy 216
molecular formulas of 221
nomenclature entries 208
Multifile searches
general notes 149
Multistep reactions 310

News databases
general search strategy 115
Nicotine
connection table 231
NLDB File 116
NMR spectra
BEILSTEIN File 284
Nomenclature
Basic Index and segmentation 211
common examples 209
functional groups in 206
IUPAC, CAS,Beilstein 205
multicomponent substances 208
segmentation rules 210
Nomenclature search
general strategy 213
multicomponent substances 215
Nomenclature search fields
table of 211
NTIS File
coverage 4
Nucleic acids
indexing of 191
molecular formulas of 222
Numeric databases
content 7
Numeric operators
table of 47
Numeric properties
files with property information 162
general search options 161
search formats 161
Numeric searches

and MF fields 225
general format of 225
NUMERIGUIDE File 161

Offline prints
delivery 71
Online searching
advantages 9
different from hardcopy 6
disadvantages 9
problems 6
Online vendors 4
Orbit
network 5
comparison chart 330
Orbit/Questel commands 14
Organic acid salts
indexing of 194
Organic bases
indexing of 195
Other Sources Field 114

PATDPA File
coverage 4
Patent application date 125
Patent Cooperation Treaty 121
Patent databases
comparison of abstracts in 132
comparisons of indexing 130
indexing of technical aspects 128
legal information, table of 125
searches on classification codes 135
searching for patent families 136
subject searching in 134
table of additional indexing 130
table of specialist 122
Patent date 125
Patent literature
the process of obtaining patents 120
Patent superfields 135
Periodic Table
Table 331
description 176
salts of Group I/II Bases 194
PHAR File 306
Physical properties
classes of 278
Physical property information
BEILSTEIN File 288
Physical property searches
units 290

olymers
  indexing of 188
  molecular formulas of 222
olystyrene
  REGISTRY File record 189
ostings for records 21
eliminary search
  in bibliographic databases 90
eparations
  from BEILSTEIN File 287
  in CAplus File 311
  P suffix in CAplus File 59
imary and secondary literature
  comparison 101
iority application date 125
ROMT File
  display scan 118
  search example 116
operty information
  chemical properties 278
  classes of physical properties 278
  finding substances with specific 289
oteins
  indexing of 190
  molecular formulas of 222
oximity operators
  general applications 37
  implied 19
  in full text databases 109
  in MF fields 224
  linking concepts 66
  spaces in 19
  table of 18
  use 18
  use for restricting answer sets 92
  use in name based fields 212
  use of (nW) and (nA) 40
  use of (S) operator in Abstract Field 49
  use of NOT options 19

JERY command
  for storing E-numbers 43
eryDef menu
  options 254
estel
  network 5

cemic mixtures 199
  REGISTRY File example of 201
dom Leo 160
actant

definition of in reaction databases 309
Reagent
  definition of in reaction databases 309
REGISTRY File
  basic sections in 179
  class identifiers 202
  crossover to CAplus File 59
      preparations and roles 59
  duplicate records and BEILSTEIN File 285
  file segments 202
  importance of Locator Field 174
  indexing 179
  number of substances 286
  simvastatin record 85
  when other files should be searched 174
  why it should be searched first 172
Regulatory information on STN 291
Repeating groups 254
Reviews
  searching for 48
Rings
  isolated or embedded 247
  isolation of 248
Roles
  for substances in the CAplus File 59
RTECS File
  EFFCODES 147
  general description 302
  help directory 146

Salts
  indexing of 192
  molecular formulas of 222
SAMPLE search
  for structure queries 255
Sapphire
  REGISTRY File record for 185
Scandinavian Journal of Metallurgy
  online records from 52
Scientists
  roles in online searching 8
Scifinder 10
SCISEARCH File
  appearance of citations 35
  citation searching in 157
  sample online record 34
Screens
  in structure searching 232
  manual addition of 258
  number based 240
  table of 232

SDI command 156
Search command
    subcommands within 255
Search scopes
    options 240
Search steps
    in bibliographic databases 70
Search term fees 165
Search types
    options 240
Section Codes
    Chemical Abstracts Database 56
    general application 56
    search examples in CAplus File 57
    searching of in CAplus File 57
SELECT CHEM
    for searching on chemical names 154
SELECT command
    general comments 151
Shortcut symbols 252
Simvastatin
    BEILSTEIN File record 279
    postings in files 85
    record in REGISTRY File 85
    review articles 95
SmartSELECT
    and FSEARCH command 139
    and the CIT select feature 160
    application for CSCHEM and CSCORP
    Files 294
    finding Index Headings 152
    finding only US patents 141
    general application 151
    patent family crossover 137
    tables for comparing companies 140
    tabular display options 152
Sodium acetate
    REGISTRY File record 194
Source Field
    appearance in bibliographic databases 30
    fields within 47
    general entries 46
    search example 49
SPECINFO File
    general information 305
Spectral data
    BEILSTEIN File 285
    HODOC File 296
    SPECINFO File 305
Spectroscopic techniques
    in structure determination 184

Stereoisomers
    definitions 199
    examples 200
Stereosearch 269
STN
    command prompt 14
    subcommand prompt 15
STN commands
    input format 14
    table of 145
STN Express
    and Scifinder 10
    checking defaults 251
    chemical reaction searching with 315
    QueryDef menu in 254
    refinement filters 258
    software capabilities 13
    spectral images 305
    structure building defaults 249
    structure searching with 230
Stop words
    finding file specific options 146
    in bibliographic databases 40
    table of 41
    typical examples 41
Structure building
    keyboard commands 246
Structure building defaults
    chains 246
    rings 247
    STN Express and 249
Structure connection tables
    for coding substances 231
Structure files
    table of 241
Structure queries
    revision of 257
Structure search
    costs 165
    system options 251
Structure search examples
    EXACT 262
    FAMILY 264
    SUBSTRUCTURE 265
Structure search queries
    blocking substitution 266
    building larger structures 268
    ring isolation 267
Structure search scopes
    table of 255
Structure search types

definitions 244
   table of 255
tructure searchable files
   table of 272
tructure searches
   command options 261
   steps in 244
ubcommands
   default options 15
   options within DISPLAY command 15
ublimation point
   BEILSTEIN File 290
ubset searches 259
ubstance based files
   general search strategy 282
   table of 173
   table of search fields 173
   why search? 282
ubstance searching
   general issues in 203
ubstances
   commercial availability 293
UBSTRUCTURE search
   example 265
   screens in 241
ulfoxides
   selective oxidation to sulfones 324
upplementary Terms
   appearance in CAplus File 31
ystem defined variables
   table of 253
ystem limits
   structure search 259

abular inorganic substances 186
automers
   definitions 235
   ketones and enols 236
axol
   search involving 117
ea tree oil
   search for 217
elecommunications networks 13
hesaurus
   display of associated terms 54
   EXPAND command in 53
   explosion of terms 54
   explosion of terms in MEDLINE File 88
   geographic
      in CIN File 54
   in CIN File 53

in EMBASE File 83
in MEDLINE File 87
in USPATFULL File 128
structure and content 53
Titanocene
   REGISTRY File record 183
Title Field
   appearance in bibliographic databases 30
   general entries 44
   search example 49
   use for finding known article 80
Toxicity information
   in substance and bibliographic files 305
   RTECS File 303
TOXLINE File
   Database Summary Sheet 61
TOXLIT File 106
Trade names 207
Truncation
   left, in CNS Field 212
   use in name based fields 212
Truncation symbols
   left-hand truncation 19
   table of 19
   use 18
TSCA 291
Type of Ring screens 238

Uniterms
   in IFI Files 132
Units
   in physical property searches 290
USAN File 307
USPATFULL File
   coverage 4
   full text availability in 133
   IPC and NCL thesaurus 128

Valence Bond structures 177
   conventions in using 178
Valency 177
   of common atoms 177
Variable point of attachment 253
Variables
   in structure building 252

Wodginite
   REGISTRY File record for 185
WPI Files
   and patent family information 136
   coverage 4

crossover to for patent family information
136
patent legal status information 127